ROYAL HISTORICAL SOCIETY

STUDIES IN HISTORY

New Series

ENGLISH PUBLIC OPINION AND
THE AMERICAN CIVIL WAR

Studies in History New Series

Editorial Board

Professor David Eastwood (*Convenor*)
Professor Michael Braddick
Dr Steven Gunn
Dr Janet Hunter (*Economic History Society*)
Professor Colin Jones
Professor Mark Mazower
Professor Miles Taylor
Dr Simon Walker
Professor Julian Hoppit (*Honorary Treasurer*)

This series is supported by an annual subvention from the Economic History Society

ENGLISH PUBLIC OPINION AND THE AMERICAN CIVIL WAR

Duncan Andrew Campbell

THE ROYAL HISTORICAL SOCIETY
THE BOYDELL PRESS

© Duncan Andrew Campbell 2003

All Rights Reserved. Except as permitted under current legislation no part of this work may be photocopied, stored in a retrieval system, published, performed in public, adapted, broadcast, transmitted, recorded or reproduced in any form or by any means, without the prior permission of the copyright owner

First published 2003

A Royal Historical Society publication
Published by The Boydell Press
an imprint of Boydell & Brewer Ltd
PO Box 9, Woodbridge, Suffolk IP12 3DF, UK
and of Boydell & Brewer Inc.
PO Box 41026, Rochester, NY 14604–4126, USA
website: www.boydell.co.uk

ISBN 0 86193 263 3

ISSN 0269-2244

A catalogue record for this book is available
from the British Library

Library of Congress Cataloging-in-Publication Data
Campbell, Duncan Andrew, 1968–
  English public opinion and the American Civil War / Duncan Andrew Campbell.
    p. cm. – (Royal Historical Society studies in history. New series, ISSN 0269–2244)
  Based on author's thesis (doctoral) – Cambridge University, 1997.
  Includes bibliographical references (p.) and index.
  ISBN 0–86193–263–3 (Hardback : alk. paper)
  1. United States – History – Civil War, 1861–1865 – Foreign public opinion, British. 2. Public opinion – Great Britain – History – 19th century. I. Title. II. Series.
  E469.8.C36 2003
  973.7'1 – dc21   2002155075

This book is printed on acid-free paper

Printed by Newton Printing Ltd, London, UK. www.newtonprinting.com

Contents

		Page
Acknowledgements		vii
Introduction		1
1	Differences of opinion	17
2	The *Trent* outrage	61
3	Observations from experience	96
4	The political debate	134
5	The Confederacy's partisans	162
6	Who supported the Union?	194
Conclusion		234
Appendix 1.	MPs' proclivities during the Civil War	247
2.	Aristocratic proclivities during the Civil War	250
Bibliography		253
Index		261

Publication of this volume was aided by a grant from the Scouloudi Foundation, in association with the Institute of Historical Research.

Acknowledgements

This book is based upon the doctoral dissertation I wrote at Cambridge, completed in early 1997, and considerably revised since. From those days to the present, many kind and thoughtful individuals have greatly contributed to the process of thought and research that this work has entailed. I owe a debt of deep gratitude to Professor Miles Taylor, of the University of Southampton, who, from my time as a PhD candidate, through the revising of this manuscript for publication, could always be counted upon for insightful counsel and invaluable advice. For all of his help, I am profoundly thankful.

I am very grateful to my former supervisor, Dr Gareth Stedman Jones of King's College, Cambridge, for listening to and critiquing my ideas and arguments, as well as reading the numerous drafts with which I presented him. Gratitude is also owed to Dr Ann Robson, at whose stimulating graduate course at the University of Toronto, the seed of this book was planted and I first became interested in, and in some cases introduced to, many of the people examined within it.

From my days at Cambridge, I should like to thank Dr Mike Sewell, Dr Beau Riffenburgh, Dr Derek Beales and Dr Graham Storey, who all provided me with information that I would never have come across on my own.

At the University of Wales Swansea, I should like to express my appreciation to my colleagues in the American Studies Department who listened to my paper on this subject and weighed in with their intelligent and perceptive comments. I would especially like to thank Dr Craig Phelan, who has listened to my ideas with a patience that goes beyond the point of collegial courtesy.

I am further grateful to the Royal Historical Society for publishing this book, particularly Professor Martin Daunton, Professor Peter Mandler and Mrs Christine Linehan, the executive editor, all of whom have helped improve this work immeasurably.

I should also like to thank Bobbie Jo for patiently putting up with this apparently never-ending project. I owe her a major debt of gratitude.

It remains to be noted that although this book could never have been started, never mind completed, without the help of everyone named above, they are in no way responsible for any errors or omissions; these are entirely my own.

Finally, I should like to thank my parents Dr Neil and Mrs Sheila Campbell, without whose support and attention this book could not have been written. It is to them that this work is dedicated.

Duncan Andrew Campbell

TO MY PARENTS

Introduction

The last Confederate unit that lowered its flag did so, not in the United States, but in Britain. This was the southern raider, the CSS *Shenandoah* that, whilst cruising off the Californian coast, encountered the British ship *Barracouta*, on 2 August 1865 and learned of the collapse of the Confederacy and the capture of its president, Jefferson Davis. Deciding against the risks of surrender at an American port, the *Shenandoah*'s captain, James Waddell, instead set sail for Liverpool some 17,000 miles away. Evading a United States navy searching for her, the vessel travelled around the horn of Africa and, on 6 November 1865, sailed up the Mersey to Liverpool. There, to quote Shelby Foote, 'she lowered her abolished country's last official flag'.[1] In a sense, it was a homecoming for the ship; Liverpool had been the centre of Confederate naval operations in Europe. It was here that the *Shenandoah* had been purchased, re-christened and re-launched.

The story of the *Shenandoah* serves to represent Britain's significance to both combatants in the American Civil War. On the diplomatic front, the Union anxiously wanted to ensure its neutrality, while the Confederate States desperately urged it to interfere on their behalf. Both sides needed to purchase materials from Britain, such as munitions, especially the South. Indeed, according to Richard Lester, had it not been for the success of their commercial activities in Britain, the Confederate cause would probably have lasted only months instead of years.[2] These same activities, as well as conflicts over maritime and neutral rights, brought Britain to the brink of war with the northern states on at least one occasion, and seriously damaged Anglo-American relations for years to come. As it was, the war ended with Britain despised by both sides – in southern judgement, for not helping them enough, and in northern opinion, for helping the former too much. The Union and the Confederacy were as divided on British neutrality as they were about everything else.

If neither belligerent could agree on the nature of British neutrality, however, nor have historians since. For although the diplomacy of the period has been comprehensively researched, less examined is its foundation: British opinion regarding the conflict. Despite the basis of a traditional interpretation, a revisionist critique and a counter-reaction against the latter, the nature of British sentiment remains unclear. This work re-examines the nature of British public and political opinion on the war in order to better

---

[1] Shelby Foote, *The Civil War: a narrative*, New York 1958–74, iii. 1031.
[2] Richard Lester, *Confederate finance and purchasing in Great Britain*, Charlottesville 1975, pp. ix–x.

understand what factors were essential to its development and its ultimate effect on Anglo-American relations. In order to place the arguments of this work in context, however, a brief synopsis of the debate until now is required, with emphasis upon the arguments of the major contributors.

A modern historiography of Anglo-American relations during the Civil War essentially begins with two studies: E. D. Adams's two-volume *Great Britain and the American Civil War* (1925) and Donaldson Jordan's and Edwin J. Pratt's *Europe and the American Civil War* (1931).[3] Although others had, to an extent, proposed similar arguments before, most notably Henry Adams in *The education of Henry Adams* (1907), Brougham Villiers and W. H. Chesson in *Anglo-American relations 1861–1865* (1919) and George Macaulay Trevelyan in *British history in the nineteenth century, 1782–1901* (1922), E. D. Adams's and Jordan and Pratt's works were the first modern, full-scale studies of the topic. Barring a few minor differences, these studies form a largely harmonious model of British attitudes towards the conflict which has since come to be called the traditional interpretation and, despite the attack to which it has been subjected ever since, this version of events has proven remarkably resilient. So durable has it proven, in fact, that every examination of the subject since has been in reaction to this interpretation. Thus, when tracing the course of the debate on British attitudes and opinions, one has to begin with this traditional interpretation.

According to this model, the British aristocracy, the upper-middle class and political conservatives were solidly pro-South while radicals, the lower-middle and working classes were firmly pro-North. The radicals, represented largely by John Bright (and, to a lesser extent, by Richard Cobden), viewed America as the bulwark of democracy, and thus its promotion, not to say its survival, depended upon a Union victory – an idea supposedly shared by the lower-middle and working classes. Further, argues this tradition, these groups were far more anti-slavery than their social superiors and quickly recognised that it was a war of emancipation, especially after Abraham Lincoln's Emancipation Proclamation (1862), which galvanized their opinion in favour of the North. Thus, Lancashire cotton operatives, driven out of work by the cotton famine, endured their hardships and remained pro-Union during the war because they recognised it as a campaign for democracy and against slavery.

The conservatives and enfranchised classes of Britain, meanwhile, according to the model, regarded America's growing military and industrial might with fear and loathing. Interpreting American democracy as a threat to their privileged positions, they blamed it for the breakdown in order that led to the conflict. Desirous of crippling not only a hated rival, but republicanism and democracy, too, these groups championed the Confederacy, and condemned the North's attempts to conquer it. Further, according to the

---

[3] E. D. Adams, *Great Britain and the American Civil War*, London 1925, and Donaldson Jordan and Edwin J. Pratt, *Europe and the American Civil War*, London 1931.

INTRODUCTION

tradition, the upper and middle classes developed an affection for what they perceived to be a South of genteel landowners, socially superior to the belligerent Yankees. The upper classes and conservatives only belatedly recognised that the war was a campaign against slavery after the Confederacy collapsed and Lincoln was assassinated, and finally accorded both the martyred president and the Union some overdue respect. The traditional interpretation concludes with the northern supporters' triumph, the passage of the 1867 Reform Act. This event, according to the model, occurred largely – or in part – because of the Union's victory. Additionally, this version of events has been accepted by several subsequent scholars working on areas outside our topic, particularly some historians of British labour, most notably Henry Pelling in his *America and the British Left; from Bright to Bevan* (1956).[4]

The traditional model of British opinion on the Civil War, in its original form, is very much an example from the Whig school of history. Indeed, H. Butterfield's *The Whig interpretation of history* (1931) appeared at almost the same time as its establishment.[5] The model's first critic, however, owed his approach to developments in the American historical profession rather than the British – namely the domination of Civil War history by the 'Progressive school' from the 1910s to the 1940s. Although lack of space precludes any close examination of their approach, the Progressive school, led by Charles A. Beard, posited a clash between interest groups and classes as the central theme of American history. In so doing, they not only generally de-emphasised slavery as a cause of the war but also called into question whether or not the Union's cause was indeed liberal, ultimately judging neither side in the conflict to be, in any way, morally superior to the other. Southern historians, in turn, took up the Progressive's school themes in the 1930s and used them to defend the Confederate cause.[6] One of these southern historians (and partisans) was Frank L. Owsley who, in *King Cotton diplomacy: foreign relations of the Confederate States of America* (1931), denied that slavery had any impact on British views of the war. Although Owsley accepts the belief that the middle and upper classes were mostly pro-Confederate, he claims they were so on the grounds of a liberal belief in the right of self-determination rather than because of opposition to democracy. He also dismisses the notion of a pro-Union working class, stating that British labour was wholly indifferent to the war, and their presence at any pro-northern rally could be attributed to 'the liberal use of small coin'.[7]

---

[4] Henry Pelling, *America and the British left; from Bright to Bevan*, London 1956.
[5] H. Butterfield, *The Whig interpretation of history*, London 1931.
[6] For a brief synopsis of Civil War historiography in the United States during this period see Gerald N. Grob and George Athan Billias (eds), *Interpretations of American history: patterns and perspectives*, 3rd edn, New York 1978, i. 363–77, and James M. McPherson, 'What caused the Civil War', *North and South* iv/1 (2000), 12–22.
[7] Frank Lawrence Owsley, *King Cotton diplomacy: foreign relations of the Confederate States of America*, Chicago 1931. For the purposes of this work, I have used the second edition, revised by Harriet Owsley and published in 1959.

Although Owsley's work had little overt impact upon the scholarly consensus of Anglo-American relations during the conflict, the changing historical interpretations of the Civil War, of which he was a representative, certainly did. Now that the conflict was no longer treated as a simple battle of progression versus reaction, nor was the British response to it. Scholars re-examining the subject began to criticise the traditional interpretation as being both too simplistic and, in many respects, simply wrong. Thus, the publication of the articles by W. D. Jones, 'British conservatives and the American Civil War' (1953), and Arnold Whitridge, 'British liberals and the American Civil War' (1962), marked the model's first genuine challenge.[8] W. D. Jones argues that, rather than having any hatred of U.S.-style democracy, conservatives had very little interest in American affairs either before or during the conflict. Nor is there any evidence to suggest that the conservatives saw the fate of democracy or republicanism as in any way related to the outcome of the American Civil War. Whitridge, meanwhile, points out that the anti-democratic duke of Argyll supported the North, believing that no part of any nation state had the right of secession. The liberal Lord Acton, in comparison, opposed what he saw as the increase of autocracy in America and supported the South's bid for independence.

Criticism of the traditional interpretation further intensified during the 1950s and 1960s, with the increased study of labour and radical history in Britain. For example, D. P. Crook's study, *American democracy in English politics, 1815–1850* (1965), examines various political groups' responses to America and argues that, apart from Cobden and Bright, most liberals and radicals felt ambivalent towards the U.S. by the time the Civil War began, their formerly high esteem for American-style democracy having been eroded because the growing belief in what is termed economic justice clashed with America's *laissez-faire* society.[9] In other words, by the time of the Civil War, radicals no longer regarded America as the ideal model from which to draw ideas for parliamentary, to say nothing of social, reform.

The labour historian Royden Harrison, meanwhile, raised further questions regarding the existence of monolithic working-class support for the Union in his three important studies: 'British labour and the Confederacy' (1957), 'British labor and American slavery' (1961) and *Before the socialists: studies in labour and politics, 1861–1881* (1965).[10] Harrison finds that many members of the radical working class were hostile towards the North during

---

8 Wilbur Devereux Jones, 'British conservatives and the American Civil War', *American Historical Review* lviii (1953), 527–43; Arnold Whitridge, 'British liberals and the American Civil War', *History Today* xii (1962), 688–95.
9 D. P. Crook, *American democracy in English politics: 1815–1850*, Oxford 1965.
10 Royden Harrison, 'British labour and the Confederacy', *International Review of Social History* ii (1957), 78–105; 'British labor and American slavery', *Science and Society* xxv (1961), 291–319; and *Before the socialists: studies in labour and politics, 1861–1881*, London 1965, 2nd edn, Ipswich 1994. For the purposes of this work, I have used the second edition, with the revised introduction.

INTRODUCTION

the war, particularly the labour press, which was mostly pro-South, although there were exceptions – particularly the *Bee-Hive*. Despite acknowledging these divisions Harrison still argues that, overall, the working class was pro-North, concluding that 'it is the record of public meetings which provide the most convincing support for the traditional account of working-class opinion on the Civil War', citing the many pro-Union rallies held by British labourers.[11]

So although Harrison's work questioned, but ultimately did not overturn, the traditional interpretation regarding British labour's sentiments, one followed that did so and yet, paradoxically, at the same time, recycled the notion of conservative and upper class opposition towards the Union. This was Thomas J. Keiser's thesis, 'The English press and the American Civil War' (1971).[12] Keiser's idiosyncratic position is that almost all Britons, from the working class to the aristocracy, liberals and conservatives alike, were hostile towards the Union and that Britain would have intervened in the war on the side of the South, but for the North's steadfast diplomacy. Unfortunately, despite making some original and important points, Keiser's thesis has some problems. For instance, his examples of anti-Union opinion are presented in a vacuum – ignoring concurrent political and diplomatic events. More problematic, however, is Keiser's basic depiction of any anti-northern opinion as pro-Confederate, pro-slavery and anti-democratic sentiment, which simply ignores the arguments against this interpretation. Other than his newspaper sources, Keiser's only basis of information is an uncritical repetition of northern propagandists' views, quoting (on multiple occasions) Henry Adams's 'They [the British] feel they went too far and they feel we know their feelings.'[13] Keiser concludes by discussing a metaphorical 'Heavenly City' of British pro-northern supporters.[14] Like all such celestial states, its membership is extremely limited (although it seems to include the entire population of the Union), containing Cobden and Bright and a select few of their allies.

The strongest attack on the traditional interpretation's portrayal of working-class and radical attitudes towards the Civil War, however, has unquestionably been led by Mary Ellison's regional study of Lancashire. In her *Support for secession: Lancashire and the American Civil War* (1972), Ellison argues that, despite what historians have assumed, most of Lancashire (especially Liverpool and regions hit by the cotton famine) was strongly pro-Confederate during the conflict, citing rallies and petitions demanding the recognition of the South.[15] According to Ellison, it was Cobden and

---

11 Harrison, *Before the socialists*, 66.
12 Thomas J. Keiser, 'The English press and the American Civil War', unpubl. PhD diss. Reading 1971.
13 Ibid. 124.
14 Ibid. passim.
15 Mary Ellison, *Support for secession: Lancashire and the American Civil War*, Chicago 1972.

Bright who misrepresented Lancashire opinion to their American and radical friends, and pro-Confederate displays were often ignored or down-played by both pro-Union supporters and an establishment that, far from wanting to become involved in the fray, was actually fearful of a war with the North. While she sometimes extrapolates too much from isolated examples, Ellison does, none the less, argue convincingly that Lancashire's working class did not view slavery as the reason for the conflict, even after the Emancipation Proclamation – and instead, blamed their misery on what they perceived to be northern imperialism.

Ellison's book has an afterword by one Peter d'A. Jones, that posits a thesis for the origins of the myth of labour support for the Union. While Jones agrees with Ellison's claim that Cobden and Bright misrepresented events, he also blames William Ewart Gladstone who, seeking support to extend the franchise, cited the patience of the workmen of Lancashire during the war as proof that they could be trusted with the ballot. Jones further argues that the Adams family – Charles Francis Adams and Henry Adams – who largely resented British society, credited the working classes for preventing an Anglo-American war by their support for the Union. The myth was also aided – albeit independently – by Karl Marx who promoted the concept of a heroic working class refusing to support a slave-power, despite the terrible hardships caused by the cotton blockade. The myth, according to Jones, has since been supported by Marxists citing it as an example of working-class solidarity and by Americans who argue that their civil war was the touchstone of English progressivism. In actual fact, as we shall see, the formation of the traditional interpretation was rather more complicated than this, but Jones has established, none the less, some of the main reasons for its foundation.

The high-water mark of the revisionist interpretation of British views of the Civil War was probably the publication of D. P. Crook's *The North, the South and the powers* (1974), which collected and expanded upon many of the revisionists' arguments.[16] Crook's remains the best broad study of Anglo-American relations during this period to date, although some parts have been superseded by more recent scholarship, such as Howard Jones's *Union in peril: the crisis over British intervention in the Civil War* (1992), which examines the cabinet discussions regarding British mediation in the war.[17] In addition to the arguments mentioned above, Crook notes that many upper- and middle-class Britons compared southern secession to Ireland and thus accepted the North's right to use force to maintain the Union. With the empire in mind, the British establishment was not prepared to support the concept of self-determination, regardless of how beneficial a divided America might have appeared. Crook also cites numerous reasons for upper- and middle-class opposition to the Union unrelated to the question of democracy

---

[16] D. P. Crook, *The North, the South and the powers: 1861–1865*, New York 1974.
[17] Howard Jones, *Union in peril: the crisis over British intervention in the Civil War*, Chapel Hill 1992.

and thus not considered by the traditional model, such as distaste of the North's protectionist Morrill tariff, which offended the widespread free-trading sentiment in Britain.

Despite criticising the traditional interpretation, most of the revisionist studies only challenge isolated points of the model yet remain, for the most part, firmly within its framework. Further, despite the revisionist criticism, more recent studies have resurrected many (sometimes all) of the arguments of the traditional interpretation of British attitudes towards the war. This has been caused, in part, by the changing interpretations of the Civil War itself that occurred in the United States during and after the Civil Rights struggle. For one thing, slavery has once again gained prominence as the cause of the conflict, which, in turn, has led to the contest being labelled, by numerous historians, as a moral war. As such, pro-Union or pro-Confederate sentiment has reacquired, to a certain extent, the clear political distinctions formerly attached to them – reaction on the side of the Confederacy, progression on the side of the Union. Although this reappraisal was first applied to events in the United States, it did not take long before it was reapplied to Anglo-American relations during the conflict. Despite the fact that precious little new research has been done on the opinions of conservatives and the upper and middle classes regarding the war since Crook's *The North, the South and the powers*, his and Ellison's pronouncements on radical and labour opinion have been questioned by, among others, Philip S. Foner.[18]

Foner's *British labor and the American Civil War* (1981) largely rebuts the revisionists generally, and Ellison specifically.[19] Accusing Ellison of accepting southern partisans' claims unquestioningly, Foner insists that the pro-Confederate newspapers and meetings in Lancashire she cites had nothing to do with the working-class or radical movements and names numerous labour leaders who were overwhelmingly pro-Union. He particularly criticises Ellison for her dismissal of the famous Manchester Free-Trade Hall meeting on 31 December 1862, where a gathering of working men and others pledged their support for the northern cause and received Abraham Lincoln's 'Address to the English Working Men,' by way of reply.

Foner's book, unfortunately while not short of interesting points, has some problems. For example, if Ellison does accept Confederate supporters' claims

---

[18] As far as I have discovered, there has been only one recent article which has specifically concentrated on upper-middle-class, aristocratic or conservative opinion: Donald A. Bellows's article, 'A study of British conservative reaction to the American Civil War', *Journal of Southern History* li (1985), 506–36. Unfortunately, Bellows's article is disappointing. First, many of the individuals he examines were not conservatives – the novelist Elizabeth Gaskell, for example. Second, he states that the conservatives were pro-secession without providing any new evidence or refuting the arguments of other historians. Third, he fails to note people's changes of opinion, calling Gaskell pro-Confederate. In actual fact, Gaskell was never pro-South and was persuaded by the American Charles Elliot Norton early in the war to adopt a pro-northern position.
[19] Philip S. Foner, *British labor and the American Civil War*, New York 1981.

uncritically, Foner essentially does the same on an even greater scale with the Union propagandists' allegations. Further, his dismissal of the revisionists generally, and Ellison specifically, is somewhat too easy. Foner insists, 'At no point does Ellison prove that meetings held in Lancashire to support the Confederacy were "workingmen's" meetings, a difficult task to be sure, since even most of the pro-Southern papers in those towns did not make this claim.'[20] This is simply untrue. Ellison specifically describes meetings of workmen cited by the local press, such as that held in Ashton-under-Lyne in January 1863.[21] This work, meanwhile, lists others in England. Foner also dismisses Ellison's arguments that the Manchester Free-Trade Hall meeting was contrived, claiming that this is her belief, not that of the Lancashire press.[22] In fact, Ellison specifically cites the *Manchester Courier*'s dismissal of it as a 'contrived enterprise' on the part of Cobden and Bright.[23] The most fundamental problem with Foner's work, 'though is his almost blind faith in the traditional model: which, upon examination, is based on no more than pro-northern supporters', and then, later, E. D. Adams's and Jordan and Pratt's, belief that the working class was pro-North while the rest of British society was pro-South.[24]

This view, of course, ignores the many studies cited above. Further, even when Foner actually does deal address opponents of his views, his rebuttals frequently lack foundation. He dismisses d'A. Jones's thesis of the myth of working-class support for the Union on the grounds that it 'strains the imagination to the breaking point to be asked to believe that so many careful and reliable twentieth-century scholars were, up to the 1950s when the reaction [against the traditional interpretation] got underway, taken in by a plot carefully hatched by John Bright, Richard Cobden, William E. Gladstone, Henry Adams and Karl Marx.'[25] The answer to this is, of course, that d'A. Jones never mentions a plot, but only suggests how over-reliance on a particular set of sources could lead to misinterpretation. In any case, the real question is *why* there has been a reaction against the traditional model; which did not start in the 1950s, as stated by Foner, but in 1931, with the first edition of Owsley.

None the less, the re-emergence of at least portions of the traditional model is evident in two of the most recent full-scale studies of Anglo-American relations during the conflict: Brian Jenkins's *Britain and the war for the Union* (volume 1, 1974, volume 2, 1980) and Dean B. Mahin's *One war at a time: the international dimensions of the American Civil War* (1999).[26] Although

---

[20] Ibid. 21.
[21] Ellison, *Support for secession*, 74.
[22] Foner, *British labor and the American Civil War*, 21–2.
[23] Ellison, *Support for secession*, 81. See Ellison for the journal's objections in their entirety.
[24] Foner, *British labor and the American Civil War*, 12–14.
[25] Ibid. 24.
[26] Brian Jenkins, *Britain and the war for the Union*, i, ii, Montreal 1974, 1980; Dean B.

both studies offer new insight on the diplomacy of the period, they are less successful on the question of British public opinion, both effectively endorsing the traditional model of hostile enfranchised classes desirous of the democratic North's downfall. Jenkins, despite providing little in the way of new evidence or even refuting the findings of Crook, Whitridge, or W. D. Jones, concludes that although Britain wished to interfere and destroy the Union it was stayed by a fear of losing its Canadian colonies in a war with the North. Further, although he dismisses the idea of working-class support for the Union, Jenkins fails to address Harrison's arguments, which is a serious omission. Mahin, meanwhile, is even more supportive of the traditional interpretation that British radicals and the working class supported the North because the survival and spread of democracy depended on a Union victory, and ignores the revisionist arguments even more completely than does Jenkins. Besides Whitridge, W. D. Jones and Harrison, the arguments of Ellison and Crook are not acknowledged, far less answered. Also absent are the arguments of Foner, which is particularly puzzling because his work would at least have provided a justification for Mahin's repetition of the traditional interpretation of radical and working-class support for the Union.

Mahin's work, published in 1999, brings us to the present and it is worthwhile looking at two very recent studies on the subject of English opinion and the American Civil War. The first, R. J. M. Blackett's 'Pressure from without: African Americans, British public opinion and Civil War diplomacy' (1995), examines, among other things, public meetings convened by pro-Union and pro-Confederate supporters.[27] Although Blackett concludes that working-class opinion was divided over the Civil War, he believes that conservatives were more likely to be pro-South and radicals pro-North for the usual democratic reasons.

The second work is James M. McPherson's 'The whole family of man: Lincoln and the last best hope abroad' (1995).[28] McPherson is one of the leading Civil War historians (and a proponent of the notion that the conflict was a moral one) and his work can be treated as representative of the present consensus on the subject of British opinion on the conflict. Although McPherson acknowledges that 'a simple dichotomy between British liberals who admired American democracy and supported the Union and conservatives who detested both does considerable violence to historical reality', he none the less believes that revisionists have overstated their case. Citing the examples of Cobden and Bright, McPherson argues that, on the whole,

---

Mahin, *One war at a time: the international dimensions of the American Civil War*, Washington 1999.
[27] R. J. M. Blackett, 'Pressure from without: African Americans, British public opinion and Civil War diplomacy', in Robert E. May (ed.), *The Union, the Confederacy and the Atlantic rim*, West Lafayette 1995, 69–100.
[28] James M. McPherson, 'The whole family of man: Lincoln and the last best hope abroad', ibid. 131–58.

liberals and the working class supported the North while conservatives and the aristocracy supported the South on the basis of democratic arguments. He declares that the United States was a symbol of freedom and democracy for the oppressed of the world, and their fate, both at home and abroad, depended upon the preservation of the Union. McPherson cites numerous Northerners who believed this was so, such as the Adams family, stating that 'the triumph of democracy in Britain was an indirect result of the American Civil War'.[29]

McPherson's description of the northern belief that the future of democracy depended upon a Union victory is probably sound. His statement that Cobden and Bright shared this belief is undoubtedly so. Unfortunately, the evidence upon which McPherson's argument is based only serves to highlight the traditional interpretation's central flaw. Its foundation is based largely on the opinions of the Union's strongest supporters – American and British alike. Their interpretation of the war, and British attitudes towards it, has been accepted far too easily. This is a type of thinking we need to move away from. As we have seen above, Foner is very quick to brush aside d'A. Jones's criticism of the Adams family, Cobden, Bright, Marx and Gladstone, which is unfortunate, because this disparate group has done so much to shape our perceptions of Anglo-American relations during this period.

The Adams family, Cobden, Bright and Marx were, to a greater or lesser extent, Union sympathisers – indeed, in the case of the first three, outright propagandists. C. F. Adams, and his son Henry, apart from viewing the war through a northern perspective that was vastly different from that of the British, saw a southern supporter in every Briton. Indeed, Adams senior told the secretary of state, William Henry Seward, after the war, that Britain did its best to help the break-up of the United States.[30] This is not only a serious allegation it is also a highly questionable one, as anyone surveying the diplomacy of the period can attest. Cobden and Bright, meanwhile, were the two most profoundly pro-American radicals in Britain and effectively served as spokesmen for the northern lobby in England during this period. As a result, their pronouncements must be subjected to far more scrutiny than they have been hitherto. Further, as this work will establish, not only was Bright, in particular, far more pro-Union than most of his erstwhile followers, but many of the latter did not even endorse his arguments that the cause of the North was that of democracy. A similar charge can be laid against Marx, who was further over-reliant on ideology – in particular, his arguments regarding the displacement of agrarian societies by industrialised ones and his belief in working-class solidarity. The last, however, was far more perceived than real.

The only individual in the group who was not a pro-northern sympathiser was Gladstone. Gladstone, however, only made his pronouncements about working-class support for the Union after the war was over, precisely because,

[29] Ibid. 147.
[30] Adams, *Great Britain and the American Civil War*, i. 1.

as d'A. Jones has argued, he was promoting the extension of the electoral franchise. During the war, Gladstone's speeches in favour of the Confederacy were cheered by working-class audiences – something the Grand Old Man found politic to forget.

If the traditional interpretation is flawed, then so too are many of its revisionist critiques. For example, apart from the fact that events have been seen largely through the opinions of northern and southern partisans, virtually all the pronouncements made on various social classes' opinions are based on the views of a small minority. Jordan and Pratt, for instance, base their arguments for a pro-southern aristocracy on the opinions of fewer than five lords, and their statements on conservative opinion on a similarly small number of members of parliament. Even W. D. Jones and Whitridge cite few specific examples. It is all very well to mention the odd reactionary such as the duke of Argyll who disliked the Confederacy intensely, but this cannot be assumed to be the view of the majority of the House of Lords. This work examines the views of a much larger number of members of parliament – from both Houses – than has previously been the case. The members include conservatives, radicals and liberals and their arguments regarding the Civil War are examined in detail.

This leads us to the most serious omission in studies of Anglo-American relations during the war: the failure to place British perspectives within their own political and social context. This includes not only British views on secession, trade, the rules of warfare, political and neutral rights, but views on race and slavery as well. For example, on the question of British thought on American democracy, virtually none of the writers mentioned above discuss the influence of Alexis de Tocqueville. As both D. P. Crook and Jon Roper have established, de Tocqueville's *Democracy in America* (1835 and 1840) profoundly shaped British views of the United States in the antebellum period, particularly by John Stuart Mill's analysis of the work.[31] Readers of de Tocqueville frequently forget that the Frenchman had numerous criticisms of the United States, and although Mill was less pessimistic than de Tocqueville regarding the failures of democracy, he was still prejudiced in favour of a middle-class version, something he believed existed in America. The resonance of de Tocqueville's ideas and criticisms of the United States can be distinctly heard in British commentary on the war and will be pointed out during the course of this work.

No issue, however, impacted upon English opinion on the American Civil War as much as did slavery. The existence of the institution caused far more damage to the reputation of the Confederacy than most historians have acknowledged. The British, however, were always suspicious of Union claims that the war was an anti-slavery campaign, even after Lincoln's Emancipation Proclamation, because of the far higher levels of anti-black sentiment in

---

[31] Crook, *American democracy in English politics*, ch. v; Jon Roper, *Democracy and its critics: Anglo-American democratic thought in the nineteenth century*, London 1989, 72–83.

American society, something which argued against the North's sincerity on the issue. This is another vital point that has also been overlooked in most studies of our subject and will be examined in this work.

Another problem besetting studies of British opinion on the Civil War is omission of the discussion of the state of Anglo-American relations before the war even began. As Martin Crawford points out in his *The Anglo-American crisis of the nineteenth century: The Times and America, 1850–1862* (1987), not enough attention has been paid to British-U.S. relations of the antebellum period.[32] This is clear not only in the discussions of slavery, but in the examinations of each country's national experience as well. The overriding concern of the British regarding the Civil War was that they were not dragged into it. Besides the Indian Mutiny in 1857–8, Britain had earlier fought the Crimean War in 1854–6. Although victorious in both neither had been an easy victory, and the latter in particular not only caused a crisis of confidence in British military ability, but reminded them just how far-stretched they were as an international power. The Crimean War impacted upon British perceptions of the Civil War in other ways that have been ignored as well, as this work will make clear. In any event, the British, just before the American Civil War, had been reminded of their limits, and it is no coincidence that isolationism was the prevailing doctrine of this period. The British were not about to abandon their empire – far from it – but there was virtually no appetite during our period for any further foreign entanglements.

The United States' experience was almost the complete opposite of Britain's and it is remarkable how little discussion of American expansionism during this period there has been – particularly by historians adhering to the traditional interpretation. In particular, Manifest Destiny, which effectively claimed the entire continent of North America (not to mention Cuba) for the United States, has been either ignored or played down. Indeed, many historians appear to concur – consciously or unconsciously – with H. C. Allen's statement that 'Manifest Destiny was not based on militarism, American expansion across a practically empty continent despoiled no nation unjustly.'[33] This is simply untrue. Besides the American Indians who were brutally dispossessed of their lands, the United States, by conquest or purchase, had seized all Spanish and French territory on the continent during the century and, in 1846–8, expanded its territory by two-fifths through making war on Mexico – a conflict which, the then Lieutenant, Ulysses S. Grant considered to be 'one of the most unjust ever waged by a stronger against a weaker nation'.[34] As late as 1855, filibuster expeditions were still

---

[32] Martin Crawford, *The Anglo-American crisis of the nineteenth century: The Times and America, 1850–1862*, Athens, Ga. 1987.
[33] H. C. Allen, *Great Britain and the United States: a history of Anglo-American relations, 1783–1952*, London 1954, 205.
[34] Grant further added, 'It was an instance of a republic following the bad example of European monarchies, in not considering justice in their desire to acquire additional territory.'

being directed at Cuba, only to be overshadowed by the impending crisis of the Civil War. Simply put, in the period just before the conflict, the United States had gained a great deal at comparatively little cost – an experience antithetical to Britain's.

Much has been made of the fact that this American expansionism was more popular in the South than in the North, and therefore connected to the expansion of slavery, but this is where the problem of Canada comes in. Although the United States negotiated with Britain over territorial disputes such as the Oregon border, its designs on Canada existed almost right up to the outbreak of the Civil War. Northerners, not Southerners held these designs on Canada and although it is true that Manifest Destiny was always far more popular among members and supporters of the Democratic Party, the Republicans had their annexationists, too. One individual in particular who needs to be named is Abraham Lincoln's secretary of state, William H. Seward, who unquestionably believed that the United States should annex Canada. The United States might have been willing to negotiate with Britain over territory, but weaker nations were not as lucky. It is therefore unsurprising that many in Britain, far from regarding the United States as a peaceful, democratic republic, instead viewed it as an aggressively expansionist power with an apparently insatiable appetite for territory. As the historian Charles Adams has cogently asked, 'What was Manifest Destiny but a label for American imperialism?'[35] It must also be borne in mind that this was the view of the British prime minister, Henry Temple, Viscount Palmerston, who experienced not only the wrangling over the border with Canada, but also American intransigence over British attempts to stop the international slave trade.

This work, then, re-examines the subject of British views of the American Civil War by taking these and other issues into account. Although the term 'public opinion' has been used above, a more accurate term for this work's subject is, in fact, public discourse – in other words, what the British thought about the war, what they said about it and how they reacted to it. Further, by concentrating closely on British, rather than American, views, this work de-emphasises the issue of the cause(s) of the Civil War. There is a good reason for this. For example, those historians who argue that slavery was the only issue at stake are prone to let it colour their views of British opinion. Emphasising slavery as the sole issue of the conflict, they tend to attribute all criticism of, or, indeed, lack of support for, the North as somehow morally dubious – even when the Union was in the wrong, such as during the *Trent* affair. This, in turn, leads to views being attributed, without evidence, to

---

Note how the United States was simply expected to act more justly than the European powers. This bland assurance, as we shall see, underpinned northern criticism of Britain: Ulysses S. Grant, *The personal memoirs of U. S. Grant*, London 1885, i. 53.
[35] Charles Adams, *When in the course of human events: arguing the case for southern secession*, Lanham, Md. 2000, 78.

anti-northern commentators that were, in fact, never held. Further, even if the cause of the Union was a moral campaign against slavery that does not necessarily explain or account for people's positions towards it – particularly if they honestly believed, albeit erroneously, that other issues were in fact at stake.

This work examines Anglo-American relations during the conflict from both a thematic and a chronological perspective. Chronology, as this work will reveal, is crucial to any understanding of British thinking on the war. To give but one example, the *Trent* affair was a watershed in Anglo-American relations during the war and there was a distinct difference between British attitudes towards the Union before the incident and afterwards. Yet the thematic perspective is important, too, because the war raised numerous issues in Britain that were repeatedly discussed throughout the conflict.

Besides personal letters, parliamentary debates and a limited amount of propaganda literature, this work is based on an examination of newspaper reports, with the emphasis on information pertaining to general common sentiment and public meetings – especially those attended by members of parliament and members of the aristocracy. A broad spectrum of journals is examined, covering a wide range of political viewpoints, from the *Saturday Review* on the right, to *Reynolds's Weekly Newspaper* on the left. What has generally been avoided are those journals which either prostituted themselves out to one side, such as the *London Standard* and the *London Herald*, which did so for the Confederacy, and the *Daily News* and the *Morning Star*, which did so for the Union, or were blatant propaganda pamphlets, such as the *Index*, for the South, and the *London American*, for the North.[36]

The journals examined in this work are weeklies, monthlies and quarterlies, which, being reviews of a longer period of time, tended to offer a calmer appraisal of the state of Anglo-American affairs than did the dailies. Further, the weeklies had a wider audience than the dailies because the higher costs of the latter made them less attractive to mid-nineteenth-century lower-middle- and working-class readers.[37] In addition, in the 1860s, the monthlies and the weeklies were generally more influential than the dailies on political issues.[38] The final advantage of these journals is that they were less prone to interference from parliamentary political parties than the dailies.[39] The dailies are not entirely ignored, however, and *The Times* is also examined. 'The Thunderer', however, is examined in conjunction with other

---

[36] Henry Hotze, the Confederate propagandist, informed Richmond that both the *Herald* and the *Standard* placed themselves at his disposal. The *Daily News*, meanwhile, had an information-exchange partnership with the *New York Tribune*. The *Morning Star* was Cobden and Bright's organ, which, to all intents and purposes, made it a northern propaganda pamphlet: Lucy Brown, *Victorian news and newspapers*, Oxford 1985, 63, 179 and ch. x passim.
[37] Ibid. 30–1.
[38] Ibid. 109.
[39] Stephen Koss, *The rise and fall of the political press in Britain*, London 1981, i, ch. i passim.

journals. Historians of Anglo-American relations have tended to overrate *The Times*'s influence during this period – too easily assuming that its views were those of British society as a whole. As Crawford points out, those historians who state that when *The Times* took snuff, England sneezed are according the newspaper a power it did not enjoy in the 1860s.[40]

Although the term 'Britain' has been used consistently above, largely because most historians of the period claim to examine British, as opposed to English, opinion, this work concentrates on the English point of view – largely through the perspective of London. The term 'Britain' or 'British' is used only in specific instances, such as when referring to diplomatic events. Palmerston's ministry, after all, represented the entire United Kingdom, not merely England. Although some meetings in both Scotland and Ireland are mentioned, both Scottish and Irish opinion often differed from that of England, and to lump them in with English perceptions would be hazardous.[41]

Beyond each side's partisans, most English observers, irrespective of class, wished to remain neutral in the struggle and distrusted (and even disliked) both sides. Initially, English opinion was hostile to the Confederate states because of slavery and because of the South's 'King Cotton' plan: a policy of withholding the southern cotton crop in order to force British intervention in the war. However, suspicious of both America's past history of slavery and its greater levels of racism, most in England doubted the Union's sincerity on the subject of emancipation – a doubt apparently justified by the North's vacillation on the issue. English exasperation with the Union grew, thanks to both the North's initially belligerent diplomacy and the Morrill tariff, the latter being regarded as an anti-British measure. This perception of a hostile Union was reinforced by the *Trent* affair which led to high levels of anti-northern sentiment in England. This situation persisted until late 1863, lessened in part only by Lincoln's Emancipation Proclamation. Although during this same period there is evidence of increased pro-southern sentiment, English opinion never wholly endorsed the Confederacy, largely because of slavery, and such sympathy as existed declined sharply when southern opposition to Britain's continued neutrality (which Davis's government correctly realised helped the Union) resulted in anti-British sentiment and activities. By 1864, Britain was despised by both sides in the conflict and the English, in turn, preoccupied with European issues, dismissed both the Union and the Confederacy.

---

[40] Crawford, *The Anglo-American crisis*, 15–18.
[41] For an examination of Scottish public opinion during this period see Robert Botsford, 'Scotland and the American Civil War', unpubl. PhD diss. Edinburgh 1955. For Ireland see Joseph Hernon, *Celts, Catholics and copperheads: Ireland views the American Civil War*, Columbus 1968.

1

Differences of Opinion

'From America the news is hardly satisfactory.'

Southern secession took Britain by surprise. Having witnessed the various state wranglings of the previous decade, the actual occurrence of secession came as something of a shock.[1] The shock subsided, however, and, as historians from E. D. Adams onward have established, English public opinion was against the Confederacy from the outset.[2] The belief that the South had no better justification for secession than defeat in a fair election, combined with contempt for its 'domestic institution', ensured that South Carolina and her fellow secessionists of the lower South were universally condemned.[3]

It was from this point, according to the traditional interpretation, that British opinion turned against the Union, when the Lincoln administration failed to make emancipation an immediate war aim; and the traditional interpretation dates the souring of trans-Atlantic relations from the Queen's Proclamation of Neutrality, issued on 13 May 1861, in response to the fall of Fort Sumter on 14 April and Lincoln's subsequent declaration of the blockade of southern ports. Hence, the Proclamation of Neutrality, according to the traditional interpretation, was the beginning of Britain's rejection of the Union, and angered Northerners, who criticised it as 'a hasty, if not hostile act'.[4] Britain, always opposed to American institutions in principle, used the Union's vacillation over emancipation as an excuse to begin favouring the previously despised Confederacy.

Although the northern reaction to the Proclamation of Neutrality did indeed adversely affect English opinion, discontent had set in earlier because of, as Crook correctly argues, 'the disenchanting march of events', rather than simple disappointment in the Lincoln administration for not embarking upon a war of emancipation.[5] Crook, however, underestimates how much hesitation regarding emancipation cost the Union in the court of English popular opinion. While it is true that there was little enthusiasm for forced emancipation that would cause war (initially, the English hoped that

---

1 For a discussion on the initial British reaction to secession see D. P. Crook, 'Portents of war: English opinion on secession', *Journal of American Studies* xxxiii (1967), 163–79.
2 Adams, *Great Britain and the American Civil War*, i. 36–57.
3 See Crook, *The North, the South and the powers*, 38–9.
4 Gordon H. Warren, *The fountain of discontent: the Trent affair and freedom of the seas*, Boston 1981, 71.
5 Crook, *The North, the South and the powers*, 39–40.

secession would be resolved peacefully), this opinion existed only while there was hope for peace. Once the South initiated hostilities by firing on Fort Sumter, it was widely believed that the North should embark upon war against slavery. Suspicion regarding emancipation was only one factor that told heavily against the North. Another, much more damaging, factor was perceived Union belligerence, especially on the part of the secretary of state, William H. Seward, but also on the part of the American minister to Russia, Cassius Clay, which was expressed in his letter to *The Times*. This perception of a menacing North was compounded by the opinions of the Union press, especially, but not solely, over Britain's declaration of neutrality. Added to this was the protectionist Morrill tariff, the impact of which, Crawford points out, 'was certainly greater than most modern historians have been willing to admit'.[6]

Although English exasperation with the North existed, opinion never, despite the claims of Union supporters (and some historians), became pro-South – not simply because of slavery, but also because of the 'King Cotton' policy, which offended most commentators. This dislike of the Confederacy was made apparent not only by the hostility of the London press, but also by the reception accorded to specific pro-southern activities, the most important of which, in 1861, being Sir William Gregory's motion in the House of Commons for the recognition of the Confederacy. This chapter examines English suspicions regarding American emancipation; their response to the North's diplomacy; the Union press and the Morrill tariff; their views of the Confederacy and the South's King Cotton tactics; as well as the opinions of MPs in the first year of the war.

The question of slavery

The impact of southern slavery on English opinion has never been adequately accounted for.[7] No subject impacted upon the debate regarding the conflict across the Atlantic more than did slavery. As we shall see, those individuals and institutions who and which have been classified as pro-North should more accurately be described as anti-slavery. Their hatred of slavery, rather than any love for the Union, was what united them in their efforts. It would probably not be too much to claim that the litmus test of whether or not one opposed the South depended almost entirely upon one's views about slavery. Initially, the North's failure to capitalise on the issue was a serious blow to its hope (or, rather, expectation) of English sympathy.

---

[6] Crawford, *The Anglo-American crisis*, 93.
[7] Crawford, for example, one of the most recent writers on the subject of Anglo-American relations during the war, states, 'surprisingly, it [slavery] would play no decisive role in the majority of British criticism during this period': *The Anglo-American crisis*, 14.

Certainly the Lincoln administration's vacillation on the issue, with the emphasis on the preservation of the Union rather than emancipation, cost the North popular support. Lincoln famously stated in his inaugural address on 4 March 1861, 'I have no purpose, directly or indirectly, to interfere with the institution of slavery in states where it exists . . . I believe I have no lawful right to do so and I have no intention to do so.'[8] As E. D. Adams observes,

> It should be no matter for surprise, therefore, that, as these efforts were observed in Great Britain, a note of uncertainty began to replace the earlier unanimity of opinion that the future of slavery was at stake in America. This offered an easy excuse for a switch-about of sympathy as British commercial and other interests began to be developed, and even dismayed the ardent friends of the anti-slavery North.[9]

The shift of opinion was apparent. *The Economist*, in May, claimed that the South was wrong to accuse the Union of interfering with slavery: 'It would be more to the credit of the North if it had.'[10] This attitude hardened as the year wore on. In September, the journal stated that had the Union made emancipation a war aim, it 'should be called upon to take a very different view of the subject'.[11] In the following month the *Saturday Review* concurred, 'England is slandered if it is said that she does not with her whole heart hate slavery and desire its extinction, or that she would not be cordially with the North if it were against slavery that the North was fighting. The North, however, vehemently disclaims any such imputation.'[12] The *Annual Register* of 1861, looking back over the events of the year, summed up the majority view when it stated, 'Its [the Confederacy's] policy was simply a defensive policy, and all it asked was to be let alone. The North, on the other hand, had undertaken the task of conquest.'[13]

Unfortunately, Lincoln's inauguration speech fails to explain fully why public opinion so quickly arrived at the belief that freedom of the slave was not an issue in the war any more than does E. D. Adams's insinuation that the English were simply looking for an opportunity to switch sympathies.[14] What, in 1861, made the Union's attitudes to emancipation so suspect was

---

8 As Lincoln himself noted, he was merely repeating what he had stated in his debates with Stephen A. Douglas: *The collected works of Abraham Lincoln*, ed. Roy P. Basler, New Brunswick 1953–5, iii. 16; iv. 262.
9 Adams, *Great Britain and the American Civil War*, i. 50. Adams's depiction of the North as 'anti-slavery' is too simplistic.
10 *The Economist*, 25 May 1861, 564.
11 Ibid. 28 Sept. 1861, 1066.
12 *Saturday Review*, 5 Oct. 1861, 339.
13 *Annual Register*, 1861, 'History', 263.
14 The idea of the British actively seeking to switch from a pro-northern to a pro-southern stance is a recurrent theme of Adams: *Great Britain and the American Civil War*, i. 175. The supposed *volte-face* from a pro-Union to a pro-Confederate position is discussed below.

America's past history on the slave trade, American racism, the John Frémont controversy and the Anderson case.[15]

The right of search

As late as 1858, the United States and Britain had nearly gone to war over the slave trade when Royal Navy vessels began boarding American ships on the high seas to search for slaves being illegally transported from Africa.[16] The right to search for slaves had vexed Anglo-American relations since the 1830s. For example, when Britain began negotiating treaties with the major European nautical powers for mutual right to search by the naval vessels of each upon the others' merchant marine, the strongest opponent of this policy was the United States. As Bernard Semmell points out, the American minister to Paris, Lewis Cass, led a very public campaign to persuade the French government not to sign any such treaty.[17] When, in 1841, Britain, France, Russia, Austria and Prussia went ahead and signed the Quintuple Treaty, declaring the slave trade to be piracy and granting each other the reciprocal right of search, Cass was again vocal in his denunciations. In fairness to Cass, he believed that Britain's anti-slavery campaign was merely a pretext to dominate the high seas, but he was not speaking only for himself. There is little doubt that his views were shared by most in the United States. As Semmell notes, Cass's campaign against British maritime policy helped secure his position as the Democratic Party's presidential nominee in 1848.[18] Further, the United States rejected the Quintuple Treaty, insisting that, in time of peace, the national flag protected a ship from being searched by foreign naval vessels, and declared that it would police its own merchant marine. This might have been acceptable to Britain if the United States had, in fact, genuinely tried to stop American slave traders – but no such attempt was made. Although it is indeed true, as some historians have pointed out, that under US law engaging in the slave trade was punishable by death, no American was successfully prosecuted, much less executed, for slave trading until the conviction of Captain Nathaniel Gordon in New York in 1862. Finally, as a last attempt at compromise, Britain offered to abandon the claim of a right to search and instead claim a right to visit – in order to verify that a

---

[15] Frémont was the correct spelling of his name. All British journals, however, left off the accent. To write 'sic' after the general's name in every quote would be tedious, so I have refrained from doing so.
[16] For a recent discussion on this subject see Richard D. Fulton, 'The London *Times* and the Anglo-American boarding dispute of 1858', *Nineteenth Century Contexts* xvii/2 (1993), 133–44.
[17] Bernard Semmell, *Liberalism and naval strategy: ideology, interest and sea power during the Pax Britannica*, Boston 1986, 44–5.
[18] Ibid. 45.

ship flying the American flag had the right to do so – but the United States rejected this, too.[19]

The British had good reason to want the right to at least visit the American merchant marine. Although, earlier in the century, the United States had contributed to suppressing the slave trade, these efforts had lapsed. As Allen points out, in October 1819, Congress empowered the president to employ the United States Navy for the seizure of American slave traders and appropriated $100,000 for the purpose. By 1834, however, this had shrunk to $5,000 and by 1842, nothing; America effectively ceased searching for slave traders. Furthermore, by the time Britain again started searching American ships, 'the United States was by far the largest importer of slaves in the world, despite the illegality of the trade'. Indeed, in 1863, the British consul in New York estimated that between 1857 and 1861, of the 170 slave-trading expeditions that were fitted out, 117 were known or believed to have sailed from American ports – 74 of them from New York. Allen sums up the situation thus, 'By 1839 Britain had largely succeeded in stopping all the holes in the net except those made under illicit cover of the American flag, which meant that this device was more and more popular with slavers.'[20] Although most of these slaves were destined for Brazil and Cuba rather than America, as far as the English were concerned the United States was supporting the international slave trade. Indeed, many slave traders were not simply flying the American flag for cover – they were, in fact, United States citizens. It was because of this situation that the British re-started the policy of stopping and searching American shipping.

The resurrection of this policy was badly received by the United States. As Fulton points out, when HMS *Styx* halted and searched the American schooner *Mobile* in the West Indies in May 1858, the *New York Times* and other New York journals, including the anti-British *New York Herald*, raised a commotion. The American government, led by the now secretary of state, Lewis Cass, demanded that Britain cease and desist all such activities. To reinforce this demand, the United States navy was ordered ready for duty and the Senate passed a bill 'enabling the President to obtain by force prompt redress for the perpetration of outrages upon the flag, soil or citizens of the United States, or upon their property'. Thus, argues Fulton, 'That the Americans were prepared to go to war with England over the issue of boarding on the high seas is undeniable.' Initially, a collision seemed inevitable, especially as the response by the British press and public was largely hostile, 'stating that Britain was in the right and that if the Americans wanted war, they could have more than they wanted'. Britain, however, had recently fought the Crimean War and there was little desire to fight a third Anglo-American war. In part thanks to the efforts of *The Times*, the Conservative administration of Lord Derby determined that stopping the slave trade was not worth going to

---

[19] Adams, *Great Britain and the American Civil War*, i. 8–9.
[20] Allen, *Great Britain and the United States*, 401–3.

war against the United States, and promised to end the search policy.[21] This act, by the way, disgusted the opposition Liberals, particularly Palmerston and Russell.[22]

Although the United States had won its point regarding right to search, it lost credibility regarding opposition to the slave trade and thus slavery itself. It had been the New York press, hence the North, not the South, that had protested most vociferously against the British attempt to foil the activities of American slave traders. Unprepared to police their own citizens engaged in the slave trade but prepared to go to war to prevent others from doing so, the Americans were placed on the same moral level as pirates in the eyes of many.[23] Further, as Martin Crawford has argued, Anglo-American relations had been improving and were generally good during the 1850s, as both nations' remaining differences were peaceably settled.[24] The fact that the slave trade was an area where no compromise could be found reinforced English beliefs that the Americans were devoted to the institution of slavery. It is no wonder then that, in June 1861, when faced with Union protests against English suspicion of northern sincerity about emancipation, the *Saturday Review* remarked, 'The insinuation that the unanimous convictions of Englishmen are notoriously hypocritical, is worthy of the nation which has systemically thwarted all measures for the suppression of the Slave-trade itself.'[25] This attitude would prevail until 1862, when the Union, partially to gain British support, signed, on 7 April, a pact for the mutual right to search off the coasts of Africa and Cuba.[26]

American racial prejudice

American racism also tainted the notion that the North was likely to embrace emancipation. The complex question of American and English racial attitudes is discussed more fully later in this work. At present, the discussion is limited to the fact that not only did there exist greater antipathy

---

[21] Fulton, 'The London *Times* and the Anglo-American boarding dispute of 1858', 139. Fulton notes that *The Times* suffered a great deal of abuse from its contemporaries for its lack of patriotism when it argued for the American case on this particular issue. One wonders if this was in the back of the mind of the editor, John Delane, when the American Civil War broke out, and had an impact on *The Times*'s attitudes towards the conflict.
[22] Semmell, *Liberalism and naval strategy*, 48.
[23] Even *The Times* arrived at this conclusion, for although it did not think the British had the right to search American ships, it detested the American complicity in the slave trade: Fulton, 'The London *Times* and the Anglo-American boarding dispute of 1858', 141.
[24] Crawford, *The Anglo-American crisis*, ch. iii passim. Crawford, surprisingly, grants the slave-trade dispute little attention. See pp. 63–4.
[25] *Saturday Review*, 8 June 1861, 570. *The Economist* also accused the North of thwarting British efforts to end the slave trade: 14 Sept. 1861, 1011.
[26] Jones, *Union in peril*, 118.

towards blacks in American society, but the English were aware of this.[27] For one thing, de Tocqueville had noted the extreme racial prejudice in America and this was supported by others' reports as well.[28] As Douglas Lorimer points out, 'English observers did not see Lincoln as a defender of blacks, for informed journalists, politicians and philanthropists were well aware of northern racial prejudice, and soon learned that even anti-slavery opinion in the west stemmed from fear of black migration.'[29]

Certainly this argument made its appearance in the English press, and not just by informed journalists either. The *Saturday Review*, while reviewing a blatantly racist book by one J. H. Van Evrie, from the northern states, condemned his specious arguments that African Americans were a different species from whites, and concluded, 'His furious hatred towards the unhappy race whom he longs to rob even of their humanity, and which a European reader finds difficult to conceive, is something which happily this country has no counterpart.'[30] *The Economist* remarked on northern prejudice towards blacks as early as January 1860, quoting an Indiana congressman's insistence that his state 'would not under any circumstances tolerate any measure designed to elevate negroes to political equality with the whites'.[31] Just over a year later, it went so far as to state, 'The great majority of the people in the Northern States detest the coloured population even more than do the Southern whites.'[32] *The Economist* was not unique in its belief that Southerners were, slavery notwithstanding, less prejudiced against blacks. Nor was *The Economist* anti-American. Its editor, Walter Bagehot, was, if anything, an admirer of the United States.[33] In October the *Athenaeum*, reviewing the American Frederick Law Olmsted's anti-slavery book, stated, 'It is well known that in the Free States of America the Whites disdain to hold intercourse with Blacks – to sit at table or exchange the ordinary civilities of life with them. Mr. Olmsted records an almost total absence of this hateful race prejudice in Virginia.'[34] This view was shared by an anonymous writer in *Fraser's Magazine* who insisted, 'The North has always despised the negroes who are free men among them, still more than the South does their enslaved brethren.'[35] Even the *Spectator*, which argued throughout the conflict that slavery was the sole cause of the war, noted the 'fanatical hatred' the North-

---

[27] As Lorimer points out, Britain was seen as a haven from prejudice compared to America: *Colour, class and the Victorians*, Leicester 1978, 39.
[28] Alexis de Tocqueville, *Democracy in America*, New York 1945, i. 356–81.
[29] Douglas Lorimer, 'The role of anti-slavery sentiment in English reactions to the American Civil War', *Historical Journal* xix (1976), 405–20, 406.
[30] *Saturday Review*, 4 May 1861, 455.
[31] *The Economist*, 21 Jan. 1860, 59.
[32] Ibid. 2 Feb. 1861, 116.
[33] Alastair Burnet, The Economist *America, 1843–1993: 150 years of reporting the American connection*, London 1993.
[34] *Athenaeum*, 12 Oct. 1861, 476.
[35] *Fraser's Magazine* (Aug. 1861), 245.

erners bore towards African Americans.[36] Thomas Ellison of Liverpool, writing in the radical *Westminster Review*, also condemned the North's antipathy towards blacks and echoed this opinion. Indeed, Ellison went so far as to inform his readers that 'In fact, to such an extent is this intolerant bearing of the white men carried, that there are instances on record of negroes going South and choosing slavery as the happier mode of existence.'[37] This was obviously nonsense, but the fact that anyone could write this in a radical journal suggests just how badly the English believed African Americans were treated in the northern states.

The Frémont controversy

That the Union was prepared to liberate a people it so openly detested seemed utterly unbelievable to many English commentators, both before and even after Lincoln's Emancipation Proclamation.[38] Besides, the government at Washington committed certain actions that seemed completely contrary to any emancipationist goal. For example, when in May 1861 the Union General Benjamin Butler ordered his troops not to return fugitive slaves to the Confederates, the administration approved his policy. In August, however, when the Union General John Frémont issued a proclamation freeing the slaves of rebels in Missouri, Lincoln countermanded it.[39] The first event suggested a move towards emancipation, the second, a move against. No wonder the English press was confused – especially *The Times*.[40] It is curious that historians have paid little or no attention to the Frémont controversy – especially considering that it caused a major debate in the Union.[41] *The Economist* used the news of Frémont's actions for a scathing attack on the notion that the North was sincere about emancipation: 'The very last arrival from America brings a curious comment on these philanthropic pretensions [of emancipation] in the announcement that in Missouri the slaves *of Rebels only* were to be emancipated, while those of loyal subjects were to be retained

---

[36] *Spectator*, 30 Mar. 1861, 333–4.
[37] *Westminster Review* (Jan. 1861), 168.
[38] Not necessarily a majority. The impact of Lincoln's Emancipation Proclamation is discussed later in this work.
[39] James M. McPherson, *Battle cry of freedom: the Civil War era*, New York 1989, 352–5. Lincoln believed he had to repudiate Frémont's proclamation in order to retain the loyalty of slave-holding Missouri. English opinion was divided over the validity of this motive.
[40] See *The Times*, 30 Sept. 1861, 3.
[41] See McPherson, *Battle cry of freedom*, 352–8. The debate surrounding Frémont in England has received surprisingly scant attention from historians. Adams fails to mention it, as do Owsley, Crook and Howard. Jenkins acknowledges it, but restricts his discussion to its effect on Canadian opinion: *Britain and the war for the Union*, i. 178. Foner, meanwhile, notes the impact the controversy had on one labour journal: *British labor and the American Civil War*, 27.

in servitude!'[42] The fact that only the slaves of disloyal citizens would be freed was regarded as hypocritical by many observers. Surely, they argued, slavery was wrong regardless of where the loyalties of the slave owner lay (this argument would be raised again during Lincoln's Emancipation Proclamation). However, Frémont's decision had some supporters, too. The *Saturday Review* was guardedly optimistic about Frémont's proclamation, calling it a 'bold defiance of his superiors and legislature', and believed it would pressurise Lincoln on a course of emancipation.[43] When Frémont's decision was overruled, the journal cited this as evidence that the issue of slavery had no bearing on the war – as shown by its later criticism of Olmsted's pro-Union book: 'The whole object of them [Olmsted's arguments] is to induce the people of England to believe that the Northern invasion and the Northern blockade are, in spite of General Fremont's repudiated proclamation and President Lincoln's reiterated avowals, a crusade of Abolition against slavery.'[44]

Just as Frémont was not without supporters, Lincoln was not entirely without sympathisers either – the most supportive being the *Illustrated London News*, which scrupulously reported the debate in the Union, acknowledging, 'Mr. Lincoln was influenced in this direction by a desire to retain his hold on the loyal population in the adhering and seceded Slave States.'[45] This, of course, was exactly what Lincoln was trying to do – and, indeed, had to do. The trouble was, this policy argued against notions that the Union would embark upon a course of emancipation. As it happened, the *Illustrated London News* was more sympathetic towards the problems facing Lincoln's administration than the *Spectator*, which had, in September, cited Frémont's proclamation as evidence that 'The news of every succeeding mail from America makes it more and more evident that the Slavery issue is the practical hinge of the civil war', only to angrily condemn the proclamation's repudiation a month later.[46] Opinions about Frémont's proclamation were as divided in England as in the Union; if the English were confused, so were their northern counterparts.[47] Generally, however, the controversy surrounding Frémont's proclamation loaned credence to the notion that the North had no intention of emancipating the slaves.

---

[42] *The Economist*, 14 Sept. 1861, 1011 [their italics].
[43] *Saturday Review*, 28 Sept. 1861, 316.
[44] Ibid. 2 Nov. 1861, 460.
[45] *Illustrated London News*, 5 Oct. 1861, 336. The journal covered the northern debate later in the month: ibid. 19 Oct. 1861, 393.
[46] *Spectator*, 14 Sept. 1861, 1000; 5 Oct. 1861, 1085.
[47] It is worth mentioning that Frémont's redoubtable wife, Jessie, when justifying her husband's activities to Lincoln, cited the need to strike a blow against slavery in order to enlist British sentiment on the side of the North: David Herbert Donald, *Lincoln*, London 1995, 315.

The Anderson extradition case

Missouri had been involved in an earlier controversy regarding the North's attitude towards emancipation. In 1853, a slave, John Anderson, escaped from Missouri and killed a man, Diggs, who tried to capture him.[48] In 1860, Anderson was discovered in Upper Canada (now Ontario) and the United States demanded his extradition. When the case was heard, two of the three judges of the Queen's Bench in Toronto concluded there was sufficient evidence to extradite Anderson on the grounds that, under the law of Missouri, the man whom Anderson killed had every right to stop him, making it a case of murder, regardless of the fact that it would not be such on British soil.[49] When, in January 1861, the news of the court's decision arrived in England, the public was shocked. *The Economist* argued that Anderson had committed '*justifiable* homicide' and insisted there were no grounds for returning him.[50] The *Saturday Review* was not only extremely critical of the court's decision, but of the whole extradition treaty with the United States, stating, 'All are agreed that a treaty which binds us (if it really does bind us) to deliver up a man whom we consider innocent to be burned alive, in due form of law under the savage code of Missouri, is a disgrace to the diplomacy which could have sanctioned so horrible a compact.'[51] The journal, however, doubted that Anderson would actually be returned to the United States.[52] Although not everyone shared the *Saturday Review*'s complacent belief that the extradition would not take place, the general consensus was that Anderson could not be returned to Missouri. The *English Woman's Journal* was another paper horrified by the court's decision and it insisted that Anderson should not be extradited.[53] *The Times*, meanwhile, stated that if there was no legal escape from the court's decision, the government should simply refuse point-blank to return Anderson, an opinion the *Saturday Review* called 'audacity worthy of an American State'.[54] The *Illustrated London News* agreed with its contemporaries, and stated that 'neither legally nor morally could we be called upon to surrender the man to be burned alive, as he will assuredly

---

48 Although a few historians have studied the Anderson case within the context of American slaves escaping to British territories, the effect of the case on English public opinion towards the North has never been either discussed or acknowledged. The best single examination I have come across of the legalities of the case is that of David M. Turley, ' "Free air" and fugitive slaves', in Christine Bolt and Seymour Drescher (eds), *Anti-slavery, religion and reform: essays in memory of Roger Anstey*, Folkestone 1980.
49 Turley outlines each of the three judges' arguments: ibid. 176.
50 *The Economist*, 12 Jan. 1861, 32 [their italics].
51 *Saturday Review*, 19 Jan. 1861, 56.
52 'We have not the smallest doubt that the law will open a door for Anderson's release without driving England to the shameful necessity of repudiating a solemn contract': ibid. 19 Jan. 1861, 56–7.
53 *English Woman's Journal*, 1 Feb. 1861, 431.
54 *Saturday Review*, 19 Jan. 1861, 56. It argued that Britain could not just simply repudiate signed treaties.

be, if yielded up'. Indeed, the writer added that to return Anderson 'would be a blot which no amount of anti-slavery speeches could ever efface'.[55] What must be noted, apart from the universal opposition to extraditing an escaped slave, is the picture of Anderson being burned alive and the implication that the southern states were barbaric. As we shall see, it was an image of the Confederacy that would remain in many quarters throughout the duration of the war.

The *Saturday Review* proved prescient. Reacting to public pressure, in particular from the British Foreign and Anti-Slavery Society, the Court of Common Pleas in Toronto reversed the earlier decision on the grounds that, under British law, Anderson had been unlawfully imprisoned in Missouri and therefore had the right to make his escape.[56] The court's decision was met with relief. The *Illustrated London News* celebrated by devoting a page to Anderson's harrowing flight from slavery – and included an engraving of the former slave.[57] The *Saturday Review*, meanwhile, devoted several pages to Anderson's release, and denounced the few protests the decision had caused in America.[58] Conspicuous by its absence among the weeklies' coverage of the Anderson case was the *Spectator*, which probably avoided discussing the issue because it reflected badly on the North.[59] As the federal government had pressed for Anderson's extradition after secession had taken place, the case marked the beginning of the erosion of the hope that the North would seek to end slavery. Indeed, during the first year of the war, Secretary of State William Henry Seward sent a message to all foreign governments asking them to refuse to grant asylum to slaves using the chaos to escape.[60] It was a request Palmerston contemptuously ignored.

There were, then, by the time war broke out, several apparently sound reasons for many English observers to distrust the arguments made by various Northerners – most noticeably Harriet Beecher Stowe of *Uncle Tom's Cabin* fame, and Britons sympathetic to the Union – that the cause of the war was slavery alone and that emancipation was the ultimate northern goal.[61]

Many historians, critical of English scepticism towards the Union, forget that the formers' suspicions were not entirely misguided. As Howard Jones points out, 'Most Northerners did not like blacks and had no inclination to

---

[55] *Illustrated London News*, 12 Jan. 1861, 30.
[56] For the court's decision see both the *Saturday Review*, 18 May 1861, 498–9, and the *Illustrated London News*, 9 Mar. 1861, 223.
[57] *Illustrated London News*, 9 Mar. 1861, 223.
[58] *Saturday Review*, 18 May 1861, 498–9.
[59] The *Spectator's* only mention of the Anderson affair was its report of the public's hostility to the extradition decision: 12 Jan. 1861, 32.
[60] Jasper Ridley, *Lord Palmerston*, London 1970, 550.
[61] Northerners' protests about British scepticism have been noted by Adams and Jenkins: Adams, *Great Britain and the American Civil War*, i. 181, and Jenkins, *Britain and the war for the Union*, i. 166. Neither writer, however, gives proper consideration to the reasons for public scepticism.

fight for them, and even larger numbers had no sympathy for abolitionism.'[62] Virtually every public and private message from Lincoln prior to late 1862 appeared to indicate that he would not venture to free the slaves. Simply put, while there were very good reasons to doubt that the Union would embark upon a war of emancipation, there was no reason to doubt the North's own avowals against a colition as a goal. Even those in England who argued that the North would make emancipation a war aim believed that it would be forced to do so by the march of events.[63]

Northerners could hardly expect the cause of Union to be a sacred one in English eyes, especially as the origin of the United States lay in revolution – against Britain no less. Although, at this stage, there was little support for the belief that a divided America was good for British interests (that would come in the wake of the *Trent* affair) the Confederacy was clearly a *de facto* state.[64]

None the less, even though the North's attitude towards emancipation was highly suspect, the South remained the real slave power. 'Lincoln's effort to dismiss slavery as the chief national issue' did *not* lead to a focus 'on commerce rather than conscience'.[65] These were separate issues. It took far more than a lack of an emancipation policy to alienate British sympathies, but the Union, by maladroit diplomacy and misconceived hostility, would provide further fuel for the fire.

William H. Seward, Cassius Clay and Union diplomacy

British government and public distrust of Seward is well-covered ground, originating with E. D. Adams who concedes that Seward's past activities towards Britain were hardly likely to win him any friends. Seward had, in the 1850s agitated against US governmental compromise over the Oregon boundary then attacked the British interpretation of the Clayton-Bulwer treaty afterwards. He had long prophesied the ultimate annexation of Canada by America, and, in political struggles in New York, had further stirred up Irish-American animosities towards Britain in order to win votes. More recently he had expressed a belief to the duke of Newcastle that civil conflict in the United States could be easily avoided, or quieted, by causing a quarrel with Britain and engaging in a war against it.[66]

---

62 Jones, *Union in peril*, 16.
63 See, for example, *Spectator*, 26 Oct. 1861, 1172. J. M. Ludlow argued the same thing in *Macmillan's Magazine* (Oct. 1861), 171, as would John Stuart Mill in his famous *Fraser's Magazine* article.
64 As Crook points out, by the time Britain declared its neutrality, 'The Confederacy had been created, had adopted a constitution, federal legislature, executive, and judiciary, begun to raise an army of 100,000 men, appropriated over two million dollars for a navy, and commenced hostilities': *The North, the South and the powers*, 77–8.
65 Jones, *Union in peril*, 16.
66 Adams, *Great Britain and the American Civil War*, i. 113–14. See also ch. iv passim, for the

Seward actually denied that he made the remark to the duke of Newcastle but later changed his tune and offered an explanation – actually several explanations – over a year later, none of which satisfied the English. Nor was Seward was not shy in voicing this threat. He mentioned it to Rudolph Schleiden, the minister for the Republic of Bremen, in January of 1861.[67] Then, in February, he repeated it to Lord Lyons, the British minister to Washington.[68] It was little wonder, then, that Seward was regarded as hostile to Britain. Now that Seward, who had so long encouraged revolutions in European nations, was faced with one at home, the situation became even more volatile.[69] Certainly a note of desperation entered his diplomacy, not the least of which being his 'foreign war panacea' on 1 April. In this, Seward sent Lincoln a memorandum which called on the North to demand that France and Spain explain their recent interventionist activities in Mexico and Santo Domingo, and, if these explanations were not satisfactory, to convene Congress for the purpose of declaring war on them; after which the Union would demand that Russia and Britain declare their support for the Union, with similar consequences if they refused. *The Times* journalist, W. H. Russell, upon hearing of the dispatch, stated that it 'amounted to little less than a declaration of war against Great Britain'.[70] Fortunately for all concerned, Lincoln wisely dismissed the plan.[71]

Seward, it must be acknowledged, was not entirely unprovoked. On 20 March, Lyons had hinted that Britain might be forced to break a Union blockade if faced with a cotton famine. Although Lyons had no authority to suggest this, it was, as Crook points out, 'the gravest of menaces, and is often forgotten in discussions of Seward's early aggressiveness to England'.[72] This is true, but Seward had been hostile to Britain long before this point. Whether or not Seward actually intended to push events to the point of war is a difficult question to answer and one over which historians still disagree.[73]

---

discussion of British suspicion of Seward. Most of the diplomatic historians of the period discuss Seward, but for an analysis of his diplomacy see Norman Ferris, *Desperate diplomacy: William H. Seward's foreign policy, 1861*, Knoxville 1976.

[67] Seward made the remarks to the duke of Newcastle when the latter accompanied the prince of Wales on the royal tour of the United States in 1860: Warren, *Fountain of discontent*, 57–8. Warren, like most historians writing about Seward, de-emphasises his anglophobia and expansionist beliefs.

[68] Adams, *Great Britain and the American Civil War*, i. 60.

[69] Warren, *Fountain of discontent*, 55. Part of Seward's predicament lay in the fact that he had tried to appease the South during the secessionist crisis and was accused of drifting. He thus needed to retrieve some eroded credibility: Crook, *The North, the South and the powers*, 45–6.

[70] Quoted in Brougham Villiers and W. H. Chesson, *Anglo-American relations, 1861–1865*, London 1919, 44.

[71] Crook, *The North, the South and the powers*, 57–63.

[72] Ibid.

[73] Crook puts forward the best argument that Seward intended only brinkmanship, pointing out, among other things, that Seward must have been aware of the relative

What historians have not adequately considered, however, is how the English would have reacted to such threats, irrespective of whether Seward was bluffing or not. It is simply not true, as some have stated, that Seward only ever advocated peaceful annexation of Canada. When President Franklin Pierce had, in the mid-1850s, picked a quarrel with Britain over the Isthmus, Seward, as a congressman, outmatched the president by advocating war and broadening the scene of action to include Canada.[74] Seward was not merely warning against intervention – he was promising conflict. Nineteenth-century America, in any case, was an aggressively expansionist power, especially during the two decades prior to the Civil War – a fact many historians appear to forget. This, coupled with the fact that Seward was a chauvinistic supporter of Manifest Destiny and 'an ardent American expansionist', meant that his threats of seizing Canada took a serious cast, whether or not the English overreacted to him.[75] He was, foremost, an American imperialist and this, plus his appointment as secretary of state, was hardly going to warm England to the cause of the North. His irredentist tendencies and subsequent activities nearly created a 'my enemy's enemy is my friend' mentality. What angered most observers was the belief that Seward's threats were unprovoked. These, and his annexationist attitudes, came to be regarded as a larger problem than those of southern politicians, and did much to reduce the moral claim of the Union.

The Economist remarked as early as January, 'Unprincipled and reckless Southerners, like Mr Buchanan, may talk of seizing on Mexico, Nicaragua and Cuba; unprincipled and inflated Northerners, like Mr Seward, may talk of seizing Canada.'[76] The threats of annexing Canada adversely affected most English thinking on the subject of America. In March, the *Saturday Review*, noting the crisis at Fort Sumter, remarked, 'Mr. Seward, though he cannot keep the Federal fort at Charleston, has several times announced his intention of annexing Canada.'[77] Even the *Spectator*, in the middle of yet another article arguing that the war was solely about slavery, stated that Seward was apparently ready to commit 'any amount of energetic folly', and warned the pugnacious secretary of state, 'There is not the slightest wish in this country for a war with the United States', but, 'The British Government has no dread

---

strengths of the European powers and 'to push bluster to the point of war would have defeated his purpose [of preserving the Union]': ibid. 63–8. The answer to this, however, is that if Seward had really believed he could preserve the Union by initiating a foreign war, he would not have seen such an act as detrimental to his purpose. Jones, meanwhile, argues that Seward's activities stemmed from a genuine fear of British intervention, and is less certain than Crook that Seward would have been content with brinkmanship had he not been restrained by Lincoln: *Union in peril*, ch. i passim, esp. pp. 11–15.

74 Crook, *The North, the South and the powers*, 35.
75 Allen, *Great Britain and the United States*, 461.
76 *The Economist*, 12 Jan. 1861, 58.
77 *Saturday Review*, 30 Mar. 1861, 303. The reference is to Fort Sumter.

of a war with the United States.'[78] By the end of the year, the belief in Seward's warmongering was complete. The comment, 'he blustered against the unoffending Government and people of England. There is little doubt that he would have forced on an unprovoked war if the military system of the Union had not exploded at Bull's Run', represents typical commentary in 1861.[79]

Seward's threats have long been identified as causing the British government to 'step warily' and thus 'served America well'.[80] The British government, however, especially in a period of isolationism, was always convinced of the need to tread warily when it came to American affairs in general – as shown by the fact that Britain backed down over the stop and search policy for slave traders in 1858 – and the Civil War in particular.[81] Seward's threats, meanwhile, neither intimidated nor impressed the English public. Indeed, his belligerence only convinced them that the North was an irrational and aggressive power, eager for a quarrel. That was not a reason for supporting the Confederacy, but it made the cause of the Union far less illustrious.[82]

If Seward had been a rogue element in Union politics as a whole, his opinions might have been discounted in England. Unfortunately for Anglo-Northern relations, the Union's somewhat misguided reaction to Britain's declaration of neutrality contributed to the sense of menace Seward initiated, especially by the remarks of Cassius Clay and the Union press – particularly after the Queen's Proclamation of Neutrality was issued.

The Proclamation of Neutrality has often been misrepresented as a hasty act of incompetence or even hostility, favouring the South.[83] In actual fact, if anything, the Proclamation favoured the Union.[84] One of the obvious advantages, for example, was that Britain formally absolved the North of responsibility for any possible future outrages committed against British subjects by

---

[78] *Spectator*, 26 Oct. 1861, 1226.
[79] *Saturday Review*, 2 Nov. 1861, 445. Although Seward had abandoned his 'foreign war panacea' well before the first battle of Bull Run, there is no way either the British government or public could have known this.
[80] Adams, *Great Britain and the American Civil War*, i. 136. Brian Jenkins concurs with this conclusion, as do Jordan and Pratt: Jenkins, *Britain and the war for the Union*, i. 396; Jordan and Pratt, *Europe and the American Civil War*, 121. As this work will establish, there was virtually no support in Britain for interference in America.
[81] See Jones, *Union in peril*, chs i–iii passim.
[82] For example, the *Saturday Review*, on 8 June 1861, 571, noted, 'No prejudice, however... ought to encourage a hasty conclusion that the South is as deserving of sympathy as the North. The presumption is always in favour of an established Government, and Mr. Seward, although his language to England is culpable and offensive, is nevertheless fully justified in putting out the whole power of the Union to coerce the seceders.'
[83] See Jenkins, *Britain and the war for the Union*, i, ch. iv passim, but especially p. 94.
[84] As Jones points out, 'Union officials did not reason out the advantages of British neutrality and mistakenly regarded the decision as purposely partial to the South, if not in motive then surely in consequence.' Jones argues that 'the declaration of neutrality in fact benefited the North': *Union in peril*, 28.

the South. It is also worth noting that the northern supporter, the Liberal member of parliament, W. E. Forster, certainly regarded the Proclamation as beneficial to the Union.[85] Indeed, Forster is alleged to have credited pro-Union supporters in Palmerston's cabinet for securing the Proclamation.[86] Further, it should also be remembered that when the rebellions of 1837 in Britain's colonies of Upper and Lower Canada took place, the United States had declared its neutrality, and those revolts were, in comparison to the Civil War, local riots. In short, the US had set a precedent by proclaiming its neutrality during a rebellion in a British colony – Britain was thus simply following an American example. Ultimately, however, the British government had simply reacted to events in America. By instituting a full-scale blockade on 19 April, the North effectively admitted a *de facto* state of war, and thus forced the question of neutrality upon the British when news arrived on 2 May.[87] Britain's recognition of the blockade as the start of hostilities would later be vindicated by none other than the United States Supreme Court which, in 1863, declared that proclaiming a blockade was conclusive proof that a state of war existed.[88] If, then, the Proclamation of Neutrality was badly timed, it was so only with hindsight.

Although English opinion was satisfied with the conduct of the government in this matter, the North felt very differently. The recognition of Confederate belligerency apparently placed the southern states on the same level as the Union and, as Warren points out, this aspect of the Proclamation 'precipitated a roar of disapproval from Northerners, who had no patience for the intricate arguments of international law that justified the British action'.[89] To be perfectly fair, as recognition of belligerency was the step before recognition, northern anger was understandable even if Britain had acted correctly. From the point of view of English opinion 'though, the government had acted with scrupulous correctness regarding events in America and it came as something of a shock when the Union disagreed.

It was an unpleasant surprise. On 20 May, *The Times* published a letter from the American minister to St Petersburg, Cassius Clay.[90] As Crawford puts it, 'Part rationalization, part threat, the letter consisted of a series of questions and answers whose transparent purpose was to convince British opinion that its true interest lay in supporting the Federal cause across the

---

[85] Jenkins, *Britain and the war for the Union*, i. 101.
[86] Villiers and Chesson, *Anglo-American relations*, 37.
[87] Crook, *The North, the South and the powers*, 79.
[88] For the details of the court's decision see Jones, *Union in peril*, 43–4.
[89] Warren, *Fountain of discontent*, 71.
[90] *The Times*, 20 May 1861, 9. As Crawford points out, 'Two of the most authoritative recent scholars, Brian Jenkins and David Crook, fail to mention Clay's letter at all, despite the evidence that Thomas Keiser has produced of its considerable impact on British editorial opinion': *The Anglo-American crisis*, 107–8. Older historians such as Jordan and Pratt, however, cite (but fail to examine) Clay's letter: *Europe and the American Civil War*, 14.

Atlantic.'[91] What offended public opinion was not the author's implication that Britain had betrayed its anti-slavery past, nor his insistence that the British were unaware that the South was the 'real hater of the British nation', but his question about whether Britain could 'afford to offend the great nation' the United States would become even without the South. Clay concluded on a menacing note: 'Is England so secure in the future against home revolt or foreign ambition as to venture, now in our need, to plant the seeds of revenge in all our future? . . . Will she ignore our aspirations? If she is just, she ought not. If she is honourable and magnanimous, she cannot. *If she is wise, she will not.*'[92] Not content with this, Clay made a similar speech in Paris, a few days later, which suggested to some that he hoped France and the Union would unite against Britain and the Confederacy.[93]

Clay's blatantly threatening tone, both in print and in public, was badly received. *The Economist*, to name one journal, strenuously objected to Clay's letter.[94] The *Illustrated London News* replied to the question of whether or not Britain could afford to offend the North thus, 'Our answer is that we do not believe that we shall ever incur the hatred of a truly great nation by preserving in a course of peaceful neutrality, but that we are quite prepared, according to English custom, to incur any risk in the path of duty.'[95] The *Saturday Review*, meanwhile, remarked, 'England can well afford to consult her own honour and interest without regarding the opinion of any foreign Power.'[96] Clay's comments provided fuel for an already smouldering fire of public anger with the North. That Clay's remarks were inflammatory was shown by the *Spectator*'s urgent efforts to play them down.[97] Clay's comments effectively complemented those of Seward and the two men were usually mentioned together – often in the company of other northern politicians who had made anti-British remarks. As the *Saturday Review* commented,

> It is not necessary to examine too closely Mr. Clay's statement that Northern politicians have always been the friends of England. Mr. Seward, a year or two ago, outdid the Southern senators in the insolence of his language with respect to cruisers in the Mexican Gulf; he has several times within the present year threatened the annexation of Canada. . . . Mr. Caleb Cushing, as Attorney-General, publicly expressed a hope that the annoyance of a vexatious prosecution of English subjects would 'rebound to Queen Victoria's throne',

---

[91] Crawford, *The Anglo-American crisis*, 107.
[92] *The Times*, 20 May 1861, 9 [Clay's italics].
[93] Jordan and Pratt, *Europe and the American Civil War*, 14. Jordan and Pratt overrate how seriously the English took this threat, apparently forgetting that France and Britain, goaded by Seward, had already entered into an uneasy alliance regarding American events by this stage.
[94] 'A very model of feeble reasoning and questionable taste': *The Economist*, 25 May 1861, 563.
[95] *Illustrated London News*, 25 May 1861, 484.
[96] *Saturday Review*, 25 May 1861, 519.
[97] See the *Spectator*, 1 June 1861, 580.

and in general it may be said that the Free States have contributed far more than their share to the vituperation by which rival American politicians have bid for the suffrages of a bigoted mob.

The above observations reveal how much the inflammatory comments made by northern politicians irritated English opinion. None the less, despite this, the English were prepared to make allowances or, at the least, to find reasons other than simple anglophobia to explain American politicians' remarks. As the writer continued,

> There is, however, some truth in the apology that Republican abuse of England has been for the most part consciously venal and insecure. Mr. Seward has never forgotten the unpopularity which New England politicians incurred by their unsuccessful opposition to the War of 1812. It is possible that the slave-owners may, after all, be 'the real haters of the British nation', though, in the absence of any conflict of interest, the motives for their animosity must be entirely arbitrary and sentimental.

In other words, the writer recognised that some of the abuse directed at Britain might be intended for American consumption only. Nor, at this stage in the war, did the *Saturday Review* wish to be identified with the South and it made a point of agreeing with Clay that the North had the right to preserve the Union by force.[98] Unquestionably, however, the prevailing belief was that Britain had done nothing to deserve the repeated threats from Union politicians. An anonymous writer in the *British Quarterly Review* noted Clay's letter, and commented, 'for thus wishing to hold ourselves neutral in a quarrel raging some 1,500 miles across the Atlantic, we have been calumniated and vilipended by some four or five American envoys', and claimed that Clay was trying to sow dissent between Britain and France.[99] This perception of victimisation was echoed:

> The press, as far as it has taken a side in the dispute, has almost uniformly advocated the claims of the North; the Government has pronounced an immutable neutrality, of which the United States reap all the practical benefit; and both Houses of Parliament have firmly refused to engage in discussions which might afford an opportunity for the use of irritating language. In return . . . the United States Minister to St. Petersburg threatened at Paris that France should sweep England from the face of the earth; and all the public writers in the Northern States season incessant vituperations of England with preposterous expressions of adulation to France, which are dictated rather by a desire to be indirectly offensive than by wanton servility.[100]

---

[98] *Saturday Review*, 25 May 1861, 519.
[99] *British Quarterly Review* (July 1861), 208.
[100] *Saturday Review*, 29 June 1861, 653.

Statements like this contribute towards understanding English exasperation. As far as English observers were concerned, their government had behaved with absolute correctness regarding events in America, and public opinion had been against the South. Yet, despite this, the Union was threatening a possible attack on Canada, to say nothing of future war, for non-existent violations of neutrality and equally non-existent pro-Confederate sentiment. Clay, like Seward, damaged the standing of the Union cause in England. Ironically, Lincoln had sent Clay to Russia as a means of getting the renowned troublemaker out of the Union.[101] It was not, perhaps, the president's best decision.

The northern press

Unfortunately for Anglo-Union relations, abuse did not originate solely with northern politicians. Another source of discord was the anti-British tone of the Union's newspapers, something that has been constantly underrated by historians who have no apparent trouble citing the supposed belligerence of *The Times* for the souring of Anglo-Union relations. So aggressively anti-British were the northern journals after the Proclamation of Neutrality that even Cobden was shocked.[102] The counter-reaction was immediate. In June, the *Saturday Review* remarked,

> we hear little else than fierce invectives and bitter denunciations levelled against Great Britain, for her supposed sympathy with the Confederate States. This irrational hatred and mistrust of England and the English is traceable to the wide-spread and carefully nourished animosity against the parent country that has been handed down from father to son since the close of the revolutionary war, ready without provocation to be fanned into a flame. In this instance, it is in full blaze because the wise and prudent policy of Great Britain declines to . . . place itself bound hand and foot at the disposal of Mr. Lincoln and his cabinet.[103]

Certainly the *Saturday Review* displayed what amounted to paranoia about the recent anti-British sentiment (reflecting much the same nature as Union fears of British involvement), but what has to be remembered is that this followed threats by both Seward and Clay. It must have appeared to some in England that the entire North was eager for an Anglo-Union war. As the *Saturday Review* continued, 'It is easy to understand that New York journalists may only wish to flatter and excite the momentary passions of the unthinking multitude which they address; but the [northern] correspondents of the London papers . . . almost unanimously adopt the insolent language of their

---

[101] Donald, *Lincoln*, 321.
[102] Crawford, *The Anglo-American crisis*, 110.
[103] *Saturday Review*, 8 June 1861, 580.

noisy and unreasonable countrymen.'[104] In other words, anti-British sentiment appeared to be universally held in the North – by all classes of its citizens.

The threats varied in tone and continued long after the Proclamation of Neutrality had been announced. In November 1861, the *Illustrated London News* reported, 'the usual raving of the ribald press is launched against England ... and that as soon as ever the war is over "such a train of disasters" shall be inflicted upon England as shall make her rue the day when she dared to say that ten millions of Americans were belligerents instead of rebels.'[105]

It is worth noting that a minority of the New York press worried about the northern denunciations of Britain. On 4 June, the *New York Tribune*, which generally tried to cool the passions raised on both sides of the Atlantic, remarked,

> The tone of the debate in the House of Lords, and of European official utterances generally, is marked by eminent dignity, moderation, and anxiety to give no just cause of offence to our Government and people. Has this evident desire to maintain amicable relations with us been fairly met on this side of the water? We think not. In many quarters a disposition to take offence at trifles and aggravate slight differences into causes of serious quarrel has been manifested.[106]

So it was not only contributors to English journals that believed the Union's politicians, press and public, were irrational at best, aggressive at worst – some in the North thought the same. Indeed, the *New York Tribune*'s writer apparently believed what some in England did, that the Union was seeking a quarrel where none was offered. There is little wonder, then, that as late as 1863 the *Annual Register* declared, 'The language held by some American politicians and a portion of their newspaper press towards this country, aroused from time to time feelings of profound irritation in the public mind.'[107]

The northern paper that caused the most foreboding in England was James Gordon Bennett's *New York Herald*. Considering that this paper had as great (and probably greater) an effect on Anglo-Union relations as the often vilified *Times* of London, some background information is necessary. Bennett, an immigrant Scot, was the paper's founder and editor, and the paper had a history of anglophobia – something which would become more pronounced during the Civil War. The fact that one of the individuals most responsible for poisoning Anglo-Union relations during this period was originally a British subject is one of the many ironies of this period. Being extremely

---

104 Ibid. 15 June 1861, 595. The 'correspondent' in question is Clay.
105 *Illustrated London News*, 23 Nov. 1861, 516.
106 Quoted in the *Illustrated London News*, 15 June 1861, 568. This journal reported on the hostility of the northern press throughout 1861.
107 *Annual Register*, 1863, 'English history', 123.

pro-slavery, the *New York Herald* opposed the Republicans and Lincoln during the 1860 presidential election. Until a threatening mob appeared outside the offices of the paper on 15 April (the day after Sumter's fall) and suggested that its policies undergo a change, the *New York Herald* pushed for the appeasement of the South, which included endorsing secession. After this, as Douglas Fermer puts it, 'the *Herald* manifested all the zeal of the newly converted'.[108]

The *New York Herald* was not an esoteric broadsheet. During our period, it had a circulation of between 85,000 and 105,000; selling 35,000 to 40,000 more copies than *The Times* of London, it was New York's biggest paper.[109] Intellectually light, the *New York Herald* always courted the popular voice and at least one contemporary wrote, 'This journal is read by all classes, and its power and influence are universally acknowledged.'[110] Its views were certainly influential enough to induce Lincoln to keep in regular correspondence with Bennett.[111] What has to be remembered then is that Bennett's paper reflected a considerable portion of northern opinion and was perceived as such. Its views, often outrageous in English opinion, were at least partially reflective of its readership. Certainly, the pro-Union journalist Edward Dicey considered the *New York Herald*'s views to be a fair representative of American public opinion.[112] The additional problem Bennett's paper posed was that, as a New York paper, it tended to arrive in Britain before journals from the rest of the Union. This meant that it was able to establish the picture of northern attitudes towards Britain before the more responsible papers did. As English journals often reprinted sections from it wholesale, the public in Britain were treated to the *New York Herald*'s ravings at first hand. Doubtless too, the paper's inflammatory contents made good copy. Journalists then, as now, tended to look for the most extreme opinions in order to provide a good story.

The *New York Herald* did not require the Proclamation of Neutrality as an excuse to urge hostilities against Britain. From January to March of 1861, the journal, along with the *New York Times*, urged that the loss of population and territory to secession be made up by the acquisition of Canada and, if either the British or their Canadian colonists disagreed with the plan, annexation

---

[108] Douglas Fermer, *James Gordon Bennett and the* New York Herald: *a study of editorial opinion in the Civil War era*, Woodbridge 1986, 44–5, 62–6, 187–90.
[109] Crawford estimates that *The Times* had a circulation of between 50,000 and 65,000 during our period: *The Anglo-American crisis*, 17. For an estimate of the *New York Herald*'s circulation figures see Fermer, *James Gordon Bennett*, 324.
[110] Lambert A Wilmer, *Our press gang*, quoted in Fermer, who puts forward an impressive argument about just how influential the *New York Herald* was: *James Gordon Bennett*, 5–7, 18–19, 86–91. The last describes how the *New York Herald* was instrumental in depriving President Franklin Pierce of a second term in office.
[111] Fermer, *James Gordon Bennett*, ch. ix passim.
[112] Edward Dicey, *Six months in the federal states*, London 1863, i. 272–3.

would be achieved by force of arms.[113] *The Economist*, upon receiving news of this proposed exchange, warned that such an action would lead to war between Britain and the Union.[114] The timing was unfortunate. Seward's earlier threats of annexation, combined with his loose talk of foreign war reinforced the *New York Herald*'s opinions, creating the illusion that its views were those of Lincoln's administration. As a result, English commentators took Bennett's threats very seriously indeed.[115] With America's past history of aggressive territorial expansion looming ominously in the background, the *New York Herald* and the *New York Times* were seen to embody northern public opinion. Certainly no mainstream British paper ever made threats of as serious a cast as those published by the *New York Times*, let alone the *New York Herald*.[116]

The impact of the *New York Herald*'s views should not be underestimated. John Delane, editor of *The Times*, blamed the turn of British opinion against the Union on the 'belligerent conduct of Seward and the *New York Herald*'.[117] That the vitriolic tone of Bennett's paper damaged transatlantic relations is shown by the efforts of anti-Confederate journals like the *Spectator* to minimise its stature: 'All we know of American opinion usually filters to us from New York, a political cesspool with the scum always at the top.'[118] The *Spectator* throughout the conflict insisted that the *New York Herald* did not represent the majority of northern sentiment, referring to it as 'The New York Herald – wicked, blind and braggart leader of the wicked, blind and braggart'.[119]

---

[113] See Fermer, *James Gordon Bennett*, 52. The *New York Times* made the same argument on 8 February, but was more circumspect in its language. As Canadian sentiment was against joining America and Britain was not prepared to yield its North American colonies to either force or threat of force, a collision was inevitable if the United States followed any course of annexation.
[114] *The Economist*, 22 Feb. 1861, 201–2.
[115] Fermer argues that *The Times* worked more mischief than the *New York Herald*, but it is hard to see how this argument can be sustained when one contrasts the relatively mild tone of the former with the warmongering tone of the latter. It is worth noting, however, that Cobden believed the same thing, remarking that *The Times* and the *New York Herald* might be paired off against each other. See Jordan and Pratt, *Europe and the American Civil War*, 15. This suggests that Cobden failed to read either paper closely and is indicative of how northern apologists tended to exaggerate negative English opinion while playing down northern hostility. In any event, one cannot take the New York journal out of the context of the menaces uttered by northern politicians, whose threats the *New York Herald* effectively echoed. For, even as he equated *The Times* and the *New York Herald*, Cobden admitted that England had nothing bad enough to offset the speeches of Cassius Clay.
[116] The chief exception being *Reynolds's Weekly*, hardly a mainstream journal. Again, we are referring to the period before the *Trent* affair. This last event obviously caused a change in tone.
[117] Crawford, *The Anglo-American crisis*, 123. Delane also stated, however, 'Not that we wish the South to win'.
[118] *Spectator*, 2 Mar. 1861, 218. It is possible that this comment was an attack on Seward, too. Seward was, after all, a New Yorker, and had been the state's governor.
[119] Ibid. 26 July 1863, 2276.

Another Union sympathiser, Thomas Hughes, repeated this argument that the *New York Herald*'s views were those of a minority in the Union. Writing in *Macmillan's Magazine* (which leaned northwards in its sympathies throughout the Civil War), towards the end of 1861, Hughes, while discussing and defending the North's position, denounced the *New York Herald* as 'a notoriously Southern paper' and 'one of the most scurrilous journals in the whole states'. Hughes concluded, 'I quite admit that the tone of the Government and people of the North has been such as to deeply grieve and disappoint every right-minded Englishman: but don't let us saddle them with the frantic slanders of the *New York Herald*.'[120] Hughes' acknowledgment that the Union's politicians had acted unfairly towards Britain needs to be noted because he was a pro-Northerner. In other words, he did not want to exaggerate Union hostility towards Britain as some others might have done. None the less, Hughes was attempting to decouple the opinions of the *New York Herald* from those of Lincoln's administration. The fact that he felt it necessary to do so gives us an idea of just how much damage Bennett's journal was causing the Union's reputation in England.

It is, however, important to note that not only Union apologists dismissed the *New York Herald*. As early as July, the *Saturday Review* was honest enough to point out that the *New York Herald* was 'long an organ of the pro-slavery party'.[121] A little earlier in the same month, the *Illustrated London News* printed a report from one of its irregular 'special correspondents' regarding Bennett's paper:

> The insane ravings of this last journal against England and Englishmen generally would do more to create an ill feeling between the two countries than anything I have ever seen published on our side of the water; but, fortunately, no respectable person here pays the slightest attention to its 'editorials', and I do not suppose they ever obtain the honour of being quoted at home.[122]

That the journal's correspondent considered the *New York Herald*'s opinions to be far worse than anything printed in England reveals, once again, how English public hostility towards the Union was in large part a reaction to the northern press. Of course the writer was far too optimistic in supposing that the *New York Herald*'s views would not be noted at home. *The Economist* also condemned Bennett's paper, but took care to criticise the English press for treating it as some sort of ambassador of northern opinion.

> Our leading journals have been too ready to quote and to resent, as embodying the sentiments and representing the position of the United States, newspapers

---

[120] Hughes's first accusation obviously stemmed from the *New York Herald*'s views until April of 1861. Hughes was being economical with the truth by implying that this was still the case in December of 1861: *Macmillan's Magazine* (Oct. 1861), 416.
[121] *Saturday Review*, 13 July 1861, 31.
[122] *Illustrated London News*, 6 July 1861, 22.

notorious at all times for their disreputable character and feeble influence, and now more than suspected of sailing under false colours, and professing extreme Northern opinions while writing in the interests and possibly pay of the South. Few Englishmen can, for example with any decent fairness pretend to regard the *New York Herald* as representing either the character or views of the Northern section of the Republic. Again: we ought to be very careful lest our just criticisms on the Unionists should degenerate by insensible gradation into approval and defence of the Secessionists.[123]

The writer, apart from denying that Bennett's views were the same as those of the Union's population, was warning his readers against allowing sympathy to flow southwards. This does show effort on the part of at least some of the commentators, not all of who were particularly fond of the Union, to prevent a complete breakdown between Britain and the North. Certainly, it shows an effort to avoid any pro-southern proclivities. Despite the problems the Union posed in the first year of the struggle, preference for the Confederacy was rare indeed. None the less, by the time the above article appeared in *The Economist* and Hughes's work appeared in *Macmillan's*, the atmosphere had been poisoned. By this point, with regard to northern opinion, the English generally felt that they were the ones more 'sinned against than sinning'. It was the apparently aggressive stance of the North, not gloating over disunion, that soured Anglo-Union relations.

Although most journals made a concerted effort to play down hostilities, the London press was not entirely innocent. *The Economist*, for example, noted that although 'neither the British Government, nor the British people nor the British journalists have done or said anything to warrant the accusation that they have embraced the cause of the South. . . . The failures and shortcomings of the Federals have no doubt been freely and provokingly commented upon.'[124] Opinions of this sort were not widespread and only a few papers would admit to the *Wesleyan Methodist Magazine*'s blunt remark that the press on both sides of the Atlantic were deliberately inflaming passions, 'for, in America, it has been most threatening, and in some instances, truculent, toward England; and in England it has been ungenerous and provoking toward America'. Writing in the period just before the *Trent* affair, and recognising that tensions were rising, the writer glumly (and correctly) predicted that 'one such case, if accompanied by circumstances of aggravation, might easily grow into a *casus belli*'.[125]

None the less, the London press was not prepared to let the threats of the northern press goad it into changing its position on the American quarrel. The *Saturday Review* was probably one of the journals most hostile to the Union and it noted that, despite the 'rude injustice and malignity' of 'the

---

[123] *The Economist*, 28 Sept. 1861, 1065.
[124] Ibid.
[125] *Wesleyan Methodist Magazine* (Dec. 1861), 1119.

New York journals', there was no reason to support either side.[126] Disturbed as they were by the tone of the Union, the English were not prepared to embrace the Confederacy.

The Morrill tariff

Faced with a North where the politicians and press were unquestionably hostile, anti-Union sentiment was bound to exist in England. This alone probably ensured English animosities, but there was yet another problem. During the height of public faith in free trade, the Union's passing of the Morrill tariff was inauspicious. By 1860, free trade was the gospel of the Liberal Party (and grudgingly accepted by the conservatives). Unfortunately for Anglo-Union relations, at the time free trade was enjoying its ascendance in Britain, protectionism, under the 'infant industry' argument, was beginning its ascendance in the North. Although the tariff was passed during the last days of President James Buchanan's administration, the Republicans had campaigned on a tariff platform.[127]

Those historians who argue that the Morrill tariff was used merely as an excuse by Britons to abandon sympathy for the Union ignore just how much of a blow it was to British commerce. From 1830 to 1860, 40 per cent of the value of American imports came from Britain and about 25 per cent of total British exports went to the United States.[128] By 1861, the United States was Britain's most important single market. Although the Morrill tariff did not impose the higher duties of earlier American tariffs, its duties were higher than the most recent tariff of 1857.[129] Further, as it was more specifically directed against manufactured goods, and passed during the secessionist crisis, the reaction to it was all the more intense. Passed on 2 February, the Morrill tariff was opposed for two reasons: first, and most obviously, it harmed British commerce; second, it was seen as an anti-southern piece of legislation which hampered re-union, raising the question of whether or not the North actually wanted the South to return to the Union.

Crawford notes that 'modern historians are divided over the wider impact of the Morrill tariff'.[130] They should not be. Depending upon the commentator, the Morrill tariff was either a monstrous act of folly or a blatantly anti-British measure. The great champion of *laissez-faire*, *The Economist*,

---

[126] *Saturday Review*, 22 June 1861, 625.
[127] McPherson, *Battle cry of freedom*, 220–1.
[128] Crook, *The North, the South and the powers*, 4–9.
[129] See Allen, *Great Britain and the United States*, 72–7.
[130] Crawford, *The Anglo-American crisis*, 163. As he notes, Jenkins gives only marginal attention to it, while Crook calls it 'a disastrous blow to Federal diplomacy': Jenkins, *Britain and the war for the Union*, i. 81; Crook, *The North, the South and the powers*, 40. Keiser, meanwhile, argues that the tariff 'had little or no effect on forming editorial opinion': 'The English press and the American Civil War', 101.

made the most thunderous denunciations, as one might expect, but it was far from being alone. As much as *The Economist* hated slavery (and, it must be added, the South), the Morrill tariff was an unforgivable action on the part of the Union: 'the narrowest oligarchy, the most arbitrary autocrat could scarcely have committed a shallower blunder, could scarcely have displayed greater ignorance and disregard of all economic laws, than have been manifested, in the matter of the new Protective Tariff by the educated, commercial, ochlocratic republic.' *The Economist*, like *The Times*, preferred the Confederate version, which, it believed, had 'at least a moderate amount of worldly wisdom in it'.[131] The journalist Francis Maurice Drummond-Davis, writing in the April edition of the *British Quarterly Review*, after making comments generally favourable to the Union, noted, 'This tariff falls with oppressive force on woollen goods and cutlery, the export produce of Great Britain and is certainly a great mistake on the part of the North.'[132] The *Saturday Review* went further,

> It would even be doing it injustice to call it Protectionist, for it is more nearly Prohibitionist than any fiscal code which has prevailed in Europe since the Great War [i.e. Napoleonic Wars]. It will crush commerce, if it be carried, not only by the duties it imposes, though they are enormous, but by a perverse system of classification expressly designed to baffle and perplex the foreign importer.[133]

Even the *Spectator* expressed anger at the tariff, remarking, 'The mad tariff, also, suggested by Mr. Morell [sic], which will almost shut out British commerce, and enable the slaveholders to conciliate all the maritime powers, is also a victory for the South.'[134] The pro-northern J. M. Ludlow, writing a defence of the Union in *Macmillan's Magazine*, agreed, calling the Morrill tariff 'an act of monstrous folly'.[135] The negative impact of the Morrill tariff continued long after it had passed. In June, the *Saturday Review* asserted,

> Individual Americans sometimes assert that the unfriendly policy of their successive Governments really proceeded from the Southern States to England; yet the feeling of the country and the acts of the Legislature have been doubly hostile since the North has been left to itself. The Morrill tariff was principally aimed at English commerce; and Mr. Seward, in repeatedly threatening a future attack on Canada, has only continued the course which, in common with his party, he has pursued in the United States senate.[136]

---

[131] *The Economist*, 16 Mar. 1861, 283.
[132] *British Quarterly Review* (Apr. 1861), 443.
[133] *Saturday Review*, 9 Mar. 1861, 234.
[134] *Spectator*, 2 Mar. 1861, 218.
[135] *Macmillan's Magazine* (Oct. 1861), 175.
[136] *Saturday Review*, 15 June 1861, 595.

The fact that the *Saturday Review* mentioned the tariff in the same sentence as Seward's threats shows that the legislation was perceived as an economic attack on Britain. In contemporary terms, we would refer to this as a trade war – something generally viewed as an unfriendly activity. In September of 1861, *The Economist* announced, 'Our *interest* as cotton consumers, we repeat it, is in favour of a termination of the war, but it is not more in favour of a Southern than of a Northern victory – unless as far as the Protective Tariff of the foolish Federalists has made it so.'[137] Exasperation increased. Later in the month, the journal found reasons for re-thinking its views of the South, 'because their behaviour is more courteous than that of their antagonists; and because they were desirous to admit our goods at 10 per cent. duty, while their enemies imposed 40 per cent'.[138] *The Economist* was by far the journal most hostile to the tariff – as was to be expected from a publication devoted to the principle of free trade. Indeed, as the above comment reveals, the journal was so affronted by the Union's starting a trade war, that it flirted with the South. In this, *The Economist* was unusual. Other journals still regarded slavery as a greater evil than restrictive trade practices.

As the English were perfectly aware that the question of tariffs was a sectional issue in the United States before the Civil War, it was obvious that such a tariff had been passed against the wishes of the South. On the question of tariffs, like slavery, the North and South were at loggerheads. The North generally favoured tariffs, believing these would protect its developing industries against Britain's cheaper manufactured imports. The South, exporting its cotton to Britain and importing manufactured goods in return, saw no reason to support any tariffs that would force it to buy more expensive northern products. Further, the South feared that any American tariff passed might provoke a British counter-tariff on raw cotton.[139] Differences came to a head in 1832, when the state of South Carolina reacted to the imposition of an increased federal tariff by passing the Ordinance of Nullification. This, the brainchild of John C. Calhoun, stated that the federal tariffs were unconstitutional and forbade all collection of duties in the state. Calhoun, who was serving as President Andrew Jackson's vice-president, resigned his post to defend the state's action. Jackson responded to Calhoun's and South Carolina's activities by issuing the Nullification Proclamation that claimed that no state had the right to annul a law of the United States. Jackson declared that the United States was a single nation and that no individual state could refuse to implement legislation, far less leave the Union. South Carolina responded by threatening to secede. Jackson replied by calling upon the rest of the Union to bring South Carolina to heel. Armed conflict was avoided primarily because none of the other southern states would support

---

137 *The Economist*, 14 Sept. 1861, 1012.
138 Ibid. 28 Sept. 1861, 1066.
139 Regarding the sectional aspect of tariffs see Van Mitchell Smith, 'British business relations with the Confederacy, 1861–1865', unpubl. PhD diss. Texas 1949, 24.

South Carolina and also because the congressman Henry Clay proposed a compromise tariff which addressed some of the state's grievances. Both Jackson and South Carolina accepted Clay's compromise.[140] Although both sides had, in essence, backed down, Jackson could at least claim to have established that the Union could not be dissolved by the unilateral action of a state (or states). Both Calhoun and South Carolina, however, refused to see this and, in a real sense, the groundwork for the Civil War was laid with the Nullification crisis. The English were aware of this dispute, in no small part thanks to de Tocqueville's discussion of it in *Democracy in America*.[141] In any event, the next time South Carolina took the path of secession, it had the support of other states. Certainly the Nullification crisis provided support for the argument that the war was about tariffs, not slavery.

Although it is true that had the lower South not seceded, the tariff could not have been passed because southern congressmen would have prevented it, the tariff was passed against the wishes of the temporarily loyal upper South. This fact hardly supported the theory that the Union was sincere about reconciliation or that peaceful re-union was intended. As early as January, *The Economist* noted that South Carolina objected to 'the protective tariff adopted by Congress' because 'She knows that, if the Federal Customs duties were abolished, she would be able to import British manufactures more cheaply than at present; and she fancies also that Charleston would thus become a sort of New York for the South, the future capital and the centre of its commercial operations.'[142] The *Saturday Review* assumed the tariff meant the Union did not want the Confederacy back.[143] The *Annual Register* of 1861 concurred with this view.[144] Francis William Newman, professor of Latin at University College London, writing in *Fraser's Magazine*, called the Morrill tariff 'a new affront and wrong to the adhering Slave States, and raises a wall against the return of the seceders'. The barrister Thomas Collett Sandars, writing in the same issue, noted, 'Argument about the Tariff Bill is superfluous when we say that it alienates English sympathy . . . and presents one more obstacle to the return of the seceding States.'[145] The *Illustrated London News* was unusual in that it was one of the few journals that actually laid part of the blame for secession on the tariff. 'There are other causes of difference between the North and the South than that of slavery' and 'Not a little of it [the secessionist movement] should be set down to the protective policy whereby Northern manufacturers have flourished at the expense of Southern planters.'[146] Later, when the tariff had passed, the *Illustrated London*

---

140 William W. Freehling, *Prelude to Civil War: the nullification controversy in South Carolina, 1816–1830*, New York 1965.
141 De Tocqueville, *Democracy in America*, i. 410–13.
142 *The Economist*, 12 Jan. 1861, 30.
143 *Saturday Review*, 9 Mar. 1861, 234.
144 *Annual Register*, 1861, 219.
145 *Fraser's Magazine* (Apr. 1861), 411, 524.
146 *Illustrated London News*, 19 Jan. 1861, 47–8.

News called it 'the very reverse of conciliatory'.[147] Most English commentators did not actually blame the tariff for causing the war, but a minority did. Charles Dickens, for example, noting Lincoln's various guarantees that he would not interfere with slavery, decided that the tariff must be at fault. He wrote two articles on this subject, blaming the tariff for the war in his journal, *All the Year Round*.[148] Belief that the tariff actually caused the war, however, was unusual.[149] While some in England did indeed blame secession on the Morrill tariff, the majority of the commentators never did.[150]

That the Morrill tariff had a negative impact on public opinion is shown by the fact that northern sympathisers had to play it down, just as they did the ravings of the *New York Herald*. The *Spectator*, in May, argued that the Union's war was against slavery and that England should not be distracted by the Morrill tariff.[151] A quote from Leslie Stephen, writing in *Macmillan's Magazine* in 1862, is worth noting:

> Although the question of Free-Trade is therefore, in our opinion, a mere collateral issue, it is still one of no small importance in itself . . . it is worth while to consider how much of the national bitterness which has been produced may be owing to this policy. Free-Trade may not be the great bone of contention between North and South, but it is, perhaps, that point in dispute between them *which most immediately affects us*.[152]

Stephen identified the problem correctly. Although the war might not have been caused by the Morrill tariff, because the Union had pushed emancipation off the agenda, the question of economics was all that was left. It made no difference as far as English commentators were concerned whether there were one or more republics on the North American continent; what did matter was how the respective nations treated Britain. Stephen's urging the public not to support the Confederacy because of the Morrill tariff was not unique – every supporter of the North was compelled to deal with the damage of the tariff.

For those in England whose livelihoods depended on the exportation of manufactured goods to America and who were thus financially harmed by the Morrill tariff, opposing a free-trading Confederacy for the sake of slavery must

---

147 Ibid. 18 May 1861, 455.
148 Charles Dickens, 'American disunion' and 'The Morrill tariff', in *All the Year Round*, 21, 28 Dec. 1861.
149 *Reynolds's Weekly* was the only other journal I found which propounded this notion and it did so only much later in the year when it demanded that the blockade be broken.
150 Some historians have suggested this, probably because John Stuart Mill argued against this thesis in his article in *Fraser's Magazine*. Although very few contemporary commentators echoed Mill, it is worth noting he was not alone. The *English Woman's Journal* stated in 1863, 'We do not suppose, as many do in England, that the desire for free trade was the cause of the war': 2 Feb. 1863, 376.
151 *Spectator*, 18 May 1861, 524 (misprinted as 324).
152 *Macmillan's Magazine* (Dec. 1862), 127–8 [my italics].

have appeared a luxury they could not afford. The South, which needed British goods, having few industries of its own, was a valuable customer to these disaffected Britons – unlike the hostile Union.[153] The North had to buy certain materials, too, of course, and there is one recorded instance of British steel manufacturers attempting to defraud the United States Revenue by exporting their goods at wholesale, and not market, prices in order to avoid paying duty.[154] In the end, however, the Confederacy, simply put, was a paying customer. This also explains why southern agents like James Bulloch and Edward Anderson pronounced British opinion so favourable to their cause – they were dealing with disaffected manufacturers (both being purchasers of munitions and materials). This was certainly the view of the Confederate agent Major Edward C. Anderson who sardonically remarked, 'money would get anything in England, even an interview with the Queen'.[155] Certainly, those individuals such as J. S. Mill, Ludlow, Forster, Stephen and other leading members of the northern apologist lobby, whose well being was not directly affected by trade with the Union, could afford to take a detached (later perceived to be more noble) view of the struggle and condemn slavery. It must be noted, however, that some northern apologists were incensed by the tariff. Harriet Martineau, for example, writing for the pro-Union *Daily News*, stated that while the sin of the South was slavery, the sin of the North was protection.[156]

Again, despite the fact that the tariff had a negative impact on public opinion, it did not drive it into the Confederate camp. The *New Monthly Magazine* remarked, in an article entitled 'North and South', that, despite the Morrill tariff, 'we cannot believe that any who have reflected on the subject can sympathise with the Southerners, for there is no use in disguising the fact that the question of slavery or non slavery is now at issue'.[157] Even *The Economist*, which, as we have seen above, at least partially sympathised with the South because of the Morrill tariff, could not quite stomach supporting the Confederacy. In April, although it argued that the North was wrong to impose the tariff and the South was wrong in seeking to expand slavery, it did not equate the two: 'We do not mean for one moment to put the two follies and two wrongs on a level as regards their social gravity or moral heinousness.'[158] Finally in September, after yet another diatribe against the tariff, it

---

[153] The Confederates had to import virtually every manufactured item from Europe in general and Britain in particular: Lester, *Confederate finance and purchasing in Great Britain*, ch. vii passim, but particularly pp. 164–8.
[154] See Miles Taylor, 'The Sheffield steel inquiry of 1869', *Transactions of the Hunter Archaeological Society* xv (1989), 38–47.
[155] Edward C. Anderson, *Confederate foreign agent: the European diary of Major Edward C. Anderson*, ed. W. Stanley Hoole, Alabama 1976, 29.
[156] Betty Fladeland, *Abolitionists and working-class problems in the age of industrialization*, Baton Rouge 1984, 87.
[157] *New Monthly Magazine* (Aug. 1861), 356.
[158] *The Economist*, 13 Apr. 1861, 395.

warned Britons never to forget that secession lay in a cause that held their 'heaviest and most deeply rooted disapprobation'.[159] The Morrill tariff unquestionably damaged the Union's standing in England, but the South's domestic institution damaged the South far more. Slavery remained far more repugnant than restrictive trade practices.

In his *Macmillan's Magazine* article, Thomas Hughes considered the majority of the press to be 'ungenerous and unfair' to the Union. This state of affairs he blamed on the Morrill tariff and 'the menacing attitude which the President's Government chose to assume towards us'.[160] Was he correct in his assessment of overwhelming anti-Union sentiment in England? Certainly, almost all northern supporters shared Hughes's belief. Most historians on the subject have agreed with the pro-Union camp, with few exceptions.

The notion of an anti-northern Britain is discussed more completely later in this work. For now, it is necessary to concentrate on the period before the *Trent* affair. Answering such a question of whether or not anti-Unionism was the prevailing sentiment depends upon what is meant by 'anti-Unionism' or, conversely, 'pro-Confederate'. By the end of 1861, although a deep dissatisfaction with the Union had set in, there was still no rush to commend the South.

English views of the Confederacy

The institution of slavery, despite the North's apparent refusal to tackle the issue, ensured that the Confederacy remained a renegade nation or rogue state. Although, as we have already seen, English commentators made their distaste for southern slavery known even as they criticised the North, it is worth noting some specific comments about the Confederacy itself.

In March, *The Economist* pronounced that Southerners 'seem actually to have no scruples, and their morality on all points seems to have been strangely warped by slavery'.[161] It retained this view of the Confederacy throughout 1861.[162] Francis William Newman wrote in *Fraser's Magazine* that 'the temper of the South is essentially barbarous'. He also, like several other commentators in England, saw some of the problems an independent Confederacy would pose, noting, 'the British Government cannot wish these States to establish their independence, when it would involve much danger of getting into a war with them ourselves on the question of the slave-trade with Africa, which, however prudent may be their present language, the moving spirits among them are bent on re-opening'.[163] In other words,

---

[159] Ibid. 28 Sept. 1861, 1065.
[160] *Macmillan's Magazine* (Oct. 1861), 414–15.
[161] *The Economist*, 2 Mar. 1861, 226.
[162] See, in particular, ibid. 14 Sept. 1861, 1010.
[163] *Fraser's Magazine* (Apr. 1861), 403, 414.

Britain's anti-slave-trading campaigns would have to begin all over again. In August, when the possibility of southern independence was first (dejectedly, it must be added) considered, Thomas Collett Sandars, also writing in *Fraser's*, predicted that the Confederacy would become a despotic, not democratic, power.[164] The conservative *Fraser's* was not the only journal whose commentators disliked the South. When relations with the North began to sour, the industrialist and social critic William Rathbone Greg, writing in the *National Review*, remarked:

> We cannot be very zealous for the North; for we do not like her ambition; we are irritated by her insolence; we are aggrieved by her tariffs; but we still have much feeling of kinship and esteem. We cannot be at all zealous for the South; for though she is friendly and free-trading, she is fanatically SLAVE, and Slavery is the object of our rooted detestation.[165]

Again, despite the activities of Seward and Clay, among others, and the Morrill tariff, slavery remained the major problem with the South.

The *New Monthly Magazine*, in September, ran two articles on the Civil War. In the first, it said of slavery, 'The "domestic institution", as it has been called, has been at the bottom of everything questionable in the policy of Government – everything wicked, everything foolish, everything impolitic, everything mischievous, done by the Congress of the United States for a long course of years.'[166] The second article, 'Americans at Home', argued, despite the Morrill tariff, Seward's belligerence and the *New York Herald's* provocations, that 'Though neither side deserves much sympathy from English readers, our feelings ought to be enlisted on the side of the North, for, try to disguise it how they may, the Southerners are fighting for the maintenance of an execrable system, which all civilised nations are agreed in condemning.'[167] The *British Quarterly Review*, in July, took pains to insist that the Proclamation of Neutrality did not confer any legitimacy on secession.[168] The *Saturday Review*, meanwhile, although certainly ungenerous and unfair to the Union, never granted the Confederacy much respect either – despite E. D. Adams's claim that it was 'pro-Southern'.[169] In July, when relations had deteriorated between Britain and the North, it stated, 'At the beginning of the struggle, the feeling of England was almost unanimously friendly to the North; and up to this time, the vulgar insolence of the Republican faction has failed to produce the faintest reaction in favour of slavery.'[170] In October it argued, 'The war between the Northern and Southern States admits of no legitimate

---

[164] Ibid. (Aug. 1861), 260.
[165] *National Review* (July 1861), 162.
[166] *New Monthly Magazine* (Sept. 1861), 6.
[167] Ibid. 234.
[168] *British Quarterly Review* (July 1861), 214.
[169] Adams, *Great Britain and the American Civil War*, i. 183.
[170] *Saturday Review*, 6 July 1861, 3.

adhesion to the cause of either belligerent. The Confederates are fighting for slavery, and their enemies are fighting, not for abolition, but for conquest.'[171]

Slavery was the perceived cornerstone of the Confederacy, and as impatient as commentators were with the Union, the stain of slavery was not to be easily effaced. Little wonder, then, that William L. Yancey, one of the first southern representatives in Europe, reported to his superiors in May that the British public opposed the Confederacy because of slavery.[172]

Despite what historians have claimed, there was no concept of the southern planters resembling English country gentlemen.[173] Certainly, in 1861, as far as English opinion was concerned, Southerners were uncultured slave owners, an image that would remain with the Confederacy in most quarters for the duration of the war. Another idea that must be discredited is that Britain was somehow flattered by the rumour that the South wanted to re-join the British empire. This notion, which arose during the secessionist crisis, was greeted with widespread derision in the press. In January, the *Saturday Review* remarked that 'letters extolling the system of this country are not now uncommon in the Southern newspapers, and it is remarkable that the writers venture on saying that they have always preferred a Monarchical Government to their own, and have never concealed their preference'. However, the writer continued, 'it is no flattery to be told that a slaveholding community considers a monarchy likely to be more conservative of its institutions than a Republic. . . . If the Southerners ever take a king to reign over them, it is not a Constitutional Monarchy but a military despotism which they will probably establish.'[174] The *Illustrated London News* was equally dismissive.[175] As the notion of the Confederacy re-joining the British empire was raised when English sympathy was almost entirely on the side of the Union, there seems little wonder why it was derided.

King Cotton

Although slavery made the South distasteful, there was yet another reason for its unpopularity, bound up with that of slavery – namely, King Cotton. The phrase 'King Cotton' originated with a writer from Ohio, David Christy, who, in 1855, published his pro-southern tract, *Cotton is King: or slavery in the light of political economy*. The theory of King Cotton was simple: Britain was in thrall to the South because of the latter's monopoly on raw cotton. In 1860,

---

[171] Ibid. 19 Oct. 1861, 391.
[172] Yancey and Ambrose D. Mann to Robert Toombs, 15 July 1861, in *The messages and papers of Jefferson Davis and the Confederacy, including the diplomatic correspondence, 1861–1865*, ed. James D. Richardson, New York 1966, ii. 37. Yancey was later succeeded by James Mason as representative to London after the *Trent* affair.
[173] Adams, *Great Britain and the American Civil War*, i. 48.
[174] *Saturday Review*, 5 Jan. 1861, 3.
[175] See *Illustrated London News*, 12 Jan. 1861, 26.

85 per cent of the raw cotton arriving in Lancashire (the world's largest manufacturer of cotton fabrics) came from the South, and some four or five million individuals were dependent upon the industry and its subsidiary trades. Cotton fabric accounted for some five-ninths of total British exports during the 1850s. As Owsley points out, the British were well aware of the perilous situation they were in. Writers and commentators frequently commented on the economic dependence on the South prior to the war: 'Operatives, manufacturers, merchants, government agents, prime ministers, all, believed alike according to their expressed opinion during the few years before the war, that the cutting-off of the cotton supply in the South would destroy England's chief industry, starve the operatives, and bring ruin and revolution upon the land.'[176] The South was certainly encouraged by this opinion, and was convinced that, should war break out, to avoid the chaos at home a cotton famine would cause, Britain would have to intervene on the side of the southern states.

King Cotton obviously proved delusive. For one thing, the pre-war bumper crop of cotton meant that Britain already had a surplus supply; for another, the British were able to encourage the growth of cotton in India; and finally, as the war progressed, the Confederacy had to ship cotton through the blockade in order to raise money for munitions. As regards English public opinion, however, it was not the failure of the King Cotton policy that was important so much as the overwhelming resentment that it caused. Opposition to being blackmailed into interference in the war was widespread in England.[177]

The *Saturday Review* was one of the first off the mark regarding King Cotton, and its view was blunt, 'it will be national suicide if we do not strain every nerve to emancipate ourselves from moral servitude to a community of slaveowners'.[178] Later, when opinion began to turn against the North, it opined, 'Neither of the belligerents has any reason to count on English assistance or sympathy, for the slave-owners are as loud in their childish threats of withholding their cotton from its principal market as the Republicans of the North in their blustering denunciations of [British] neutrality.'[179] This position remained unchanged by the end of 1861, when the journal again repeated its insistence that Britain would not fight a war for cotton.[180] This opposition has to be noted, because it was commonly claimed by Bright, Marx and other northern supporters (and, subsequently, by certain historians) that the Lancashire workers were constantly induced to agitate for

---

176 Owsley, *King Cotton diplomacy*, 3–15. Owsley provides the most thorough depiction of the King Cotton foundation of Confederate diplomacy. See ch. i passim.
177 For a thorough discussion of the reasons behind King Cotton's failure see *King Cotton diplomacy*, ch. xviii passim.
178 *Saturday Review*, 12 Jan. 1861, 28.
179 Ibid. 13 July 1861, 31. Lest this be interpreted as even the slightest move in favour of the Confederacy over the Union, further down the page, the writer insisted: 'The social condition of the North is safer and wholesomer than a system founded on slavery.'
180 Ibid. 2 Nov. 1861, 445.

the breaking of the Union blockade (the persons concerned were never named, but catch-all phrases like 'Tories' were usually tossed freely about), so as to provide an excuse for Britain to interfere in the American quarrel. Bright's and others' lobbying efforts will be discussed later. What needs to be established here is that the English were aware that they were being blackmailed and were opposed to going to war for the sake of cotton.

Despite what E. D. Adams claims, *The Economist* was resolutely opposed to any surrender to King Cotton from the start.[181] In January, it had this to say about the cornerstone of southern diplomacy:

> Have South Carolina and Georgia really persuaded themselves that mercantile men in England would even wish that their Government should interfere in a struggle between the Federal Union and revolted states, and interfere on the side of those they deem wilfully and fearfully in the wrong, simply for the sake of buying their cotton at a cheaper rate?[182]

In February, it remarked, 'the stock of cotton in our ports has never been so large as now'.[183] Thus, there was at least a dim awareness in England of the cotton surplus that would foil the designs of the Confederacy. *The Economist* continually dismissed the idea of King Cotton. In June, it remarked that the South was trying to hold back its cotton to force Britain's hand; in August it predicted that the Confederacy would have to sell Britain cotton for munitions; and finally, in September, it informed the South that Britain would not go to war for cotton, remarking, 'Cotton is *not* King.'[184]

It must be admitted, however, that not all of *The Economist*'s readers concurred. In October 1861, *The Economist* reported that it had received letters urging Britain to either recognise the Confederacy or break the blockade in order to get cotton. Disturbed to have its wisdom questioned (*plus ça change*), the journal put forward its arguments against intervention: that Britain had no legal claim to the cotton, interference with the blockade or recognising the South would be an act of war, and that recognition would not end the war or expedite the delivery of cotton to Britain.[185] The following week, it again repeated its point that the Confederacy was deliberately holding back cotton to force Britain to interfere.[186] This debate raises two points: one, that the British were aware that southern intransigence, not the Union blockade, could cause a potential cotton famine; two, that there was general recognition that to interfere with the blockade meant going to war with the North – something public opinion was clearly against. Indeed, *The*

---

[181] Adams, *Great Britain and the American Civil War*, i. 55.
[182] *The Economist*, 26 Jan. 1861, 89.
[183] Ibid. 2 Feb. 1861, 117.
[184] Ibid. 22 June 1861, 674; 31 Aug. 1861, 953–54; 21 Sept. 1861, 1040 [their italics].
[185] Ibid. 12 Oct. 1861, 1123.
[186] Ibid. 19 Oct. 1861, 1149.

Economist recognised that the conflict prevented a cotton glut, something it viewed as positive.[187]

The example from *The Economist* proves the existence of a school of thought that argued for breaking the blockade and getting cotton into England. However, as *The Economist* shows, the cost of this action would be war with the Union. No mainstream journal was prepared to pay that price except the anti-establishment *Reynolds's Weekly*.[188] In fact, the *British Quarterly Review* was snobbishly dismissive of those (mostly mill owners, it claimed) who opposed the blockade on the grounds of a cotton shortage: 'these fears are not shared by men in the position of statesmen, and administrators, or by the better classes of our general merchants, who are accustomed to take larger views of mercantile questions'.[189] This suggests that opposition to the blockade was confined to the middle classes and below – in other words, not the aristocracy as the traditional interpretation has claimed. As it was the working-class journal, *Reynolds's Weekly*, which was conspicuous among the few journals in favour of forcing the blockade to prevent a cotton famine, this idea may well have been valid.

Further, recognition of the Confederacy's King Cotton policy was widespread – and resented. *Fraser's Magazine* was not much slower than *The Economist* regarding King Cotton. In February, T. C. Sandars declared, 'The South has been buoyed up to encounter all the risks of secession by the conviction that we must have cotton at any price, and that they would be able to dictate terms to us, and grow richer and richer while we become humbler and humbler. It is now the greatest kindness we can do ourselves and to them to show them their mistake.'[190] This sentiment was repeated in April, when F. W. Newman discussed the southern belief 'that England, through her desire to get cotton, will not permit the blockade of their ports; the making much of this hope shows how wretched is their weakness. We cannot imagine that any English Ministry would enter into conflict with the Northern States for such an object.'[191] The *Illustrated London News* was more phlegmatic. Condemning British reliance on slave-grown cotton, it remarked, 'it does seem to us to be an obvious duty, a duty enforced upon us just now by the arrangements of Divine Providence, that we strenuously exert ourselves to defeat an experiment so largely fraught with evils to humanity'.[192] Even in October, when relations had greatly deteriorated with the North, the *Illustrated London News* maintained the general consensus: 'A most miserable subject for contemplation is no doubt furnished by the present condition and future prospects of

---

187 Ibid. 16 Nov. 1861, 1262.
188 Throughout 1861 *Reynolds's Weekly* agitated for the blockade to be broken. The position of *Reynolds's Weekly* towards America is, for various reasons, discussed separately in a later chapter.
189 *British Quarterly Review*, 1 July 1861, 211.
190 *Fraser's Magazine* (Feb. 1861), 268.
191 Ibid. (Apr. 1861), 413.
192 *Illustrated London News*, 8 June 1861, 520.

our cotton trade, and of the hundred thousands implicated in it; but even this, the South may be well assured, will not tempt us to force the blockade.'[193] The *National Review* toed the party line as well. In October, it published a circular from Neill Brothers and Co. (dated Manchester 21 August 1861). Noting that the Confederacy had withheld its cotton from Britain, the note read,

> No doubt a shallow, confounded conception has taken possession of their minds that 'Cotton is King' . . . that Great Britain and France are entirely dependent on the American supply for the employment of their capital, the profits of their trade, and the subsistence and tranquillity of their industrial populations; and that their wants and fears will soon force both Governments to interfere and compel the Federal Republic to abandon the blockade. . . . But as soon as the leaders of the Southern Confederacy have had leisure and calmness to inquire and reflect, they will become aware, first, that England and France, having recognized the indisputable belligerent rights of the North, have far too strong a sense of the requirements of international law, decency and usage to dream of such an act of direct and unwarrantable hostility against the United States as a forcible violation of their blockade.[194]

With all of this then, it is incredible that the *Spectator* actually argued that Britain might attempt to break the blockade for cotton[195] – a statement *The Economist* brutally dismissed.[196] One individual who believed that Britain would go to war against the Union because of the blockade, in spite of the evidence, was Cobden, who wrote to Charles Sumner on 12 December 1861, saying, 'By raising the blockade, except for articles contraband of war, you get rid of all pressure from abroad, and the tone of public feeling in Europe would naturally become favourable to the North. *It is the suffering and misery that your blockade is bringing on the masses in Europe that turns men against you.*'[197] Cobden's letters to Sumner were, to say the least, alarmist. Besides revealing his own ignorance about why there was a shortage of cotton being sent to Britain – an ignorance not shared by his countrymen – Cobden was also confusing the impact of the blockade with that of the Morrill tariff.

As all of the above commentary establishes, clearly the majority of opinion was against challenging the northern blockade in order to get cotton into Britain. Whoever (assuming such a party actually existed) encouraged the Lancashire cotton workers to agitate for hostilities against the Union belonged to a minority whose views cannot be cited as the general opinion of the English middle classes or above. Indeed, if anything, the press was convinced that breaking the blockade would make matters worse rather than

---

[193] Ibid. 5 Oct. 1861, 340.
[194] *National Review* (Oct. 1861), 460.
[195] *Spectator*, 7 Sept. 1861, 970.
[196] *The Economist*, 14 Sept. 1861, 1012.
[197] Quoted in Villiers and Chesson, *Anglo-American relations*, 65.

better. This argument remained in force even while the cotton famine was at its height. Clearly, if the Lancashire cotton workers' social superiors told them anything, it was *not* to agitate against the blockade.

MPs' opinions on the conflict

There were, none the less, seemingly from the first, a minority of individuals who openly supported the South, and the year 1861 bore witness to the birth of pro-Confederate lobbyists. One of the first of these was the Liberal member of parliament for Galway, William Gregory. Gregory has the dubious distinction of being the first member to forward a motion in the House calling for the recognition of the Confederacy as an independent nation, which he did in June. Like every other attempt in parliament to recognise the South, it was an ignominious failure. The *British Quarterly Review* reported in its July edition, 'so determined were sensible men, on both sides of the Speaker's chair, not to express any public opinion on American difficulties, so resolved were they to be as a Parliament neutral, that efforts were made by men of all parties to get rid of the threatened motion'.[198] Faced with so little support and so much opposition, Gregory had to withdraw his motion. As the *Spectator* succinctly put it: 'Mr. Gregory's motion . . . elicited only four cheers in the House of Commons and was silenced before it had been withdrawn.'[199] Although the House of Commons was never to be the hotbed of pro-Confederate sentiment portrayed by the traditional interpretation, future motions for intervention would at least spark debate – something Gregory's motion did not. Gregory, in fact, had miscalculated and acted prematurely. Events in America were, as yet, too inchoate from the English point of view – the first Battle of Bull Run, for example, had not yet been fought at the time of the motion. Even though Sumter had been taken, the blockade initiated and Britain's neutrality declared, it was still not completely beyond the realm of possibility (remembering that we have the advantage of hindsight) that cooler heads might prevail in America and the conflict might somehow be averted. Further, if from the British point of view the North was behaving intolerably, so too was the South. Yes, the Union had the Morrill tariff, Seward, Clay and the *New York Herald*, but the Confederacy had King Cotton and slavery.

In fact, parliament was generally quiet about America during 1861. There were general questions on the Proclamation of Neutrality, certainly, but non-intervention seemed to be the agreed consensus. Members of parliament were equally cautious outside the House regarding American affairs. There were few truly pro-southern speeches – indeed, northern supporters were the most vocal, as several meetings in constituencies (and elsewhere) establish.

---

[198] *British Quarterly Review* (July 1861), 204.
[199] *Spectator*, 15 June 1861, 635.

Russell, it is true, made a speech at the Newcastle town hall on 14 October, in which he characterised the Union's and the Confederacy's respective causes as 'the one for empire and the other for independence'.[200] Historians such as Keiser who cite it, however, usually fail to point out that Russell also insisted on British neutrality in the same speech.[201] Further, faced with northern insistence that slavery was not going to be interfered with, Russell's depiction was not entirely inexplicable. In any event, other members of parliament begged to differ.

On 1 October, after relations with the Union had deteriorated, William Edward Forster, the pro-reform Liberal member for Bradford, who would become one of the major northern apologists, spoke at the Mechanic's Institute to a large audience. Forster was quick to blame the South for King Cotton, and, to defend his statement that slavery was the only issue of the war, he quoted Confederate Vice-President Alexander Stephens's speech that slavery was the cornerstone of the Confederacy. To great cheering, he predicted the North would beat the South, and noted the Frémont controversy, saying, 'For a time the President has forced General Fremont to lower the standard of freedom which he had hoisted, but military necessities might compel him to raise it again.'[202] The meeting passed a vote of thanks – no one opposed his pro-Union position. What was interesting was Forster's prediction that necessity would compel the Lincoln administration to embark upon a war of emancipation – it was to be frequently repeated by pro-Northerners.

Towards the end of October, the duke of Argyll held a banquet attended by eighty gentlemen in the Argyll Arms Hotel. Argyll, speaking to a group composed of members from his social class, condemned the Confederacy for the institution of slavery and announced to cheers, 'Gentlemen, I think we ought to admit, in fairness to the Americans, that there are some things worth fighting for, and that national existence is one of them.'[203] Argyll held the traditional conservative view that no part of any nation-state had the right to unilaterally secede. It was an argument that he, and many other political conservatives, would maintain throughout the war. Argyll's distaste for the Confederacy was pronounced. Besides secession, he hated slavery and he corresponded with Harriet Beecher Stowe during the conflict. Argyll's views on the war were thus at least in part shaped by his friendship with the author of *Uncle Tom's Cabin*.[204]

---

200 *Reynolds's Weekly*, 20 Oct. 1861, 1.
201 Keiser, 'The English press and the American Civil War', 175.
202 *Reynolds's Weekly*, 6 Oct. 1861, 9. I have used *Reynolds's* for speeches generally simply because I have found its coverage the most effective – the members' speeches are usually quoted in full, as are the audiences' reactions. Further, *Reynolds's* – unlike other journals – often reported who made up the audience, franchised or not – an important detail when discussing reactions of class. None the less, the speeches have been cross-referenced with other journals' reports.
203 Ibid. 3 Nov. 1861, 11.
204 Ridley, *Lord Palmerston*, 550.

John Locke, a barrister by profession and one of the Liberal members for the borough of Southwark, made two pro-northern speeches at meetings which contained electors and non-electors of his constituency: one on 5 November, another three weeks later, both of which called for neutrality and declared that no one was agitating to challenge the blockade. Locke was cheered at both meetings and a vote of thanks was passed.[205]

Southwark's other member of parliament, the Liberal Austen Henry Layard, the archaeologist who excavated Nineveh and now the under-secretary for foreign affairs, spoke on 28 November at a meeting of the borough's electors. Like his fellow member, Layard also made a pro-Union speech. By blaming slavery as 'the great error or great crime in the institutions' of America, he made it clear where his sympathies lay – something his electors clearly supported.[206]

This is not to say that all members of parliament made speeches friendly to the Union. Besides Gregory, two members made speeches that must be considered hostile to the North. Only one of these two, however, actually called for intervention. This was the speech given by Captain Henry Jervis, the member for Harwich. Speaking at Colchester on 24 October, Jervis argued that neutrality would not get Britain cotton, and that secession was comparable to the American Revolution. Condemning the war, which caused 'only misery, not only to this country but to all the nations of Europe', Jervis concluded, 'I am no advocate of slavery, but at the same time I think it is high time for us to take some steps for obtaining supplies for our manufacturing population.' Although he was cheered for this last statement, there was definitely evidence of dissent.[207] In any event, the London press, as we have already seen, opposed views such as Jervis's. Further, one solitary voice calling out in Colchester for some kind of interference with the blockade (though Jervis was never specific on this) again suggests that such views were those of a minority.

The other member of parliament who spoke in favour of the South in 1861 was rather more important, because he became the leading Confederate spokesman during our period. This was the radical Liberal – not Conservative – William Schaw Lindsay.[208] Lindsay was a self-made man. He had begun life as an ordinary seaman in the merchant marine and had gone on to establish a shipping company that had made him wealthy. Lindsay never forgot his humble origins, however, and had, along with Cobden and Bright, championed both free trade and an extension of the franchise. Lindsay had in fact been in America during the secessionist crisis, having gone abroad to encourage better shipping links between the United States and Britain. In

---

205 *Reynolds's Weekly*, 10 Nov. 1861, 2; 1 Dec. 1861, 5.
206 Ibid. 1 Dec. 1861, 5.
207 Ibid. 27 Oct. 1861, 1.
208 Despite the regular misspelling of Lindsay's middle name as 'Shaw', Schaw is the correct version.

the United States he had spoken in Boston and New York and he had travelled extensively throughout America.[209]

Speaking to the Sunderland Ship-Owner's Society, on 21 April 1861, Lindsay declared that on 'travelling through the States he saw secession as a mere question of time'. Lindsay blamed secession on tariffs, making references to the Nullification crisis and the Morrill tariff. As Lindsay saw it, the North and South were two distinct economic entities, each with their own particular needs and requirements. He praised Russell for the Proclamation of Neutrality, but declared, 'when the proper time arrived, it would be desirable that he [Russell] should take another step in advance and acknowledge the Southern Confederation as an independent power'. Lindsay declared that he did not believe the South could, or, indeed, should, be conquered, and predicted that, should the North embark upon such a course, mass destruction would be the only end result.[210]

Lindsay's speech, as he put it, occasioned 'very great excitement on the other side of the Atlantic'. Because of his visit to the United States, Lindsay was known in America. The speech undoubtedly confirmed many Northerners' worst fears that British neutrality was merely a prelude to recognition of the South. Particularly – and understandably – aggrieved were Northerners who had provided Lindsay with hospitality on his trip. It did not take long for them to respond. Before long, circulars advertising Lindsay's company were returned by the United States postal service, which none the less managed to deliver batches of hate mail. One letter addressed to the 'Dishonorable W. S. Lindsay' contained a sample of 'hemp used in America for hanging traitors'. Another included a crude, hand-drawn pencil cartoon of a scrawny chicken looking at a pot of tar and a pile of feathers, with the caption: 'If Mr. Lindsay were to visit America again, he will be furnished with a warm suit of clothes.'[211]

Considering that Lindsay was a radical, and that his shipping business was severely damaged by his speech at Sunderland (and by later, far more blatant pro-Confederate activity), some explanation for his actions is required. Doubtless Lindsay's faith in free trade had been damaged by the Morrill tariff, but there was another reason for Lindsay's actions. Lindsay was a committed pacifist and his record on this subject was consistent. He had opposed the Crimean War and, throughout our period, he would oppose war in America. For Lindsay, there was no such thing as a just war and, so far as America was concerned, peaceful separation was preferable to the inevitable bloodshed of civil war. Lindsay was undeterred by hate mail from America and remained

---

[209] Details of Lindsay's speech at the New York Chamber of Commerce and Boston Board of Trade, are related in Lindsay's collection of reminiscences about the Civil War: Lindsay papers, National Maritime Museum, Greenwich, LND 7, 7–15. The pagination in Lindsay's collection is extremely faulty.
[210] Lindsay papers, LND 7, 41–5.
[211] Ibid. 51–63. The collection of such material is extensive.

convinced that British recognition of the South would end the war. It never seems to have occurred to him – so far as his personal correspondence reveals – that British recognition would lead to an Anglo-American war. He continued to agitate for recognition throughout 1861. In May, he wrote to Gladstone, saying,

> If the Great Powers of Europe make no move the terrible war in America may continue for years – I do not think it possible now for the American people to settle it among themselves – the protest of Europe against its atrocities by the acknowledgement of the South or some such move, or the sheer exhaustion of one or the other of the contending parties, can alone bring it to a close. In the latter case, from the determined spirit which is displayed, there must be an awful sacrifice of life, so awful that if the war continues for 3 years, which is more likely than the '3 months' which Mr. Seward predicts, there will be more lives sacrificed in the struggle, than were ever sacrificed in any war ancient or modern.

In the same letter, he said of the Confederate states: 'They are a nation.'[212] Gladstone would later borrow that quote when speaking publicly at Newcastle. Lindsay got a lot wrong about the conflict, but he saw more clearly than many in America – including its secretary of state – what was about to happen. The fact that Lindsay could also overlook slavery as a cause of the war, and thus deny it any moral ground can only be attributed to the Union's promise not to interfere with the institution. This left the subjects of tariffs and self-determination as the only issues of contention.

None the less, Lindsay, Gregory and Jervis represented a minority opinion. As we have seen above, there were, at this stage, more pro-northern than pro-southern speeches. So, clearly, by the end of 1861, while there were divisions on the question of America, there was no decisive shift of sympathy from the Union to the Confederacy. Indeed, while the North's belligerent conduct, vacillation over slavery and the Morrill tariff caused a great deal of anger and resentment, the South, thanks to King Cotton and slavery, was disliked even more.

The English position prior to the *Trent* affair

There was a great deal of divided opinion on almost every subject relating to the war. For instance, the very question of whether or not the American constitution condoned secession was keenly disputed. The *Athenaeum*, *The Economist*, the *Illustrated London News*, *The Times* and *Westminster Review* all argued that southern secession was legitimate under the constitution; *Fraser's Magazine*, *Macmillan's Magazine*, the *National Review*, the *New Monthly Maga-*

---

[212] Lindsay to Gladstone, 12 May 1861, ibid. 84–5. The underlining is Lindsay's.

DIFFERENCES OF OPINION

zine, the *Quarterly Review*, the *Saturday Review* and the *Spectator* all denied it.[213]

It is true that after the first Battle of Bull Run a general consensus arose that the Union would find it difficult to conquer the Confederacy.[214] This, however, was more firmly rooted in the belief that it would be hard for a victorious Union to re-establish a sundered allegiance, rather than any belief in innate northern weakness, an argument that would apparently grow in strength as the struggle became more protracted.[215] Even then, it must be remembered that there were dissenting views. The *Annual Register* noted that the Confederacy was 'fearfully overmatched' and stated, 'it is idle to speculate on the future course of this tremendous conflict'.[216] The *Spectator*, meanwhile, cited the fact that America had fought Britain for 'twelve years' in the Revolution as proof that 'The enthusiasm may die away, but there is no chance of Northern determination growing cold.'[217] It must also be remembered that Britain had recently suppressed rebellion in India and fought Russia, and had, in the past, skirmished in Ireland. 'Few', as Crook points out, 'denied the abstract right of the North to use coercion.'[218] This probably goes some distance in explaining the refusal, especially on the part of conservative journals, to accept the right of secession. *Fraser's Magazine*, for instance, insisted that if Britain could hold Ireland, the North could conquer and hold the South.[219]

Although some jeered at the North's humiliation at Bull Run, it is too simple to merely say that it 'occasioned sarcasm and sneers throughout Western Europe'.[220] A number of voices remarked that the defeat would

---

[213] For the right of secession see *Athenaeum*, 23 Nov. 1861, 686; *Illustrated London News*, 17 Aug. 1861, 151; *Westminster Review* (Oct. 1861), 501. *The Economist*, as we have seen, stated that it believed the South should be allowed to leave peacefully; earlier, on 25 May 1861, 564, however, it had argued the opposite. For the arguments against secession see *Fraser's Magazine* (Aug. 1861), 258–60; *British Quarterly Review* (July 1861), 207; *Saturday Review*, 2 Feb. 1861, 109. The *New Monthly Magazine* stated, 'For our part, we are strongly on the side of the North' (Aug. 1861), 392; the *National Review*, meanwhile, took a neutral view of the right of secession, saying it could not be defended or denied, but only determined by force of arms. It did, however, state that the South's secession was 'insolent, traitorous and dishonourable' (July 1861), 151, 155. I judge from the position taken by *Macmillan's* and the *Spectator* – namely, that the cause of the war was slavery alone – that they opposed the right of secession.
[214] Adams, *Great Britain and the American Civil War*, i. 176–7; Jones, *Union in peril*, 8.
[215] See, for example, *Saturday Review*, 5 Oct. 1861, 347; *Illustrated London News*, 16 Nov. 1861, 493. *The Economist* even posited this on 26 July 1861, 731, before news of Bull Run had arrived.
[216] *Annual Register*, 1861, 'History', 263.
[217] *Spectator*, 25 May 1861, 553. Later in the year, after Bull Run, the journal would again insist on the possibility of a northern triumph: 16 Nov. 1861, 1253.
[218] Crook, 'Portents of war', 176.
[219] *Fraser's Magazine* (Aug. 1861), 262. Later on, northern apologists would frequently make the equation between Ireland and the Confederacy.
[220] Crook, *The North, the South and the powers*, 89.

galvanize the Union, including *The Economist* and *The Times*.[221] The *Illustrated London News*, meanwhile, noted, 'Let it be understood, however . . . that the victory of the South places its cause in no better position in English eyes.'[222] In any event, the reaction to Bull Run has to be taken in the context of the atmosphere of Anglo-American relations. There was real concern about northern hostility towards Britain; Bull Run proved that the defeat of the Confederacy (assuming it was actually going to be achieved) was going to take time to effect. This meant that the Union was going to be otherwise engaged.

That the Union was hostile to Britain was the one point where there was a genuine consensus. As the *Spectator* remarked in June,

> The Americans are, for the moment, transported beyond the influence of common sense. . . . With all of England sympathising, more or less heartily, with the North, they persist on regarding her as an enemy, and seem positively anxious to change an ally, who happens to be quiescent, into an open and dangerous foe.[223]

What the North never understood – especially the Adams family – was that threats of hostilities served only to irritate, not intimidate, the English.[224] None the less, there was a real determination to stay clear of the conflict. Further, by the end of November, with the war begun in earnest, many English commentators believed that it was unlikely Britain would be dragged into the fray. Whatever else it established, the Battle of Bull Run had proven that the defeat of the South was going to demand the North's full attention. There were, however, a few dissenters. Besides the *Wesleyan Methodist Magazine*, the *Saturday Review* remarked on 2 November, 'The Government at Washington ought to take care that ill-will or ill-breeding is not allowed to exaggerate itself into practical outrage.'[225] Unfortunately, a practical outrage was only a few days away – although the news would not arrive in England until over a fortnight later – when Captain Charles Wilkes, commanding the USS *San Jacinto*, stopped the British mail carrier the RMS *Trent* in international waters and removed the Confederacy's diplomatic representatives from it.

---

[221] See *The Economist*, 10 Aug. 1861, 869; Crawford, *The Anglo-American crisis*, 117–22.
[222] *Illustrated London News*, 10 Aug. 1861, 132.
[223] *Spectator*, 15 June 1861, 635.
[224] See Jones, *Union in peril*, 54. E. D. Adams meanwhile states, 'The public anger of America expressed in her newspapers, astonished the British press and, temporarily, made them more careful in comment on American affairs': *Great Britain and the American Civil War*, i. 103.
[225] *Saturday Review*, 2 Nov. 1861, 445.

2

The Trent *Outrage*

> 'The idea of war with America should be to every
> Englishman unnatural and revolting.'

Among all the aspects of Anglo-American relations during the Civil War, the *Trent* affair has been the most closely examined. The actual capture of the Confederate envoys, the opinions of the British and northern cabinets, and the complex legalities surrounding Captain Charles Wilkes's actions have all been studied by historians of Anglo-American affairs. Additionally, in recent years, two separate studies on the incident itself have been published.[1] Despite all this research, however, both parliamentary and popular opinion – as opposed to the diplomacy – remain either misunderstood or, worse, misrepresented. The controversy surrounding the *Trent* affair was very much a product of the preceding six months – it would also have a major impact on subsequent British views of the war. In the case of the *Trent* affair, English public opinion, as often during the war, was shaped by events in America. The incident began as a minor outrage when the news of the commissioners' seizure arrived in England, and subsequently grew into a major crisis when reports from the North arrived thereafter.[2] The chronology of these events is crucial to any understanding of why English public opinion took the form it did, and this chapter examines popular sentiment both as it unfolded during the crisis and within the wider context of Anglo-American relations at the time.

The boarding of the *Trent*

The two Confederate commissioners, James Mason and John Slidell, appointed to the courts of Queen Victoria and Napoleon III respectively, were sent to replace Yancey and Mann in Britain and T. Butler King and Pierre A. Rost in France. The two were dispatched essentially to obtain what their predecessors had attempted and failed: international recognition of southern independence.

---

[1] Norman Ferris, *The Trent affair: a diplomatic crisis*, Knoxville 1977; Warren, *Fountain of discontent*.
[2] E. D. Adams was the first to note this important point, subsequently ignored by successive historians. He attempts, however, little analysis: *Great Britain and the American Civil War*, i. 225.

The commissioners departed from South Carolina on 12 October 1861 and, avoiding the Union warships blockading Charleston, sailed to Cuba. From there, they booked a passage on the mail carrier the RMS *Trent*, sailing on 7 November for the Danish island of St Thomas – the connecting point for British ships headed to Southampton. *En route*, the *Trent*, in international waters, proceeding from one neutral destination to another, was halted by the USS *San Jacinto*, commanded by Captain Wilkes, and a party of armed marines was sent across to arrest the Confederate envoys, plus their secretaries, George Eustis and James MacFarland. After some actions of questionable intelligence on the part of the Union officers and crew, Mason and Slidell 'yielded to force under protest' and were taken aboard the *San Jacinto*, doubtless hoping that their seizure, illegal under international law, would provoke a military response from Britain.[3] Once the Union warship had secured its prizes, the *Trent* was allowed to proceed on its way.

There has been, ever since the event, a suspicion that Mason and Slidell somehow orchestrated their seizure by the Union so as to bring Britain into the war. Generally historians have dismissed this suspicion, but an examination of Mason's letters to his family (whom he left behind in Virginia, unlike Slidell who had his family accompany him) suggests that the Confederate commissioners did indeed bait Wilkes into seizing them. For, when and while the commissioners were in Havana, so too was the *San Jacinto*, which was refuelling with coal. As Mason wrote, after his arrest,

> Our presence in Havana and our mission to Europe as well as our purpose to embark on the mail steamer which was to leave Havana on the 7th of November was well known in the city. We knew it had been spoken of and commented on by the consul of the United States at Havana and thus, would of course, reach the ears of Captain Wilkes, besides which I had visits at my hotel from the officers of that ship. Of course, in conversation with these gentlemen, I imported nothing touching our plans or purposes, but in the manner above noted, it became fully known to Captain Wilkes that we were to embark upon the mail steamer for England via St Thomas on the 7th of November.[4]

Of course, Mason might simply have been bragging, but it seems unnecessary to have done so in a private letter to his wife. The question does arise, if he and Slidell did ensure that their mission became known in order to provoke capture, why did Mason not just say so? The answer to this is that Mason wrote the above letter from prison where it was read first by Union officials. If Mason had openly stated that he and Slidell provoked their capture, the North would doubtless have passed on such a confession to the British.

---

[3] For more details of Mason and Slidell's departure from Charleston and capture see Warren, *Fountain of discontent*, 7–25.

[4] Mason to his wife, 15 Nov. 1861, in *The public life and diplomatic correspondence of James M. Mason with some personal history by his daughter*, ed. Virginia Mason, Roanoke 1903, 214–15.

Indeed, such a confession could be used to argue that the Confederacy was trying to provoke war between Britain and the Union – something that would not have suited Mason at all. Whether or not the commissioners did deliberately ensure their own seizure cannot be definitively answered, but entertaining enemy naval officers at one's hotel, as Mason claims to have done, should certainly raise suspicions.

None the less, whether he had been tricked or not, the controversial Captain Wilkes, as Warren points out, had done his best to rationalise the capture, poring over authorities on international law, scrutinising neutral rights and responsibilities. Wilkes concluded he had the power to capture vessels carrying enemy dispatches, but was uncertain if this could be applied to the Confederate commissioners. For, as he wrote, they 'were not dispatches in the literal sense, and did not seem to come under that designation'. In the end, Wilkes decided that since Mason and Slidell were traitors, they were the embodiment of dispatches, subject to arrest if they lacked American passports. As Warren points out, 'It was a novel theory and a good example of quarter-deck justice, but for all his homework, Captain Wilkes did not find a single precedent to support his dubious enterprise; subsequently, neither could anyone else.'[5] Unfortunately, while such 'quarter-deck justice' might have satisfied the Union navy, it failed to satisfy the somewhat more stringent views of the British government.

There has been some past confusion regarding the legality of Wilkes's seizure and historians are still somewhat divided. Some suggest the Union did no more than follow British precedents, confusing the *Trent* affair with the issue of impressment during the Napoleonic Wars – a confusion made by many in the northern states at the time.[6] Crook, meanwhile, argues that 'the legal matters were by no means clear cut'.[7]

The one issue which is clear-cut is that impressment was (and is) irrelevant to the case of the *Trent*. Impressment by the British, during the Napoleonic Wars, in so far as it concerned the Americans, involved stopping neutral ships on the high seas and removing British deserters. Mason and Slidell were neither pressed into the Unites States navy, nor removed for their alleged status as American nationals.[8] Further, by the time of the *Trent*, impressment had effectively ended with the Napoleonic Wars, almost half a century ago. Although there had been no official abnegation on impressment, British views on neutral rights had changed; new precedents had since been set, as evidenced by Britain's, as Crook puts it, 'novel self-restraint' in the Crimean

---

[5] Warren, *Fountain of discontent*, 7, 14–15.
[6] Jenkins appears to believe that British precedents supported the seizure: *Britain and the war for the Union*, i, ch. viii passim, esp. p. 198. Mahin, meanwhile, specifically equates the seizure of the envoys to the impressment issue: *One war at a time*, 78.
[7] Crook, *The North, the South and the powers*, 107.
[8] Some English journals noted this. See, for example, *Saturday Review*, 30 Nov. 1861, 548.

War.[9] In any event, individuals in the Union were on shaky grounds citing a precedent the United States had always opposed.[10]

Crook argues that there might have been grounds for rationalising the capture, provided Wilkes had brought the *Trent* to a prize court, noting that, 'On British precedents, but not on American, dispatches could be contraband', and that although Foreign Secretary Russell argued that the *Trent* did not carry such contraband because it travelled between neutral ports, there was an argument in Henry Wheaton's collection of United States Supreme Court cases supporting confiscation despite a neutral destination. Where this argument fails is in Wilkes's assessment that men could be the embodiment of dispatches. The only authority Crook can cite to support Wilkes's argument is that of the American, Francis Wharton, over twenty years later. By Wharton's time, however, the rules had changed. The erosion of distinctions between neutral and belligerent theatres (partially resulting from the American Civil War) was more generally acknowledged. As Crook points out, 'The new American doctrine, although logical, raised scarifying vistas of ruthless wartime interference with commerce which really require a twentieth century mind to accept.'

The trouble is, we are not talking about twentieth-century (or twenty-first-century) minds, but mid-nineteenth-century ones. Although warfare and its rules may have been changing, this is obvious only with hindsight. There was simply no precedent for Wilkes's seizure. The Civil War may have forced America to 'take a leading role in eroding neutralist conventions it had previously championed', but it did not follow that neutrals would, or should, accept this erosion.

There was, however, a far more important flaw in the Union's argument: that although belligerent vessels had the right to visit neutral ships in order to determine identity and to seize contraband of war, 'These arguments applied, of course, only if a state of war existed, and during the crisis, serious argument was conducted on the premise that the rebels were belligerents. The British were obliged to do so by their neutrality decree, the Americans by the fact that if they did not their case was lost at once.'[11]

The problem for the North was that, by November of 1861, it had still not officially recognised Confederate belligerency – indeed, Seward was still trying to get the British government to withdraw the Proclamation of Neutrality. Although Britain had accepted the role of a neutral with its rights and duties, the North had not officially recognised such status – the blockade

---

[9] Crook, *The North, the South and the powers*, 107–8.
[10] Further, it should be remembered that in 1812, when America believed its neutral rights were violated by Britain in its struggle against Napoleon, the United States did not send an ultimatum, but declared war and invaded Canada. Palmerston's actions during the *Trent* affair were, by contrast, extremely moderate.
[11] Crook, *The North, the South and the powers*, 108–10; Henry Wheaton, *Cases argued and decided in the Supreme Court of the United States*, Albany 1883.

notwithstanding. No official Union recognition of a state of war meant that federal warships had no legal status as belligerents with the right of search. Thus, the Union could not cite the right of a belligerent to search a vessel sailing between neutral ports for contraband. According to the Union's own logic, Wilkes had illegally stopped a foreign ship on the high seas in time of peace, searched it, and removed four passengers from it. Considering that, in the past, the United States had prevented Britain from merely visiting American ships to ensure that they were not slave traders sailing under false colours, made the Union's position less tenable. It is, therefore, impossible to escape the conclusion that the North violated international law.[12]

The reaction of the press and public

These arguments aside, what has to be remembered when discussing English opinion during the *Trent* affair is that the government and public believed Britain's neutral rights had been violated – violated by a nation which, over the last several months, had become increasingly bellicose. It was also a slap in the face to those sympathetic to the North who had tried to play down Union hostility. Surprisingly enough, most European governments united behind the British interpretation of the affair's legality. Certainly, some nations, such as France, had their own reasons for doing so, but even Russia, the pro-Union stance of which derived from its ongoing imperial rivalry with Britain, supported Palmerston's government.[13]

The news of the northern captain's actions arrived in Britain on the afternoon of 27 November and was common knowledge by the following day.[14] Unsurprisingly, the general reaction was hostile. The idea of foreign powers stopping and seizing passengers from British ships at will was an extremely emotive issue in England. This alone would have caused discontent, but the ill-will and suspicion which had arisen between Britain and the Union over the previous seven months greatly contributed to English anger. Indeed, the name of the event most used by historians, 'the *Trent* affair', is of American coinage. Nineteenth-century Britons called it 'the *Trent* outrage'.

Irritation with the Union was also stoked by the report of the *Trent*'s

---

[12] Warren argues that, ironically, had Wilkes taken the *Trent* to a prize court, it would have been condemned because Commander Williams secured Mason's dispatch bag in the *Trent*'s mail room when the Union halted the ship. At that point, the vessel was guilty of a violation of neutrality; there was even a British precedent to support an American confiscation of the ship in such a case. Warren, however, does not take into account the Union's failure to recognise Confederate belligerency: *Fountain of discontent*, ch. ix passim.
[13] See Jones, *Union in peril*, 86–7; Warren, *Fountain of discontent*, 158–63. Crook, meanwhile, notes 'The opinion of neutral nations was depressingly unsympathetic towards America's untraditional championing of belligerent rights': *The North, the South and the powers*, 154, 128–30.
[14] *Saturday Review*, 30 Nov. 1861, 547.

Commander Williams, whose description of the federal navy's actions has generally been ignored by historians – including careful ones such as Warren, who relies almost entirely on the American Lieutenant Fairfax's account. Williams, for example, denied American reports that the *San Jacinto* had requested the *Trent* to heave to before firing a warning shot across the latter's bows. According to Williams, the first he knew of the Americans' wish to search the vessel was when the Union ship fired its warning shot. Williams also declared that the marines sent across to the *Trent* were rather too free in the use of their rifle-butts and had threatened innocent passengers with their bayonets. Williams repeated his accusations after the affair had been resolved. He went so far as to call Fairfax's description of good behaviour on the part of the search party a 'fabrication'.[15] By this point, without a doubt, Williams was responding to the very unflattering portrait painted of him by Lieutenant Fairfax – including the claim, denied by Williams, that Captain Moir of the *Trent* had to send the bumptious commander below decks. It is worth noting, though, that James Mason's account of his capture bears a closer resemblance to Williams's version of the seizure than Fairfax's. In particular, that the *San Jacinto* did not request the *Trent* to heave to before firing a shot across its bows and that the marines treated the passengers roughly.[16] What is far more important, though, than whose account of the event was more accurate, is that it was Williams's account – not Fairfax's – that the English public first heard and his description did little to help the Union's case.

Most important, however, was that initially, beyond knowledge of the actual seizure of Mason and Slidell, nothing was known. The question of whether or not the Union had finally decided to pick the quarrel many believed it wanted could not be answered, simply because there was no immediate way of telling whether or not Washington had authorised the act. Even the American minister, C. F. Adams, was completely ignorant on this point. For those suspicious of the Union, the timing was ominous. It would be winter in Canada and thus difficult to reinforce the colony. If the Lincoln administration, led by Seward, was planning to seize Canada to make up the territory lost to the Confederacy, it had picked itself as advantageous a time as was possible. It was under these conditions that English perceptions of the *Trent* incident took place.

Despite appearing to be 'the climax of American arrogance', the tone in England was far more moderate than the irrational explosion of anti-northern sentiment that historians have often portrayed.[17] Although

---

15 Williams's speech to the Royal Western Yacht Club: *Western Morning News*, 15 Oct. 1862, 3.
16 Mason to his wife, 15 Nov. 1861, in *Correspondence of James M. Mason*, 215–25.
17 Adams, *Great Britain and the American Civil War*, i. 203, 217. Adams, besides greatly exaggerating the belligerence of the British press during the first few weeks of the crisis, relies too heavily on the opinions of the Adams family and American visitors to England at

Crook states, 'The hysteria was indeed extraordinary, matched in the mid-Victorian period perhaps only by the emotion over the Papal Aggression of 1851 and the Indian mutiny of 1857', there is little evidence of any such hysteria.[18] Henry Adams, who certainly exaggerated the English response to the act, claimed that if the Atlantic telegraph had been in operation in December 1861, Britain would have gone to war with the North.[19] As Dean Mahin points out, however, had the telegraph been in operation, Washington could have sent London an immediate telegram informing Palmerston's government that Wilkes had acted without authorisation – something that would have certainly changed the situation.[20] In the first week of the crisis, there was only one true anti-Union meeting, held on the day the incident became known in Britain, in Liverpool, England's capital of pro-southern sentiment, by one of the chief spokesmen of English pro-Confederate sympathy, James Spence.[21] Further, the London press, trying to cool passions, was quick to heap scorn upon Spence's efforts in Liverpool.[22]

Certainly, the press, as a whole, preached calm and praised it too, noting the general moderation of public temper it perceived. The anti-North *Saturday Review* remarked,

> We may be reasonably proud of the manner in which the news of the seizure of the Confederate Commissioners, while under the protection of the British flag, has been received in England. There has been the most serious determination to uphold our rights, and the keenest jealousy of our national honour; but there has been an honest wish to abide patiently by the rule of law.[23]

---

the time who would, considering the circumstances, probably have exaggerated the public temper (they, after all, had probably been on the receiving end of any personal expressions of anger). The oft-quoted '999 men out of every thousand would declare for immediate war' was the observation of an American visitor. I have not found sentiment this hostile repeated by any English commentator. C. F. Adams, the American minister, was meanwhile dealing with an outraged Palmerston, a fact which coloured his (and his family's) views. Palmerston believed that he had received a verbal agreement from Adams that the North would not molest British shipping in order to capture the two envoys. Jones, meanwhile, largely repeats Adams's quotes: *Union in peril*, 84. See also Warren, *Fountain of discontent*, ch. v passim.
18 Crook, *The North, the South and the powers*, 119–20.
19 Ridley, *Lord Palmerston*, 553.
20 Mahin, *One war at a time*, 66–7. Mahin fails to mention that Henry Adams came up with the idea that war would have broken out had the Atlantic telegraph been in operation.
21 *Reynolds's Weekly*, 1 Dec. 1861, 5. Warren cites this meeting, but fails to note Spence's involvement (he was chairman). Although there was initially a resolution calling on the government 'to assert the dignity of the British flag by requiring prompt reparation for this outrage', cooler heads prevailed, and the phrase demanding prompt reparations was struck out: Warren, *Fountain of discontent*, 104–5.
22 See, for example, *Saturday Review*, 7 Dec. 1861, 583–5.
23 Ibid. 30 Nov. 1861, 547.

The *Illustrated London News* agreed with this assessment.[24] The *Spectator*, meanwhile, was less sanguine than its contemporaries. It noted, however, that although

> The public throughout the country are calling for war, and the irritation which New York bluster has for some months produced, threatened for a moment to overbear the needful respect for international law. It is creditable to the English people that, touched on their sorest point – the right of their flag to protect all which it covers – they are content to await the tardy effect of a calm but decisive remonstrance.[25]

The 'New York bluster' must be noted. The reason the *Trent* affair caused so much disquiet was directly owing to the escalating tensions between Britain and the Union since the Queen's Proclamation of Neutrality. Further, although there was a great deal of anger, there were no cries to descend upon Washington. Despite the claims of some historians, no jingo press clamouring for war can be observed.[26] One of the few journals that actively sought conflict was the anti-establishment *Reynolds's Weekly* that was agitating against the northern blockade.[27]

Nor, despite what some historians have claimed, was the assumption that Wilkes's seizure was an affront authorised by Washington universally accepted. True, *The Economist* suspected Seward's involvement in a deliberate outrage upon the country, 'We remembered the antecedents of Mr Seward; his language as to Canada'; but other journals were more circumspect.[28] The editorial of the *Illustrated London News* noted that, because Britain would not tolerate having passengers seized from its ships in international waters, 'If, as has been asserted, it has been the object and design of the Federal Government to force Great Britain into an attitude of hostility, without question full reason and justification has now been afforded.' None the less, the editor also pointed out that 'American naval officers have been always somewhat hasty in asserting what they conceive to be the rights of their country', concluding, 'When the matter is looked at, considered with that coolness and calmness which its importance requires, it seems almost impossible to suppose that so flagrant a trespass on the rights which by international law are covered by a flag can have been deliberately planned by the American Government.'[29] The *Saturday Review* held a similar view. Although the journal took care to blame the current climate on Seward's activities, stating that his 'conceptions of policy since his accession to office are known to have been so wildly

---

[24] *Illustrated London News*, 14 Dec. 1861, 591.
[25] *Spectator*, 30 Nov. 1861, 1297.
[26] See, for example, McPherson, *Battle cry of freedom*, 390.
[27] For insistence that Britain make war on the North see, in particular, *Reynolds's Weekly*, 1 Dec. 1861, 1; 8 Dec. 1861, 1; 15 Dec. 1861, 1.
[28] *The Economist*, 30 Nov. 1861, 1318. The journal, however, refused to commit itself to this idea.
[29] *Illustrated London News*, 30 Nov. 1861, 540.

extravagant that there is scarcely any conceivable piece of folly from which we can confidently exonerate him without inquiry', the journal added, 'Yet, unless all judgment has left him, he can hardly have given such orders as Captain Wilks [sic] has acted upon, if orders he had.'[30] The fiercely anti-Confederate *Spectator* expressed the most concern. Believing that Wilkes could not have acted without authority, being 'too old and too distinguished an officer', the journal found itself on the side of *The Economist*, suspicious that the incident was a calculated affront. The *Spectator* insisted that the Union had absolutely no justification for seizing the Confederate commissioners and likewise condemned Seward's past conduct. The journal further warned the secretary of state that if he was attempting to provoke an Anglo-American war, the Union would find the conquest of Canada more difficult than he bargained for.[31]

Over the first week, then, speculation reigned. The question of whether or not the act was deliberately hostile remained. This appeared unlikely, for it did strike commentators that for the North to embroil Britain in a war, now that the South had proven so resilient, would be tantamount to national suicide. The only answer to this was the possibility that the Lincoln administration had determined to make up the loss of the Confederacy with Canada at a time when it would be difficult to defend the colony. As the *New York Herald* had first suggested the idea of this 'exchange', it is unsurprising that it gained some currency. Despite the concern expressed, however, the agreed position was to wait for the Union's response to the outrage. Unfortunately, the news from the North only worsened the situation.

The news from America

The news from America was that Captain Wilkes was lionised in the Union – in particular in Boston, New York and Washington.[32] Among the thousands who turned out to congratulate and defend Wilkes's actions were, in Massachusetts alone, Chief Justice George T. Bigelow, Governor John Andrew, Boston's mayor Joseph Wightman, veteran politician Edward Everett, and a number of Harvard law professors. Besides this distinguished company, Wilkes also found defenders and supporters (it was, and is, often hard to discriminate between them) in Caleb Cushing, the War Department's secretary Simon Cameron, and others within the Lincoln administration. This included Gideon Welles, secretary of the navy, who, despite his misgivings, wrote Wilkes a congratulatory letter.[33] Although much of the celebration

---

[30] *Saturday Review*, 30 Nov. 1861, 548.
[31] *Spectator*, 30 Nov. 1861, 1305.
[32] For a complete description of Wilkes's celebratory tour of the northern states see Warren, *Fountain of discontent*, ch. ii passim.
[33] Ibid. 37. Welles's congratulation, however, included a rider reprimanding Wilkes for

reflected northern desperation for good news since secession and war, many, if not most, in the Union shared Governor Andrew's smug satisfaction that 'Commodore Wilkes fired his shot across the bows of the ship that bore the British lion at its head.'[34] Or, as Jones puts it, 'Starved for good news after Bull Run, they [Northerners] praised Wilkes for avenging that humiliation and all British maritime encroachments with one blow.'[35] Clearly, the British had been put in their place and Wilkes was the hero of the hour. The culminating honour came from the House of Representatives, which passed a resolution thanking Wilkes for his 'brave, adroit, and patriotic conduct'.[36]

Northern enthusiasm appeared unanimous, but it was not entirely so.[37] If the House of Representatives was satisfied with the legality of Wilkes's deed, Lincoln's cabinet was divided. Controversy still surrounds the president's position, whether or not he feared that Mason and Slidell would turn out to be white elephants or whether he believed the Union had acted legally.[38] Although E. D. Adams and several others have insisted that Seward doubted the legality of Wilkes's actions from the start, cabinet member Gideon Welles's report that Seward was initially 'elated' by the act proves this to be untrue.[39] As does the threat to 'wrap the whole world in flames' he made to the journalist, W. H. Russell, shortly after the British ultimatum arrived in Washington.[40] Although some historians have claimed that Seward was only speaking for effect, the problem with this theory is that when the secretary of state said this, Lincoln's cabinet was still divided over whether or not to release the envoys. The two cabinet members who opposed Wilkes's actions from the beginning were the secretary of the Treasury, Salmon P. Chase, and the Postmaster General, Montgomery Blair. Indeed, Chase wrote in his diary on 25 December 1861: 'We cannot deny this [the illegality of the act] without denying our history.'[41] Also, despite the lack of enthusiasm expressed by some western newspapers, the New York press, including the belligerent *New York*

---

failing to bring the *Trent* to a prize court for adjudication. He was certainly 'hedging his bets', as Crook puts it, but the British government (and public) missed or ignored Welles's codicil: *The North, the South and the powers*, 116–17.
34 Warren, *Fountain of discontent*, 27.
34 Jones, *Union in peril*, 83.
36 Warren, *Fountain of discontent*, 169–70.
37 Crook cites a number of minor American officials and publications that opposed the seizure from the start: *The North, the South and the powers*, 111–14.
38 Both Warren and Crook are extremely uncertain regarding Lincoln's view during the crisis: *Fountain of discontent*, 35–8; *The North, the South and the powers*, 115.
39 Adams, *Great Britain and the American Civil War*, i. 231; Warren, *Fountain of discontent*, 39. Crook also reports that Seward's son Frederick, acting as his father's secretary, insisted on the legality of Wilkes's act in an official state department notice: *The North, the South and the powers*, 115.
40 Jones, *Union in peril*, 88.
41 Salmon P. Chase, *Inside Lincoln's cabinet: the Civil War diaries of Salmon P. Chase*, ed. David Herbert Donald, New York 1954, 53–5. See also Warren, *Fountain of discontent*, 35–8.

Herald, and eastern newspapers generally, 'rushed to the defence of Wilkes'.[42] Unfortunately, the English used these newspapers as barometers of northern public opinion.

The response

From the vantage-point of England, then, it appeared as if the entire Union was engaged in fierce competition to honour and celebrate both the offensive act and its author. Any hopes for quick repudiation from Washington disappeared. As *The Economist* put it, '*we* are right no doubt; but the Americans, as we see by their papers and speeches, have no doubt also that *they* are right'.[43] A new question was now raised: could the Lincoln administration disown so popular a deed, assuming they were even prepared to do this? This was a serious question. After all, de Tocqueville had called into question the power of American public officials when faced with the opposition of a large majority.[44] Palmerston also believed that the Lincoln administration would be unable to resist the popular chorus, writing to Russell on 5 December that 'nations in which the masses influence or direct the destinies of a country are swayed much more by passion than by interest'.[45] In any case, the British had experienced their own groundswells of popular support for unjustifiable wars in the past, such as the Crimea. The possibility of a collision was now clearly faced. It was not a reality taken either eagerly or lightly – the exact opposite, in fact. Not only did commentators dislike the thought of wantonly going to war with the Union, they were also disgusted with Britain's inevitable ally, the Confederacy. Despite Bright's, and Marx's, misrepresentations of the English – often blindly accepted by historians – serious efforts were made to prevent a complete breakdown in relations not only by much of the press, but also by numerous private individuals.

Fears about whether or not Lincoln's administration could, or even would, repudiate such a popular act were immediately aired. The *Illustrated London News* was less worried about the president than about his secretary of state, 'We wish that we could believe the Seward party wise enough and patriotic enough to consider the question only on its merits. They have never given any proof of such a statesmanlike disposition. They have sought nothing but popularity and the applause of that part of the populace whose good opinion is a reproach to honest men.'[46] Notice how the journal referred to the 'Seward party' as opposed to the 'Lincoln party'. The secretary of state's reputation

---

[42] Warren, *Fountain of discontent*, 39.
[43] *The Economist*, 7 Dec. 1861, 1345 [their italics].
[44] De Tocqueville, *Democracy in America*, 254–70.
[45] Ridley, *Lord Palmerston*, 554.
[46] *Illustrated London News*, 4 Jan. 1862, 6.

had by this time sunk to the point where any wrong committed by the Union was attributed to him. As W. R. Greg writing in the *National Review* put it,

> If the mob of New York, the multitude of Americans who fancy, in their elegant phrase, that they can 'wop the whole world'; – if such people as Mr. Seward, who stimulate passions which they do not share, and simulate prejudices that they do not feel, are permitted to rule the policy of the United States, war is inevitable.[47]

As the above quote establishes, however, it is too much of a simplification to state that commentators saw a Machiavellian Seward forcing conflict upon Britain. There were fears that it was not the secretary of state but the supposedly unreasonable northern populace (a theory based on the opinions of such journals as the *New York Herald*) who would cause an Anglo-Union conflict. In other words, although Seward might have previously worked the mob, it did not logically follow that he could control it. Events, at that point, could rapidly spiral out of control. This was the belief of *Fraser's Magazine*, which argued that northern politicians (such as Seward) had believed that, because Britain had borne insults, it would also tolerate aggression. Now that they were about to learn differently, 'they will perhaps do their best to extricate themselves from their difficulty. It may be more easy, however, to wish to extricate themselves than to succeed. Infatuated with vanity, the American democracy may prefer to run all risks than humiliate themselves to England.'[48] By 'American democracy', the journal meant nothing more than the mob. The *New Monthly Magazine*'s fear of the unreasonable mob was made more explicit:

> We think too well of the president, and of one or two of the leading American officials, to credit that they have any desire to force on an unnatural contest, which must be injurious to their country. Our fear is, that the wisdom of the government and reflecting men in America will not be backed by sufficient power to master a senseless and rabid mob, which has no regard for consequences, domestic or foreign.[49]

Part of the problem was, of course, that it had not only been the popular voice that had cheered Wilkes's actions, but the voices of those who held positions of power and responsibility. Not that English observers always professed to see the difference. *The Economist*, noting the plaudits the House of Representatives heaped upon Wilkes, described it as 'the lower Chamber of their Congress' and 'therefore a very just index of common opinion. It is composed of average persons representing the ordinary political opinion, not of the more intelligent and educated minority, but of the ordinary rude and practical

---

[47] *National Review* (Jan. 1862), 266.
[48] *Fraser's Magazine* (Jan. 1862), 129.
[49] *New Monthly Magazine* (Jan. 1862), 64.

mass which rules beyond the Atlantic.'[50] As the *Illustrated London News* succinctly put it, 'The one topic of the day is the great question whether the American democracy will permit the American statesmanship to do right.'[51]

Despite the belief that conflict would be forced upon them, opposition to unnecessary war with the North was widespread in England. As the *British Quarterly Review* remarked, 'The idea of war with America should be to every Englishman unnatural and revolting.'[52] The *Illustrated London News* pointed out that, despite the kudos Wilkes received, there was still no evidence that the captain had acted under orders from Washington. Indeed, stated the journal, 'The probabilities all lie the other way . . . we may well make some allowance for the difficulties which surround the Lincoln administration', adding that 'we firmly believe [the British] will be prepared to make any sacrifice of feeling, not inconsistent with national honour, in order to avert a war with their American kin'.[53] The *Illustrated London News* did not state whether this included accepting northern offers of arbitration, but other commentators did not rule mediation out. Although despondent, *The Economist* predicted that the Union would propose arbitration: 'Any proposal of this sort will require much caution and consideration before it is accepted. The Americans scarcely (to use a felicitous legal phrase) come into court with clean hands. They have been so overbearing and insolent formerly, that we are entitled to scrutinise with rigid care every part of their policy now.' Despite this obviously suspicious tone, *The Economist* urged that any honourable proposal for mediation be accepted.[54] It was not alone. Although the *National Review* maintained a slightly harder tone, regarding Wilkes's act as 'the most grave outrage' that could be committed against Britain, it added, 'We have taken generous pride in making our territory and our ships a refuge for political exiles; we have taken a selfish pride in making the safety of our commerce a proverb upon the ocean. Both feelings have now been outraged.' None the less, the writer added, 'if the United States should apologize for the aggression of Captain Wilkes, and should engage never again to commit or tolerate such an act, some arbitration might, we think, be possible'.[55] In other words, the notion of arbitration was considered acceptable in at least some quarters in England.

Fraser's Magazine did not consider arbitration, but it opposed aggressive action, doubting any particular perfidy on the part of the North: 'If we are driven to fight with them, we should rather they should have fair play, and not to be taken at a fatal disadvantage. In spite of appearances, it is hard to believe that they will really throw down the gauntlet to us.' The journal, like

---

[50] *The Economist*, 21 Dec. 1861, 1401–2.
[51] *Illustrated London News*, 7 Dec. 1861, 573.
[52] *British Quarterly Review* (Jan. 1862), 236.
[53] *Illustrated London News*, 7 Dec. 1861, 568.
[54] *The Economist*, 21 Dec. 1861, 1402.
[55] *National Review* (Jan. 1862), 263–4.

the rest of the London press, had no doubt where the blame for the current state of affairs lay: 'It is more likely that Captain Wilkes was but acting in the spirit which has characterised lately the whole conduct of the Americans towards us. Mr. Seward makes political capital by being impertinent to us. Captain Wilkes desires to make himself popular by imitating Mr. Seward.'[56] The *Saturday Review* also warned against seeking a quarrel: 'we none of us wish that the demand [for the return of the commissioners] be put in any but a conciliatory way'.[57] As did *The Economist*, which noted, 'we would not even appear to force a quarrel upon the United States at a time of weakness and rebellion. . . . We shall demand our rights very firmly, but we shall demand them also very quietly.'[58] Although Britain was placed in a relatively advantageous position should hostilities have broken out, there was, despite the clear determination to go to war if the North refused any form of reparation, an evident desire to avoid needless conflict. The impact of the Crimean War still lingered. Even if the Union had not yet developed an aversion to war, England clearly had.

The prospect of war against the Union was never taken lightly.[59] *The Economist* devoted an article to the subject in its 28 December edition, remarking,

> we must bear in mind that the Northern Americans are, in several of our most ineradicable qualities, alarmingly like ourselves. They do not know any better than we do, nor so well, how to give in when beaten. They grow more obstinate with every month of conflict. Those who are clamorous for war will grow daily more virulent with every fresh privation and every fresh defeat we inflict upon them. Those who are averse to war now, will gradually become among the most resolute for continuing it when once begun.[60]

There was definite respect in this tone and a clear warning that a war with the North would be no easy undertaking. *Fraser's Magazine* essentially noted the same thing, stating, 'We shall not begin by underrating our antagonists. They will fight better against us than the Southerners; and we will gather no hasty conclusions from Bull's Run.'[61] *The Times*, meanwhile, dwelt upon the problems of northern privateers.[62]

What everyone realised was unavoidable in any conflict with the Union was an alliance with the South. Despite Jordan and Pratt's claim that 'It is remarkable that during the whole crisis so little was said about the Confeder-

---

[56] *Fraser's Magazine* (Jan. 1862), 129.
[57] *Saturday Review*, 30 Nov. 1861, 547.
[58] *The Economist*, 21 Dec. 1861, 1403.
[59] The *Saturday Review* was the most confident of the journals, but even it had reservations about fighting a war with the North: 7 Dec. 1861, 574–5.
[60] *The Economist*, 28 Dec. 1861, 1433.
[61] *Fraser's Magazine* (Jan. 1862), 132.
[62] Adams, *Great Britain and the American Civil War*, i. 228.

acy', rather a lot was, in fact, written about it.[63] In January, the *Eclectic Review* promoted Olmsted's anti-slavery work and commented, 'We have little occasion to feel any emotions of interest in, or respect for, the Northern States; but we pray earnestly that God may avert from us the great calamity of finding ourselves striking hands with Southern slavery.'[64] It appears, then, that distaste for a British alliance with the Confederacy favoured peaceful resolution. *Fraser's Magazine* toed the same line: 'the largest civil war which the earth has ever witnessed is raging with unceasing fury; and in the rear of it we are ourselves likely to be dragged into the conflict, the unwilling allies of the slaveowners, whose crimes we have been the loudest to denounce'.[65] If Britain went to war, it was going to have a slave power as its ally. Virtually every commentator faced this stark truth. If the South was able to preserve its independence and thus maintain slavery, that was the judgment of history, Britain's guaranteeing Confederate independence was something else entirely. As the *Wesleyan Methodist Magazine* pointed out, recognition of the South 'would naturally follow' any declaration of war on the Union. 'In fact', the journal pointed out, 'we should become the allies of a Confederacy which – the first in the history of nations – has been formed for the defence and extension of the odious institution of slavery!' This situation, for the *Wesleyan Methodist Magazine*, was intolerable. Although the journal supported war if the North refused to release Mason and Slidell, the inevitable alliance with the South meant that, 'If for no other reason than this, – that England, the friend and guardian of the Negro, should be saved from helping to secure and prolong the bondage of the Southern slaves, – we should pray fervently that the threatened war may be averted.'[66]

This argument was not confined to anti-Confederate journals. No one would accuse the *Saturday Review* of harbouring any pro-Union sentiment, yet it too reminded its readers of Britain's inevitable allies: 'There can be no peculiar sympathy between England and the new Confederacy as long as slavery is the basis of Southern institutions, and while the revival of the Slave-trade is an open question at Charleston and New Orleans.' The journal also pointed out that 'The statesmen of the South, while they remained in the Union, bid against the demagogues of the North for popularity by constant vituperation against England.'[67] The *Saturday Review*'s antipathy towards the South actually increased as the crisis worsened, insisting, 'It is not even true that any active sympathy is felt for the Southern Confederacy, though it would at once be relieved from pressure by a war between the United States and England.' The reason for this state of affairs was, as the journal pointed out, 'The existence of slavery is an impediment to cordial

---

63 Jordan and Pratt, *Europe and the American Civil War*, 43.
64 *Eclectic Review* (Jan. 1862), 55–6.
65 *Fraser's Magazine* (Jan. 1862), 128.
66 *Wesleyan Methodist Magazine* (Jan. 1862), 68.
67 *Saturday Review*, 7 Dec. 1861, 569.

co-operation, nor is it forgotten that the Democrats and their Southern allies formerly vied with the Republicans of the North in venal and factious vituperation of the much-enduring English nation.'[68] It appears, then, that the Confederacy gained precious little from the hostility directed at the Union. It is also surely significant that the military plan drawn up by Palmerston's ministry to strike at the North if it defied the British ultimatum did not include an active alliance with the South.[69] Further, neither Palmerston nor Russell conferred with any Confederate diplomats during this period. Yancey, Rost and Mann did indeed again apply for recognition on 27 and 30 November, but Russell flatly refused to communicate with them 'in the present state of affairs'.[70]

John Bright's misrepresentations

If there is one individual whose views have hampered our understanding of English sentiment during the *Trent* affair (and indeed throughout the entire American Civil War), that individual is unquestionably John Bright. Bright and his colleague Richard Cobden were referred to as the 'Members for America' in the House of Commons for their strenuously pro-American views. Bright, a radical, was a major spokesman for electoral reform in Britain, having cut his political teeth in the campaign against the Corn Laws, in which he, a passionate advocate of free trade, served as a leading spokesman for the anti-Corn Law league. A pacifist, an opponent of the British aristocracy and often accused of being a republican, Bright (and, to a lesser extent, Cobden) looked to the more democratic United States as the model for political reform in Britain. Although one might reasonably have expected this free-trading pacifist's boundless admiration for the United States to been slightly tempered by both the war and the tariff, veneration of America was probably Bright's only consistent characteristic. Indeed, during the conflict, he probably never missed a single opportunity to promote the North's interests and activities – even if they were in direct opposition to Britain's. Cobden's views on America, in contrast, were slightly more mixed. Although he was pro-Union too, Cobden was far more critical of both the tariff and the North's activities overall. Bright, however, by portraying himself and Cobden as the two lone voices for peace during this period, has misled some historians into believing that Britain actually hoped to use Wilkes's actions as grounds for intervention on the side of the Confederacy.[71]

---

68 Ibid. 28 Dec. 1861, 650.
69 For the Palmerston ministry's plans see Warren, *Fountain of discontent*, ch. vi, esp. pp. 124–41.
70 Adams, *Great Britain and the American Civil War*, i. 214.
71 For example, see Keiser, 'The English press and the American Civil War', 198. Crook, meanwhile, is under the impression that 'Bright had made his lonely stand against an infuri-

An examination of Bright's oft-referred to – but not quoted – speech at Rochdale, on 3 December 1861, makes this clear.[72]

Speaking at the town hall, on what was essentially home ground, Bright expressed his hope that 'we would not attempt to force our exclusive interpretation of international law upon the 20,000,000 of Americans who are now united under the Federal Government. We could not impose our laws on the Americans when they were three millions of colonists, and we could not reasonably hope to do so now.'[73] The trouble was, that it was not Britain's 'exclusive interpretation' of international law but the opinion of the European and other neutral powers which all acknowledged that Wilkes's actions were illegal. Any comparisons between the current crisis and the American Revolution, meantime, were simply fatuous. Bright argued for arbitration (as we have seen, so did a number of publications and individuals) and then, as usual, 'spoke at great length' and delivered a 'glowing panegyric' on all things American, promising his audience that the northern government would act justly. Considering that the Lincoln cabinet had not even decided at this point whether or not to free Mason and Slidell, and, indeed, was actually divided on whether or not Wilkes's actions could be justified, Bright was being extraordinarily presumptuous in his assumptions. Bright then continued in much the same vein, 'Our leading newspaper . . . had never yet one fair, honourable, or friendly article on the subject [of the North].'[74] If 'leading newspaper' referred to *The Times*, Crawford has established that, for the first year of the conflict at least, these accusations were groundless.[75] Bright then concluded by accusing Britain of seeking a quarrel, and furthermore,

> There may be those persons in England who are jealous of the States. There may be men who dislike democracy, and who hate a republic; there may even be those whose sympathies warm towards the Slave oligarchy of the South. But of this I am certain, that only misrepresentation the most gross, or calumny the most wicked, can sever the tie which unites the great mass of people in this country with their friends and brethren across the Atlantic.[76]

---

ated people', when he spoke at Rochdale: *The North, the South and the powers*, 136. Cobden, meanwhile, railed at his fellow countrymen's 'cowardice' for wanting to go to war against a conveniently divided America, as wild a misrepresentation of the situation as could have been imagined: Jenkins, *Britain and the war for the Union*, i. 236–7. Perhaps unsurprisingly, as a northern propagandist, Cobden made no comparisons to 1812.

[72] See, for example, Adams, *Great Britain and the American Civil War*, i. 221–3. Adams notes that *The Times*, 5 Dec., editorially attacked Bright's speech, accusing him of speaking at an 'inconspicuous' place where he was sure of a warm welcome. However, Adams fails to examine the reasons for the paper's criticism of Bright, and also fails to note the positive comments *The Times* made about Bright, despite disagreeing with him. This is the sort of oversight that has muddied our understanding of English opinion on the American Civil War.

[73] *Spectator*, 7 Dec. 1861, 1329. In addition, see *Reynolds's Weekly*, 8 Dec. 1861, 1.

[74] *Spectator*, 7 Dec. 1861, 1329.

[75] See Crawford, *The Anglo-American crisis*, passim.

[76] *Spectator*, 7 Dec. 1861, 1329.

This was creating a false syllogism. What Bright effectively insinuated was that any individual who opposed the violation of Britain's neutral rights, or criticised the Union, was either opposed to democracy, or in favour of slavery, or both. This was patently false – the position taken by the *Spectator* is but one example. Further, very few individuals in England wanted a war with the North. Finally, the Confederacy, with universal white male suffrage, was arguably as much a democracy as the Union – slavery notwithstanding. To call refer to the South as an 'oligarchy' was a misrepresentation.

It is unfortunate that too many historians since have simply accepted Bright's propaganda, because his contemporaries were quick to take issue with him. Although, as Warren states, 'journalistic reaction was predictably hostile', it was not simply unfriendly because Bright spoke out against war.[77] The debate was far more complex than that. Everyone else, after all, was also denouncing conflict. The criticism levelled at Bright was based on specific and logical grounds. For one thing, commentators were aware that Bright was blindly infatuated with America generally, and the Union specifically, and they recognised that his speeches had to be taken for what they were – northern propaganda. The *Saturday Review*, noting Bright's past opposition to the Crimean War, accused him of trading pacifism for militarism when the Union's interests were involved: 'War is culpable when it is undertaken by an English Government in defence of English rights or interests; but foreigners, and more especially American Republicans, are entitled, if fair means prove insufficient, to maintain their system of freedom and equality by force.' More important, though, than the fact that zealots rarely make for good pacifists was Bright's analysis of how Anglo-Union affairs had plunged to such low levels:

> It is not to 'misrepresentation the most gross, or calumny the most wicked', that the evils of a rupture must be attributed, although the malignant falsehoods of the American press and platform, always uncensured by Mr. Bright, have done much to produce that feeling in the States which tempts a weak and corrupt government to violence against England.[78]

Clearly, Bright had forgotten the naked aggression of the *New York Herald*, William Seward and Cassius Clay; either that, or he had used the remaining Confederate cotton in Lancashire to cover his eyes and stuff his ears. Indeed, one of the reasons Palmerston believed that the Union would not surrender the commissioners was because of the hatred whipped up by the northern

---

77 See Warren, *Fountain of discontent*, 150. That Warren so easily accepts Bright's prevarications shows just how pernicious the latter's influence remains. It is certainly interesting that Warren can cite few actual examples of hostility to Bright in the British press.
78 *Saturday Review*, 7 Dec. 1861, 570. The journal, which had attacked the suspension of *habeas corpus* in the Union earlier, was being sarcastic in its reference to 'freedom and equality'.

press.[79] As the *Saturday Review* had little sympathy for the Union, one would expect it to be critical of a northern agitator. No such excuse can be made for the *Spectator*, which, if not sympathetic to the North, certainly condemned the South and slavery more vocally than virtually any other mainstream publication. It, too, criticised Bright's views, noting,

> On the dispute with England, he was however, less satisfactory. He allowed that the seizure of the two Commissioners was a 'bad and impolitic act' and only urged the people to calmness, and the Government not to drift into war. But his remarks lacked national feeling, and leave the impression – not embodied indeed, in one sentence, but pervading the speech like a bad scent – that rather than war with America, he would relinquish the right of asylum.[80]

The right of asylum was important. Britain had long been a haven for European radicals and rebels seeking sanctuary. Its colony, Canada, was a refuge for American slaves seeking sanctuary, too – soon to be joined by Union draft dodgers and escaped Confederate prisoners of war. That Britain and its territories served as sanctuary for those individuals fleeing repression elsewhere was something the English were rightly proud of. It was also something that they were determined to defend – by force if necessary. Granted, Mason and Slidell were not the perfect embodiment of oppressed individuals seeking sanctuary, but their rights were none the less sacrosanct. Thus, it was not just English pride that was on the line, but something far more important – asylum. Hence, the *Spectator* recognised what Bright failed to grasp, that the anger directed at the North originated from neither anti-democratic nor pro-slavery sentiment, but from the transgression of Britain's neutral rights and the right of political asylum. Further, considering the level of tension when the act had taken place, public opinion was remarkably restrained.

We should be careful in placing too much credence in Bright's carefully cultivated image of being metaphorically martyred by an anti-northern English press. *The Times*, despite being slandered, treated Britain's 'political shrew' magnanimously, regarding the latter as a necessary devil's advocate.[81] The *Illustrated London News*, meanwhile, noting that Bright had been left 'high and dry' by the circumstances, was extremely tolerant: 'it is but simple justice to say that in his speech at Rochdale he has shown tact and good sense, combined with just such warmth of feeling as might have been expected of him'.[82] What must be remembered, in spite of this patronising tone, is that war with the Union appeared to be a distinct possibility. Bright's opponents granted him far more generosity and courtesy than he ever showed them.

Bright probably worsened the situation between Britain and the northern

---

[79] Ridley, *Lord Palmerston*, 554.
[80] *Spectator*, 7 Dec. 1861, 1325.
[81] *The Times*, 6 Dec. 1861, 6.
[82] *Illustrated London News*, 7 Dec. 1861, 576.

states through his (and Cobden's) letters to Charles Sumner, in which he told the American that Britain sought a war with the Union. These letters were subsequently passed on to the Lincoln cabinet.[83] Although some historians believe that these warnings alerted the Union to the danger they faced and thus prevented the dreaded Anglo-American war, this argument remains unproven.[84] It is equally likely that their letters damaged Anglo-Union relations by convincing the North that the British, far from wanting to avoid the conflict, hoped to join it on the side of the South.

The only justification one can find for Cobden and Bright's belief (one must assume that it was honestly held) that England wanted conflict with the Union is their experience during the Crimean War. Cobden and Bright were implacably opposed to that war – something that made them very unpopular in Britain, especially amongst liberals and radicals, the majority of whom supported the conflict. The pair was probably genuinely shaken at the war mania that swept the country and resulted in the conflict. They paid for their opposition to the war, too – both lost their parliamentary seats because of it.[85] It is thus probably fair to say that, mindful of the experiences of the Crimea, they overreacted to the display of determination on the part of English commentators. They probably, of course, did not have as much faith in the Union acting honourably as they claimed. Yet, as we have seen, and will further see, Cobden and Bright did exaggerate the temper of the English public.

Views of other members of parliament

The inaccuracy of Bright's portrait of an England eager for war is further exposed by an examination of meetings held throughout December and January by members of parliament who favoured a peaceful resolution. Interestingly, the speakers were usually politically unrelated. One of the first public figures to talk on the crisis was not in fact, as historians have claimed, Bright, but Charles Newdegate.[86] Newdegate, a staunch opponent of political reform and Catholic emancipation, was referred to as a 'Conservative of the old school'. Representing the constituency of North Warwickshire, Newdegate should, in accordance with the traditional interpretation, have called for fire and brimstone to rain down upon the Union. In fact, speaking on Friday 29 November, at the annual dinner for the Rugby and Dunchurch Conserva-

---

[83] Cobden to Sumner, 29 Nov. 1861. Cobden papers, British Library, London, MS 43676.
[84] Warren gives Cobden and Bright credit for this: *Fountain of discontent*, 181.
[85] Miles Taylor provides an excellent study of the problems Cobden and Bright faced because of their opposition to the Crimean War: *The decline of British radicalism, 1847–1860*, Oxford 1995, chs vii–viii.
[86] 'As might be expected, Bright was first in the field with peaceful counsels.' Jordan and Pratt, *Europe and the American Civil War*, 37.

tive Association, Newdegate did no such thing. The member of parliament began by citing past American objections against the right of search in order to prevent the slave trade, but stated that 'the English Government would deeply consider before they undertook retaliation, and that the English people would be patient until they were clearly informed whether our flag had been insulted or not. If it had been insulted, he trusted retaliation would be ample. But he had a most friendly feeling towards the American people.' Newdegate deprecated war for, in his opinion,

> It appeared to him that the position of England was this: we have stood by as a neutral while two parties have been engaged in active strife; and if a man stands by while two fellows are having a match, he must not take it hard if he gets a black eye, unless he is sure that the blow was given with the intent of insulting him. He trusted that they would be sure of that before the power of England was used against a people of the same blood and origin as ourselves. (Applause).[87]

The reactionary Newdegate was not the only one to urge a wait-and-see approach. On Tuesday 10 December, H. B. W. Brand, the Liberal member of parliament and government whip, spoke at the Lewes Fat Stock Show dinner. Although Brand would not venture to predict how the crisis would resolve itself, 'Of this he was quite sure, that England regarded with the most friendly feeling the people of the United States. They looked at the civil war between themselves as a great calamity. They would look upon a war between England and America as a greater calamity. (Hear, hear).' Mr Brand's fellow Liberal member for Lewes, J. G. Blencowe, stated that he agreed with his fellow representative's sentiments regarding America.[88]

Other members of parliament trying to defuse the situation used other rhetorical methods. Speaking on the same day as Brand, the Liberal member for Stroud, Edward Horsman, addressed his constituents. Horsman pointed out what numerous journals had already noted: a war against the Union meant an alliance with the Confederacy. The problem with this, the member of parliament explained, was 'that gulf placed between us, between the English nation and any community that subsists by slavery, that makes it impossible that we can ally ourselves either by sympathy, community of feeling, or affection with any nation that exists upon that which I can call nothing but a disgrace and curse to mankind. (Cheers)'.[89] Horsman was an unlikely pacifist. His main claim to fame at this point was his participation in a duel with one James Bradshaw in 1840 over remarks the latter had made about the Queen. Further, despite his membership of the Liberal Party,

---

[87] *Spectator*, 30 Nov. 1861, 1302.
[88] *Reynolds's Weekly*, 15 Dec. 1861, 4.
[89] Ibid. 2.

Horsman had been a strong opponent of Chartism and would, in 1866, join Robert Lowe in opposing the extension of the franchise in Britain. Once again, if the traditional interpretation is correct, Horsman should have been a staunch opponent of the Union and a champion of the Confederacy. Yet, Horsman, like so many others in England, was more concerned about the South's institution of slavery than the supposed democratising influences of the North. Indeed, Horsman wanted the British demand 'to be couched in terms the most conciliatory, so as to give the American Government every possible opening to recede with honour, and not imposing upon them the slightest humiliation. (Hear, hear).'[90] During the same week, William Williams, the Liberal member for Lambeth, attended a meeting in Kensington and also spoke out against unnecessary war. Williams 'hoped the American government would have sense enough to deal with the question justly'.[91]

These were not to be the only honourable members preaching calm. The following week, on Monday 16 December, H. B. Sheridan, the member for Dudley, spoke. Openly doubting that the Union actually wanted a war, he expressed the anger felt, but left the door open to arbitration: 'Explain this if you can; apologise and place those men in a neutral position, so a neutral Power may decide upon the question between us; if not, then we will fire our broadside, which is at the door of the northern States, and settle the American question forever. (Cheers).' Although this was certainly grave talk, Sheridan was careful to add, 'we must remember that if we are victorious the colour of our ensign would be deepened with our brother's blood'.[92] Once again, there was the resolve to defend Britain's perceived rights, mixed with a desire that this would prove unnecessary.

There was another flurry of speeches after a very tense Christmas. On Monday 30 December, the two Liberal members for Brighton, W. Coningham and James White, made speeches very favourable to the Union. In fact, Coningham 'expressed his conviction, his earnest hope, that no intervention would be allowed to take place on the part of England which would prevent the Federal states from bringing back their erring children within the fold. (Repeated cheering).'[93] Although Coningham believed that an emancipation programme was evolving, he had no doubts about Britain's rights; he, like the other members, called for war if Mason and Slidell were not released. The crowd approved of these sentiments, too.

More devious tactics were in evidence at the meeting held by A. W. Kinglake, Liberal member for Bridgewater, at the town hall on the same day. Kinglake relied on shameless francophobia to sustain his arguments in favour of arbitration instead of war by pointing out that an

---

[90] Ibid.
[91] Ibid.
[92] Ibid. 22 Dec. 1861, 1.
[93] Ibid. 5 Jan. 1862, 1.

Anglo-northern conflict would give Napoleon III a free hand in Europe.[94] Although these sentiments went down well with Kinglake's constituents, he slandered the French; Louis Napoleon's government supported Britain's claims against the Union, thus helping to secure a peaceful settlement.[95] Kinglake, however, was a long-standing opponent of Louis Napoleon's government. He had carried this to the extent of opposing the alliance with France in the Crimean War – a conflict he had otherwise supported.[96]

Forster needed no cunning to defend his preference for arbitration instead of an ultimatum to his constituents in Bradford when he spoke to them on Tuesday 31 December. Forster spoke strongly in favour of the Union (although not as strongly as Bright), and declared that Britain did not want a war with the North (a very different position from that Bright had taken). None the less, although Forster's constituents unanimously passed a resolution in favour of arbitration, they added a rider that stated that if the North rejected even this, conflict must ensue.[97]

Potential members of parliament shared this anti-war sentiment, too. M. Mills, one of the candidates for the Finsbury by-election, spoke at a meeting held in the Spafields schoolroom, on Monday 2 December 1861. During his speech, Mills stuck to domestic politics, but when a 'voice' asked him about America, Mills replied 'he should first understand how that question stood before he attempted to answer. At present he thought that it best to leave the question in the hands of the Government, hoping that the means might be found of securing an honourable peace. (Hear).'[98] Clearly, there was little political capital to be made by inciting conflict or denouncing the Union – or so believed the cautious Mr Mills.

There were apparently only two speeches by members of parliament clearly hostile towards the North during the affair.[99] At a meeting on Monday 9 December, J. M.Cobbett, Liberal member for Oldham, spoke in the town hall. Cobbett, representing Lancashire's interests, was understandably more critical of the Union. He condemned the abuse of Britain 'not only by the press, but by public men, in America'. Cobbett also insisted that Britain's 'interest had been very much damaged by that which, upon all hands, was considered the unjustifiable blockade of the Southern ports of America'. After pointing out, for Bright's benefit, that much of the hostility directed at the Union had been caused by northern politicians and press, Cobbett heaped scorn on the notion that England favoured the South, stating, 'Some said that the press had favoured the South against the North. He said, looking

---

[94] Ibid. 3.
[95] Crook, *The North, the South and the powers*, 159–60.
[96] Taylor, *The decline of British radicalism*, 257.
[97] *Illustrated London News*, 4 Jan. 1862, 10; *Spectator*, 4 Jan. 1862, 6.
[98] *Reynolds's Weekly*, 8 Dec. 1861, 5.
[99] Crook cites a number of other anti-Union meetings in Lancashire, which, in light of Mary Ellison's findings, is to be expected: *The North, the South and the powers*, 139.

at both sides of the question, that he could not see anything to justify that remark with regard to our people.'[100] To prolonged cheering, Cobbett then disparaged the Manchester school for its lack of patriotism and warned of war if Mason and Slidell were not returned to British custody. Cobbett was clearly affronted both by the Union and its chief propagandists. Much of his intolerance towards the former, however, probably lay in the fact that, coming from Lancashire, he represented the region most adversely affected by the Civil War, where opinions were bound to be more partisan.

If there were gains to be made fomenting anger against the Union in Lancashire, doing it elsewhere proved less profitable. On Friday 6 December, Lord Fermoy and John Harvey Lewis, the members for Marylebone, spoke to their constituents at Hall's Riding School. Lord Fermoy confidently asserted that the North would not dare push events to the point of war, but, 'if they refused redress, and drove us to take vengeance upon them, and sweep their navy from the sea, let responsibility be on the aggressor and not upon us'. There were interruptions at this point as some members of the crowd believed they detected an aggressor closer at hand.[101] However, order was restored and both members received a vote of confidence.

None the less, Cobbett's and Fermoy's speeches cannot be cited as warmongering. In both cases, the men believed Britain's rights had been violated and were prepared to accept a repudiation of the deed. Neither insisted that war was the only recourse. Further, all of the above speeches by members of parliament are in addition to the efforts cited by Warren made by nonconformist preachers and their congregations and other religious spokesmen in urging the government against precipitate action.[102] For example, the Quakers sent copies of a signed circular opposing war against the Union to every single member of parliament. Yet the circular acknowledged several basic truths, such as: 'There have been many words or deeds on the part of the Government of the people of the United States which have tried the temper and the patience of both our Statesmen and of our fellow-countrymen generally', a clear recognition of the fact that English hostility towards the North was hardly unprovoked. None the less, the circular pointed to the obvious perils of Britain allying itself with the slave-holding Confederacy, carefully adding the following words: 'though in saying this, we do not intend to express our approval, in all respects, of the course pursued by the North in reference to slavery'.[103] This was a reference to English suspicion regarding the Union's plans for emancipation.

---

[100] *Reynolds's Weekly*, 15 Dec. 1861, 2.
[101] *Spectator*, 7 Dec. 1861, 1328–9.
[102] See Warren, *Fountain of discontent*, 151; Jordan and Pratt, *Europe and the American Civil War*, 38–9. Unfortunately, neither Warren nor Jordan and Pratt attempt any analysis of the meetings, and this makes it difficult to establish whether the various bodies sought mediation or simply expressed a wish for peace.
[103] 'Memorial of the Religious Society of Friends'. Ramsden papers, West Yorkshire

The fact is, when looking at public meetings and speeches as a whole, considering the level of anxiety (greatly increased when it became apparent that the North celebrated, rather than disowned, the deed), sabre-rattling was not widespread. Although public opinion was unquestionably largely behind the Palmerston government's ultimatum that Mason and Slidell be returned or a rupture would take place, it is impossible to tell whether or not an offer of arbitration from the Union would have been accepted in Britain. As we have seen, there were a number of voices arguing in favour of it. Jones may be correct in stating, 'In truth, the chances for England's accepting arbitration would have been minimal at best', but there was no eagerness for a quarrel.[104] This was certainly the view of Russell who, on 16 December, informed Palmerston, 'I do not think the country would approve of an immediate declaration of war.'[105] This was after the Union's reaction to Wilkes's deed had become known.

There were, of course, some isolated individuals who wanted a war with the Union. The Liberal member of parliament, Sir John Ramsden, for example, received a letter from a constituent saying, 'I hope the Federal States will not be able to find some dodge by which they can slip out of their little difficulty, we cannot expect to be in a better position than at present to give them a lesson on the effects of bullying.'[106] The writer was clearly furious with Union diplomacy and commentary before the crisis. These views were, however, held by a small minority. Most in England disliked the idea of entering the war and being forced into an alliance with the Confederacy. Indeed, the position of English public opinion during the *Trent* crisis was probably best expressed by the *Wesleyan Methodist Magazine*:

> If there be a war-party in this country, eager for conflict, it must be very fractional and insignificant. The number who desire war with the Federals through sympathy with the Confederates; or who wish for it as a means of letting the cotton of the South find its way to Lancashire; or who long for it as an opportunity of humbling a proud and provoking insolence; or who, with a pugnacity unrestrained by a fear of God or man, love it for its own sake; – the number of all such, we are convinced, must form but a small proportion of this peace-loving nation.[107]

Archives, Leeds, RA 66/8. Ramsden scrawled on the form that all members of the House had received one.
[104] Jones, *Union in peril*, 91. Jones bases this assessment on the views of Palmerston and Russell. Crook also notes the acceptability of arbitration in certain quarters: *The North, the South and the powers*, 138.
[105] Russell to Palmerston, 16 Dec. 1861. Palmerston papers, University of Southampton, Southampton, GC/RU/685.
[106] J. W. Tottie to Sir John Ramsden, 20 Dec 1861. Ramsden papers, RA 66/8. This was the only letter Ramsden received expressing a desire for war.
[107] *Wesleyan Methodist Magazine* (January 1862), 68.

Any reading of the English press and examination of public meetings upholds this view. Although the public was angry at the violation of neutral rights and determined to uphold these rights, there was no desire for war so long as the Union was willing to address the grievance.

Karl Marx's commentary

Having examined the opinions of the English press and numerous members of parliament, it is now necessary to detour slightly and look at the writings of Marx on the issue of the *Trent* affair. This needs to be done because Marx's belief, that a calculating and aristocratic British ruling class hoped to interfere in the war on the Confederacy's behalf, remains one of the cornerstones of the traditional interpretation – and his remarks are still sometimes cited by historians. During the period of the *Trent* crisis, Marx was contributing articles to the *New York Daily Tribune* – something he continued to do until early 1862. An examination of one of these articles – published on 25 December 1861 – is especially important because it reveals just how wildly inaccurate Marx's reporting was and how carefully it needs to be scrutinised.

Marx's article, 'The progress of feeling in England', was a long diatribe against perfidious Albion, which ended advising the North to surrender the prisoners rather than provide Britain with an excuse to enter the war. Marx, displaying his ignorance of the legalities of the affair – he confused Mason and Slidell's seizure with the issue of impressment – accused Britain of using the incident as an opportunity for aggression. For example, he informed the American public that 'a large and influential party of the mercantile community has for months been urging on the government to violently break the [northern] blockade and thus provide the main branch of British industry with its raw material'. As we have already seen in the previous chapter, not only did there exist widespread opposition – particularly on the part of the mercantile community – against breaking the blockade, but it was already recognised in England that the shortage of cotton was owed to the Confederacy's King Cotton policy. Marx also informed his American readers that Palmerston was seeking 'a legal pretext for a war' with the Union, but met with 'a most determinate opposition on the part of Messrs. Gladstone and Milner-Gibson'.[108] This, as it happened, was completely untrue but unsurprisingly so as Marx had no access to cabinet discussions whatsoever.[109]

If the above inaccuracies were not bad enough, Marx then accused the English press of trying to stir up an Anglo-American war – a spurious charge if ever there was one. To prove his accusation, he quoted a statement from *The Economist* to the effect that if Britain had to fight the Union, the former was

---

[108] Karl Marx, 'The progress of feeling in England', *New York Daily Tribune*, 25 Dec. 1861, 3.
[109] For cabinet discussions during the *Trent* affair see Warren, *Fountain of discontent*, passim.

placed in an advantageous position, thus giving the distinct – and wholly false – impression that the journal was agitating for war.[110] This was an example of selective quotation at its worst. Nowhere in his series of articles did Marx bother to acknowledge that *The Economist* not only opposed a war with the North, but also had, in fact, called for mediation instead of conflict. Some historians have pointed out that selective quoting, or outright misquoting, was a hallmark of Marx, to the extent that he deliberately misquoted both Gladstone and Adam Smith, among others, in *Das Kapital*.[111] It was thus unlikely that he would act any differently when reporting on the Civil War. Clearly, Marx had little interest in accurately reporting the mood of the English public, and his comments, like Bright's, require a far closer scrutiny than they have previously received.

The resolution, the reply and the reaction

The reaction to the news that the Lincoln cabinet had decided to accede to Palmerston's ultimatum reflected the earlier views of the English press and public. Although there were serious misgivings about Seward's announcement of the release of the commissioners, the overwhelming emotion was that of relief. Further, although there was a sense of vindication, displays of triumph were discouraged – as was any lionisation of Messrs Mason and Slidell, as E. D. Adams pointed out over seventy-five years ago.[112]

The Lincoln cabinet, in receipt of the British ultimatum, and swayed by both justice and pragmatism, decided, on 26 December, to release the commissioners.[113] Unquestionably, that the northern press had, by and large, made an about-face and accepted that the envoys had to be released, helped the cabinet.[114] The overall situation was also doubtless helped by Prince Albert, who managed to lift himself out of what was literally to be his deathbed, to soften the contents of the British ultimatum. Albert insisted that the ultimatum state that Britain had no doubt that Wilkes acted without authority – providing the Union with a face-saving means of retreat. Seward, as secretary of state, penned the reply to the British government. He was not, unfortunately, to make a good job of it.

---

[110] Marx, 'The progress of feeling in England', 3.
[111] See, for example, David Felix, *Marx as a politician*, Carbondale 1983, 161–2, 269–70, 147.
[112] Adams, *Great Britain and the American Civil War*, i. 237–41. Unfortunately, Adams also states that the press, public and politicians only made anti-southern and anti-slavery comments *after* the North agreed to release Mason and Slidell, calling it 'a complete reversal, not to say somersault'. This is, as we have seen above, completely untrue.
[113] See Warren, *Fountain of discontent*, 181–2. Further, by this time, enthusiasm for the continued detention of Mason and Slidell was beginning to fade in the Union: Crook, *The North, the South and the powers*, 149–51.
[114] Crook, *The North, the South and the powers*, 154–6.

Repudiating American precedent, Seward insisted that enemy ambassadors were contraband of war, hence the *Trent* was liable to capture despite sailing between two neutral ports; Wilkes should have taken it to a prize court for adjudication. Having thus declared the capture legitimate, Seward now needed an excuse to repudiate it. In this vein, he wrote that had Wilkes involuntarily released the *Trent*, the Union would have been able to keep the commissioners, but because the captain had himself freed the ship, the North lost the right to hold the prisoners. As a result, Mason and Slidell would be returned to British custody.

Seward was thus claiming that the Union had the right of a belligerent, even though both he and the government he represented had, until the crisis took place, denied that a state of war existed. None the less, absurd though Seward's reasoning was, his response would have been sufficient, but the secretary of state went further. After implying that the 'guarded language' of the British ultimatum meant Palmerston's government was afraid of war – a response to Albert's efforts that was both ignorant and crass – he added that had the Union's security required the retention of the prisoners, they would not have been surrendered. It was only their 'comparative unimportance' that made their further detention unnecessary. In other words, Seward admitted that the Union had violated Britain's neutral rights but was only making reparation because it happened to feel like obeying international law on this occasion. This 'monument to illogic', as Warren correctly calls it, proves that, insults aside, Seward grossly underestimated English determination – unsurprising as he had previously underestimated the determination of his former fellow-countrymen in the South – all of which must cast doubt upon the wisdom of his earlier and subsequent activities regarding Britain.[115]

Seward also made the erroneous comparison of the seizure of the commissioners to the issue of impressment, arguing that the British now accepted the American view of neutral rights (including, one presumes, his newly minted prerogative to respect those rights only when they felt like it). None of this, however, could disguise the fact that his document completely repudiated America's former position on neutral rights at sea – the Union had effectively adopted the British policies the United States had opposed for the previous eighty years – all for the sake of insulting Palmerston's government.[116] Seward should have simply written that because, under both American and international law, the unauthorised capture could not be sustained, the Union was surrendering the men solely out of respect for the rights of neutrals. Despite the praise some historians have heaped upon Seward's response to Palmerston's ultimatum, it was an example of poor diplomacy and sounded

---

115 Warren, *Fountain of discontent*, 184.
116 'In effect he had capitulated to a high British view of belligerent prerogatives, contrary to American tradition, on every issue at stake except that of adjudication': Crook, *The North, the South and the powers*, 160.

THE *TRENT* OUTRAGE

suspiciously like sour grapes.[117] For all his posturing, the secretary of state had indeed, as Warren points out, 'surrendered the men for the wrong reasons'.[118]

That the Union was to surrender the commissioners was satisfactory, despite Seward's statement that the Union could defy international law at will if the security of the North depended upon it. This last statement caused dissatisfaction, and was seized upon by those hostile to the Union such as *The Times* which noted:

> Mr. Seward missed a great opportunity when he failed to act as a European statesman would have acted under similar circumstances. At this moment there is no sympathy here for either party. The attraction we feel towards a weaker nation invaded by a stronger and a richer nation is repelled by the very detestation of slavery; and, if Mr. Seward had seized the opportunity for a graceful and courteous act we would not answer for how far our countrymen might have been tempted from their rigorous neutrality. It was a gross blunder for the shrewd Minister of a shrewd people to miss the chance of a great advantage only to do the same act at last under circumstances of unavoidable humiliation.[119]

Yet Seward's response annoyed even those sympathetic to the Union. For example, *Macmillan's Magazine*, which had been the publication most generous to the North during the crisis, regarded the secretary of state's arguments to be unacceptable. The barrister Charles Synge Bowen (later Baron Bowen), after reviewing the legal arguments of the affair in the journal, remarked, 'Viewing the matter as impartially as we can, we must confess that Mr. Seward's policy of delay was neither graceful nor intelligent, nor did his letter recover for him any lost ground.'[120] J. S. Mill stated much the same in his famous defence of the North in *Fraser's Magazine* in February.[121] Most pessimistic was the *Spectator*, which opined that it was 'a very grave augury for the future. We believe that no legal ground for such a decision, in the case of an ordinary mail packet, carrying between neutral port and neutral port, could be sustained at all. And we should fear for the permanence of peace should such a case actually arise.'[122] In other words, although the present crisis was settled, its cause remained, possibly to flare up again. There remained no agreement on the rights of neutrals.

[117] Both Jenkins and Mahin highly rate the response by Seward to Palmerston's ultimatum: *Britain and the war for the Union*, i. 227; *One war at a time*, 77–8.
[118] Warren, *Fountain of discontent*, 182–5.
[119] *The Times*, 9 Jan. 1862, 8.
[120] *Macmillan's Magazine* (Feb. 1862), 350. This journal's January edition carried an article by the northern apologist J. M. Ludlow that was actually critical of British mobilisation. None the less, Ludlow insisted that the Union was in the wrong and that there was cause for war if the Confederate commissioners were not returned. The fact that *Macmillan's* took a far harsher view of the Union in its February edition suggests just how disappointed the magazine was with Seward's stance: (Jan. 1862), 253–65; (Feb. 1862), 349–56.
[121] *Fraser's Magazine* (Feb. 1862), 261: Mill's footnote.
[122] *Spectator*, 11 Jan. 1862, 29.

Most journals, however, concurred with *The Economist*'s assessment: 'An old proverb tells us not to scrutinise gifts too closely, and under the circumstances we will consider the act of Mr Lincoln a free gift.'[123] The *Illustrated London News*, although unimpressed by Seward's equivocations, none the less remarked, 'That Mr. Lincoln has performed this act of justice is sufficient.'[124] It was interesting that after blaming Seward for causing the crisis, English commentators credited Lincoln with successfully resolving it. In part this had to do with Seward's note, which destroyed any goodwill he might have garnered, but commentators also believed the president had reined in his secretary of state. This was to be the start of an increasing appreciation of the President, despite its basis on erroneous grounds.

The general relief, of course, was mingled with a little self-satisfaction. The *Illustrated London News* laughed off Seward's response as mere grandstanding and remarked, 'We have, however, made the demand for reparation in the most considerate way, we have done everything to conciliate ... we are therefore clear of all blame in the whole transaction, and legally, morally, and even sentimentally, we have shown ourselves friends to the Americans.'[125] Despite this smugness, the *Illustrated London News* did not suggest that the Union had been stared down. Indeed, the relief was palpable. For, the following week, the journal again reminded its readers what had been avoided:

> England allied with a Confederation of slaveholding States, the corner-stone of whose constitution is not merely the lawfulness but the expediency of slavery, and the thinly-veiled object of whose policy is the wide extension of slave territory and the speedy revival of the slave trade – England, recognizing such a confederation, and thereby imparting to it a vitality and strength it neither possesses nor deserves, and assisting it to make good its position against the Free States of the North, from which, for the sake of perpetuating and extending slavery it wantonly seceded; – such a position as this would have been a cruel necessity, entailing upon it a humiliation, and exhibiting to the world a scandal, for which no military or naval success could have been accepted as adequate compensation. Thank God, we have escaped the danger.[126]

There was certainly far less boasting in England that the North had yielded to the threat of war than E. D. Adams supposes.[127] True, the *Saturday Review* was highly critical of the Union in general, and Seward in particular, whose arguments were all wrong. Indeed, the journal opined, 'If he had frankly acknowledged that the capture was untenable and indefensible, he might have fairly

---

[123] *The Economist*, 11 Jan. 1862, 29.
[124] *Illustrated London News*, 11 Jan. 1862, 38.
[125] Ibid.
[126] Ibid. 18 Jan. 1862, 58.
[127] Adams, *Great Britain and the American Civil War*, i. 237. The only evidence that Adams actually cites is a mildly offensive *Punch* cartoon.

claimed the credit of yielding to reason and not to force.'[128] The *Saturday Review* had no doubt as to why Mason and Slidell had been given up: 'It is remarkable that, until the arrival of the news from England, not a single public writer in the northern States had taken that sound view of International law which appears to Mr. Seward so clear and irrefragable.' The journal's verdict was that the North had acted out of fear rather than out of a sense of right: 'In the long run they have done justice, and have done it frankly and courteously; but they were quite prepared to shirk doing justice if possible.'[129]

Not everyone, however, shared the anti-Union *Saturday Review*'s opinions. The *Wesleyan Methodist Magazine* remarked that those, such as the *Saturday Review*, who claimed that 'the American people yielded to fear and not to a sense of right, – to the logic of armstrong guns and mustering of squadrons, more than to the logic of diplomacy – misjudge to some extent our transatlantic kindred'. The journal was not completely satisfied with the North's conduct, admitting that 'No doubt our preparations for war had a share of influence in settling the question; but to deny them all credit of acting from a sense of righteousness is ungenerous.'[130] The main point, as far as English observers were concerned, was that the dreaded Anglo-American war had been avoided. Britain was not to be allied with the Confederacy and the right of asylum had been vindicated. Seward's insults could not disguise the fact that the Union had backed down.

Palmerston replies to Bright

If everyone else in England was satisfied with the outcome of the *Trent* incident, the dissenting voice was that of Bright. He believed the British government had been unfair, for he raised the issue in parliament on 17 February. Bright made a number of claims and accusations, which require discussion. Bright's complaint was not the ultimatum itself, which he wrongly referred to as 'the request', but the British mobilisation that accompanied it. He also hypocritically criticised the press for using language of 'the most violent and offensive character', noting,

> I have not the smallest doubt myself that the only thing which made it a question whether these men would be surrendered and war avoided was not the tenor of the dispatch from the Foreign Office, but the tone of the organs of the press . . . and the movements of regiments and ships in a manner which must have been intended and understood as a menace to the cabinet of Washington.

---

[128] See *Saturday Review*, 18 Jan. 1862, 57.
[129] Ibid. 11 Jan. 1862, 29.
[130] *Wesleyan Methodist Magazine* (Feb. 1862), 68.

Bright further insisted 'that there was an intention on the part of some section of the Government, or of some powerful classes in this country, if opportunity offered, to engage in a war with the United States'. Citing past 'American practice and American principles' regarding neutral rights, Bright again reiterated his argument that 'I had no doubt, whatsoever, that the matter would be amicably settled, except the menaces from this side might make it difficult for them to concede to the demand of Her Majesty's Government.'[131]

This speech only confirms that Bright's views on events in our period must be treated with caution. He was not a reliable witness. As this chapter has established, the English press had, throughout the *Trent* affair, opposed war and, on at least two occasions, proposed arbitration. Anger was, of course, expressed by numerous journals, but this arose because of the violation of neutral rights. The failure to mention the same journals' efforts to promote peace was dishonest.

Despite Bright's claim of a conspiracy by 'a powerful class', or 'a section of the Government', desirous of making war on the North, there is no evidence of this to be found in any examination of meetings or publications during this period – just the reverse, in fact. Indeed, Bright's very terms were hopelessly nebulous. He produced no proof, no specifics and failed to mention a single name. In fact, the only specific thing he said was that by 'Government' he did not mean Palmerston's ministry.[132] If Bright's remarks were, as E. D. Adams argues, 'intended for American consumption', they would have exacerbated, not eased, Anglo-Union differences.[133] Bright's chief argument, meanwhile, that the Union would have freed the envoys without Britain's mobilisation, is a thesis not even the traditional interpretation is prepared to entertain.[134]

It was Palmerston's reply, however, which illuminated the gaps in Bright's assertions. If the North had determined all along, in concordance with American interpretations of neutral rights, to release the men, Palmerston asked, 'why did they keep those four gentlemen so many weeks in prison?' The prime minister then pointed to the tension of the preceding months: 'My hon. Friend says that . . . it was criminal in us to take measures ostensibly in defence, but in reality calculated to provoke a war with the United States. But Sir, had we no ground for thinking that it was very doubtful whether our demand would be complied with? (Hear, hear).'

It had not, however, been solely the events of the previous year that had caused disquiet in Britain, as Palmerston pointed out, but the reaction in the Union itself when Mason and Slidell were seized:

---

[131] *Hansard*, clxv, 7 Feb. 1862, 380–4.
[132] It should be noted that no historian examining parliamentary documents has found any evidence to support Bright's claims either. Despite this, they are often accepted as true.
[133] Adams, *Great Britain and the American Civil War*, i. 241.
[134] See, ibid. 241–2.

THE *TRENT* OUTRAGE

Well, Captain Wilkes declared that he had done the act without authority and instructions. But did the people, did the public of the United States hesitate as to whether what had been done was right or wrong? Did they wait to be informed whether it was consistent or not with . . . international code? It is well known that Captain Wilkes was made a hero of; and for what? Why, the reason was distinctly avowed and put forward – namely, because he had the courage to insult the British flag. There was a great ovation at Boston, where, I believe, persons holding judicial situations, among whom was a person in high office, the Governor of a State, joined in the general chorus of approbation. But you may say, that that took place at a public meeting, and we have heard a great many foolish speeches made at public meetings ('Hear, hear', and laughter).[135]

Palmerston further cited Wilkes's reception in New York and by the House of Representatives, reinforcing the point that the celebrations in the Union had much to do with English hostility. Palmerston, however, neglected to mention that he had sent the ultimatum before news of these events was known in England.

Bright's failure to recognise English concerns about northern aggression hampered him even when he got his facts right. It was certainly true, as Bright claimed, that several newspapers had predicted that Lincoln's government possibly, but Seward definitely, 'was anxious to get into war, or difficulty, with this country, with the view of enabling him, with something like credit, to get out of the difficulty in the South – in fact, under cover of a war with England, peace upon, I presume, terms of separation of the Union, was to be made with the South'.[136] Unless, however, one mentioned that this belief originated in the *New York Herald*'s proposal – that the territory lost to the South be made up by the acquisition of Canada – which was made early in the secessionist crisis and was reinforced by Seward's avowed annexationist tendencies, one was not providing a complete picture. Further, by the time Bright made his speech in parliament, this thesis had been discredited by the Union's surrender of Mason and Slidell. Clearly, Bright's version of events demands a far more careful scrutiny than it has hitherto received.

Although the *Trent* affair added to an already virulent anglophobia in the North, historians are divided over the long-term results of the incident in England.[137] Just as this is difficult to measure, so too is it hard to provide conclusive answers. There were, however, some clear results. Unquestionably, for many in England, the entire *Trent* affair – the outrage itself, the Union's behaviour during it, and Seward's note – was the final straw. These persons had no time for the South, but they never forgave the North, either.

---

135 *Hansard*, clxv, 7 Feb. 1862, 390; *Reynolds's Weekly*, 23 Feb. 1862, 3. When Palmerston referred to the 'four men' he meant Mason's and Slidell's secretaries.
136 *Hansard*, clxv, 7 Feb. 1862, 382.
137 Numerous Northerners believed that Britain had sought a quarrel while America was divided. This probably owes something to Cobden and Bright: Warren, *Fountain of discontent*, 205–7.

Without a doubt, 1862 was the year anti-northern sentiment reached its peak in England (although it continued into 1863). Several journals, including those formerly sympathetic to the Union, were notably less kind throughout 1862.[138] Certainly, the view of the 1863 *Annual Register* cannot be discounted:

> It is difficult to estimate exactly the relative forces of public sentiment upon any question, but so far as observation may be trusted, it would appear that opinion in England at this time leaned rather in favour of the Southern than northern states. Some of the causes for this inclination of feeling are sufficiently obvious. In the first place, it is certain that the arrogant and boastful language of the northern leaders, the scornful and menacing tones which they occasionally use towards England, and especially the spirit they evinced in the matter of the 'Trent', had excited great offence in this country against President Lincoln's government and its partisans.[139]

Memories of the *Trent*, then, still rankled in some quarters – almost two years after the incident first took place. This increase in anti-northern sentiment naturally contributed, in part, to southern sympathy, and the complicated nature of this phenomenon will be discussed in the following two chapters. It is also no coincidence that 1862 was the only year that Palmerston's ministry seriously considered offering to mediate in the American Civil War.

On the other hand, there were some positive developments. The incident came as a sobering shock to intelligent commentators in both England and the North. Seward, for one, suddenly became more guarded and circumspect in his language to Britain – at least until the Union won the war. He still managed to irritate the English public but, generally speaking, the days of extravagant threats were over. Further, future diplomatic disputes such as Wilkes's activities in the West Indies, not to mention Union threats to pursue suspected Confederate sympathisers into Canada, were dealt with with far more alacrity, not to say courtesy, by both parties. It had been made plain to the North that Britain was determined to uphold her neutral rights; it had been made clear to Britain that the Union was uninterested in quarrelling. The *Spectator*'s hope that 'The Northerners will lose the delusion that England dreads war with them; we shall lose the delusion that they are seeking war with us' was largely fulfilled.[140] Although concern was still expressed about the Union's intentions, the belief that the North wanted a war with Britain in order to extricate itself from its attempted conquest of the Confederacy largely disappeared. Clearly, the Union's priorities lay southwards, not northwards to Canada. Fears for the colony's security did not return until after Appomattox. After the *Trent* affair, English observers

---

138 I have found this to be true of *Fraser's Magazine*, the *English Woman's Journal*, the *Spectator*, the *British Quarterly Review* and even *Macmillan's*.
139 *Annual Register*, 1863, 5.
140 *Spectator*, 4 Jan. 1862, 9.

tended to view the war as an event in which they would not become involved. There were, of course, exceptions to this, for, unfortunately, having sunk to such a low, Anglo-northern relations were, unsurprisingly, to remain generally poor for the remainder of the conflict and, indeed, for years afterwards.

3

Observations from Experience

'They are collectively to us the most disagreeable of people.'

With the conclusion of the *Trent* affair, and as the likelihood of immediate British intervention in the war receded, the North and the South could again turn their attention to one another. After avoiding becoming involved in the war against their wishes, the public in England resumed their observations of the conflict as outsiders. As the struggle in America progressed and changed, so too did English observations of it. These changing circumstances, and the evolving English views, are the subjects of this chapter, which follows broadly thematic lines rather than chronological ones and, generally, covers the period from 1862 until mid-1863.

After the *Trent* affair, English opinion was never especially friendly to the Union. Unfortunately for the Confederacy, the English were never particularly enamoured with it either. Certainly, a degree of sympathy developed for a people defending themselves against overwhelming odds, but even this sentiment, fuelled in part by the perceived northern aggression that culminated in the *Trent* affair, was hampered by the issue of slavery and had largely peaked in 1862. In 1863, Lincoln's emancipation edicts, combined with Confederate anti-British measures, arising from Britain's continued neutrality, effectively eroded what southern sympathy existed. From the end of 1863 to 1865, evidence of widespread partiality for either side is difficult to find. Furthermore, as Jordan and Pratt first pointed out, the Polish rebellion and the Schleswig-Holstein crisis, in 1863 and 1864 respectively, replaced America as the chief area of English interest, greatly reducing commentary.[1]

Contrary to what has been so often asserted, beyond the confines of a small minority, Union or Confederate sympathy was rarely based on political or social grounds. There is little evidence that the majority of conservatives leaned southwards in their sympathies while the majority of radicals inclined northwards. Nor did the aristocracy favour the Confederacy while the working class favoured the Union. Both sides drew support from a cross-section of social and political groups, with the vast majority of northern

---

[1] Jordan and Pratt note that Poland diverted attention from America and 'the Continental crisis over Schleswig-Holstein, following shortly, absorbed a further share of interest when the United States was becoming something of a bore': *Europe and the American Civil War*, 188–9. They fail, however to realise how the North's friendship with Russia damaged the Union. For the diplomatic impact of these two crises see Crook, *The North, the South and the powers*, chs x–xii passim.

apologists motivated by anti-slavery arguments and the vast majority of southern apologists driven by self-determination arguments. Most English commentators, however, wished a plague on both houses and favoured a cautious neutrality – especially by the end of 1863.[2]

English opinion was extremely varied and complex. Virtually every argument posited by any commentator drew a counter-argument or rebuttal. On almost every issue and incident during the war, there was a plethora of opinion. Simply put, English public opinion cannot be divided into distinctive and antagonistic blocks. This perception of public sentiment owes its origins to each side's partisans and was rarely adopted by the majority who maintained a neutral stance. The only view upon which a real consensus existed was that the Confederacy could not be conquered. This view was shared not only by southern apologists, but by northern ones, too.

Studies of English interpretations of the American Civil War have been marred by a number of failings. In the case of the North, there has been a tendency to ignore Union belligerence during the period, and a failure to place the English commentary within the context of its own mid-nineteenth-century political thought. This combination has led to criticism directed at the North being simplistically classified as anti-democratic sentiment. In the case of the South, meanwhile, there has been a tendency to gloss over the inherently mixed (not to say fragile) nature of the sympathy the Confederacy engendered, and a failure to recognise how the anti-slavery opinion militated against that sentiment. This has led to the levels and nature of southern sympathy being both overrated and misunderstood respectively.

Nationhood, empire, the Confederacy and the Union

The failure to place English commentary within its own political tradition is shown by the argument of some historians that English condemnation of the Union for fighting to preserve its territory while the British had recently fought to preserve their own empire, such as the suppression of the Indian Mutiny in 1857–8, smacked of hypocrisy. The problem with this argument is that it ignores significant avenues of thought and other international events which shaped English opinion. For example, in 1859, Piedmont led the war against Austria for Italian independence and unification. English sympathy,

---

[2] Although most historians trace the turning point of the war from the capture of Vicksburg and the battle of Gettysburg (both occurred in the first week of July 1863), this was not obvious at the time. The outcome of the conflict still appeared uncertain as late as mid-1864, when it appeared that Lincoln would lose his bid for re-election. The Union capture of Atlanta on 1 September 1864 marked the change in Lincoln's electoral fortunes. See McPherson, *Battle cry of freedom*, ch. xxv passim. In other words, English opinion on the war was established before it became obvious that the Confederacy was doomed.

by and large, went out to the Italians, and southern sympathisers often equated the two struggles. The Italian struggle bore a closer resemblance to America than India. The Indian Mutiny was viewed as an undisciplined uprising, not a war for liberty and independence. This interpretation was shaped by a combination of ethnocentrism, the mutiny's essential regionalism (it was confined largely to the Ganges valley), brevity (it lasted roughly a year), and by atrocities such as Cawnpore (and the inevitable reprisals), which stripped any guise of romanticism from the entire affair. Or, to put it more bluntly, the English viewed the Indian Mutiny in much the same way Americans saw their periodic Amerindian uprisings. Both the Italian and Confederate causes, in contrast, were bettered-organised and more clearly defined national struggles. Indeed, when American commentators equated the suppression of India with that of the South, the *Saturday Review* specifically denied the comparison had any legitimacy.[3] Besides Italy, there was also Poland, in which there was an uprising in 1863. It is no coincidence that certain Confederate sympathisers such as Lord Campbell and the radical George Potter were in the forefront of organising public displays in favour of Polish independence.[4] It is also worth noting that both Cobden and Bright were largely uninterested in both the Polish uprising and the Italian struggles – despite the considerable amount of working-class sympathy they engendered.[5] Indeed, as Margot Finn has pointed out, this indifference on the part of Cobden and Bright caused something of a rift between them and the radical working class[6] – a clear indication, if ever there was one, that the Manchester school did not always see eye-to-eye with the working class in international affairs.

Indeed, as far as Poland was concerned, the Union, to a certain extent, made a rod for its own back. The North's suspected sympathetic alliance with Russia greatly disturbed many English radicals, particularly working-class ones.[7] When Russia crushed the Polish rebellion in 1863, northern boasting of a Russian–Union alliance caused problems. The American abolitionist Henry Ward Beecher toured England during 1863, speaking at meetings held by the Union and Emancipation Society, ostensibly to educate the public about the facts of the war. The meetings did not go well. At Manchester and Glasgow, working-class audiences heckled Beecher and turned the proceedings into a shambles. This occurred, *Reynolds's* noted, despite the fact that, because 'the meeting might be disturbed by partisans of the Confederate

---

[3] *Saturday Review*, 2 Jan. 1864, 13.
[4] *Reynolds's Weekly*, 3 May 1863, 1; 6 Dec. 1863, 1.
[5] Margot C. Finn, *After Chartism: class and nation in English radical politics, 1848–1874*, Cambridge 1993, 213.
[6] Ibid. 188.
[7] It is unclear whether there was ever a formal alliance between Russia and the Union although there was definitely a sympathetic one. Crook notes the enthusiasm felt for Russia in the North even during the suppression of the Polish rebellion in 1863. For a discussion of Russian–Union friendship see Crook, *The North, the South and the powers*, 285–6.

States', 'Arrangements had, therefore, been made for the prompt suppression of disorder.'[8] In response to this, admission to the meeting at Exeter Hall in London was subject to a more stringent policy. None the less, despite the fact that the meeting was attended by individuals amenable to Beecher's views, when he discussed the North, 'a voice' asked, 'What about [the] Russians?' Beecher was forced to denounce the supposed alliance stating, 'But you will say "Is it not an indecent thing for America now that Russia is engaged in suppressing the liberties of Poland, to make believe to flirt with her?" (Hear). I think it is. (Cheers).'[9] Considering that this was a meeting organised by and containing individuals friendly to the Union, with policies in place to keep out those who opposed it, the demand that Beecher denounce the Russian alliance is noteworthy. It is also true that *Reynolds's Weekly*, after it had abandoned its hostility to the North, took the Union to task for its friendship with Russia.[10]

Nationalist uprisings, by white Europeans at least, often won English sympathy. The country that might have placed the English in an embarrassing position was Ireland. Those in England hostile to Irish aspirations who condemned southern secession had at least absolved themselves of any charges of hypocrisy. Those who supported southern secession were the ones in difficulty when it came to Ireland. As it happened, many of the English commentators sympathetic to the Union later opposed Irish Home Rule and further, like those who condemned secession without supporting the Union, frequently made the comparison between the North's attempts to subjugate the South with Britain's approach to Ireland. Those in the pro-northern camp who would come to oppose Home Rule included Edward Dicey, Goldwin Smith, Henry Fawcett, John Bright, J. S. Mill and W. E. Forster. Many of them, rightly or wrongly, saw the Home Rule position as the thin edge of the wedge of outright Irish independence that would weaken Britain. Dicey absolutely saw matters in this light. James Bryce, meanwhile, was a supporter of a federal system with Ireland and the colonies that would, he hoped, eventually involve the United States (clearly making his political position vastly different to that of the Lincoln administration's). Numerous of these pro-Northerners opposed Gladstone's Home Rule bill precisely because

---

[8] *Reynolds's Weekly*, 18 Oct. 1863, 5.
[9] Ibid. 25 Oct. 1863, 3.
[10] Ibid. 18 Oct. 1863, 7. *Reynolds's* was scornful of Beecher who, it noted, along with his sister, had always admired the British aristocracy before the conflict. Earlier, Harriet Beecher Stowe had published *Sunny memoirs of foreign lands*, which the journal deemed to be 'one of the most slavish and sycophantic books ever written' and which betrayed the principles of republicanism. Further, in the case of Beecher, Foner notes that after the war, 'he turned against workingmen and denounced labor activities and aspirations'. The fact is that Beecher had never been particularly pro-labour and his speeches in England concentrated on slavery, not political reform. This, once again, should serve to remind us that anti-slavery individuals and political radicals were not necessarily one and the same: ibid. 25 Oct. 1863, 1; Foner, *British labor and the American Civil War*, 118.

of his Confederate sympathies. If he supported secession in America, how could he be trusted over Home Rule? Pro-northern opponents repeated Leslie Stephen's complaint that no one could be certain of Gladstone's principles, during the Home Rule debate. There was, as well, a considerable amount of anti-Irish inclination to be found amongst numerous northern supporters, in part because they believed that Irish immigrants to America were responsible for anti-British sentiment there. There was, however, more to it than that. Leslie Stephen, Goldwin Smith and James Bryce all blamed corruption in American politics on Irish immigrants, too.[11] Most importantly was that, in the period immediately before and then during the American Civil War, Ireland was quiet and very much off the public agenda.

It is worth acknowledging, though, that, as Peter Mandler points out, the English were lagging behind Europeans in thinking seriously about 'nationality'.[12] This meant that national struggles such as that in Italy tended to be seen as libertarian. Conservatives, in particular, were uncomfortable with the notion of 'national struggles'; Benjamin Disraeli and Robert Gascoyne-Cecil, later Lord Salisbury, and, like the former, a future Conservative prime minister, were both hostile to the idea. Disraeli, in particular, called it a 'modern new-fangled sentimental principle of nationality', which, he believed, destabilised governments.[13] This, in part, explains the existence of conservative discomfiture regarding southern secession and probably acted as a restraint on sympathy towards the Confederacy. Unfortunately for the North, such thinking also hurt the Union. The extent of the North's devotion to the Union was probably never really grasped by the majority of English commentators. Notions of national exceptionalism (believed by most Northerners) were concepts they did not really understand. The idea that the United States was some kind of experiment on behalf of mankind, or that it had to remain united in order for democracy to flourish, was not one that found much resonance in England. This is not to say that the English had no concept of the nation-state – they did, of course – only that European and, to a lesser extent, American, ideas of 'a people' with a national destiny carried little weight.

All of this, of course, still raises the question of whether or not there were reasons for viewing the South's activities as an uprising similar to Poland's or Italy's. That is, did there exist reasons for believing that the South would be better off, politically, as an independent nation-state? Unfortunately for the Union, there were indeed reasons for doing so. Beyond the disputes over

---

[11] Christopher Harvie, *The lights of liberalism: university liberals and the challenge of democracy, 1860–86*, London 1976, 221–7.
[12] Peter Mandler, 'Race and nation in mid-Victorian thought', in S. Collini, R. Whatmore and B. Young (eds), *History, religion and culture: essays in British intellectual history, 1750–1950*, Cambridge 2000, 224–44 passim.
[13] Paul Smith, *Disraeli: a brief life*, Cambridge 1996, 190–1. I should like to thank Professor Mandler for bringing this to my attention.

tariffs, slavery, and states' rights, or the fact that the Confederacy was effectively a *de facto* state, generally united in its efforts to obtain independence, the South and its society had been viewed as inherently different from the rest of the United States by the English before the conflict even took place. The travel literature (from which the English largely drew their opinions of America), published before the war, lent a good deal of support to notions of the Confederacy as a nation-state different in political character and culture. As Richard Rapson observes, 'It is interesting to note that when the British wrote of the United States and her values, they meant the northern and Western states. Both before and after the Civil War, the travellers usually considered the South as a separate land, and they referred to the South specifically by name.'[14] Observers could scarcely fail to notice the difference between the industrialising North and largely agrarian South. What is interesting to note is the lack of positive commentary about the South before the war began. Max Berger informs us,

> No sooner was the Mason-Dixon line crossed than poverty, decay and retrogression stared the traveller in the face. . . . Arriving at Richmond, travellers were amazed by what they saw. The city presented the appearance 'so unusual in America of retrogression and decay.' The great Charleston of which they had heard so much, turned out to be equally disappointing to most visitors.[15]

The notion of an aristocratic South, or rather, a self-styled one, was not held by the English. Although de Tocqueville, it is true, did compare southern society to an aristocracy, he none the less noted that it was based on slavery, making it a different entity from the European version he admired.[16] Apart from de Tocqueville, notions of an aristocratic South are owed, in large part, to the southern planter society itself, which had something of a fascination with the novels of Sir Walter Scott. Indeed, so keen on Scott's works was the planter society that Mark Twain is alleged to have accused the author of being in great measure responsible for the Civil War, having had so large a hand in making the southern character. Although this was hard on Scott, just because an element of southern society saw itself as a region of chivalrous cavaliers (and the image has persisted, witness Margaret Mitchell's *Gone With the Wind*), it did not follow that the English shared this view. Indeed, the view the English had of the South was diametrically opposed to notions of Confederate aristocratic cavaliers. As Berger also informs us, the main house of a slave-plantation 'was always disappointing to those who had conjured up visions of magnificent mansions'.[17] This view of a backward South was, as we shall see, reinforced by visitors to America during the conflict and was

---

[14] Richard Rapson, *Britons view America: travel commentary, 1860–1935*, Seattle 1971, 53.
[15] Max Berger, *The British traveller in America, 1836–1860*, New York 1943, 43.
[16] De Tocqueville, *Democracy in America*, i. 356–81.
[17] Berger, *The British traveller in America*, 110.

retained by many English commentators throughout the conflict, despite Confederate successes.

The Union's cause, however, was damaged by other strains of mid-nineteenth-century English thought, too. Geoffrey Best's study of Britain during our period notes a strong English distaste for centralisation and a preference instead for local government.[18] It did not take much imagination to apply this favourably towards the Confederacy's 'states' rights' arguments, or unfavourably towards the increasing powers assumed by the Lincoln administration in Washington. Some English commentators shared John C. Calhoun's belief that the American Constitution was a compact among the states, not over them. Although Calhoun's works did not receive wide dissemination in England, Jon Roper is substantially correct when he says that the champion of states' rights might well have found a home in nineteenth-century Britain, although his slaves would have had to remain behind.[19] Finally, it should be remembered that the empire was held in comparatively low esteem at this point in British history, despite the skirmishing in the various far corners of the world.

The impact of 'total war': civil liberties and casualties

It was almost universally believed – even by northern sympathisers – that the Union was permanently sundered. Even British visitors to America during the conflict such as Lieutenant-Colonel Arthur J. L. Fremantle, author of *Three months in the Southern States, April–June 1863* – who, as a military man and witness to the battle of Gettysburg, should have known better – also declared that the South would emerge victorious.[20] This persisted as the prevailing belief up to at least the end of 1864. Why did the English believe Confederate defeat was impossible? Obviously, they shared this delusion with the South and, indeed, with many Northerners – C. F. Adams Jr. and Horace Greeley, just to name two. But warning signs that the Confederacy was not invincible were there – particularly by 1862. The capture of New Orleans (remembering Britain's defeat there in 1815) and Grant's success in the West, all pointed to the possibility of a Union victory. In response to this, one can remark that warning signs are usually such only after the fact. Had the Confederacy won the war – and this was not entirely impossible, as McPherson and other historians have shown – the English would have

---

[18] Geoffrey Best, *Mid-Victorian Britain*, London 1971, 35–55.
[19] Roper, *Democracy and its critics*, 65.
[20] Surprisingly little attention has been paid to Fremantle's memoirs by historians of this subject, even though he is regularly cited by Civil War historians: Arthur J. L. Fremantle, *Three months in the southern states, April–June, 1863*, ed. Gary Gallagher, Lincoln, Neb. 1991, 309.

appeared to be prescient.[21] The fact is, however, the Union won the war and, in any case, none of the above answers the question of why the English believed the South would not be conquered. An event in the year 1862, however, does provide a possible answer. The event is the battle of Antietam (or Sharpsburg, as the South called it) which took place on 17 September. There were over 23,000 casualties (killed and wounded) at Antietam – more than twice as many as in all of America's previous wars combined. Add to this examples such as Shiloh, which took place in April 1862 and cost 5,000 men their lives, and then Gettysburg in 1863, where at least 46,000 men perished.[22] Ultimately, more than 620,000 soldiers would be killed in the war – some 260,000 Southerners and 360,000 Northerners.

This was what stunned the English, the Union's determination to carry on fighting in the face of such appalling losses. Casualty numbers like these were virtually unprecedented. By way of comparison, the British lost 19,584 men in the Crimean War – *in total*.[23] The only precedent to the Battle of Gettysburg the English could draw on from personal experience was the Battle of Waterloo, where some 47,800 men perished on both sides.[24] Waterloo, however, by the 1860s was the experience of an earlier generation and, in any event, that battle and Gettysburg were not much of a comparison because the former had at least ended the Napoleonic Wars. Gettysburg, on the other hand, was followed by almost two more years of fighting. How, the English wondered, could the North do it? The mid-nineteenth-century English mind found it difficult to conceive of destruction of human life on this scale. Contemporary society (and, by extension, its historical profession) is, to a certain degree, less shocked by the idea of such losses in battle because of the experiences of the First and Second World Wars. The American Civil War, however, was the precursor to these wars – or, at least, their killing rates. It was the first example of its kind and, as such, difficult to conceive of, much less grasp. Not until the First World War and battles like the Somme did Britain undergo a similar experience and, like the Union (not to say the Confederacy), see the affair out to the bloody end. This was the first modern war and no civilised society, the English believed, could tolerate such losses for long. Bloody stalemate seemed the only likely end result.

The fact that the Civil War was the first modern conflict brings us to another point. In order to defeat the Confederacy, the Union had to fight what amounted to total war. This meant not only directing the economy

---

[21] James M. McPherson, *Drawn with the sword: reflections on the American Civil War*, Oxford 1996, ch. ix, 'How the Confederacy almost won', passim.
[22] Peter J. Parish, *The American Civil War*, New York 1975, 288.
[23] J. B. Conacher, *Britain and the Crimea, 1855–56: problems of war and peace*, New York 1987, 218.
[24] Lawrence James, *The Iron Duke: a military biography of Wellington*, London 1992, 262. It should also be remembered that the casualty rates at Waterloo were extremely high by the standards of the Napoleonic Wars. As James notes, 'the losses at Waterloo far outstripped those of his [Wellington's] earlier battles'.

towards the war effort, but it also meant instituting conscription, suppressing rights such as freedom of speech and the writ of habeas corpus, and making war on civilians (by destroying private property of non-combatants). Again, to a twenty-first-century mind, after two world wars, this is almost par for the course. To a mid-nineteenth-century mind, however, this was anathema. Conscription, for example, appeared to be a return to the press-gangs of the Napoleonic Wars. On the question of enemy civilians' property rights, meanwhile, Britain had largely respected these in her wars, especially against the Americans during both the Revolution and the War of 1812. Lincoln's suppression of freedom of speech and the suspension of the writ of habeas corpus, meanwhile, simply smacked of despotism.[25]

In a sense, the Lincoln administration was placed in a no-win situation. To defeat the South (and, coincidentally, prove English predictions wrong), it needed to fight the kind of war to which mid-nineteenth-century English thought was opposed. What must be continually remembered is that total war, or, rather, the aspects introduced (or, in some cases, resurrected) by the Union, was new. Coupled with what appeared to be an impossible cause (re-union), such measures boded ill for freedom in America. The strategies and tactics needed for the conquest of the South flew in the face of mid-nineteenth-century ideals of progress and freedom. It is this vital aspect of English thinking about the American Civil War that has been almost entirely ignored.

Worries about the Union sliding into tyranny were expressed early in the struggle. The *Illustrated London News* remarked in late 1861:

> Had anyone hinted some twelve months back at the possibility of the United States being the next arena for the display of the antiquated resources of martial law, suspension of *habeas corpus*, and the passport system, he would have been met with a shout of derisive laughter. We have lived, however, to see these things as living, tangible facts.[26]

It did not take long before this strain of thinking developed into smug insularity. Very soon, the journal made fresh comparisons between English and American versions of liberty, stating, 'Blessed ourselves with a really free and constitutional Government, a responsible Ministry, an unfettered press, and tribunals of unquestionable integrity, it has been difficult – perhaps we ought rather to say unpalatable – to our imaginations to picture the actual condition of internal affairs on the other side of the Atlantic.'[27] The *Illustrated London News*, like other journals, regularly posted bulletins on the suppres-

---

[25] Crook is one of the only historians to even mention the civil liberties issue, but does not consider its importance in English thought: *The North, the South and the powers*, 219, 244, 250.
[26] *Illustrated London News*, 7 Sept. 1861, 236.
[27] Ibid. 5 Oct. 1861, 340.

sion of liberties in the Union, maintaining the view of an illiberal society.[28] *Reynolds's Weekly* regularly fulminated against the measures passed by the Lincoln administration and published a list of newspapers and periodicals which were shut down by either the federal government or mobs on at least one occasion.[29] Needless to say, the English press particularly disapproved of this last development. For some commentators, the ultimate blow was the suspension of the writ of habeas corpus and the introduction of martial law in areas loyal to the Union.[30] These concerns were widespread. The *New Monthly Magazine*, the sympathies of which fluctuated, went so far as to remark, 'we say advisedly that, except as one of the majority, there was no country in which a man had less freedom of speech or action at any time than in the United States'.[31] *The Economist* remarked as early as 1861,

> For a long time now, the true liberty of the individual citizens has been as little regarded and as ruthlessly trampled down in the United States as in Austria or France – and in Washington as New York as in Charleston or Louisiana. The oppression has been exercised in a different name by a different despot – that is all. The violent oppression of unpopular opinions, the ostracising of the more moderate and wise of the public men, the Lynching of the few courageous citizens who stood up for their conscience and their civil rights, have not been confined to the wild West or slavery-stained South. Real liberty, as *we* understand it, – liberty to act and think and speak as each man chooses, – we have no scruple in saying, did not exist in the United States before the disruption, and does not exist there now.[32]

The journal maintained this view throughout the conflict.[33] Even periodicals friendly to the Union such as the *Spectator* expressed concern, criticising the Lincoln administration for 'shutting up suspected people who could never have done anybody any harm'.[34]

Such activities were often cited as rebuttals to the assertions of Union apologists. The *Saturday Review* reported on one of Forster's pro-northern speeches and noted, 'The large majority of educated Englishmen according to

---

[28] Take, for example, this report: ' "peace party" newspapers suspended since the commencement of the war:– Papers suspended by the authorities, 17; destroyed by mobs, 10; died naturally, 5; denied the mails, 5; changed politics, 7; whose editors are in prison, 6': ibid. 12 Oct. 1861, 361.
[29] The journal listed thirteen northern newspapers which had either been suppressed by the federal government or whose staff and offices had been attacked by mobs. *Reynolds's Weekly*, 15 Sept. 1861, 4.
[30] See *Illustrated London News*, 11 Oct. 1862, 373–4; 22 Aug. 1863, 181–2.
[31] *New Monthly Magazine* (Oct. 1864), 203–4. As a reminder of how much English thinking on America fluctuated, it is worth noting that, in the pages of the same journal, the journalist Cyrus Redding argued in favour of Lincoln's activities and stated that the president should have even more powers to quell dissent: ibid. (June 1862), 216–23.
[32] *The Economist*, 14 Sept. 1861, 1012 [their italics].
[33] See, for example, ibid. 10 Sept. 1864, 1135.
[34] *Spectator*, 20 Sept. 1862, 1043.

Mr. Forster's admission ... think that the struggle is for independence in the one side and empire on the other, and they find the champions of political liberty on the side of the South.' The journal dismissed Forster's claims that the war was solely about slavery, as well as the member of parliament's insistence that Britain would follow exactly the same course of action as the North if Ireland tried to secede, something it called 'a strange doctrine to be seriously propounded by a liberal politician', and sarcastically remarked that Forster's 'land of freedom is a land where the press is interfered with, and *Habeas Corpus* set aside, and where one man's proclamation is above all law, and is enforced upon a whole city, even pending a judicial inquiry, by an army of thirty thousand men and a fleet of gunboats commanding its wharves and quays'.[35]

This last reference was to General Benjamin Butler's command of the occupation of New Orleans. The general's activities there have been well covered by historians, in particular his infamous instruction that women who insulted either northern soldiers or the flag of the United States would be treated as common prostitutes.[36] Some historians have argued that the above sentence was an English misinterpretation of Butler's orders. Unfortunately, this argument becomes unstuck once one actually reads what Butler proclaimed: 'Any lady who shall by word or gesture express contempt of any Federal officer or soldier shall be liable, without protection or redress, to be treated as common prostitutes are treated.'[37] Although this was not incitement to commit rape, as some nineteenth-century commentators believed, in an age with concepts such as 'the fallen woman' it suggested rather more than the night in prison that Jordan and Pratt glibly describe.[38] In a sense, the women of New Orleans were lucky – one New Orleans citizen was hanged solely for tearing down the Stars and Stripes.[39] The incident received more coverage than has generally been acknowledged, although some historians conspicuously fail to mention the atrocity.[40] What remains most interesting about Butler's reign in New Orleans is the surprise expressed by the same historians that the English would object to such activities and that they might contribute to anti-Union sentiment.[41]

---

[35] *Saturday Review*, 10 Oct. 1863, 417. Note how it was the northern apologist Forster, rather than the journal, who asserted that the majority of English opinion favoured the South.
[36] See Crook, *The North, the South and the powers*, 206–7; Adams, *Great Britain and the American Civil War*, i. 302–4.
[37] Published in *Saturday Review*, 14 June 1862, 672.
[38] Jordan and Pratt, *Europe and the American Civil War*, 112.
[39] *Saturday Review*, 17 Jan. 1863, 67. The journal, interestingly enough, was uncertain whether Butler could be fairly held responsible for Mumford's murder.
[40] Crook, *The North, the South and the powers*, 206–7. The Mumford atrocity is absent from the studies of Jordan and Pratt and Adams.
[41] See, for example, Jordan and Pratt, *Europe and the American Civil War*, 112–13; Keiser, 'The English press and the American Civil War', 222.

Another incident that damaged the North's pretensions to freedom was the Vallandigham affair. Briefly put, Clement Vallandigham, a Democratic gubernatorial candidate for Ohio, was arrested in May 1863, for denouncing the war at a public meeting. Found guilty by a military court, Vallandigham was sentenced to imprisonment for the war's duration (Lincoln later commuted the sentence to banishment, although Vallandigham returned to the Union before the war's end and was not molested).[42] This was immediately denounced as an infringement of the right of political dissent. The *Saturday Review* remarked, 'It is difficult to find any explanation for the marvellous acquiescence of the Americans, who were reputed to be a freedom-loving people, in such a tyranny as this.'[43] Even the *Spectator* was shocked by the incident and reported,

> the mode of his [Vallandigham's] punishment suggests that court-martials have been adopted as part of the machinery of government; that the President holds a military sentence on a civilian for scurrilous chatter to be a legal and just proceeding. This view is, moreover, supported by a number of other incidents.[44]

One of the few individuals who vocally supported Lincoln's actions in the affair was, predictably, Bright, who argued 'that there is a vast difference between speech that is free and speech that is licentious'.[45] The *Saturday Review* was quick to reply: 'The distinction has often been drawn by the enemies of freedom, but the institutions which Mr. Bright abhors, enable him, with absolute impunity, not only to proclaim Republican doctrines, but to libel the existing form of Government and all who administer its authority.'[46] The journal then sarcastically asked Bright if he believed that the British government had enjoyed the right to expel him from the country during the Crimean War because of his public opposition towards it. This argument establishes the foundation of the *Saturday Review's* and, by extension, English criticism of the Union. Simply put, Lincoln's administration violated basic liberties, and this was in no way mitigated by the fact that the North was engaged in fighting a different kind of conflict from, to maintain the comparison, the Crimean. Indeed, the majority of English commentators did not see a difference between the two struggles. The right of dissent applied as much to the American Civil War as it did to the Crimean. At this point, it must again be reiterated that the cause of Union was sacred to the Northerners, not to the English, and thus the latter saw no reason to justify the suspension of liberties. This was certainly the opinion of the novelist Charles Dickens (not a conservative), who wrote in *Once a Week*, 'The

---

[42] McPherson, *Battle cry of freedom*, 596–7.
[43] *Saturday Review*, 6 June 1863, 711.
[44] *Spectator*, 6 June 1863, 2083.
[45] *Saturday Review*, 20 June 1863, 773.
[46] Ibid. 773–4.

sacking of homesteads and undermining railway bridges; the infliction of torture and murder for supposed opinions; the suspension of laws and rights – these scandals and miseries are of a nature and extent never required or imagined in international wars.'[47]

What also needs to be remembered about English criticism of the suppression of rights in the North is that there was opposition in the Union, too. When, in April 1861, a Maryland secessionist, John Merryman, was arrested and imprisoned, he secured a writ of habeas corpus from Chief Justice Roger Taney of the Supreme Court, who denied Lincoln's right to suspend habeas corpus. Lincoln simply ignored Taney's judgment and Merryman remained imprisoned without trial, a situation which caused some controversy in the North.[48] The controversy was to grow when, on 24 September 1862, Lincoln suspended habeas corpus throughout the North and occupied Confederate territory, which resulted in individuals being imprisoned merely for criticising conscription policies. This, as David Herbert Donald tells us, 'had resulted in hundreds of cases of violations of civil liberties, when civilians were subjected to arbitrary and quite often unreasonable arrests'. By mid-1863, curtailment of the freedom of speech and of the press, arrests of dissenters and the disloyal – always called 'arbitrary arrests' by his [Lincoln's] opponents – and, above all, suspension of the privilege of the writ of *habeas corpus* deeply troubled many Americans. Of course, the Peace Democrats vigorously protested against these measures, and, after the arrest and trial of Vallandigham, many of the War Democrats joined them. But they were not alone. Within the President's own party a Conservative like his friend [Orville Hickman] Browning believed that the arrests ordered by the Lincoln administration 'were illegal and arbitrary, and did more harm than good, weakening instead of strengthening the government.'[49] Lincoln, of course, always protested that the measures were temporary and would end with peace – as proved to be the case. This, however, was only obvious with hindsight. Especially as the suppression of dissent in the Union appeared to tally with the image the English had of America before the war.

Many in England were reminded of de Tocqueville's claim that 'I know of no country in which there is so little independence of mind and real freedom of discussion as in America'[50] – a claim echoed, as we have seen above, by *The Economist*. But antebellum travel writers to the United States were also unimpressed by what they believed to be the lack of political dissent in American politics and supported de Tocqueville's claim. English liberalism, if one may simplify, which looked back to John Locke and, later, J. S. Mill, was less concerned with the idea that all men should have a voice in government than with the notion that all official interference with men's free thought

---

47 Charles Dickens, 'New phase of the American strife', *Once a Week*, 30 Nov. 1861, 638–9.
48 See McPherson, *Battle cry of freedom*, 288–9.
49 Donald, *Lincoln*, 380, 441.
50 De Tocqueville, *Democracy in America*, i. 263.

must be stripped to the barest minimum. Or, as Richard Rapson puts it, 'American political democracy concerned itself with *all* men, rule by the *demos*. To the English, this bore little resemblance to authentic political democracy in which rational exchanges between free men would *select* the *best* ideas, in which maximum dissent must be tolerated.'[51] This is, of course, a simplification of mid-nineteenth-century English political thought, and numerous radicals, such as Reynolds, to name just one, would have rejected it immediately. None the less, the notion of maximum intellectual dissent and freedom of speech had a large number of adherents. Rightly or wrongly, their concept of what constituted a liberal state was violated by Lincoln's measures. This was to have a profound impact upon English interpretations of the American Civil War.

Just as Butler caused controversy, so too did Sherman's 'march to the sea'. The *Illustrated London News*, early in the conflict, had expressed the common English belief that 'War is now carried on under far different conditions than those which prevailed in olden times. Armies are not now allowed to devastate private property in the countries in which they are engaged.'[52] The rule of 'olden times' returned when Sherman devastated Georgia. As expected, the *Illustrated London News* expressed disgust at this development.[53] The *Saturday Review* made some of the most vociferous denunciations throughout Sherman's manoeuvres: 'It is argued that the destruction of food and the means of raising it has the effect of weakening the Confederacy by diminishing its resources. The same argument would justify any kind of barbarity practised under the pretence of war.'[54]

Sometimes American correspondents expressed opposition to such activities. Moncure David Conway, the former American minister to England, writing in *Fraser's Magazine*, described Sherman's activities as simply wanton, and, concerned about the progress of emancipation, remarked, 'It were idle to say that the victories of the Union are now the victories of emancipation. Sherman's progress through Georgia is traceable in burning towns, but not, so far as the world learns, in broken fetters.'[55] By the time Sherman was devastating Georgia, however, the American Civil War was relatively minor news in England. Poland and Schleswig-Holstein now dominated the public discourse.

The similar abuses of freedom that occurred in the Confederacy were rarely covered, but this was not merely due to English partiality. The South was, in fact, far more tolerant of dissent than the North. Davis's government maintained the traditional liberal rights of freedom of speech, freedom of the press and freedom from arbitrary arrest. Indeed, Donald has argued that this

---

51 Rapson, *Britons view America*, 63 [his italics].
52 *Illustrated London News*, 9 Nov. 1861, 464.
53 Ibid. 8 Oct. 1864, 354.
54 *Saturday Review*, 2 Apr. 1864, 404–5; 6 Aug. 1864, 173; 29 Oct. 1864, 524.
55 *Fraser's Magazine* (Jan. 1865), 20.

upholding of civil liberties was one of the reasons the Confederacy lost the war.[56] The fact that the South was more tolerant of dissent (slavery notwithstanding) unquestionably had an impact on English thinking. For example, the mild-mannered philanthropist and social reformer, Antony Ashley Cooper, the Earl of Shaftesbury, was moved to condemn the North for its conduct, but at the same time wrote a letter to James Mason, praising the Confederacy for not behaving in the same fashion.[57] Southern conduct contrasted even more favourably with that of the North because the Confederacy was viewed as a newly founded rebellious state – much higher standards of behaviour were expected from the established Union. It is also true, however, that not as many southern papers made their way into Britain as northern ones, thus Union abuses of personal liberty, not to mention protests against, were much better reported upon. This is not to deny, however, that some English commentary was misguided and some was indeed malicious – anti-Americanism certainly played its part – but neither misapprehension nor malice satisfactorily explains the deluge of criticism directed at the suppression of rights in the North. Further, at least some anti-Union sentiment must be attributed to these same such activities by the federal government.

The northern press and politicians

Historians have underrated just how little northern politicians and commentators helped their own cause. Union foreign policy, for example, was viewed as abrasive – even by those sympathetic to the North. The two individuals who once again distinguished themselves in their crassness were Seward and Clay. In 1862, and again in 1863, Clay publicly called for a Union–Russian alliance to be formed against Britain. This was hardly conducive to good relations, and no British minister of anything like comparable rank ever made remarks as remotely hostile towards the North – and this includes Gladstone's speech at Newcastle. The *Illustrated London News* and the *Saturday Review* both expressed disgust at Clay's maladroit diplomacy.[58]

Seward, however, remained the least popular northern politician in England. Although the secretary of state's open aggression markedly decreased after the scare he received over the *Trent* affair, Seward published his diplomatic correspondence in 1862, which openly revealed his virulent anti-British sentiments.[59] What was probably more damaging still was the

---

56 David Herbert Donald, 'Died of democracy', in David Herbert Donald (ed.), *Why the North won the Civil War*, Baton Rouge 1960, 81–92.
57 Shaftesbury to Mason, 19 Aug. 1862, in *Correspondence of James M. Mason*, 308–9.
58 *Saturday Review*, 15 Feb. 1862, 169–70; *Illustrated London News*, 29 Aug. 1863, 210.
59 *Saturday Review*, 15 Feb 1862, 183–4. One of the documents published was Dispatch No. 10, which virtually promised war if Britain communicated officially or otherwise with

Spectator's associating Seward with editorials in the *New York Herald* in early 1862, the anglophobia of which has already been discussed.[60] The regular attacks and abuse from the *New York Herald* then became identified as the official opinion of Seward and, to an extent, the Lincoln administration.[61] It is thus unsurprising that the *Spectator*, while favouring the North, made a point of stating, 'We have not the slightest sympathy with American ways or American foreign policy. They are collectively to us the most disagreeable of people, and we have as contemptuous a pity for the half-bred vapouring of their public dispatches as any European diplomatist, or as Mr. Roebuck himself.'[62]

The fact that one of the Union's most adamant apologists could state this proves beyond any doubt that the North's foreign policy was extremely distasteful to English opinion and did much to foster antipathy towards it. For the *Spectator* to agree with the pro-Confederate member of parliament John Arthur Roebuck – who, as we shall see, would later put forward a motion for the recognition of the Confederacy in the House of Commons – on the merits of the Union required some incentive. It says little for northern diplomacy that such was provided. There was much truth to the *Saturday Review*'s comment made in 1864 that, 'If an English minister were to speak of a nominally friendly country in the language which is familiar to Mr. Seward . . . all parties would concur in declaring that he had disgraced his office.'[63] It is difficult to overestimate the negative impact of Seward's activities on English opinion.

Even the traditionally highly-thought-of Adams was not always judicious in his public remarks. In late 1864, the minister informed a deputation of the Emancipation Society, a pro-Union lobby group, 'that the North resents the neutrality of England with a bitterness which must eventually lead to war'.[64] After a remark like this, the real miracle is that the Emancipation Society continued to agitate in favour of the Union. Speeches such as these, made by northern officials, remain under-examined, or, worse, unreported, by

---

the Confederacy or its representatives – effectively an impossible demand for a neutral nation to meet.

[60] *Spectator*, 4 Jan. 1862, 1. Although the journal insisted, 'It is unfair, however, to consider the *Herald* as the organ of the Federal Government or of any respectable body of politicians', the damage was done. I have been unable to discover why the *Spectator* highlighted Seward's connection to the paper. (Seward did, as Crook points out, edit one or two of its reports on the Lincoln government.) After all, despising Seward was the one trait Bennett shared with his former compatriots: *The North, the South and the powers*, 85.

[61] A year later, the *Saturday Review* reviewed the diary of an American, who accused Seward of dictating many of the anti-British articles to the *New York Herald*, and wondered why the secretary of state was so keen to pick a quarrel, noting, 'Even my Anglo-phobia cannot stand it': *Saturday Review*, 14 Feb. 1863, 218.

[62] *Spectator*, 16 Aug. 1862, 901.

[63] *Saturday Review*, 24 Dec. 1864, 769.

[64] Ibid.

historians adhering to the traditional interpretation of English opinions of the conflict.

Efforts were, of course, made by certain conscientious northern diplomats to ease the tension. William L. Dayton, the United States minister to France, made a point of informing English correspondents that the Union had no desire for conflict with Britain. Such correspondence sometimes found its way into the national press.[65] Unfortunately, the atmosphere, which had deteriorated since the Proclamation of Neutrality and the *Trent* affair, only damaged Anglo-Union understanding and poisoned the negotiations surrounding delicate subjects such as the building of Confederate ships in England and interference with British shipping in the West Indies.[66]

The last case caused particular irritation in England and was cited as a further example of northern aggression. Wilkes, of *Trent* affair infamy, harassed neutral shipping in the West Indies in an effort to foil the blockade-runners. This continued until Vice-Admiral Milne, commander of the North American fleet, ordered the Royal Navy to protect British shipping in the area – by force if necessary. Russell, recognising the danger of the situation (had Royal and US naval vessels opened fire on each other, events would have probably spiralled out of control), commanded Milne to rescind his order, and shortly afterwards, in what was probably a reciprocal gesture, Gideon Welles removed the offending Wilkes from the scene.[67]

Although some historians have claimed that the acrimonies of the northern press only matched those of England's press, in most respects, the former outdid the latter in virulence. The *New York Herald*'s career has already been discussed, but it was not alone. Promises of future war and that 'America will hate England . . . until the last American now living goes to his grave', by journals such as the *New York Times*, were scarcely likely to foster a pro-northern spirit.[68] The *New York Times* was a particularly interesting case. It regularly fulminated against Britain, and on 9 December 1862 claimed not only that nine-tenths of members of parliament 'sided with the rebels in their public addresses', but that 'the great body of the upper and middle classes of England have from the outset, through almost every organ of their opinion, not ceased to defame, malign and damage the sacred cause to which we have pledged our lives and fortunes'.[69] The inaccuracy of the paper's remarks on members of parliament's public addresses is discussed in the next chapter. As for 'the great body of the upper and middle classes' opposing the Union from

---

[65] See, for example, Dayton's written discussion with Mr Nassan in *Reynolds's Weekly*, which took the form of what we would now call an interview: 6 Sept. 1863, 2.
[66] The myth that Britain actively aided the Confederacy by allowing privateer vessels to be built and armed in British ports has been completely discredited by modern studies. See, in particular, Frank J. Merli, *Great Britain and the Confederate navy: 1861–1865*, Bloomington 1970, chs iii–xii passim.
[67] Jenkins, *Britain and the war for the Union*, ii. 259–66.
[68] Quoted in the *Saturday Review*, 6 Dec. 1862, 669.
[69] Quoted in *Reynolds's Weekly*, 28 Dec. 1862, 2.

the outset, the *New York Times* had clearly forgotten the widespread opposition secession had initially engendered. Whether or not the upper and middle classes did 'defame, malign and damage' the Union is one of the questions this work attempts to answer, but at least the *New York Times*, unlike Bright, frankly identified its erstwhile foes. What was also forgotten by the journal, however, in a curious fit of amnesia, was the *New York Times*'s very own suggestion of annexing Canada upon the receipt of Britain's Proclamation of Neutrality, discussed in chapter 1.

One member of the northern establishment who deserves credit for seeking to reduce tensions was Thurlow Weed, one of the Republican Party's bosses. In an open letter to the municipality of New York, written after a fact-finding trip to England, Weed discussed English perceptions of the Union with remarkable accuracy. Pointing out the hostility the Morrill tariff had caused, Weed noted that 'In England it was believed that we not only cherished unfriendly feelings towards that country, but we desired a rupture of friendly relations.' After pointing to the successful conclusion to the *Trent* affair, and English suspicion of Seward (which, he insisted, was 'egregiously unfounded'), Weed concluded his speech stating,

> the Union has many ardent, well-wishing friends in England, and can [have] many more if we act justly ourselves and labour to correct erroneous impressions. . . . Nor, in forming our estimate of the degree and value of English sympathy during our domestic troubles is the fact that her Queen and the House of Commons modified harsh dispatches, and resisted unfriendly legislation, without significance.[70]

Earlier, while in England, Weed had written a letter to *The Times* during the *Trent* affair, insisting that, despite appearances and Seward's comments to the duke of Newcastle, the Union did not want a war with Britain.[71] In other words, Weed had made an earlier attempt to ease Anglo-American differences. Unfortunately, as was so often the case regarding Anglo-American relations during the conflict, calming voices such as Weed's were exceedingly rare on both sides of the Atlantic. With perhaps the exception of the *New York Tribune*, the tone of the major organs of the North was hostile to Britain – from the Proclamation of Neutrality to the end of the war.

One can detect the exasperation in the tone of the *Illustrated London News*'s comments on the reaction of the northern press to Britain's refusal to join the French efforts at mediation: 'Some writers say that we were afraid to interfere, others that we rejoice in the war because it tends to weaken the

---

[70] *Reynolds's Weekly*, 27 July 1862, 1.
[71] Thurlow Weed to the editor of *The Times*, 12 Dec. 1861; 14 Dec. 1861, 7. It is worth pointing out that Weed was a long-standing friend and political ally of Seward and, therefore, naturally wished to place the secretary of state in the best possible light. Despite this, Weed appears to have been honestly sincere in his sentiments in both the letter to *The Times* and his open letter to New York.

Union. Nor are the comments of such of the Southern papers as have reached us much more civil.'[72] Clearly, by 1862, the British were damned if they did, damned if they did not. The *Saturday Review* was not alone when it stated, 'Everything we do, right or wrong, is so misrepresented in America – we give so much offence, however we behave – that we can only come to the conclusion that the Federal Government will pick a quarrel with us whenever war promises to be an advantageous speculation, but not before.'[73] The *New Monthly Magazine*, meanwhile, remarked, 'we are told openly that all pending hostilities will be directed against us'.[74] Even the *Spectator* expressed concern, and resurrected the old idea of the North seeking to fix a quarrel upon Britain in order to abandon the task of suppressing the South.[75] Indeed, so frequently were northern threats directed at Britain that the Confederate secretary of state, Judah P. Benjamin, gleefully observed to Mason at the end of 1864 that, 'The administration papers in the United States, by their party cry of "one war at a time", leave England with little room for doubt as to the settled ulterior motive of that Government to attack England as soon as disengaged from the struggle with us.'[76] If the unquestionably very able and talented Benjamin believed that the Union intended at some point to go to war with Britain, is it any surprise that numerous English columnists concurred?

Historians wedded to the traditional interpretation of English attitudes towards the American Civil War have largely ignored the regular threats made against Britain by Union politicians and by the northern press, and often accept the same organs' dubious and unproven accusations as fact.[77] The *Saturday Review*'s challenge to Cobden was perceptive: 'It would be interesting to hear what Mr. Cobden would say if any English paper habitually proposed an unprovoked invasion of American territory; yet he must be well aware that the conquest of Canada is one of the most ordinary subjects of American leading articles.'[78]

It should also be remembered that bouts of anti-northern sentiment were often a reaction to anti-British activities in America (and, of course, vice versa). For example, on 28 March 1863, the *Illustrated London News* levelled (by its standards) an unusually savage attack on the Union.[79] The week before, however, the New York Chamber of Commerce held a public meeting where speakers savagely denounced Britain and its allegedly pro-southern

---

72 *Illustrated London News*, 13 Dec. 1862, 626.
73 *Saturday Review*, 1 Aug. 1863, 136.
74 *New Monthly Magazine* (July 1862), 344.
75 *Spectator*, 18 Apr. 1863, 1882.
76 Benjamin to Mason, 30 Dec. 1864, in *Correspondence of James M. Mason*, 544.
77 Foner, for example, reproduces the above-quoted *New York Times* article without any critical comment whatsoever, despite the fact that much of the article contained charges that are, at the least, debatable: *British labor and the American Civil War*, 47–8.
78 *Saturday Review*, 26 Nov. 1864, 645.
79 *Illustrated London News*, 28 Mar. 1863, 341–2.

neutrality.[80] Although many of the charges levelled against Britain were wildly exaggerated, there was an interesting pattern to the Union's attacks. First, as the *Saturday Review* reported, northern criticism of Britain became more severe whenever the South won a victory – when the Union won, Britain was largely ignored.[81] When this consideration is coupled with the *New York Herald*'s regular charge that Britain was the cause of the rebellion (precisely how was not mentioned), the picture becomes clear.[82] The idea of their fellow citizens actually wanting to break away from the sublime Union flew in the face of American nationalist ideals – some foreign scapegoat was required, and few nations could apparently fulfil that role better than Britain.

Discussions of Anglo-Union relations during the conflict are fundamentally incomplete unless it is noted that the North's secretary of state, its diplomats (including its resident representative), and its national press threatened war on occasions. On the British side, no politician of Seward's status, nor any diplomat (certainly not Lord Lyons, the British minister to Washington), ever made public menaces as grave as the Union's. In retrospect, the United States, fighting for its existence, was bound to be exceedingly touchy on certain topics. Many of the threats were indeed merely for effect. This, once again, however, is obvious only with hindsight. Further, the English, not having the advantage of hindsight, could only draw from the experience of the past. For example, although northern supporters claimed that the South was the most pro-expansionist part of the Union, responsible for all antebellum acts of aggression, Northerners had, before the war, angrily denounced President James Polk for negotiating with Britain over the Canadian boundary while going to war with Mexico.[83] This, of course, made the Union, in English eyes, a greater threat. From 1860 to 1865, the United States underwent what amounted to a revolution, the end results of which could not be easily foreseen. The North appeared (and was) an aggressive, unstable and unpredictable entity. English criticism and dislike of the Union reflected that reality.

English divisions and doubts about the conflict are shown by the debate surrounding *realpolitik* arguments. Historians who argue for a pro-southern England cite the *realpolitik* argument that in a divided America two separate republics could serve as counterweights to one another and keep each other in check.[84] It is certainly true that this argument existed; it had adherents by early 1861, being advanced by the Liberal Edward Bulwer-Lytton in September and given further support by the *Trent* affair.[85] Bulwer-Lytton's

---

[80] Ibid. 21 Mar. 1863, 295.
[81] *Saturday Review*, 24 May 1862, 575–6. My own reading of the national press largely tallies with the journal's suggestion.
[82] Quoted in *Reynolds's Weekly*, 20 Apr. 1862, 4.
[83] See McPherson, *Battle cry of freedom*, 53.
[84] See Keiser, 'The English press and the American Civil War', passim, esp. ch. iv; Jordan and Pratt, *Europe and the American Civil War*, xi.
[85] Bulwer-Lytton's speech was commented upon by the *Spectator*, 28 Sept. 1861, 1058.

realpolitik approach was derived entirely from his experience of American territorial ambitions; he had led the British delegation during the tortuous negotiations of the 1850 Clayton–Bulwer Treaty that determined the Canada–United States boundary.[86] Although some journals such as *The Economist* considered *realpolitik* arguments, *realpolitik* beliefs were never as widespread as has often been argued, largely because there were a number of competing notions.[87] The *realpolitik* argument was based on the premise that the two American republics would be at permanent loggerheads – a leap of faith not everyone would take. For instance, the *Saturday Review* and the *Illustrated London News* both believed that an independent Confederacy would probably re-join the Union at some point.[88]

Another scenario which suggested itself and which was at least as prominent as *realpolitik* was that, once the two combatants made peace, there was nothing to stop the Union from expanding northwards into Canada (remembering northern suggestions that territory lost to the South be made up with Britain's largest colony) and the Confederacy from expanding southwards into Mexico and Central America, to say nothing of resurrecting the slave trade. Certainly, this was the fear Cairnes played upon in his anti-southern work *The Slave Power*, wherein he predicted that an independent Confederacy would follow exactly both these courses.[89] Southern independence, then, could very well place Britain in the nightmare scenario of fighting two outraged nations at the same time. As Crook has established, Gladstone viewed matters in precisely this light.[90] The northern sympathiser (and one of the very few observers who constantly correctly predicted the conquest of the South), Edward Dicey, argued in a similar vein when he wrote that a Union victory was in Britain's interests because the North would be too preoccupied holding the South to contemplate war against Britain.[91] The unwritten assumption was, of course, that a thwarted Union might drive northwards to wipe out the anguish of defeat.

Dicey's argument underpinned the only *realpolitik*-type argument that offered Britain future peace, that the two sides would permanently disable each other. This, however, smacked of desperation. None the less, it had

---

[86] Bulwer-Lytton remarked, 'The United States Government is honorable, just and prudent; it is not likely to originate a war of ambitious or aggressive character, but the people who live under this government are of a wild, adventurous and conquering character.' Quoted in Allen, *Great Britain and the United States*, 418. Bulwer-Lytton's attitudes to America were thus shaped by its imperialism rather than any anti-democratic reasons. Indeed, in 1832, as a Liberal MP, he had reformed himself out of a seat.
[87] *The Economist*, 15 Feb. 1862, 171.
[88] *Saturday Review*, 19 Apr. 1862, 401; 31 Jan. 1863, 132; *Illustrated London News*, 22 Aug. 1863, 181.
[89] Cairnes first announced this idea in *The Economist*: 8 Feb. 1862, 145–6; 1 Mar. 1862, 231–2.
[90] Crook, *The North, the South and the powers*, 228.
[91] *Macmillan's Magazine* (Sept. 1862), 419.

adherents. In a letter to Benjamin in the final days of the Confederacy, Mason noted, 'a tacit consideration in the English mind that the longer the war lasted in America, the better for them, because of the consequent exhaustion of both parties'.[92] Only individuals who distrusted both North and South alike, of course, would hold such 'a tacit consideration'.

British travel and propaganda literature

English opinion was divided even in the field of pamphlet literature on the war. Although the sheer number of publications precludes any full-scale study here, it is worth looking at a number of examples. It is interesting to note that, despite the war and the blockade, a fair number of British subjects none the less entered the Confederacy and published their impressions of it. Such travellers sometimes went North too, and commented on the Union as well.[93] The works of British travellers are varied in tone. John Francis Campbell's *A short American tramp in the fall of 1864* (1865) was a highly flippant work, even regarding slavery.[94] Although Campbell was generally kind to both sides, he declared that both 'were darned fools for fighting' the war.

A more serious work was the businessman William Carson Corsan's *Two months in the Confederate States* (1863) that is still cited by Civil War historians for its observations.[95] Corsan actually visited the Confederacy to determine whether or not the pre-war debts owed by Southerners to English and foreign merchants would eventually be repaid. Corsan was a Sheffield native, and his cutlery company, Corsan, Dentin and Burdekin, which had exported a third of its produce to America, had been hit hard by the Morrill tariff and the blockade of its former customers.[96] Corsan was generally sympathetic to the Confederacy and doubted that it could be conquered, so united was it in its efforts to remain independent. As Corsan remarked, 'No language, however, could convey an adequate idea of the loathing with which the Yankee was regarded, and that, too without regard to age, sex or condition.' Despite his business interests and his general respect for the South,

---

[92] Mason to Benjamin, 31 Mar. 1865, in *The messages and papers of Jefferson Davis*, ii. 710. The earl of Clarendon held this view, arguing that as long as the Americans were fighting each other, they were not fighting Britain. See Jenkins, *Britain and the war for the Union*, ii. 64.
[93] See E. Merton Coulter, *Travels in the Confederate States: a bibliography*, Oklahoma 1948; Baton Rouge 1994.
[94] John Francis Campbell, *A short American tramp in the fall of 1864*, by the editor of 'Life in Normandy', Edinburgh 1865.
[95] William Carson Corsan, *Two months in the Confederate States: including a visit to New Orleans under the domination of General Butler by an English merchant*, London 1863.
[96] Benjamin H. Trask, Introduction, *Two months in the Confederate States: an Englishman's travels through the South*, by William Carson Corsan, Baton Rouge 1996. This edition of Corsan's work uses the book's American title instead of the British one.

Corsan none the less remained unimpressed with slavery. Although he stated that the institution was not as bad as it had been made out to be, he also insisted, 'There is nothing, however, either less or more offensive in the business than there used to be; it is a hateful trade, and one which I hope the South herself will soon stop.'[97] Considering how important the South was to his business interests, Corsan could scarcely be expected not to feel some affection towards it. Napoleon Bonaparte's description of the English as a nation of shopkeepers has hardly been more apt. This, however, should again remind us just how significant an impact the Morrill tariff and the blockade had on many English businesses. Certainly Sheffield suffered. As we shall see, it was a stronghold of Confederate sympathy in the war and its member of parliament, the radical John Arthur Roebuck, was one of the leading southern supporters in the House of Commons.

Another important publication was Lieutenant-Colonel Arthur James Lyon Fremantle's *Three months in the Southern States, April–June 1863* (1863). Like Corsan's, this is another work regularly cited by Civil War scholars.[98] Fremantle was initially a pro-northerner because of slavery, until he met the Confederate Captain Raphael Semmes of the CSS *Sumter* at Gibraltar, where the lieutenant-colonel was then stationed. Fremantle was a strong southern supporter after that, and became an even stronger one after he visited the Confederacy.[99] Fremantle's account is predominantly famous because of the friendships he struck up with leading Confederate generals such as James Longstreet and Robert E. Lee, and because he witnessed the Battle of Gettysburg. Indeed, his presence at the battle has recently been immortalised in the film *Gettysburg*.[100] Despite the strong friendships he developed (and continued after the war), making him probably the most popular Briton to visit the Confederacy, Fremantle's account is no hagiography of the South. Although he believed the Confederacy would preserve its independence, he did not fail to record some uncomplimentary observations, including some on slavery. Fremantle attended a slave auction, 'certainly not a very agreeable spectacle to an Englishman', and admitted that 'complete emancipation cannot be expected'. Unfortunately for the Union, though, Fremantle was also present to witness the draft riots in New York, which resulted in attacks on, and lynchings of, African Americans.

> I saw a negro pursued by the crowd and take refuge with the military; he was followed by loud cries of 'Down with the b—y nigger! Kill all niggers!' &c. Never having been in New York before, and being totally ignorant of the state of feeling with regard to negroes, I inquired of a bystander what the negroes

---

[97] Ibid. 16, 85.
[98] Fremantle, *Three months in the southern states*.
[99] Gary W. Gallagher, Introduction, *Three months in the southern states*, p. viii.
[100] *Gettysburg*, Turner Pictures 1993, directed by Ronald F. Maxwell.

had done that they should want to kill them? He replied civilly enough – 'Oh sir, they hate them here; they are the innocent cause of all these troubles.'[101]

Fremantle's account confirmed a number of English suspicions. Despite his sympathy for the Confederacy, Fremantle could not deny that the South was determined to retain the institution of slavery. It was embedded in the culture. Further, despite his picture of Confederate bravery, Fremantle's depiction of the South (particularly Texas) as a place of bad roads, poor facilities and so forth ensured that its backward image was retained. The assaults on African Americans in the North, however, convinced many in England that the Union was insincere on the subject of emancipation. Clearly Northerners hated their black fellow-citizens too much to fight for their liberty.

Another account worth noting is Catherine Cooper Hopley's *Life in the South: from the commencement of the war, by a blockaded British subject* (1863), which was published under the pseudonym Sarah L. Jones.[102] Hopley's work has been unfairly neglected. She was an English schoolteacher who went to America to visit relatives in Indiana and moved south to teach in 1860. Hopley taught in Virginia and Fredericksburg before moving to Florida to teach the family of the governor of that state. She met numerous leading Confederates, including Lee, but, to her credit, Hopley remained neutral in sentiment. Although she opposed slavery, Hopley also declared that it was not as bad as it had been portrayed. Further, Hopley cited examples of northern opposition to emancipation. On one occasion, she quoted a Union officer she met:

> We don't really want to interfere with slavery, it isn't *that* we care so much about; but it's this thing of having the Union broken up: we can't allow *that*. I have been in the South myself, and I don't find so much fault with slavery; but you see the niggers stay at home and work while all the white men go and fight. Now if it were not for them, their masters would be obliged to stay at home and cultivate their own land, as our men do, or starve, and that would so reduce their army that there would be no chance for them. That's what our government is up to.[103]

This excerpt was published in the *New Monthly Magazine*, where it attracted the ire of the journalist and former editor of the magazine, Cyrus Redding, who condemned Hopley's 'superficial' analysis of both the South and the war itself.[104] Despite her commendable neutrality, Hopley's citation of Union

---

[101] Fremantle, *Three months in the southern states*, 300.
[102] Catherine Cooper Hopley, *Life in the South. From the commencement of the war. By a blockaded British subject. Being a social history of those who took part in the battles from a personal acquaintance with them in their homes. From the spring of 1860 to August 1862*, London 1863.
[103] *New Monthly Magazine* (May 1863), 15 [Hopley's italics]. The same issue of the magazine contained a pro-northern piece, 'Story of a Union spy'. Once again, we see a variety of opinions on the war in English journals.
[104] Ibid. (Aug. 1863), 438–9.

hostility to emancipation – such as that quoted above – doubtless confirmed the widespread English belief of northern insincerity on the subject.

There were, of course, works written by Britons who went to the South and defended every aspect of its culture, including slavery. One example is Samuel Phillips Day's *Down South: or, an Englishman's experience at the seat of the American war* (1862).[105] Day was a journalist on the pro-southern *Morning Herald* and spent most of his time in Richmond. Besides slavery, Day defended the habit of chewing tobacco – a serious social *faux pas* as far as the English were concerned, who regarded it as a barbaric habit. Day's strident southern partisanship, especially the open defence of slavery, was unusual, if not unique. His was probably the most blatantly pro-Confederate work of all the English publications.

Edward James Stephen Dicey held a view entirely opposite to Day's in his book *Six months in the federal states* (1863).[106] Dicey, whom we have already encountered, began his career with the *Daily Telegraph*, but by the time of the Civil War was a special correspondent for *Macmillan's Magazine* and the *Spectator* – two journals which, if not pro-North, were certainly far more sympathetic to it than to the Confederacy. Some portions of Dicey's work appeared in these publications. Dicey was an implacable foe of slavery and the South. Although Dicey never actually visited the Confederacy, he visited portions of the border states and parts of the South under Union occupation. The South, in Dicey's eyes, was backward, riddled with dirt and decay, its inhabitants a much lower species of man than those found in the North. Dicey was no uncritical admirer of the Union or American government – he believed the elections were hopelessly corrupt – but he certainly sympathised with the cause. What made Dicey particularly unusual, however, was that he was one of the only Englishmen who not only predicted that the North would win the war, but that it would be able to re-absorb the South back into the Union. Not even Bright was ever as confident as Dicey.

The comparison between Dicey and Day is important to note in so far as that for every pro-Confederate publication, there was a northern sympathiser's reply. Thus, works like the former Conservative member of parliament Alexander James Beresford Hope's *The American disruption* (1863), and Lord Robert Montagu's *A mirror on America* (1861), have to be paired off against Anthony Trollope's *North America* (1862) and William Howard Russell's *My diary, North and South* (1863).[107] Although neither Trollope nor Russell believed the Union could conquer the Confederacy (though Trollope

---

105 Samuel Phillips Day, *Down South: or, an Englishman's experience at the seat of the American war*, London 1862.
106 Edward James Stephen Dicey, *Six months in the federal states*, London 1863.
107 See A. J. Beresford Hope, *The social and political bearings of the American disruption*, London 1863; Robert Montagu, *A mirror on America*, London 1861. Beresford Hope's pamphlet was originally delivered as a talk at a mechanic's institute.

did not rule it out completely), both authors supported the North's attempts to suppress the South.[108]

Russell's account was influential. He was the respected journalist of *The Times* whose reports on the Crimean War exposed the incompetence of that campaign. Russell actually managed to offend both the North and the South with this book. Southerners were outraged by his hatred of slavery and those who sought to defend it, while Northerners were angered by his account of their defeat at the first Battle of Bull Run and uncomplimentary descriptions of their mannerisms. It is fair to say that, like his homeland, Russell managed to get himself despised by both sides in the conflict.

Trollope's account was far friendlier towards the Union and its citizens, and it had to be, for he wrote his book with the reputation of his mother Frances Trollope's caustic *Domestic manners of the Americans* (1832) hanging about his neck. Trollope's account of the North and its people was reasonably fair. An opponent of both secession and slavery, Trollope defended the Union's attempt to subjugate the Confederacy and wrote that if they were to

> succeed in rescuing from the South and from slavery four or five of the finest states of the old Union, – a vast continent, to be beaten by none other in salubrity, fertility, beauty and political importance, – will it not be admitted that the war has done some good, and that the life and treasure have not been spent in vain?[109]

Although Trollope did not actually visit the Confederacy, this did not stop him from portraying the South as backward and uncivilised, unlike the Union. At the time he wrote *North America*, Trollope was at the height of his powers as a novelist and had a huge readership. Indeed, *North America* outsold *Barchester Towers*. Clearly, some in England believed him to be a better travel-writer than novelist.

One work which cannot be neglected is Frances 'Fanny' Anne Kemble's *Journal of a residence on a Georgia plantation in 1838–1839* (1863).[110] Fanny Kemble came from a family of actors – her aunt being the legendary Sarah Siddons.[111] She clearly inherited her aunt's talent, for she became a star of the English stage in the 1830s. In 1834, on a tour of America, she met and married Pierce Butler, the second-largest slave owner in the state of Georgia. Kemble came from an anti-slavery family, so why she married Butler is a question that not even her latest biographer can satisfactorily answer. If her anti-slavery sentiment had been dormant, it was swiftly re-awakened when

---

[108] William Howard Russell, *My diary, north and south*, London 1863; Anthony Trollope, *North America*, London 1862.
[109] Trollope, *North America*, 520.
[110] Frances Anne Kemble, *Journal of a residence on a Georgia plantation in 1838–1839*, London 1863.
[111] See Catherine Clinton, *Fanny Kemble's civil wars: the story of America's most unlikely abolitionist*, New York 2000, 9.

she moved to Butler's plantation. Horrified by the institution, she published, in 1835, *Journal of residence in America*, which, among other things, attacked slavery in no uncertain terms.[112] The marriage, predictably enough, did not last and, after separating from her husband she returned to the English stage in the 1840s, only to return to America to engage in a particularly scandalous (and very public) divorce. By any stretch of the imagination, Kemble was a celebrity. Despite the notoriety caused by her divorce, she remained accepted in many social circles in England and was friendly with such luminaries as Harriet Martineau, Robert and Elizabeth Browning and William Thackeray. She cut quite a figure in both the United States and Britain.

Kemble was in America when the war broke out and was an ardent supporter of the Union. As one observer remarked, 'She is very enthusiastic about the war & predicts from it the destruction of slavery.'[113] Visiting England during the war, Kemble was surprised by the lack of support for the North and, after the Emancipation Proclamation was passed, she published her *Journal of a residence on a Georgia plantation*. This work was far stronger than her previous one, no doubt because she was now divorced from Butler. Reviewers praised the book and excerpts from it were read out by speakers at anti-slavery gatherings as well as by pro-northern politicians in the House of Commons.[114] Kemble's description of the squalor, the abuse and the inhumanity of slavery was probably timely. Perhaps the best tribute to the book was paid by the allegedly pro-southern *Athenaeum*: 'A more startling and fearful narrative on a well-worn subject was never laid before readers.' Of the Southerners themselves, the journal remarked,

> For many a long day we have heard enough, and rather more than enough, about the chivalry of Southern gentlemen, the moral and physical graces of Southern women, the patriarchal character of the peculiar institution, the devotion of slaves to their masters, the tenderness of overseers who with aching hearts flog their blackies mercifully, just as mothers whip their children, to do them good, and make them upright members of society.[115]

Kemble's book pulled no punches. She frankly described slaves being flogged and women being forced to labour in the late periods of their pregnancies. She described duelling (her husband fought one), depicted southern men as inveterate gamblers and also noted that masters raped their slaves. Undoubtedly the fact that Kemble had an insider's view of the South ensured the credibility of the book. Unquestionably the fact that she was such a celebrity ensured that it received the attention it was due. Kemble's work added to English perceptions of a backward and depraved South. How effective it was in improving the image of the Union may be questioned, but it unquestion-

---

112 Frances Anne Kemble, *Journal of residence in America*, London 1835.
113 Clinton, *Fanny Kemble's civil wars*, 176.
114 J. C. Furnas, *Fanny Kemble: leading lady of the nineteenth century*, New York 1982, 403.
115 *Athenaeum*, 6 June 1863, 737.

ably damaged the standing of the Confederacy in England. It is probably fair to say that no Southerner made a worse marriage than did Pierce Butler.

The two propaganda works that must be examined are James Spence's pro-southern *The American union*, and J. E. Cairnes's anti-Confederate *The slave power*. Spence's work, published in 1861, followed the course of most pro-southern propaganda and argued that the Confederacy was fighting for self-determination and that the American constitution condoned secession.[116] Like all southern apologists, he dismissed the issue of slavery as having little importance. Spence has often been cited as influential, but this has been difficult to substantiate.[117] The *Saturday Review* indeed acknowledged that 'he is likely to succeed with English readers, because all his views are taken from a thoroughly English standpoint', but this was because it regarded Spence's as the first acceptable pro-southern work, its predecessors, mostly written by Southerners, being too blatantly enamoured with Confederate institutions such as slavery. Nor was the *Saturday Review* particularly ecstatic in its review, criticising several of Spence's main arguments: 'we are decidedly of the opinion that Mr. Spence fails, in spite of much ingenuity, in making good any legal justification for the revolt'.[118] Furthermore, when Spence published another, more aggressively pro-southern work in 1862, the journal dismissed it.[119]

The *Athenaeum* toed a similar line when it reviewed *The American union*:

> Although Mr. Spence takes the right side of the main questions raised in his book, and arranges with lucidity and force the arguments which establish the existence of a constitutional right to secede in the states of the American Union, he commits some errors of judgment, employs some unsound reasoning, and consequently we are unable to award to this volume as a whole, the praise which is due to it in certain parts.[120]

The *Athenaeum*, like the *Saturday Review*, was unimpressed with Spence's second publication, remarking, '[It] has all the faults and none of the merits of his more ambitious essay in "The American Union." '[121] Considering that these two journals have traditionally been classified by historians as 'pro-southern', a modicum of support for the leading Confederate propaganda

---

[116] James Spence, *The American union; its effects on national character and policy with an inquiry into secession as a constitutional right and the cause of the disruption*, London 1861.
[117] Ibid. ch. iv, 'The slavery question', passim. For the debate surrounding Spence's work see Owsley, *King Cotton diplomacy*, 172–4; Keiser, 'The English press and the American Civil War', 178–9; Jordan and Pratt, *Europe and the American Civil War*, 75–6. All of these historians state that Spence was influential, but all fail to provide evidence to support this statement. Certainly, members of parliament and London journals rarely repeated his ideas.
[118] *Saturday Review*, 16 Nov. 1861, 515.
[119] Ibid. 9 Aug. 1862, 150.
[120] *Athenaeum*, 23 Nov. 1861, 685.
[121] Ibid. 23 Aug. 1862, 232–3.

work would have been expected. Thus, contrary to what some historians have asserted, Spence's arguments were not accepted without reservation.[122]

Cairnes's work, meanwhile, followed the course of most pro-Union propaganda and argued that slavery was the sole issue at stake in the war.[123] Cairnes, however, put forward a pseudo-scientific argument that slavery, by nature, was not only inefficient, but actually exhausted the soil where it existed. A society based on slavery, Cairnes argued, was thus inevitably naturally expansionist because it had to continually conquer new territory in order to remain productive. Cairnes concluded by warning that a strong and independent South would be a menace to the world.

Cairnes was unquestionably Spence's rival. Spence's work may have sold more copies, but he had the advantage of publishing his work in 1861, before the market began to become saturated with books on America. None the less, despite what some historians have claimed, Cairnes was unquestionably influential.[124] After reviewing Cairnes, the *Westminster Review* changed from an anti-Union to an anti-Confederate stance, and *Fraser's Magazine*, meanwhile, largely abandoned its southern sympathies.[125] *The Economist* favoured Cairnes over Spence, praising the former for his attacks on the latter's 'sophistries'.[126] The *British Quarterly Review* meanwhile, in 1864, argued that the Confederacy wished to 'diffuse' slavery – something it had denied in 1863.[127] This was too close to Cairnes's arguments to easily deny any influence.

Changing the views of at least four major nineteenth-century journals was no mean feat and at least one historian has stated, 'probably no book exercised more influence in educating and shaping British public opinion on the American Civil War'.[128] Certainly, Cairnes's book provided Union sympathisers with a well-argued (if partisan) case against the South, and many of his ideas were repeated at anti-slavery and pro-northern meetings. Cairnes, then, must be held to be at least as influential as Spence, and probably more so.

Race, slavery and emancipation

The subjects of slavery and emancipation were, of course, the focus of much of the debate on America. Commentators, both neutral and anti-North, were highly critical of the Union's emancipation policy and suspicious of the

---

[122] See, for example, Keiser, 'The English press and the American Civil War', 179.
[123] John Elliot Cairnes, *The slave power, its character, career and probable designs*, 2nd edn, London 1863.
[124] Keiser, 'The English press and the American Civil War', 178.
[125] The *Westminster Review*'s career is discussed in ch. 5 below, *Fraser's* in ch. 4.
[126] *The Economist*, 14 June 1862, 651.
[127] *British Quarterly Review* (July 1863), 222; (Jan. 1864), 243.
[128] Adelaide Weinberg, *John Elliot Cairnes and the American Civil War: a study in Anglo-American relations*, London n.d. [circa 1970], 3.

Lincoln administration's plans for the blacks. Commentators sympathetic to the North, meanwhile, although less critical on this score, expressed reservations none the less. Despite this criticism of the Union, slavery remained the millstone around the neck of the Confederacy. Although northern supporters and activists always tried, with mixed success, to exploit this weakness, they were, in large part, hampered by the Union's often-dubious stance on emancipation. This suspicion surrounding the North's dedication to abolitionism was what damaged Lincoln's Emancipation Proclamation, but it was, none the less, better received in England than some historians have argued, and news of its arrival caused irretrievable damage to southern sympathy.

Just as it is crucial to note the divergence between British and American opinion on racial issues, it is important to note that the former's thinking on the subject was undergoing a change by the late 1850s and early 1860s.[129] Although more racially tolerant than Americans, generally, by 1860 at least, English attitudes towards blacks were changing from an ethnocentric to a racist position. Earlier, the English view on race had been that non-whites needed to be 'brought up', as they saw it, to the level of western civilisation. This, 'the civilizational perspective' as Peter Mandler terms it, remained the dominant view throughout our period.[130] By the time of the Civil War, however, it was under increasing pressure from another school of thought that claimed that blacks were congenitally inferior to whites and forever in need of white guidance. The reasons for the appearance of this new school of thought can be blamed on social Darwinism which developed from the debates surrounding evolution, which placed blacks below whites on an evolutionary scale. Members of this school of thought cited the economic decline of the West Indies as proof that blacks were innately lazy. Thomas Carlyle, for example, expressed this argument in his essay, 'Occasional discourse on the negro question', where he effectively called for a form of state-run slavery to increase productivity amongst black workers in Jamaica.[131] Blacks' erstwhile supporters may also have done damage, too. Harriet Beecher Stowe depicted African Americans in *Uncle Tom's Cabin* (1852) as more simple, more docile and more childlike than whites – an important consideration in light of the popularity of the novel in England.[132] Certainly, as Christine Bolt points out, the anti-slavery forces in Britain were

---

[129] The two historians who have most closely examined these issues, Christine Bolt and Douglas Lorimer, disagree over precisely when these changes began. Bolt argues for the 1850s, Lorimer for the 1860s. I would argue for 1859 with the publication of Charles Darwin's *On the origin of species*, but see Christine Bolt, *Victorian attitudes to race*, London 1971, p. xi, and Lorimer, *Colour, class and the Victorians*, 60.
[130] Mandler, 'Race and nation'.
[131] Thomas Carlyle, 'Occasional discourse on the negro question', in *Fraser's Magazine* (Jan. 1850).
[132] Lorimer, *Colour, class and the Victorians*, 16, 120–5, 142–7.

on the wane.[133] All of this probably militated against, at least to a certain extent, stronger condemnation of the Confederacy.

None the less, the change was not yet as profound as some historians have argued.[134] The challenge to the civilisational perspective was only beginning to gain ground during 1861–5, and ideas usually take time before they become widespread. For example, J. M. Ludlow claimed that the Indian Mutiny meant India needed to be made 'more English', not less. A. H. Layard held a similar view.[135] Throughout the conflict, Britain still remained more racially tolerant than America. Most historians cite the Jamaica Insurrection in 1865 as the major turning point in English racial attitudes, and this did not occur until after Lee's surrender at Appomattox earlier in the same year.[136] Although Bolt argues that English criticism of American racism was, in reality, an attack on the latter's institutions as a whole, there is no evidence for this.[137] Indeed, even during the 1860s, black Americans such as Frederick Douglass still described Britain as a haven from racial prejudice compared to America, lending credence to English criticism.[138] Further, leading spokesmen for the increasing racism such as James Hunt always had more opponents than supporters, despite the fact that Hunt always took care to distance his beliefs from those of American racists.[139] In fact, when Hunt informed a meeting in 1863 that blacks were inferior to whites he was booed and jeered.[140] Lorimer also points out that Dr Robert Knox, identified by some historians as something of a founding father of modern racism, 'saw himself as an outsider, advancing an unpopular but none the less truthful case' during the 1860s.[141] It was only later in the nineteenth century that his opinions came into wider currency. Carlyle meanwhile, who re-titled his paper 'Occasional discourse on the nigger question' in 1853 (and it has been called this ever since), was always something of an intellectual maverick. Contrary to what some historians have claimed, the word 'nigger' did not enjoy popular usage after Carlyle's pamphlet or, indeed, after the Indian Mutiny – English journals throughout the Civil War used the word only in quotation marks and only in reference to the American usage. Carlyle, and his noxious views, definitely became prominent when he formed the committee to defend Governor Edward Eyre who had brutally suppressed the

---

[133] Bolt, *Victorian attitudes to race*, 30.
[134] See Jenkins, *Britain and the war for the Union*, ii. 155–8. Jenkins overstates the shift in attitudes.
[135] Taylor, *The decline of British radicalism*, 269.
[136] See Bolt, *Victorian attitudes to race*, ch. iii passim; Lorimer, *Colour, class and the Victorians*, ch. ix passim.
[137] Bolt, *Victorian attitudes to race*, 31.
[138] Lorimer, *Colour, class and the Victorians*, 30–9, 46–7.
[139] Bolt, *Victorian attitudes to race*, 6, 19.
[140] Lorimer, *Colour, class and the Victorians*, 138.
[141] Idem, 'Race, science and culture: historical continuities and discontinuities, 1850–1914', in Shearer West (ed.), *The Victorians and race*, Aldershot 1996, 12–33, 15.

Jamaican rebellion, but that, again, was after the Civil War.[142] Certainly, the Confederate agent, Edward C. Anderson, stationed in England in 1862, confessed his surprise to see a black man being 'on perfectly equal terms' with the gentlemen around him.[143] Even after the Jamaican uprising, the British still appeared to be more tolerant; as late as 1868 James Horton regarded racism as an American, not British, problem.[144] It is also interesting to note that, as R. J. M. Blackett has established, black abolitionists who spoke at public meetings during our period were often challenged by members of the audience to explain why they championed a government that discriminated against them.[145]

It should also be remembered that just because the anti-slavery forces in England were less active, this does not mean that slavery was an acceptable institution. It is true that *The Times* made a half-hearted attempt to defend slavery in one of the paper's more violent anti-Union tirades, but it received no support from the rest of the press establishment, and most journals, even anti-northern ones, denounced the institution.[146] Historians sympathetic to the Confederacy have noted how even English southern spokesmen, such as James Spence, always took care to denounce slavery. Indeed, Spence, in the end, made too many predictions about the abolition of slavery for Richmond, which, in December 1863, dispensed with his services.[147] Thus, by any consistent measurement, slavery remained repugnant to English morality, as shown by the obstacle Lincoln's Emancipation Proclamation proved to be to southern sympathies.

Essentially then, by the 1860s, although Britain was beginning to emulate American views on race (something forgotten by historians citing the influence of American progressivism), the changes were still under way and the decisive incident, the Jamaica Insurrection, was yet to occur. British racism was still less virulent than the American version, and this difference in viewpoints greatly shaped English thinking about both the Union and the Confederacy.

There was a great deal of suspicion regarding the Union's plans for the emancipated slaves; particular controversy surrounded Lincoln's dabbling in deportation to Liberia or elsewhere. Notions of deporting freed blacks to

---

142 For a recent discussion on Carlyle's involvement in the Eyre Defence Committee see Catherine Hall, *White, male and middle-class: explorations in feminism and history*, Cambridge 1992, ch. x, 'Competing masculinities: Thomas Carlyle, John Stuart Mill and the case of Governor Eyre'.
143 Anderson, *Confederate foreign agent*, 27.
144 Lorimer, *Colour, class and the Victorians*, 62.
145 Blackett, 'Pressure from without', 90.
146 Jordan and Pratt, *Europe and the American Civil War*, 132, 155. Jordan and Pratt concede that the article 'did not go very far' and fail to note not only the opposition it engendered from other publications, but also the regular denunciations made against slavery by anti-northern journals. Further, despite their claims, the *Saturday Review* never supported slavery. It is on these untenable grounds that Jordan and Pratt base their assertion that the British began to regard slavery as an acceptable institution.
147 Owsley, *King Cotton diplomacy*, 383–4.

Africa (it was called 'colonisation' in America) had a sizeable following in the North prior to (and indeed during) the conflict. Although completely impracticable, Lincoln was certainly in favour of the idea. As Donald notes, 'Though reality sometimes broke in, Lincoln persisted in his colonisation fantasy until well into his presidency.'[148] Indeed, in late 1862, Adams actually sounded Russell out on whether or not the Union could ship freed slaves to the West Indies.[149]

Most English commentators opposed the idea of forcible deportation. Once more, those who distrusted or disliked the Union, such as the *Saturday Review*, were the most vociferous in denouncing the 'impracticable project of removing the coloured population from American soil'.[150] However, even the *Spectator* was critical and remarked, 'the negroes are Americans, and entitled to remain in the country to which their fathers were brought'.[151] The *Athenaeum*, meanwhile, remarked that if Lincoln endorsed views of repatriation, 'his right to the title of "Honest old Abe" will rest on disputable grounds'.[152]

Reports of northern distaste for both emancipation and blacks were a regular feature of the English press. As the *Saturday Review* asked in early 1862, 'Could four million newly enfranchised negroes live in the same States as fellow-citizens with men who will not sit at the same table, nor kneel at the same aisle, nor ride in the same "car" with free negroes whose liberty dates two generations back?'[153] The *Athenaeum*, which sympathised with the southern claim that secession was legal under the American constitution, defended the lack of English support for the Union by stating, 'We stand aloof from this conflict because (apart from considerations which arise from the moral questions at issue between the North and the South) we do not see our way to any good resulting to the negro from this unhappy war.'[154] This was not only the view of the Union's opponents. In 1862, the *Spectator* published a letter it had received from a travelling reader who remarked: 'With regard to the abolition of slavery, it seems to me to be still popularly regarded as a possible eventuality rather than a probability, as, in fact, a last resource to be adopted if all other measures fail for the subjugation of the South; but not till then.'[155] In that same year, *Macmillan's* pro-Union correspondent Edward

---

[148] For a discussion on the northern arguments for colonisation (or repatriation, as it was sometimes called) see Donald, *Lincoln*, 166–7.
[149] *Illustrated London News*, 10 Jan. 1863, 34.
[150] *Saturday Review*, 20 Dec. 1862, 726.
[151] *Spectator*, 28 Dec. 1861, 1418. Lest one be accused of giving an exaggerated view of English mid-nineteenth-century thinking on race, one should report that the journal argued the blacks should live in Florida on the grounds that the climate would be more appropriate to them than whites.
[152] *Athenaeum*, 2 Mar. 1861, 288.
[153] *Saturday Review*, 4 Jan. 1862, 6.
[154] *Athenaeum*, 17 Jan. 1863, 79.
[155] *Spectator*, 22 Feb. 1862, 212.

Dicey cited numerous Northerners making comments such as, 'We do not claim to be carrying on a war of emancipation. We are not fighting for the blacks, but for the whites. . . . The object of the war is to preserve the Union.'[156] Dicey tried to justify this by writing that just as the empire was a source of pride to the English, so too was the Union to Americans. In other words, as a liberal, he used a typically conservative defence against secession. As late as 1864, the *Saturday Review* was able to report, 'General Sherman adds that, in his opinion, the negro is neither equal to the white man, nor fit for military purpose.'[157] The *Spectator*, although it argued that English criticism of the Union's view of emancipation was unfair, made certain to note,

> We do *not* maintain that the mass of Northerners have any elevated views on the question of slavery. We do *not* assert that the mass have any sympathy at all with the blacks. We have scarcely a doubt that if the Northerns could get rid of the question by selling the whole black population to Brazil, they would accept that evil solution without hesitation.[158]

English suspicion was not merely owing to America's past history, but also to the anti-black riots that occurred in New York, and elsewhere in the Union. The riots were publicised in the English press, particularly in *The Times*, as well as in Fremantle's book, and their occurrence did little to help those who argued that the war would lead to the emancipation of the slaves.[159] Unquestionably the fact that the English first received accounts of events in America from the New York press had a profound impact upon this question. None the less, New York cannot be held wholly responsible. After all, there was very little sympathy for emancipation amongst the ranks of the northern army, as McPherson has noted.[160]

In any case, as Lincoln spent most of 1862 publicly denying any intention of interfering with slavery, it is unsurprising that the English press took him at his word:

> the President's candid declaration to Mr. [Horace] Greeley that this is not an anti-slavery war, but that, on the contrary, Mr. Lincoln is ready and anxious to place the slave system on a basis most acceptable to the South, if only the Union can be preserved, has drawn angry comment from his friends in America and in England, and not unnaturally, for he has cut away the only ground upon which Englishmen could be asked to take an interest in the success of the North.[161]

It is no coincidence that 1862 was the height of anti-northern sentiment (and, in some cases, height of Confederate sympathy) in England. The *Trent*

---

[156] *Macmillan's Magazine* (July 1862), 410.
[157] *Saturday Review*, 10 Sept. 1864, 322.
[158] *Spectator*, 21 Dec. 1861, 1389 [their italics]. At this point, slavery was legal in Brazil.
[159] *The Times*, 'The riots in New York', 28 July 1863, 12.
[160] See McPherson, *Battle cry of freedom*, 497–8.
[161] *Illustrated London News*, 18 Sept. 1862, 282.

affair and Lincoln's vacillation on slavery cost the Union dearly in the court of English public opinion.[162]

None the less, the South's adherence to slavery cost it still more especially after the Emancipation Proclamation. When France proposed joint mediation in 1862, Palmerston refused, citing the fact that the cabinet and the Confederacy could not reconcile their deep differences on slavery.[163] The impact of southern slavery certainly worried the Confederate propagandist Henry Hotze, who, noting the anti-slavery rallies in 1863, reported to Richmond:

> Great efforts have been made to arouse the anti slavery feeling of the country by emancipation meetings, but so far with remarkably little success. The largest of these meetings, Exeter Hall, was indeed numerously attended, but not a single one of the well-known names of the emancipationist school was among the number. . . . But although the agitators have failed, there is always a latent danger in the agitation of this subject; and of this public men are aware, which may account in part for the timidity of their American policy.[164]

The reason Hotze feared agitation on the slavery issue was obvious: most individuals in England hated the institution. The *British Quarterly Review* remarked in 1863,

> We reject utterly the doctrine of Negro inferiority, as it is taught by the deliberate apologists of slavery. With one of the most famous and also infamous passage of Mr. Stephens' speech, delivered at a time of extreme excitement more than two years since, it is surely unnecessary to say we have nothing in common. It appears to us to be a damnable heresy, a most selfish and cruel lie.[165]

As *The Economist* noted, 'We fear little can be said for the kindness of the anti-slavery North to her black children, but at least she leaves them liberty.'[166] Even the allegedly pro-southern *Saturday Review* noted in 1862, 'The military vigour and fortitude of the South has been fully appreciated; but, as long as the Confederate cause is identified with slavery, it will never obtain perfect sympathy in Europe.' The journal again remarked in 1864, 'The Confederates would have earned by their unequalled heroism the sympathy of the world, if their cause had not been identified with an intolerable evil.'[167] Nor did the journal accept the argument some historians have portrayed as a widespread belief in Britain, that the South would have to free their slaves even if they won their independence. 'What may be the result to

---

162 Even staunch Union supporters such as Harriet Martineau denounced Lincoln's vacillation on emancipation: Adams, *Great Britain and the American Civil War*, ii. 79.
163 Palmerston to Russell, 26 Oct. 1862. Russell papers, Public Record Office, Kew, 30/22/14.
164 Hotze to Benjamin, 14 Feb. 1863, in *The messages and papers of Jefferson Davis*, ii. 434.
165 *British Quarterly Review* (July 1863), 224.
166 *The Economist*, 31 May 1862, 594.
167 *Saturday Review*, 6 Sept. 1862, 265; 12 Nov. 1864, 584.

the slaves when the Confederates finally become a recognised independent State, it were vain to speculate. We cannot say we look for any great alteration in the national or State laws respecting slavery from any merely political changes.'[168]

Indeed, the more apparently sympathetic to the South a journal was, the more it expressed repugnance towards slavery and the more it attacked the institution's defenders. The *Athenaeum*, for example, remarked, 'What we like in Lee and Jackson is their conduct, not their opinions. But our respect for the men must not be confounded with respect for their principles and toleration for their cause.'[169] Unqualified approval of the Confederacy was extremely rare in England.

The Emancipation Proclamation itself was better received than historians have acknowledged.[170] Part of the problem was the timing. News of the proclamation became widespread in England just after South routed the North at Fredericksburg, making it look like an act of desperation.[171] James Mason was certainly contemptuous of the proclamation. Writing to the Confederacy's secretary of state, Judah P. Benjamin, he reported,

> Even the Emancipation Proclamation, which it is believed was issued under the promptings of their Minister Adams, as a means of warding off recognition, had little other effect than to disappoint the anti-slavery party here, and met with general contempt and derision. It was seen through at once, and contemned accordingly.[172]

None the less, despite Mason's optimism, the proclamation's reception was not entirely hostile. *The Times*, it is true, believed that Lincoln intended to start a slave uprising, as did several individuals in Britain, but other commentators demurred.[173] Insisting that *The Times*'s attacks on the Emancipation Proclamation were unjust, *The Economist*, despite reservations, stated, 'we consider it commendable on several grounds'. It dismissed notions of a slave insurrection, insisting, 'we do not anticipate any such consequences, nor do we believe that Mr Lincoln designed nor desired them'. According to *The Economist*, a slave insurrection was unlikely, as 'The African race are not, as a rule, either bloodthirsty or vindictive.' *The Economist* believed that Lincoln's intention (which it doubted would prove successful) was to force southern soldiers to return home to guard their plantations and family, thus weakening the Confederate war effort – this, the journal insisted, was a legitimate

---

[168] Ibid. 4 July 1863, 29.
[169] *Athenaeum*, 17 Jan. 1863, 78.
[170] For example, E. D. Adams insists (falsely in my opinion) that the press was opposed to the proclamation, believing that it would cause a slave uprising: Adams, *Great Britain and the American Civil War*, ii. 103–5.
[171] Sheldon Van Auken, *The glittering illusion: English sympathy for the Confederacy*, London 1988, 89.
[172] Mason to Benjamin, 17 Nov. 1862, in *Correspondence of James M. Mason*, 354.
[173] *The Times*, 7 Oct. 1862, 8.

strategy.[174] In fact, *The Economist's* chief criticism was consistent with the stance it had maintained throughout the war: Lincoln was wrong to free only southern slaves, as opposed to all slaves. It also worried that Congress would repudiate Lincoln's proclamation.

The *Illustrated London News* also argued against any intention by Lincoln of causing a slave insurrection, remarking, 'He does not think that his notice that the slaves are free will set four millions of revengeful Africans firing, plundering, and slaying; but he probably does hope that he will embarrass the Confederate Generals.'[175] None the less, noting that without congressional approval the proclamation was useless, and believing that the South would not be conquered, the journal remained sceptical:

> The tone of this proclamation, the circumstances under which it was issued, the conditions upon which it is to take effect, and the party views which it is understood to represent, compel us to regard this instrument as having been rather forged for war purposes than fashioned as a basis of national policy – as a weapon against the foes of the United States' Government, rather than as a frank but tardy exposition of what is just between man and man.[176]

Robert Vaughn, writing in the *British Quarterly Review*, also found Lincoln's proclamation generally commendable, despite the fact that he doubted the South could be subjected. None the less, such reservations aside, Vaughn pronounced, 'The North can no longer be said to be wanting in its duty.'[177]

The anti-slavery *Spectator* actually delivered a harsher verdict upon the Emancipation Proclamation, remarking, 'We are not disposed to exalt over the President's manifesto. It is only a hopeful promise. . . . The principle asserted is not that a human being cannot justly own another, but that he cannot own him unless he is loyal to the United States.'[178] Much friendlier was the journalist Bernard Cracroft who, writing for the *National Review*, decided against looking a gift-horse in the mouth: 'In whatever light we view it [the Emancipation Proclamation], one thing is indisputable, that abolitionism has penetrated from the closets of philanthropists into practical discussions of statesmen. The step may be a timid one. It may be dictated, most probably is, by a warlike policy intended to secure the border states. But it is an *abolition policy*.' Lincoln, according to Cracroft, 'has aimed the first great blow at the true root and cause of the present American troubles'.[179]

There was opposition from the anti-Union *Saturday Review*, which was utterly contemptuous of Lincoln's proclamation; and although it believed that the president intended to cause an uprising, the journal explicitly stated

---

174 *The Economist*, 25 Oct. 1862, 1177–8.
175 *Illustrated London News*, 17 Jan. 1863, 63.
176 Ibid. 11 Oct. 1862, 373.
177 *British Quarterly Review* (January 1863), 209.
178 *Spectator*, 11 Oct. 1862, 1125.
179 *National Review* (April 1862), 505 [Cracroft's italics].

that this aim would not be achieved.[180] The *Saturday Review* also remained unconvinced that Lincoln was sincere in his abolitionist policies, and not without reason. In August 1864, faced with possible defeat in the presidential election, Lincoln actually considered sacrificing abolition as a condition of peace between the North and the South.[181] Some aspects of English suspicion, then, were not entirely unfounded.

None the less, once the Emancipation Proclamation took effect, the Union's anti-slavery stance gained some badly needed credibility. It also provided the impetus for the anti-slavery bodies in England to begin (and effectively conclude) their agitation during the first part of 1863, when the proclamation took effect. The vexed nature of these meetings, and their impact, requires more space than can be provided here. As a result, they are discussed in Chapter 6. What needs to be noted is that, despite the fact that the Emancipation Proclamation did not make England pro-North, it did damage southern sympathy, the nature and levels of which have been misunderstood and exaggerated.

---

[180] *Saturday Review*, 11 Oct. 1862, 436–8.
[181] Lincoln, writing to a war democrat, Charles D. Robinson, on 17 August 1864, insisted: 'If Jefferson Davis wishes . . . to know what I would do if he were to offer peace and re-union, saying nothing about slavery, let him try me': *The collected works of Abraham Lincoln*, vii. 499–501.

4

The Political Debate

'It is a very pleasant thing to show them that we entertain no ill-feelings towards them, and that we consider what has been said as so much idle wind that has passed by.'

It is surely one of the most enduring myths of the nineteenth century that the English aristocracy and conservatives favoured the insurgent Confederacy because its establishment would check democracy in general and demands for an expanded suffrage in England in particular. Beyond the unsubstantiated accusations by certain members of the pro-northern lobby there is little evidence that the British establishment believed Confederate independence would slow demands for an extension of the suffrage at home. It goes beyond H. C. Allen's statement that 'it is difficult to find a great deal of positive evidence of specific aristocratic fellow feeling for the upper classes of the South'.[1] It is not that there is little evidence it is that there is virtually no evidence. Below them, in the House of Commons, the situation was much the same. Precious few members of parliament viewed the American Civil War as a test case for either democracy or reform in Britain, and this was especially true of conservatives in particular – both inside the House of Commons and out. All of the above is made clear not only by their speeches in parliament, but by their constituency (and other) speeches outside of it. The politicians were not alone in their opinion that the conflict in America had little influence on the debate surrounding democratic reform in Britain – the English press shared this view – a view, by the way, held especially by the conservative press that was extremely reluctant to draw lessons from the American experience. This chapter thematically examines the views of British politicians and political journals towards the war, with emphasis on the period from 1862 to 1864.

---

1 Allen, *Great Britain and the United States*, 458. Allen admits that even those such as Sheldon Van Auken who believe that they have found distinct southern sympathy in England have difficulty proving it. McPherson, meanwhile, although he believes revisionists have overstated their case, concedes that 'The correlation between class and British attitudes toward the American conflict should not be exaggerated': *Battle cry of freedom*, 552. None the less, despite the fact that they admit the evidence is scant at best, both McPherson and Allen continue to treat the traditional depiction of a pro-southern aristocracy as valid.

THE POLITICAL DEBATE

The opinions of the aristocracy

As the British aristocracy was, for the most part, extremely reticent in its views on America (exceptions are noted below), its opponents' denunciations have been almost completely accepted as fact. Yet, despite this, accusations that the aristocracy supported the South did not go unchallenged. The *Saturday Review*, for example, regularly replied to Bright's and others' accusations of a pro-southern British aristocracy, arguing that he and they simply levelled accusations without providing any proof.[2] Sometimes the journal had to go further than this. When, in 1863, Bright vilified British neutrality at the Trades' Union's meeting at St James's Hall, and claimed that 'privilege' in England supported the Confederacy, the *Saturday Review* pointed out,

> Northern animosity will receive a new impulse when Mr. Bright and his irresponsible followers assure the President that all Englishmen above the working class are enemies of the United States. If war should unhappily arise, no small part of the blame will attach to the reckless partisans who have calumniated their own Government and country by echoing the vituperative falsehoods of the Northern press.[3]

Bright's claim, that everyone other than the working class in Britain opposed the Union, was, as the journal pointed out, false. Indeed, as far as the *Saturday Review* was concerned it was an outright lie – and one that could cause serious damage. The journal proved to be correct in its assessment. Bright's misrepresentation of English attitudes towards America would be cited in the United States after the war as evidence that Britain supported the Confederacy. Bright, however, continued to make these spurious claims. In 1863, after he again accused the aristocracy of supporting the South, the *Saturday Review* pointed out: 'Four or five days ago, the arrogant aristocracy assembled in the House of Lords approved, with but one dissentient voice, Lord Russell's declaration that it was inexpedient to interfere between the belligerents even by the tender of good offices.'[4] As the *Saturday Review* made clear, the behaviour of the House of Lords largely belied any pro-southern sentiment. Indeed, an examination of the debates in the House of Lords supports the statements of the *Saturday Review*, rather than the opinions of Bright. There were very few pro-southern speeches in the upper House, and those few were restricted, as in the House of Commons, to a small clique. The anti-northern speeches in the House of Lords tended to be directed at specific Union violations of

---

[2] For example, *Saturday Review*, 20 Dec. 1862, 727; 20 June 1863, 774. This last issue shows just how careless Bright could be, for the journal had the pleasure of informing him that his guest speaker, invited to talk on slavery, 'had, a few days before, formally offered, under certain conditions, to promote the recognition of Southern independence'. See *Reynolds's Weekly*, 21 June 1863, 1, for details of the speech.
[3] *Saturday Review*, 28 Mar. 1863, 390.
[4] Ibid. 389–90. The 'one dissentient voice' was that of Lord Campbell. He did, indeed, receive no support. For details see *Hansard*, clxix, 23 Mar. 1863, 1714–41.

neutrality, such as Wilkes's harassing British shipping in the West Indies and federal recruiting in Ireland. Nor were the Lords being over-zealous in the last instance; northern recruiting in Ireland was one of the reasons it turned anti-Union during the American Civil War, as Joseph Hernon has established.[5]

The sentiments of the aristocracy are extremely difficult to measure on the question of the Civil War. Very few of them expressed an opinion on it, and, as a social class, they did not congregate in large numbers to express their views on a particular issue – the House of Lords excluded. None the less, an examination of what individual members of the aristocracy said about the war at public meetings is interesting in itself. Most took a neutral position and a few were clearly sympathetic to the Union.

Edward Adolphus Seymour, the twelfth duke of Somerset, notorious for duelling in 1835, a former Liberal member of parliament and now first lord of the Admiralty, spoke on American affairs in Exeter in early November, 1862. Speaking at the meeting convened to express sympathy with, and to raise money for, the distressed Lancashire operatives, Somerset urged calm with respect to the North and argued that allowance had to be made for the position in which both sides – but especially the Union – were placed. Besides avoiding criticism of the North, Somerset also opposed intervention or offers of mediation.[6] The Union could hardly have asked for more from this particular member of the aristocracy.

Charles Philip Yorke, the fourth earl of Hardwicke, a former admiral, Conservative member of parliament and now lord-lieutenant of Cambridge, addressed a public meeting in his former constituency's town hall in January of 1863. His references to America need to be reprinted in full:

> We are supposed by many persons to be dependent upon the United States for our peace and happiness, for our security and wealth; but we have shown them, and we shall be able to show them for the future, that this country has a power which they never supposed to possess, and that with its love of order, its obedience to the law, its great charity, and its powerful resources, there are no circumstances which can bring upon us that depression which I will not say they desired to see, but that which they felt confident would be caused if the supply of cotton should be deficient.

The earl was referring to both the Union's Morrill tariff and the Confederacy's King Cotton policy when he spoke of dependence on the United States for security and wealth, clearly establishing that he believed both sides had acted badly towards Britain. By condemning the activities of both, Hardwicke clearly favoured neither side, although he stated, 'It is a very pleasant thing to show them that we entertain no ill-feelings towards them, and that we consider what has been said as so much idle wind that has passed

---

5 Hernon, *Celts, Catholics and copperheads*, 23–38.
6 *Reynolds's Weekly*, 9 Nov. 1862, 2.

by (Hear, hear).'⁷ This, clearly, was a not too subtle reference to both the opinions of the northern press and the Union's diplomatic efforts. None the less, such a statement by Hardwicke establishes that he did not support retaliation or any escalation in the transatlantic contest of insults.

Yet the question of King Cotton remains important. As Hardwicke's speech reveals, even by early 1863, people were still blaming the cotton famine on Confederate intransigence rather than the Union blockade. Indeed, the southern commissioner, James Mason had recognised the danger this presented to his cause. Of his first meeting with Russell, Mason reported to the then Confederate secretary of state, Robert Hunter: 'So much as related to the cotton supply and its importance to this country, I thought it best to omit, as I had reason to believe, from very intelligent sources, that it might be considered obtrusive, having been urged until England had become a little sensitive.'⁸ In other words, he recognised that the King Cotton policy had caused serious offence in England. By this point in time, however, the Confederacy had to smuggle cotton through the Union blockade in order to pay for desperately needed munitions.

Hardwicke's speech contained another important reference regarding the cotton question. This was, aside from the usual praise of the Lancashire operatives for not agitating against the blockade, that of Britain's 'great charity'. As studies on the cotton famine have revealed, there was a great deal of effort expended not only by the government but also by private organisations, to alleviate Lancashire's distress. As Geoffrey Best notes, over a million pounds was raised for Lancashire and it was fairly, humanely and economically administered.⁹ Yet the very social classes – according to the traditional interpretation – who were eager to interfere on the side of the South raised this money. If members of these social classes hoped that a cotton famine would cause an Anglo-American war, why did they expend so much effort trying to alleviate distress in the north of England? The answer is, of course, that no one in England wanted to see hardship in the cotton districts, let alone a mass movement calling for war to re-open the cotton supply. The very fact that discontent in Lancashire never reached such a point is surely owing to the efforts of men like the duke of Somerset and the earl of Hardwicke – and all those others who generously contributed to the various charities.

It is also clear that when members of the aristocracy addressed working-class meetings, they were able to denounce the Union to the delight, not disapprobation, of the audience. For example, Henry Peter Brougham, Baron Brougham (who had earlier in the conflict expressed hopes for re-union), spoke at Edinburgh under the auspices of the Social Science Association in October 1863.¹⁰ As *Reynolds's* put it, 'The largest and most commodious

---

7   Ibid. 11 Jan. 1863, 2.
8   Mason to Hunter, 11 Mar. 1862, in *Correspondence of James M. Mason*, 260.
9   Best, *Mid-Victorian Britain*, 137.
10 For Brougham's speech in favour of re-union see *Hansard*, clxii, 10 May 1861, 1833.

building in Edinburgh proved wholly inadequate to accommodate the thousands of working men who were desirous of being present at the meeting.' Brougham frankly stated that Lincoln's Emancipation Proclamation 'was not for the sake of emancipating the slaves, but for the sake of beating the whites'. Brougham, however, like most individuals who have so often been sloppily classified as 'pro-Confederate', denied either side had any claim to British sympathy and insisted on neutrality.[11] After the speech a blacksmith, speaking on behalf of the workmen of Edinburgh, congratulated Brougham on his words.

This speech, and the reaction to it, further damages the arguments of the traditional interpretation when one examines Brougham's past career. A former Liberal member of parliament with a radical streak, Brougham had, over a long career, opposed the infamous 'Six Acts' (repressive measures designed to deal with the radical reform agitation which culminated in the Peterloo massacre of 1819), moved bills for the freedom of the press and championed law reform. All of the above ensured that he had a good reputation in radical circles – hence the support of Edinburgh's workers. More interesting, however, is that Brougham had, earlier in the century, been a major anti-slavery spokesman and a friend of William Wilberforce. Considering his anti-slavery background, Brougham should have been a friend of the North. Yet Brougham's hostility towards the Union and his refusal to believe that Lincoln was sincere in his emancipation policies can probably be traced back to the Anglo-American right-of-search dispute of 1858. Brougham had been a strong supporter of the search policy and was angered when the British government backed down to the United States. He was further angered when he found himself abused by Lewis Cass for his public speeches in support of the right of search.[12] It is possible that Brougham never forgave the United States for its past conduct, but it is also likely that his neutral stance was equally owed to the Union's vacillation regarding emancipation. Whatever the reason, the failure of the North to win the support of a committed liberal and abolitionist like Brougham shows just how low the Union's reputation had sunk – and in liberal circles, too.

George Leveson Gower Granville, the second earl of Granville, a former Liberal member of parliament, along with Gladstone, addressed a working-class audience at Burslem, Staffordshire, on 26 October 1863. Gladstone was by this time known to have southern leanings, and the earl of Granville went so far as to tell the audience that neither side could have a claim of English sympathy, to cheers.[13] Granville was a champion of free

---

[11] *Reynolds's Weekly*, 18 Oct. 1863, 4. It is interesting to note, however, that one of *Reynolds's* regular columnists, 'Northumbrian', criticised the working-class audience for supporting Brougham's 'coarse misrepresentation and stale slanders of the institutions and people of the northern states of America': ibid. 3.
[12] Semmell, *Liberalism and naval strategy*, 45–6.
[13] *Reynolds's Weekly*, 1 Nov. 1863, 3.

THE POLITICAL DEBATE

trade and despised the Union's Morrill tariff, but he disliked slavery and the Confederacy, too. Granville's antipathy to both sides and his declaration that Britain could favour neither was very much an anti-interventionist stance. If Granville hoped that all of this would mean hearing less from the Americans, he was to be sadly disappointed. He was later to head the British delegation at the Alabama arbitration in Geneva. One can only speculate whether Granville pondered, at Geneva, whether intervention might have proved the less costly option.

Another member of the aristocracy speaking to a working-class audience who disliked both the North and the South was Lord Hurlington, who spoke on American affairs at the Lancashire Union of Mechanic's Institutions in December 1863. Hurlington argued that although the Northerners were 'exceedingly clever and energetic', they possessed 'a somewhat exaggerated idea of the merits, not only of their own country, but of all the people that dwell therein'. Further, argued Hurlington, they 'were somewhat arrogant [and] somewhat intolerant of opposition'.[14] Although Hurlington strongly opposed intervention, he also took care to criticise Cobden's and Bright's misrepresentations of America generally, and the North specifically. The crowd agreed with his sentiments and passed a vote of thanks.

These meetings are, in many respects, more representative of working-class opinion than the anti-slavery rallies of 1863 that will be examined in Chapter 6. The former meetings, after all, were composed of individuals who came simply to hear a speech on a variety of (mostly) domestic issues. The latter gatherings, on the other hand, were directed specifically at anti-slavery audiences and were unlikely to be attended by those who held a neutral position on the conflict.

These meetings exclude those where aristocrats, such as Lord Fermoy, spoke to their constituents as members of parliament, which are dwelt with below. Also excluded are individuals such as Lord Ashburton, whose bank, Baring Brothers and Co., invested heavily in the northern states, and whose pro-Union speeches angered former Confederate agents in England such as James D. Bulloch, years after the conflict.[15] Another consideration regarding aristocratic thought about the war which has been ignored by historians pertains to those members of the aristocracy who were involved in anti-slavery activity in the antebellum years. These individuals were, if not necessarily sympathetic to the North, hardly likely to support the South.[16]

---

14 Ibid. 13 Dec. 1863, 1.
15 Bulloch also complained that the son, T. Baring, as an MP was a warm supporter of the North – perhaps unsurprisingly, as Barings Brothers and Co. loaned large sums of money to the Union: *The secret service of the Confederate States in Europe: or, how the Confederate Cruisers were equipped*, New York 1959, i. 358–65.
16 Brian Harrison lists a number of aristocrats who were involved in anti-slavery organisations and the like: 'A genealogy of reform in modern Britain', in Bolt and Drescher, *Anti-slavery, religion and reform*, 121–38, 132.

The real democratic debate

Conservatives (both adhering to the political philosophy and/or the political party) tended to make rather more comments about the American Civil War, and an examination of their arguments casts doubt on the belief that they saw the break-up of the Union as a set-back for democracy. It is, in fact, impossible to establish that conservatives ever viewed the conflict in this light at all.

Our understanding of conservative attitudes towards the United States has been hampered in part by American interpretations of the war – for example, Lincoln's insistence that it was 'essentially a People's contest' and that the Union was 'the last, best hope' for the preservation of republican freedoms in the world.[17] Besides the fact that very few conservatives either encountered or even accepted this nationalist interpretation of events, caution has to be applied in interpreting what conservatives meant when they referred to democracy, and, in particular, American democracy. Finally, because supporting the South meant endorsing the doctrine of secession, conservatives had reasons for disliking the Confederacy as much as the Union.

Lincoln's notion that the Union was 'the last, best hope' for democracy, or popular government, as he expressed it in his Annual Message to Congress on 1 December 1862, has, for a long time now, bedevilled historians' perceptions of Anglo-American relations during the conflict. Leaving aside the fact that in this same speech Lincoln asked for Congress's help in deporting African Americans from the soil of the United States, few in England ever believed that the future of democracy depended upon the integrity of the Union.[18] Even fewer still argued that the collapse of the United States was caused by democracy and thus proved the institution to be unworkable. How and why the misperception arose that the English ever believed that the futures of the United States and democracy were intimately connected is examined more completely in Chapter 6, but, at this point, a few words need to be said about the state of political affairs in Britain, while using the United States as a point of comparison.

First of all, neither the United States nor Britain was a true democracy. If the franchise in Britain was limited by class, the franchise in the United States was limited by race. Very few northern states – to say nothing of southern ones – allowed African Americans the vote. Whatever may be said of a franchise based on class, one can at least, although often with difficulty, change one's class – one cannot change one's race. Further, neither the United States nor Britain allowed women (always slightly over 50 per cent of the population) the vote either. The franchise, however, was much more

---

17 Lincoln, *The collected works of Abraham Lincoln*, iv. 438.
18 This was first pointed out by Lerone Bennett Jr.: *Forced into glory: Abraham Lincoln's white dream*, Chicago 2000, 509–17.

limited in Britain: only about 20 per cent of adult males could vote.[19] Yet despite various claims that have been made by numerous historians of our subject about an entrenched opposition to an extension of the franchise, by the 1850s, the Liberal Party (and, to a far lesser extent, the Conservative Party) was seriously considering it. For example, bills to expand the electoral franchise were proposed in 1852, 1854, 1859 and 1860 – the campaign for reform was under way long before the American Civil War even began. Further, Palmerston, for one, was not quite the reactionary he has been painted by the traditional interpretation. In 1859, he moved his own bill for parliamentary reform, which, although moderate, as Miles Taylor puts it, 'at least it was moving in the direction of change'.[20] As for Russell, meanwhile, far from being the 'Finality John' of the traditional interpretation – that was an earlier incarnation of the foreign secretary – he and Bright had met in 1858 to discuss the issue of reform.[21] Bright, of course, wanted to go far further than Russell, but the point to be remembered is that the question asked by members of the Liberal Party was not whether or not there was to be reform but, rather, to what extent? Palmerston and Russell had further invited pro-reform members of the House into the cabinet, including Thomas Milner Gibson and A. H. Layard. Indeed, Russell had wanted to invite Bright into the cabinet and Palmerston actually offered Cobden a position.[22] Without a doubt, both Russell and Palmerston thought that they could bring the two 'Members for America' under something akin to party discipline by including them in the cabinet, but Palmerston also wanted Cobden for his expertise in foreign affairs. This is perhaps something that should be remembered when one reads about Cobden's and Bright's complaints about their Government's conduct towards the Union – the former, at least, had turned down an opportunity to shape Britain's foreign policy.

It must also be noted that the Conservative Party during our period was considering the nature of the shape parliamentary reform should take. Indeed, the Conservative Party had proposed its own reform bill – Disraeli's in 1859. So it is fair to say that the question of reform in England had a life previous to the events in America. Further, those involved in the debate – liberal, radical, conservative or reactionary – rarely, as we shall see, ever referred to the United States to support their arguments.

One of the very few Conservative members of parliament who did make a comparison between reform and the American Civil War was Robert Lowe, and why adherents of the traditional interpretation have not mentioned him remains a mystery – especially as he was arguably the most strenuous oppo-

---

[19] Eric J. Evans, *The forging of the modern state: early industrial Britain, 1783–1870*, London 1983, 379. David Thomson estimates that about one million out of a population of twenty-two million could vote: *England in the nineteenth century, 1815–1914*, London 1950, 74, 117.
[20] Taylor, *The decline of British radicalism*, 321.
[21] Ibid. 314.
[22] Ibid. 326–7.

nent of the 1867 Reform Act.[23] Yet Lowe did not annunciate these views during the war and there is no evidence that he had any time for the Confederacy. Lowe, in fact, only cited the American Civil War as an example of what democracy could lead to *after* the surrender of the South, in the pages of the *Quarterly Review*. Further, in his article in the *Quarterly Review*, Lowe was responding to the pro-Northerner Goldwin Smith and James Bryce's essays in the collection *Essays on reform*.[24] In their essays, Smith and, to a lesser extent, Bryce argued that the Union victory was a vindication of democracy. Lowe, looking at a devastated South and a body count of over 620,000 men, begged to differ. Further, Lowe's critique was as much based on the system of government in the United States as on its wider franchise.[25] This, again, is the problem with the traditional interpretation: any criticism directed at the mechanics or system of American government is simplistically classified as anti-democratic sentiment. There are other examples to follow.

During the war itself, one of the very few individuals who has ever been clearly identified as equating the breakdown of the United States with the breakdown of democracy was the Liberal – not Conservative as some historians have claimed – member of parliament, Sir John Ramsden, representative from West Yorkshire, in his speech in the House of Commons on 27 May 1861. Even so, there are some questions surrounding the meaning given to Ramsden's comments. Much has been made of Ramsden's speech largely because Adams's private secretary, Benjamin Moran, was present at the debate where Ramsden sarcastically informed the House that they 'were now witnessing the bursting of the great republican bubble which had so often been held up to us as a model on which to recast our own English Constitution'.[26] Moran noted, 'His [Ramsden's] remark was very warmly cheered by the Tory side and not much disapproved of by the Liberal. I was very surprised, but only a little, at this.'[27] What Moran declined to note, as at least one modern historian has observed, was that a large majority in the Commons condemned Ramsden's remarks.[28] Further, although it is always dangerous to argue from negative evidence, it is surely significant *when* the oft-cited remarks of Ramsden were made – namely, in mid-1861. The fact that no further such speech was made in the House of Commons throughout

---

[23] For a discussion of Lowe's activities in this regard see Asa Briggs, *Victorian people: a reassessment of persons and themes, 1851–67*, Chicago 1955, ch. ix, 'Robert Lowe and the fear of democracy'.
[24] *Essays on reform*, London 1867. Goldwin Smith's and Bryce's essays are discussed in greater detail in ch. 6 below.
[25] Robert Lowe, 'Essays on reform', *Quarterly Review* (July 1867), 263.
[26] *Hansard*, clxiii, 27 May 1861, 131–6. Jordan and Pratt base almost their entire argument of upper-class opposition to democracy and the Union on Ramsden's remarks: *Europe and the American Civil War*, 57.
[27] Benjamin Moran, *The journal of Benjamin Moran*, ed. Sarah Agnes Wallace and Francis Elma Gillespie, Chicago 1948, ii. 820.
[28] Jones, *Union in peril*, 48.

the duration of the war suggests that Ramsden's notion had been discredited from the outset. Indeed, Ramsden's comments were rebutted by his fellow members of parliament both at public meetings and in the House throughout the war, and not merely by northern apologists either. For example, in July 1862, in the House of Commons, the Independent F. H. F. Berkeley argued in favour of the ballot and remarked, 'Discredit had been thrown on the ballot in consequence of the civil war now raging in America. But civil war was no test of an institution. If it were, what became of Monarchy? (hear, hear).'[29]

It is, however, worth briefly examining Ramsden himself, because it raises some interesting questions about members of parliament's views on both political reform and America in general. Ramsden had, in fact, been elected on a reform platform. He was a member of the West Yorkshire Reform Association and had declared at Bradford in 1859:

> I am prepared to vote for a large extension of the franchise to the working classes. They must have reform. For the first time since 1832 the attention of the country is thoroughly concentrated upon reform. Reform will be the main duty of the constituent body of this country, by the measures they will take at this election, to stamp the parliament which is now about to be elected with the impress of the measures which they desire to see carried into law.[30]

Besides the fact that this speech reveals how the reform debate had already begun in earnest, Ramsden also accepted a petition from his constituents demanding the secret ballot (which he supported) which he presented to the House of Commons.[31]

None the less, it must be noted that although Ramsden claimed to support reform, he was no radical. Further, he was not in favour of reform at any price. In 1859, for example, he voted against Disraeli's reform bill. Ramsden claimed that he had done so because the bill discriminated against the electorate of Yorkshire's West Riding by splitting it in an arbitrary fashion. No one, however, had more to fear from such a division than Ramsden himself. His shrewd election agent, G. Childers, had warned him that he would probably lose his seat if the West Riding were split in the fashion it would be by Disraeli's bill.[32] Ramsden had thus, in the time-honoured fashion of politicians, put his own interests before those of the nation's.

This electoral self-preservation, however, did not come without a price and Ramsden was criticised for reneging on his pro-reform election platform. The Armley Reform Association, at a public meeting, reviewed his speeches in support of reform and demanded he resign his seat because of his 'renegade

---

[29] *Hansard*, vol. clxvii, 2 July 1862, 1302–3.
[30] Speech at Bradford, Ramsden papers, RA 17.
[31] Ramsden to W. Hickes, 15 June 1863: ibid.
[32] Ramsden and Childers had a long communication about this subject. Ramsden summed up his situation in a letter to Childers on 27 Jan. 1860. He also discussed the issue with B. Dixon on 18 Mar. 1860: ibid.

conduct in Parliament'.[33] Further, Ramsden's reluctance to state clearly how low he thought the franchise should be set also drew criticism. So too did some of his speeches in parliament, which were judged to be equivocal. As one exasperated elector, George De Main, wrote to Ramsden in 1860, 'You say, "that you want a Bill which would satisfy all parties;" a thing clearly impossible because the Tory's [sic] want no Reform at all.'[34] Although Ramsden replied to both the Armley Reform Association and De Main, protesting that he was in favour of extending the franchise, his credentials on the subject were unquestionably damaged.

What is interesting is that none of Ramsden's pro-reform critics cited his bursting republican bubble speech in parliament. The two 'indignation letters', as he scrawled on them, which he received on the subject from angry constituents were based on anti-slavery arguments, not radical ones.[35] Further, Ramsden's speech in the House of Commons was one of the very few comments he made on the subject of America. For example, although subjects such as Schleswig-Holstein were discussed in his diary and correspondence, events in America were barely referred to at all. It seems that both Benjamin Moran and subsequent historians have imputed far more significance to Ramsden's speech than he did himself. There remains, however, the question, why did he make the speech? A likely answer lies in Ramsden's antipathy towards John Bright.[36] If one considers the latter's endless panegyrics on the United States and the former's (limited) reform sympathies, the bursting republican bubble speech looks more like a calculated insult directed at Bright, rather than democratic reform itself. Indeed, considering all the above, Ramsden's speech appears to support the argument of Jordan and Pratt, who acknowledged that criticism of American democracy was, in fact, often simply personal attacks on Cobden and Bright.[37] Clearly, if Ramsden's speech is any indication, when it comes to members of parliament's comments on America, far more attention needs to be paid to both the individual's background and the personal politics of the day than has been done in the past.

Even if Ramsden's remarks were a sincere expression of his political beliefs, which they probably were not, there should still be far greater reluctance than has hitherto been shown to base the entire view of the Conservative Party and conservatives in general on the views of a single Liberal member of parliament. Besides the views expressed by Conservative members of parliament at public meetings examined below, there is the conservative press to

---

[33] Address of the Armley Reform Association to Sir John Ramsden, Bart., MP: ibid.
[34] It must be noted that Ramsden wrote a reply insisting that, despite De Main's remarks, he did favour reform: George De Main to Ramsden, 12 May 1860; Ramsden's reply, 14 May 1860, ibid.
[35] 'Anonymous' to Sir John Ramsden, 30 May 1861; Rev. Raymond Portal to Sir John Ramsden, 9 Dec. 1861, Ramsden papers, RA 66/8.
[36] See, for example, Ramsden to Sir John Potter, 22 Feb. 1859, ibid. RA 17.
[37] Jordan and Pratt, *Europe and the American Civil War*, 55.

consider. An examination of three of the major conservative periodicals – the *Saturday Review*, the *Quarterly Review*, and *Fraser's Magazine* – establishes that there was a great deal of scepticism regarding the argument that America's break-up proved democracy was unworkable.

The *Saturday Review*, for one, never endorsed Ramsden's notion. As early as February 1861, it had noted:

> If we turn our attention to the influence of the American rupture on England, the first thought which suggests itself is, that the quarrel has a material bearing on the question of parliamentary reform. That there is so close a connection between the two topics is not the fault of reflecting politicians in this country. They, at all events, have always denied that, except within certain limits, American experience had any value for English legislators. The shallow demagogues of Birmingham and other kindred platforms must bear the blame of the inference, drawn nearly universally at the present moment that, if the United States become embroiled in hopeless difficulties, it would be madness to lower the qualifications for the suffrage in England.[38]

Jordan and Pratt cite this article as an example of indirect attack on the Manchester school, rather than on American democracy, but here the *Saturday Review* was arguing something else[39] – namely, that the American question had little bearing on electoral reform in Britain, and that insisting that it did endangered the prospects for reform. This is important to note in the *Saturday Review*'s case because it had, a fortnight earlier, endorsed a speech of Bright's calling for reform. Remarking that the radical had spoken 'earnestly and well', the journal declared that 'As far as personal arguments and parliamentary reasons could go, Mr. Bright's demonstration was conclusive. Half-a-dozen Ministries have, on a score of occasions ranging over ten years, declared the necessity of extending the suffrage and of readjusting the distribution of electoral power.'[40]

Although historians have been quick to note the *Saturday Review*'s animosity towards the Union and the Manchester school, they have been slow to note its guarded support for reform and an expanded suffrage during this same period. The *Saturday Review* maintained this argument throughout the conflict. Indeed, the *Saturday Review* accepted the argument that both the Union and the Confederacy were democracies. As it opined in late 1862, 'one man shudders at the name of democracy – another thinks democracy the finest thing in the world. The one rejoices to see a democracy, as he thinks,

---

[38] *Saturday Review*, 23 Feb. 1861, 181.
[39] Jordan and Pratt, *Europe and the American Civil War*, 55–9. Compare Jordan and Pratt's truncated version of the above complete quote from the *Saturday Review*. Their abbreviated version supports their arguments, but it also distorts the writer's intentions. This is an example of the sort of simplification of English interpretations of the American Civil War that has dominated our understanding of the subject.
[40] *Saturday Review*, 9 Feb. 1861, 134. The journal perceptively predicted that reform would come about by a Gladstone–Bright alliance.

split up and weakened – the other weeps over the sight.' But, as the journal pointed out, 'Neither stops to remember that the two Federations are equally democratic in their political constitution, and that, if you split a democracy in two, it is at least a matter for discussion whether the general democratic interest gains or loses.'[41] As the above quote shows, if the *Saturday Review* could be accused of having southern sympathies, it did so on the basis that secession was a right, that the cause of democracy included the right of self-determination. Even so, the *Saturday Review* was never a partisan of the Confederacy. The journal constantly refuted Bright's assertion that opposition towards the North was based on a dislike of republicanism, and its criticisms of the Union's government make this clear:

> The exclusion of the best men in the country from power and influence is one of the worst features of American politics, but it arises from another cause [other than republicanism]. The main reason for this evil is not that they are rejected by the people, but cannot get at the people. The wretched system of Tickets, Platforms, Conventions and so forth – the whole machinery of the American party warfare – really transfers the elections from the people at large to an oligarchy of professional electioneering agents. . . . It is the oligarchy of Caucuses and Conventions which has kept the real leaders of all the parties out of the highest place in the Commonwealth, and has handed the chair of Washington to Polk, Pierce, and Abraham Lincoln.[42]

Clearly, the *Saturday Review*'s criticism was directed at the American system of government, rather than at democracy as a whole. This school of thought has to be borne in mind when mentioning criticism of the American political system. The *Saturday Review*, then, did not oppose the Union in the hopes of discrediting democracy, but frankly denied that the interests of democracy were dependent upon events in America.

If the *Saturday Review*'s position on the American Civil War has been thoroughly misunderstood or misrepresented, the *Quarterly Review*'s, at least, has been somewhat more accurately presented.[43] Lord Robert Cecil's articles in the journal did treat the breakdown of the United States as a reason to examine democracy critically, particularly in his article, 'Democracy on its trial' (not 'Democracy on trial', as some historians have called it).[44] To state that Cecil asserted democracy (and, by extension, reform) was on trial because of events in America, however, is something of an over-simplification. Most of Cecil's criticisms were open attacks on Bright and his radicalism, rather than on democracy. For example, he wrote in April 1861 that:
For the last ten years the hon. member for Birmingham has been unceasingly

---

41 Ibid. 27 Dec. 1862, 765.
42 Ibid. 6 Dec. 1862, 675. Presidents Pierce and Polk were considered to be anglophobic. Thanks to Seward, the journal held the same of Lincoln.
43 See Keiser, 'The English press and the American Civil War', 61–3; Jenkins, *Britain and the war for the Union*, ii. 161–2; Jordan and Pratt, *Europe and the American Civil War*, 85.
44 Lord Robert Cecil, 'Democracy on its trial', *Quarterly Review* (July 1861), 247–88.

appealing to the example in America in reference to administration, to government, to expenditure, to morality, and to religion; but if the social, civilized, and religious life which recent tourists in America give – the writers themselves being American – be true, as we believe them to be, well may England felicitate herself that she has not become so desperately enamoured of American institutions as the hon. Member for Birmingham professes himself to be.[45]

Cecil's article certainly fits Jordan and Pratt's assertion that attacks on America were merely attacks on Cobden and Bright and, indeed, most of Cecil's articles on the conflict were direct rebuttals of Bright's endless panegyrics of the United States. Although Cecil agreed with Sir John Ramsden that the great republican bubble had burst, it was not democracy that worried him so much as the form it had taken in the United States. In other words, most of his criticisms were directed at the institutions of the United States, rather than their democratic foundations. Further, although a Tory, Cecil shared numerous liberals' concerns about the lack of protection of civil liberties in America, quoting from de Tocqueville, and (very selectively) from Mill, at length about the tyranny of the majority. Cecil complained of 'Judge Lynch', 'the repression of free thought and free speech', and pointed out that even if slavery was the cause of the conflict, Britain had managed to abolish the institution within its territories without resorting to war. None the less, despite all of this, Cecil still found things to admire about the United States, claiming that 'America has special claims on us which are shared by no other country in the world', and referred to it as 'the advanced guard of liberty'.[46] Nor did Cecil argue against extending the franchise in Britain because of what had occurred in the United States.

Cecil's tone became harsher towards the Union in the January 1862 issue of the *Quarterly Review*, wherein he listed all previous Anglo-American quarrels and blamed them on the United States, but this was surely in large part owing to the fact that his article had been written during the height of the *Trent* affair.[47] Cecil's next article, in October of 1862, contained all the familiar complaints made by other commentators – for example, that 'the Habeas Corpus Act has been suspended, the press muzzled, and judges prevented by armed men from enforcing on the citizens' behalf the laws to which they and the President alike have sworn'.[48] Because of these activities, Cecil regarded Lincoln as a dictator, 'a poor plagiarist in the arts of tyranny. . . . He suppresses newspapers, manipulates news, seizes the telegraph, imprisons hostile speakers and writers.'[49] Despite all of this, Cecil never held the South in any particularly high esteem and he certainly did not regard the

---

[45] Idem, 'America', *Quarterly Review* (Apr. 1861), 425–6.
[46] See, for example, idem, 'Democracy on its trial', *Quarterly Review* (July 1861), 247–88.
[47] Idem, 'The American Crisis', the *Quarterly Review* (Jan. 1862), 232–80.
[48] Idem, 'The Confederate struggle and recognition', *Quarterly Review* (Oct. 1862), 558.
[49] Ibid. 559.

southern administration as an aristocratic form of government. Nor was he in favour of interfering in the war on the Confederacy's behalf, although he believed that the South would win its independence. The *Quarterly Review* generally ceased trying to draw lessons from America after this. In April 1863 it carried an article relating the history of the war up until that point.[50] The only other article discussing the war was a review of several books on the subject in the April 1864 issue.[51] In short, the war provoked a relatively small amount of commentary in the pages of the *Quarterly Review*, lending support to D. P. Crook's claim that America had little impact on English conservative thought.[52]

That the conservative press was distinctly hesitant to draw lessons regarding democracy from the American Civil War is also evident in *Fraser's* discussions of the conflict. If the *Quarterly Review* was unsure of what to make of the conflict, *Fraser's* was even less certain. It did, however, contain an article by Anthony Trollope in 1862 specifically declaring that, 'In the first place, this is not a struggle to test Democratic institutions. It is idle to say that Democracy has failed. What *has* failed is the attempt to bring together under one homogenous Government two apathetic and discordant civilizations.'[53] This was not a bad description of the struggle. The North largely was a rapidly industrialising nation while the South remained a widely agrarian one. Further, *Fraser's* published a series of articles by apologists from both sides, including a pro-Confederate American from the Union, Hiram Fuller. Fuller's articles appeared under the pen name of 'a white Republican' and he claimed that American democracy had come unstuck by immigration and mob rule. In one issue he wrote that the

> judgement of native-born male citizens of the United States over twenty one years of age, who could read the constitution' was overruled or 'nullified by some raw and ragged emigrant [sic] who cannot even speak the American language, whose 'politics' are bought for a glass of rum, and who does not know or care whether he is voting for General Jackson or the fourth of July![54]

This, of course, was not the same thing as opposing democracy as a whole. Fuller was, judging by his anti-immigrant stance, a nativist (nativism had a popular following in the United States during this period). This was no English Tory using the problems of America to discredit the democratic movement at home. In any case, Fuller's inflammatory opinions provoked protest from *Fraser's* readers. After Fuller's penultimate article, the editor felt compelled to publish a defence:

---

[50] 'The American war – from Fort Sumter to Fredericksburg', *Quarterly Review* (Apr. 1863), 322–53.
[51] 'The prospects of the Confederates', *Quarterly Review* (Apr. 1864), 289–311.
[52] Crook, *American democracy in English politics*, ch. iv passim, esp. p. 121.
[53] *Fraser's Magazine* (Aug. 1862), 260 [their italics].
[54] Ibid. (July 1862), 22–3.

Mr. John Stuart Mill has said in the pages of this Magazine that the present war in America is carried on by the slave-owners for the privilege of burning negroes alive. A Northern American, who is neither slave-owner nor has any interest in slavery, desires to state what he himself has seen ... and the Editor feels it is his duty to allow him the opportunity.[55]

Unquestionably, Fuller's articles were too extreme. His nativist arguments would have been particularly offensive – many immigrants to the Union would have been British, after all.

It should also be noted that *Fraser's Magazine* effectively shifted northwards in its sympathies after its October 1863 edition, when it published an exceedingly positive review of Cairnes's *The slave power* by Sir James Fitzjames Stephen. Stephen agreed with most of Cairnes's arguments, and concluded that Britain must 'Be perfectly neutral, be civil to each party, and sympathise fully with neither.'[56] After this, *Fraser's* published only two more articles on the American Civil War: a review of events in June of 1864 and an article on abolitionism in January 1865. Neither article favoured either side.

It would be wrong to deny that some individuals believed or hoped the conflict in America would damage democracy, but it is clear that the majority of conservatives, let alone those individuals who sympathised with the Confederacy, never held that view. Further, despite some historians' assertions, *The Times* refused to consider democracy to be at stake in America, noting, 'Far be it from us to dogmatise about democracy or to attribute the Civil War to republican institutions. The secession of the South is certainly not a necessary result of any form of government.'[57] The *Athenaeum*, which argued in favour of the South solely on the grounds that secession was a constitutional right, made a point of defending American republicanism. Reviewing a publication that denounced American democracy, in 1864, it remarked,

> The author's undertaking is by no means original. Of late years a fashion has grown up amongst writers of a certain school, on both sides of the Atlantic, to attribute every unpleasant feature of American society to democratic institutions, and then to cast the odium of its parentage on the memory of the illustrious man whose pen drew up the Declaration of Independence.[58]

The reviewer went on to disparage the publication. There does, therefore, seem to be evidence, then, for the assertion of the *British Quarterly Review* that although 'a few old Tories of the school of Sibthorpe, have, indeed,

---

[55] Ibid. (Feb. 1863), 192.
[56] Ibid. (Oct. 1863), 420–37.
[57] *The Times*, 18 Oct. 1861, 9.
[58] *Athenaeum*, 5 March 1864, 329. The work in question was *Alexander Hamilton and his contemporaries* by Christopher Riethmüller. This was an American publication that appears to have had little circulation in Britain.

exulted in the heat of debate at the breaking up of the great democracy', the clear majority never did.[59]

It is also worth mentioning that even those opposed to conservatives of any stripe contradicted themselves in their accusations levelled against the conservatives' views of America. *Reynolds's Weekly*, for instance, initially argued that conservatives were pro-North because they admired the Union's determination to crush the Confederacy: 'What they admire is strong, remorseless Government, which upon the slightest symptom of disaffection, on the part of any portion of its subjects, would sweep them out of existence with discharges of grapeshot, or trample their bodies under the iron hoofs of ferocious dragoons.'[60] This melodrama aside, it should be noted that any support of the South effectively meant endorsing the right of secession. This was hardly an argument that would find much support among mid-nineteenth-century conservatism. J. F. Stephen, writing in *Fraser's*, defined the problem the doctrine of secession posed for conservatives: 'principles from which nothing but universal anarchy would follow . . . such a principle was probably never held by any sane man'.[61] It is also surely no coincidence that numerous Union apologists were careful to cite Ireland every time they dismissed the right of secession.[62]

The idea that conservatives were pro-southern was an argument asserted largely by their opponents, rather than by conservatives themselves. Indeed, conservatives were largely disinclined to be associated with Confederate sympathisers. As Stephen Koss has noted, the Conservative Party took pains to distance itself from newspapers sympathetic to the South such as the *London Standard*.[63] This raises the question, if the conservatives were pro-southern, why did they deny it, especially if, as it has been alleged, the British electorate was so sympathetic to the Confederacy? The answer must be that either the conservatives were never as fond of the South as has been claimed, or being pro-Confederate did not endear one to the British electorate. Certainly, there seemed to be no political capital to be made by defending the South.

---

[59] *British Quarterly Review* (Oct. 1861), 471.
[60] Ibid. 17 Feb. 1861, 8.
[61] *Fraser's Magazine* (Oct. 1863), 421.
[62] For example, see the *Spectator*, 23 March 1861, 300, and see below. Hernon, meanwhile, notes that Irish nationalists leaned southwards in their sympathies as the war progressed and equated the Confederates' struggle for independence with that of Ireland. This cannot have been a coincidence: *Celts, Catholics and copperheads*, 92–5.
[63] Koss, *The rise and fall of the political press*, i. 159.

THE POLITICAL DEBATE

Addressing the public: MPs' verdicts

Reviews of members of parliament's meetings during the conflict shows just how diffuse politicians' opinions on America were. The meetings have the same advantage as those of the aristocrats as barometers of public opinion, which is lacking from the oft-cited (and under-examined) anti-slavery and pro-recognition rallies – namely, that they were not convened by each side's propagandists and partisans (unless the MP in question was such), and thus filled with participants amenable to the speakers' views. The members of parliament spoke to either electors or constituents (hence an audience not necessarily partisan regarding the war) on public affairs generally, and thus could not simply promote prejudice unchallenged. Besides the speeches previously examined in Chapters 2 and 3, references to America were quite common throughout 1862 and 1863. In 1864, references to America became fewer, and remained so until the defeat of the Confederacy in April 1865.

Charles Gilpin and Joseph Warner, Lord Henley, the Liberal and Conservative members for Northampton respectively, spoke at the Corn Exchange on 14 January 1862. Gilpin's view on Anglo-American affairs was:

> There was a complaint – and to some extent it was a just complaint – that English people showed little sympathy with the efforts of the North. He could tell them why for a moment that was apparently true. It was because the North had not identified themselves with the first principle of their great constitution – viz., that all men are free and equal (Loud cheers).[64]

Gilpin was, of course, referring to the Declaration of Independence rather than the constitution. Yet he was essentially doing what, as Garry Wills has established, Lincoln would do with the Gettysburg Address – import the equality spoken of in the declaration into the constitution.[65] More important, however, was Gilpin's assertion that English sentiment was not, in fact, pro-Confederate, but, rather, unsympathetic to the Union – and with good reason, one of the main reasons being the North's unwillingness to act against slavery. Indeed, so far as the Confederacy was concerned, Gilpin hoped the British government would never 'recognize a nation of slave-owners (hear, hear)'. Gilpin also took care to insist, 'It was no Republican bubble which burst there (cheers); it was no failure of the principles of democracy (cheers) that was shown by the quarrel between North and South.'[66] Gilpin's fellow member, Lord Henley, warmly supported Gilpin's remarks, including the positive ones on America – this, despite the fact that Henley strongly opposed extending the franchise. The two men again addressed their constituents the following year. Gilpin discussed Lincoln's Emancipation Proclamation and urged the Union to free all the slaves – not merely those in the southern

---

[64] *Reynolds's Weekly*, 19 Jan. 1862, 5.
[65] Garry Wills, *Lincoln at Gettysburg: the words that remade America*, New York 1992.
[66] *Reynolds's Weekly*, 19 Jan. 1862, 5.

states – if it wanted England's sympathy. Again, he took pains to argue that the American Civil War did not reflect badly on democracy. Lord Henley again supported him.[67]

Gilpin's speech, which was largely sympathetic to the Union, was far better received than those of members of parliament who spoke in favour of the South – even though the speech in question was made in Lancashire. On 21 January 1862, the Liberal member for Salford, William Nathaniel Massey, proposed to his constituents, 'it was the duty of the great maritime powers to consider whether the time had not come, by mediation and friendly interposition (hisses and applause) to endeavour to put an end to this state of affairs'.[68] There was, as we shall see, virtually always some opposition towards any member who spoke in favour of the South, something that was not true for those who remained neutral, or leaned northwards in their sympathies. Massey, however, did not get a chance to take up the issue with his constituents again. In 1863 he vacated his seat to go and serve in the colonial government in India.

In the same week, the Liberal member for Brighton, William Coningham, shared Gilpin's and Lord Henley's views and told his constituents that the North would not win until they began emancipating the slaves: 'If they proclaimed emancipation, then they would conquer and the South would fall before them like a pack of cards (cheers).'[69] Coningham spoke again on 1 December 1862, with his fellow member, James White, at the town hall. Both men expressed their sympathy with the Union.[70]

On 3 February 1862, William Angerstein, the Liberal (and pro-reform) member for Greenwich, spoke at the Literary Institute. Angerstein leaned southwards in his sympathies, believing that the South had the right of secession under the American constitution, and praised their free-trading policies; he did, however, insist, 'He was no Southerner, and should indeed be sorry to express sympathy with the views of those who had for many years upheld slavery.' Further, Angerstein opposed both interference and recognition, and concluded, 'that whether the Americans chose to have two or even three separate Governments mattered not to us'.[71] Angerstein spoke to his constituents again a year later. Once again he spoke against the Union, stating, 'The Government there was absolutely irresponsible, and the most gross speculation and jobbery universally prevailed with regard to the conduct of the war. He denied that the American struggle was entirely a question of slavery (cheers and dissent).' Unlike in 1862, Angerstein this time urged southern recognition and there were cheers and cries of 'No, no.'[72] Once again, there

[67] Ibid. 8 Mar. 1863, 1.
[68] Ibid. 26 Jan. 1862, 1.
[69] Ibid.
[70] Ibid. 7 Dec. 1863, 5.
[71] Ibid. 9 Feb. 1862, 3.
[72] Ibid. 1 Feb. 1863, 3.

THE POLITICAL DEBATE

were clear divisions regarding America. Despite this disagreement, however, Angerstein received a unanimous pledge of support from his constituents.

Just as Bright regularly fulminated against the Confederacy from Cobden's constituency at Rochdale (his pro-Union speeches tended to receive a mixed reception in his home constituency of Birmingham), the radical and pro-Confederate MP John Arthur Roebuck regularly denounced the Union in his constituency of Sheffield. Speaking at the Annual Cutler's Festival in Sheffield, in mid-August 1862, Roebuck found himself in the august company of Palmerston and the mayor of Manchester (who was sympathetic to the North). Addressing a crowd predominately made up of working men, Roebuck made the usual denouncements of the North and caused a minor sensation by openly demanding of Palmerston whether or not it was time to recognise the Confederacy. Palmerston refused to answer Roebuck's demands and the mayor of Manchester requested that Roebuck refrain from pursuing the matter. Roebuck was probably able to gain approval from his audience because producers of cutlery's interests (and by extension their labour force's) had been damaged by the Morrill tariff.[73]

On 20 October 1862, Alexander Colquhoun Stirling Murray Dunlop, the Liberal member for Greenock, addressed his constituents at the new town hall. One of Dunlop's claims to fame was his bill which ended the Gretna Green marriages. Having dealt with marriages, Dunlop strayed into the field of divorce, declaring that the Union was committing a 'perverse injustice' by attacking British neutrality and that, although he despised the South, the North should let it go. Dunlop, however, also expressed the 'most intense repugnance' towards recognition of the Confederacy.[74] Dunlop spoke to his constituents again at the Greenock town hall in November of 1863, and although he confessed to not knowing how the contest would resolve itself, noted, 'Whether the Union was restored or not he thought they had reason to congratulate the lovers of freedom on the shock which had been sustained by the atrocious system of slavery.'[75] Although not necessarily a northern sympathiser, Dunlop was clearly opposed to the South.

The member of parliament Western Wood spoke on 21 October 1862 at the West Kent Agricultural Society at Bromley. After praising the Lancashire operatives' patience,

> He hoped, for the sake of the honour and glory of this country, that Her Majesty's Government would persevere in the course which they had laid down and so religiously followed, and which received the approbation of the country at large, and that they would continue to observe a strict neutrality between the contending parties.[76]

---

[73] Ibid. 17 Aug. 1862, 4.
[74] Ibid. 26 Oct. 1862, 8.
[75] Ibid. 29 Nov. 1863, 4.
[76] Ibid. 26 Oct. 1862, 8.

If Wood was correct in his assertion, neutrality was the most popular course of action, even during 1862. Wood, unfortunately, did not live to see the wisdom of his stance vindicated, for he died the following year.

Some tried to have it both ways. Edward Pleydell Bouverie, the Liberal member for Kilmarnock, addressing his constituents at the George Inn on 27 October 1862, argued that he believed the South would win its independence, but added, 'When I talk of the United States, you will always bear in mind that their misfortunes, their distress, their losses, and their sufferings are all our distresses, our losses, and our sufferings.'[77] In other words, although Bouverie doubted that the Union could defeat the Confederacy, he was eager, desperate almost, not to appear anti-North.

That same week the two Liberal members for Plymouth, Robert Porrett Collier (later Lord Monkswell) and W. Morrison, spoke at the Mechanic's Institute. Collier denounced both intervention and recognition to cheers; Morrison agreed with his fellow member and stated that even the cotton famine did not justify intervention on Britain's part.[78] Collier did more than just denounce the Confederacy in public speeches. As Judge Advocate of the Fleet, he served as counsel to the Admiralty and was instrumental in preventing the escape of the Laird's Rams. As this was Plymouth, rather than Lancashire, this was not a controversial proposal; it does, however, reinforce the fact that the notion of going to war for cotton was widely decried.

Another meeting where a member of parliament leaned northwards in his sentiments was held in December. E. A. Leatham, Liberal member for Huddersfield, spoke to 2,000 of his constituents on American affairs at the Philosophical Hall on 9 December 1862. He denounced the argument that recognition would force the North to realise that re-union was impossible, stating, 'he was not by any means convinced of the hopelessness of that cause'. Leatham also expressed his view of claims made by southern propagandists of Britain's forming a profitable alliance with the Confederacy,

> if you recognize the South you will ensure the perpetual friendship of the South. Don't let them be so sanguine. If all that had been written and said against England in the South, since this war commenced, had been retailed with the same fidelity with which all that had been written and said against us in the North had been retailed, he had a shrewd suspicion that they should not trouble themselves very much about the friendship of the South.[79]

Leatham clearly, although not necessarily a champion of the Union, certainly had no time for the Confederacy either.

Apart from Bright, most members of parliament usually expressed satisfaction with the government's cautious neutrality. The Liberal John Locke, for

---

[77] Ibid. 2 Nov. 1862, 1.
[78] Ibid. 3.
[79] Ibid. 14 Dec. 1862, 5.

example, while speaking to his electors in the borough of Southwark, on 16 December 1862, at the Bridge House Hotel, took pains to silence a heckler who accused the Palmerston administration of tolerating slavery.[80] When Locke spoke to his constituents a year later, he stated, 'There was no doubt great difference of opinion in this country upon the present struggle in America, but in his opinion, whichever side was victorious, slavery was doomed (Cheers).' Locke said he supported non-intervention and, to an elector who asked, 'Are you in favour of the recognition of the South?' Locke replied, 'Decidedly I am not (Loud cheering).'[81] Although Locke was not pro-North, he, like his constituents, opposed slavery and the South.

Two days later, on 18 December 1862, Bright and his fellow radical member for Birmingham, William Scholefield, addressed their constituents in the town hall. Scholefield, speaking first, 'stated that his decided conviction was that the Government was bound immediately to recognize the Southern States – a sentiment which created a very considerable uproar, in which it was impossible to tell whether the cheers or the groans and hisses preponderated'. Bright, no longer preaching to the converted at Rochdale, none the less to his credit spoke in favour of the Union, although the audience was as divided over his views as they were over Scholefield's. It was here that Bright made his famous remark, 'Remember that there will be one wild shriek that will startle all human kind if that American Republic is overthrown', to which the crowd signally failed to respond. Bright also stated, 'There has been every effort that money and malice could make to stimulate amongst the suffering people of Lancashire an opinion in favour of the Slave States, but they have not been able to get it.'[82] It is from here that the myth that the Lancashire operatives were pressured to agitate for the Confederacy originates. As we have seen, the national press (with the signal exception of the republican *Reynolds's Weekly*) and numerous members of parliament had opposed going to war for cotton, and effectively discouraged the unemployed operatives from agitating (there was none the less, as Mary Ellison has established, some agitation on the part of the Lancashire operatives for intervention). This was misrepresentation on a grand scale.[83] Needless to say, Bright could not cite any examples to back up these frankly false assertions, and historians since have not found any evidence whatsoever of this alleged 'money and malice'.

Bright and Scholefield sparred again at Birmingham in January 1863, where both men divided the crowd once more.[84] Almost exactly a year later, in January 1864, Scholefield, speaking first, made another pro-southern speech. After insisting on the right of secession, Scholefield cited Lincoln's

---

[80] Ibid. 21 Dec. 1862, 5.
[81] Ibid. 13 Dec. 1863, 2.
[82] Ibid. 21 Dec. 1862, 5.
[83] See ch. 1 above as well as Ellison, *Support for secession*, passim.
[84] *Reynolds's Weekly*, 18 Jan. 1863, 8.

famous words, 'If I could save the Union without freeing any slaves I would do it', and remarked, 'After such an expression of opinion, he was surprised to hear people say that the object of the President was to put down slavery ("Hear, hear" and marks of disapprobation).' Scholefield declared, 'He believed that it was impossible to restore the Union by war (cheers and uproar).'[85] Bright refused to debate the right of secession, but restricted himself to denouncing slavery, and thus avoided Scholefield's challenge.

What is interesting about Bright's comments in Birmingham is that, unlike his speeches in Rochdale and at St James's Hall in London, he avoided claiming that 'privilege' was pro-South while the working class was pro-North. This was a curious omission, but its cause is explicable. William Scholefield was, in fact, even more politically radical than Bright. Son of Joshua Scholefield the Chartist, Scholefield *fils* was even more radical than his father and was one of the twelve members of parliament who had voted for the People's Charter in the House of Commons. Bright could not possibly pretend in Birmingham – as he did elsewhere – that pro-Confederate sentiment was the exclusive preserve of reactionaries. Not, at any rate, so long as Scholefield stood next to him. Nor, indeed, could he do so in a place like Birmingham where there existed strong radical sentiment and where the people were divided on the merits of the American Civil War. Bright, as he did so often on the subject, prevaricated, equivocated and evaded at Birmingham. We have already seen how Bright deliberately misrepresented English public opinion on the conflict. His actions at Birmingham are yet further evidence of this.

The Liberal member for Southwark and the under-secretary for foreign affairs, Austen Henry Layard, made one of the last speeches of 1862 when he spoke to his electors at the Bridge House Hotel on 22 December 1862. Layard was strongly in favour of non-intervention and insisted that the government had always shown the deepest sympathy towards the northern states. Layard particularly noted: 'During the session several attempts were made to induce the Government to recognize the Southern States, but those attempts were defeated, and he believed the country approved of the policy of the Government in resisting the motions made on the subject of the House of Commons. (Cheers).'[86] Layard also noted that 'the men of Lancashire knew that it was not by the recognition of the Southern States by this country that they would get cotton (Hear, hear)'.[87] He further made a point of criticising Bright's claims of English hostility towards the Union.

At this point, after having examined political meetings throughout 1861–2, from the outbreak of secession through to the *Trent* affair and the end of the year, one is tempted to ask what source the *New York Times* was

---

[85] Ibid. 31 Jan. 1864, 2.
[86] Ibid. 28 Dec. 1862, 7. Layard was referring chiefly to Lindsay's motion. Roebuck's attempt to force recognition was still to come.
[87] Ibid.

using when it claimed that 'nine out of ten members of Parliament sided with the rebels in their public addresses'.[88] Certain American sources, it seems, must be treated with caution.

Members of parliament continued speaking on America throughout the following year; the number of speeches in which the conflict was discussed only tapered off in 1864. In January 1863, the reactionary Liberal member for Stroud, Edward Horsman, spoke again on American affairs at the annual dinner of the Stroud Rifle Volunteer Corps. Horsman bemoaned northern hostility in general and cited Seward's published dispatches in particular, but argued that neutrality was the best option. He also paid a glowing tribute to the Lancashire operatives for their respect for neutrality, stating: 'the rich feel that the poor, instead of being as formerly a dangerous class, are now the strength and security on which the nation can rely'.[89] In other words, Stroud praised the Lancashire operatives for their patience regarding the blockade and King Cotton – not because they defied the wishes of their social superiors, but because they obeyed them.

Some members of parliament who had formerly been sympathetic to the Union betrayed signs of exasperation with the North as the struggle bore on. On 12 January 1863, the Liberal Alexander W. Kinglake addressed his constituents at the Bridgewater town hall. Kinglake continued to support non-intervention, but he accused the Union of disparaging the goodwill of the British government and of trying to seek a quarrel where none was offered.

> They have been indulging in language which, had it been used by a state in Europe, would undoubtedly have brought about long before this an interruption of diplomatic relations between the two Powers (Hear, hear). But, after all, there is a sort of cousinship between us, which prevents us from taking these things in too serious a way (Hear, hear).[90]

Kinglake also insisted that Britain could not mediate so long as there were no grounds to do so.

In the same week, the two Liberal members for Halifax, Sir Charles Wood (First Viscount Halifax after 1866), secretary of state for India, and Sir James Stansfeld, junior lord of the Admiralty, addressed their constituents. Both men spoke strongly in favour of reform, but when it came to the American Civil War, their paths diverged. Wood equated the Confederate struggle with that of Italy (despite the fact that Garibaldi favoured the North), a struggle for independence and self-government, and, calling the South a *de facto* state, said re-union was impossible. For this, Wood was cheered. Stansfeld, a long-time champion of Italian independence, however, begged to differ, saying, 'he regretted with a profound grief the current of public opinion, as

88 Quoted in *Reynolds's Weekly*, 28 Dec. 1862, 2.
89 Ibid. 4 Jan. 1863, 1.
90 Ibid. 18 Jan. 1863, 6.

interpreted by society and the press, for the Southern cause. The success of the South would be a triumph of our day and generation of a system of society founded on slavery (cheers).'[91] This meeting is important for several reasons. For one, notice how politicians who opposed the Confederacy did so on the grounds of slavery rather than on democratic principles. For another, despite the fact that Stansfeld claimed English society was in favour of the southern cause, his anti-Confederate speech was none the less cheered. The trouble with those commentators who regarded the war solely on the grounds of slavery is that they reduced the conflict to a case of black or white morals. This kind of viewpoint inevitably casts those who occupy the neutral grey area as black. Hence, pro-Union supporters tended to label those who held neutral views as pro-South, even when they were not. Bright, for example, effectively levelled this accusation when, from the safety of Rochdale, he claimed that those who were neutral were ignorant of the issues at stake in the war.[92] The other important point this meeting raises is that it is yet another example of a politician being sympathetic to both reform (which started its ascendance as an issue about now – two years before Appomattox) and the Confederacy. There are further examples of this to follow.

The cabinet minister Thomas Milner Gibson (who was anti-Confederate if not sympathetic to the Union) spoke to his constituents at Ashton-under-Lyne town hall on 21 January 1863. As expected, Milner Gibson blamed the war on southern slavery and insisted, 'I have often been astonished to hear it asserted that slavery had nothing to do with the war, for somehow slavery must have to do with it, because it constitutes such a great distinction between the two communities.'[93] Milner Gibson, as a cabinet member, was, unlike Bright, satisfied with the government's handling of American affairs. What is particularly interesting about this meeting is that Ashton-under-Lyne had been the site of at least one large operatives' meeting in favour of southern recognition.[94] This, of course, raises the question of whether or not specific meetings in certain places necessarily represented the widespread view of that particular area. Milner Gibson made another anti-Confederate speech in January 1864, telling his electors, 'I sympathise with nations struggling for independence, but this is not the question here (hear, hear).'[95]

The two members for the constituency of Marylebone, Lord Fermoy and John Harvey Lewis, spoke at the Literary Institute to their constituents on the same day. Perhaps mindful of the reception they had received during their anti-Union *Trent* affair speech, the two men leaned northwards in their sympathies this time. Indeed, Lord Fermoy 'denied that republican institu-

---

[91] Ibid.
[92] Ibid. 8 Feb. 1863, 3.
[93] Ibid. 25 Jan. 1863, 5.
[94] See ibid. 4 May 1862, 5.
[95] Ibid. 24 Jan. 1864, 5.

tions had had anything to do with that war, and said that if monarchical institutions had been introduced into America, the States would not have held together for as long as they had'.[96] This was not merely a criticism of Ramsden's remarks – it was a strong statement in favour of American republicanism – something that, according to the traditional interpretation, someone such as Lord Fermoy would never have made. Lewis, meanwhile, made a point of agreeing with his fellow member. The two men may have changed tack because it was expedient (suggesting an electorate sympathetic to the North), but a less cynical explanation is that they were genuinely outraged with the Union over the *Trent* affair. After that issue was settled, they had no further complaints about the North – or its political structure. Certainly they remained neutral – they spoke to their constituents again in January 1864 and again reiterated their support for neutrality.[97]

Another interesting meeting was that held by the Liberal member for Tower Hamlets, Acton Smee Ayrton, who met his constituents at the Beaumont Institute in Mill End Road on 22 January 1863. Ayrton appeared sympathetic to the South, and, as *Reynolds's Weekly* put it, in uncharacteristically dispassionate prose: 'On the American question, the views of the hon. gentleman did not harmonize with those of his hearers, by whom he was frequently interrupted.' Ayrton stated that he opposed slavery, but asked rhetorically if the North was truly 'warring for the freedom of the slaves (cries of yes yes and no no)'. Ayrton, after some bizarre remarks, regarding the Americans using human heads as cannon-balls, finally dropped the subject, stating, 'The fact was that, considering the entire question, he had no sympathy with either.'[98] Ayrton then championed reform, and made a point of criticising those politicians who claimed to support it, but failed to vote in favour of it (Sir John Ramsden may have been one of the individuals on his mind). Despite the fact that there were clearly members of the audience who disliked Ayrton's stand on America, he received a unanimous vote of thanks, suggesting the lack of impact America had on the politics of the day. On the subject of politics, once again we have a strongly pro-reform MP who, if not sympathetic to the Confederacy, certainly opposed the Union. We also see the familiar divisions on the subject of America.

Commentary on America was sometimes provoked by certain events. For example, when the Conservative Jonathan Peel, son of Sir Robert Peel, addressed his constituents at Bury on 3 February 1863, he made a point of thanking the Union for the *George Griswold* (a ship loaded with goods from America destined for Lancashire's deprived operatives), and cited it as an example of lessening northern hostility towards Britain. Peel was, however, critical of Lincoln's Emancipation Proclamation, stating that it was 'less for the welfare of the slave than for the ruin of his master; the motive was not in

---

[96] Ibid. 25 Jan. 1863, 8.
[97] Ibid. 31 Jan. 1864, 2.
[98] Ibid. 25 Jan. 1863, 8.

sympathy towards the slave, but antipathy towards his master'. Peel further compounded his ingratitude by calling for intervention, stating: 'If the war in America should continue, it becomes a call of duty upon us to intervene for the purpose of endeavouring to stop it (applause).'[99] Peel then went on to predict the independence of the Confederacy to cheers.

Lancashire, judging by the speeches of Massey and Peel, seemed to be the source of most anti-Union sentiment. It was noticeable again in the speech the Liberal member for Oldham, J. T. Hibbert, made to his constituents at the Oldham town hall on 2 February 1863. Hibbert declared himself unimpressed with Lincoln's Emancipation Proclamation, arguing that it 'must be looked upon more as a military measure rather than a social measure (applause)'. Furthermore, 'he thought the time was coming, if it had not already come, when in the interests of peace, in the interests of humanity, in the interests of the suffering population of Lancashire, this country ought to try offer its mediation between the two contending Powers (applause)'.[100] Hibbert also spoke strongly in favour of both reform and the ballot and thus must be added to the numbers of politicians antipathetic to the North, but in favour of reform.

The Liberal members for Lambeth, William Williams and F. Doulton, held an anti-slavery meeting at Lambeth Baths, Westminster Road, on 19 February 1863. They were somewhat lukewarm regarding Lincoln's measures. Williams 'expressed his regret that the Lincoln proclamation had no effect in abolishing slavery, and he was sorry to see that those who professed themselves abolitionists in America had not shown a proper feeling to men of colour'.[101] Doulton, however, pointed out that southern success meant the perpetuation of slavery. The men then proposed a resolution against southern secession and intervention by the British government, which was passed and forwarded to C. F. Adams – adding to the minister's collection of addresses in support of the Union. The opinions expressed by the two men were typical of English support for the North – namely, based on opposition to southern slavery rather than any particular admiration of the Union. Doulton spoke to his constituents again in January 1864, and again argued for neutrality.[102]

The two Liberal members for Wolverhampton, Charles Pelham Villiers and T. M. Weguelin, spoke to their constituents at a dinner held on 9 November 1863. Villiers compared southern secession to Irish rebellion and

---

[99] Ibid. 8 Feb. 1863, 3.
[100] Ibid. 4.
[101] Ibid. 22 Feb. 1863, 5. By having 'no effect in abolishing slavery', Williams presumably referred to the fact that only the slaves of rebels would be freed. Notice, too, the criticism directed at the Union for its treatment of blacks. It is also worth noting that when Williams spoke again to his constituents in December 1863, he spoke strongly in favour of reform and the ballot, but failed to make any reference to America. This suggests he did not regard the contest in America as having any significance in relation to reform. See ibid. 13 Dec. 1863, 2.
[102] Ibid. 31 Jan. 1864, 2.

called for neutrality, stating, 'I think the Americans ought to be allowed to settle their own affairs without more interference.'[103] It should be noted, however, that Villiers was a friend of Bright, having been a member of the Anti-Corn Law League, which probably had a bearing on his position regarding the Civil War.

Some politicians did adopt Bright's accusations of upper-class support for the South, but they were in a minority. Apart from Forster and Cobden (both of whom were Bright's allies in any case), only the Liberal member for Dudley, H. B. Sheridan, speaking at the Rosehill schoolrooms on 26 January 1864, concurred with the member for Birmingham's assessment. Sheridan stated that 'the educated classes were on the side of the South, (shame on them) the masses on the side of the North (hear, hear)'. Whether or not Sheridan really supported the Union is unclear, however, as he added, 'All that we could do was to look on and watch the struggle, in the hopes that some means might be found by which the discords and troubles of the contending parties might be satisfactorily settled (Hear, hear).'[104]

As we have already seen, some politicians openly sympathetic to the South found that their constituents opposed their views. The same was true for at least one pro-Confederate member of parliament. In August 1864, Lindsay spoke to his electors in Sunderland. Although Lindsay claimed that he opposed slavery, for which he was cheered, the electors responded very differently when he stated, 'I would say that the state of the slaves cannot have been so bad as it has been described (hisses and cries of "put him out").' Lindsay continued, arguing 'it is not right to give us exaggerated pictures of what these men are suffering ("put him out! The masters are tyrants")'.

The dissent continued to grow: 'The renewed hissing and uproar, which continued for several minutes' resulted in 'Lindsay being interrupted again and again when he attempted to proceed'.[105] Finally, Lindsay changed tack and claimed that the South would have to free their slaves in any event, which mollified the crowd to the extent that he was able to not only denounce the Union, but recommend mediation, to his electors' approval. The fact that the crowd's strong anti-slavery sentiment neither excluded anti-northern opinion nor considerations of mediation is something that should be borne in mind when examining the anti-slavery rallies.

As regards slavery, however, Lindsay's views unquestionably clashed with those of his electors. The root of Lindsay's beliefs lay in his friendship with the Confederate commissioners, Mason and Slidell, who, in numerous letters, convinced Lindsay that southern slavery was not as bad as it was reputed to be. Indeed, Lindsay had struck up a close relationship with Mason, remarking, 'in my intercourse with mankind, I have met few men whose

[103] Ibid. 15 Nov. 1863, 1.
[104] Ibid. 31 Jan. 1864, 3.
[105] Ibid. 21 Aug. 1864, 1.

society I have enjoyed more than that of Mr. Mason'.[106] No one in parliament (even Roebuck) was as pro-southern as Lindsay, who effectively served as the member for the Confederate states. Yet Lindsay held an extreme position, one that, as we have seen, clashed with that of his electors. His views also brought him into conflict with other British politicians such as Lord Enfield, who openly opposed Lindsay's calls for mediation at the annual dinner of the Middlesex Agricultural Society.[107] The fact is that calls in favour of helping the Confederacy were generally opposed in England throughout our period – as were speeches deemed too favourable to the South or slavery.

It needs to be further noted that the examination of the meetings above has not included the many meetings that Cobden and Bright held in Rochdale, nor the numerous meetings held by Forster in Bradford. It also excludes members of parliament who spoke at anti-slavery rallies, such as Samuel Gurney, J. E. Denson, and Peter A. Taylor.[108] In other words, numerous pro-northern speeches by members of parliament have been excluded from this account. Bearing this in mind, judging by what we have examined above, the views of the aristocracy, the conservative press and speeches made by politicians at their constituency (and other) meetings cast serious doubt on the notion of a pro-Confederate press, parliament or aristocracy. As varied and as contradictory as opinion on the Civil War was, it is clear that very few in England believed that the future of democracy was at stake in the conflict and that most wished to avoid becoming entangled in it at all.

Of course, the existence of Lindsay and others establishes clearly that the Confederacy did have its champions, even if they were in the minority. Further, despite their minority status, some of these southern champions in the House of Commons hoped to use their position to press parliament into recognising the Confederacy. Their tactics, and their failures, are the subject of the next chapter.

---

106 Lindsay papers, LND 7, 236.
107 Ibid. 639.
108 For Denson see *Reynolds's Weekly*, 8 Feb. 1863, 4; for Gurney see ibid. 3 July 1864, 1. Taylor, the member for Leicester and the then youngest member of the House of Commons, has long been identified as a northern sympathiser: Crook, *The North, the South and the powers*, 215; Foner, *British labor and the American Civil War*, 127.

5

The Confederacy's Partisans

> 'The truth would seem to be that the people of the
> Southern States are deficient in the knowledge
> and habits of civilisation.'

Having now examined both the contradictory views of English public opinion and the speeches of members of parliament on the American Civil War, we need to look at the efforts made by pro-southern members of parliament to obtain recognition of the Confederacy in the House of Commons. Besides looking at these attempts, we also need to measure the strength of pro-Confederate sympathy in England and determine the following pro-southern societies enjoyed. In addition, Confederate views of English opinion also need to be examined. This chapter examines the attempts to obtain formal recognition of the Confederacy made by pro-southern members of parliament from 1862 to 1863, the activities of the pro-southern societies in England and the public view of the Confederacy during this same period, and concludes with the breakdown of Anglo-Confederate relations at the end of 1863.

The attempts to obtain recognition

The examples of politicians' opinions on the merits of the American Civil War, examined in the last chapter, do much to explain why every effort by southern sympathisers to obtain Confederate recognition ended in ignominious failure. Further, by far the two most serious (and famous) attempts were made not by Conservative members of parliament, but by two radicals – namely, William Schaw Lindsay and John Arthur Roebuck. Although historians have discussed both of their attempts, the characters and motivations of the men themselves, the conditions under which the debate took place, as well as the reaction of the press to their efforts, have been largely unexamined.

Neither Lindsay nor Roebuck was the first MP to attempt to gain recognition of southern independence by the British government. As we have already seen, the MP William Gregory had made a first attempt in 1861. Gregory tried again in March 1862, but finding only two backers, the Liberals Lindsay and G. W. P. Bentinck, withdrew his motion at the Solicitor

General's request.[1] Lindsay's first motion was as unsuccessful as Gregory's, but the former at least found more than two backers, and provoked a minor debate.

Speaking on 18 July 1862, Lindsay urged that the British government mediate in the conflict.[2] He gained the support of fellow party-members Adolphus Vane-Tempest, Gregory, John T. Hopwood and the Conservative James Whiteside. Forster and P. A. Taylor opposed the motion. Ironically, it was the pro-southern Conservative, William Robert Seymour Fitzgerald, who stopped Lindsay by insisting upon adjourning the debate. It was Palmerston, however, who effectively ended the affair by ultimately declining to accept any motions pertaining to mediation. Palmerston, it must be noted, was unquestionably helped by the refusal of the Conservative Party (barring Whiteside) to become involved in the fray.[3]

Too much has been made of Lindsay's motion by historians who have uncritically cited the American Benjamin Moran's reports on the debate in his diary.[4] Moran, genuinely fearful about British intervention in the war, exaggerated the hostility shown towards the North. For example, he overrated the importance of Whiteside's speech, erroneously believing that his views represented those of the conservatives.[5] What historians have particularly quoted from the diary, however, is Moran's observation of the shouts of disapproval Lincoln's name received when mentioned by Taylor. Some historians have even cited the existence of the jeers as proof of a pro-southern House of Commons.[6]

What Moran did not see, and could scarcely admit to, was that Taylor's speech contained just as much blatant propaganda as Lindsay's, except, of course, that it was in favour of the Union. Thus, in light of previous Anglo-American problems, most notably the *Trent* affair, it was scarcely a speech the House would applaud. None the less, when Taylor announced that advocacy of the South meant support of slavery, Moran observed, 'The jeers to this were feeble, as the truth it contained was felt.' Before the veracity of Taylor's statement is applauded, we should perhaps remember that, at this point in time, Lincoln was still publicly denying any policy of emancipation.

---

1 *Hansard*, clxv, 7 Mar. 1862, 1158–230.
2 Ibid. clxviii, 18 July 1862, 511–78.
3 See Crook, *The North, the South and the powers*, 213–14. Crook reveals that the conservatives saw 'nothing good to be got out of the American question' – yet more evidence against a pro-Confederate Conservative Party.
4 This is true of Adams, Jenkins and even Jones. See Adams, *Great Britain and the American Civil War*, ii. ch. ix passim; Jenkins, *Britain and the war for the Union*, ii. 97–100; Jones, *Union in peril*, 132–7.
5 Moran, *The journal of Benjamin Moran*, ii. 1042. Considering that the conservatives had decided not to enter the debate, it seems likely that Whiteside, like the rest of his party, were intent on scoring easy political points from the debate amongst Palmerston's liberals.
6 See Jenkins, *Britain and the war for the Union*, ii. 97–100.

The more significant fact to be noted is that the Confederacy's advocacy of slavery was clearly recognised by the Commons.

More important, however, is that the House accorded Taylor more respect than it did Lindsay, and what has been less frequently cited by historians is Moran's observations of the Commons when Lindsay spoke: 'He is a wretched speaker and soon drove half the members of a very full House away.' Indeed, 'Taylor soon brought back the crowd that hobbling Lindsay drove away and was met both by applause and condemnation.' Considering, too, that Lindsay made a 'positive declaration that the South meant nothing to him', the behaviour of the Commons was hardly an endorsement of pro-Confederate sentiment.

This fact is underlined when Moran's observations of Lindsay's supporters, such as Vane-Tempest, are noted: 'I thought he was drunk, and so did the House, for he came near to falling over the back of the bench in front of him on several occasions.' If we compare this to the fact that 'Great respect was paid to Mr. Forster's speech' (which also contained a great deal of pro-Union propaganda), the Commons' pro-southern sentiment appears virtually non-existent.[7] How seriously was the House taking Lindsay's, to say nothing of Forster's and Taylor's, remarks? Not very – if the speeches made and individuals who made them suggest anything. This, as we shall see, was also the verdict of the English press.

To sum up, the pro-Confederates' display was a very poor one, and if the House had scant respect for the pro-Northerners, it had even less time for Lindsay's semantics and Vane-Tempest's drunken performance. This, added to the conservatives' disinclination to become involved in the debate (beyond jeering at a divided Liberal Party), explains why Palmerston so easily terminated the discussion. One cannot claim, on the basis of this, that the majority of the House of Commons favoured of recognition of the Confederacy, as some historians have claimed. If anything, the evidence points to the opposite conclusion.

Also important was the opinion of the press, which was almost entirely opposed to Lindsay's motion. The *Illustrated London News* expressed complete satisfaction at the outcome of the debate and noted, 'we are glad to say that the Commons preserved the self-control which has so creditably characterised their proceedings in reference to America'. This was an important point – the journal was opposed to both recognition and fomenting ill will against the Union. Perhaps most importantly of all, the *Illustrated London News* viewed the debate as one occurring among a collection of mediocrities with a peculiar obsession regarding the events in America. For example, the journal reported that 'No speaker of first-class position took part in the debate except Lord Palmerston, who spoke only to deprecate discussion and to urge that so difficult and important a subject should be left to the Government.' Indeed,

---

[7] Moran, *The journal of Benjamin Moran*, ii. 1040–2.

the criticism of the northern and southern partisans went further: 'There was little that fell from any of the debaters that should annoy either Northern or Southrons, at least such among them as are aware that Mr. Whiteside is rather liked for a vituperation which disturbs the dullness of the House, but is nobody when heads are counted. The other speakers displayed the most laudable moderation of language.'[8] It was not only that 'No speaker of first-class position took part in the debate' but also that those who did, such as Whiteside, the violently anti-Union speaker who so alarmed Moran, was contemptuously dismissed as a 'nobody'. The press in England had a far better idea of where individuals ranked on the scale of parliamentary influence than Moran ever had. Their verdict on the debate was thus the more accurate one.

The *Illustrated London News* was not at all alone in its view of Lindsay's motion. The *Saturday Review*, as much as it disliked the Union, opposed the motion as well: 'Mr. Lindsay's motion was properly rejected by the House of Commons as inadvisable or premature. There is no ground for simple mediation so long as the belligerents have no common basis of agreement.'[9] Simply put, there were no grounds for offering mediation and no interest on the part of Britain in becoming entangled in the conflict. Most other journals toed the same line.

It is worth noting that by the time Lindsay put forward his motion for the recognition of the Confederacy, his reputation was at something of a nadir as far as Palmerston and Russell were concerned. Lindsay had visited the emperor of France, Louis Napoleon, on 11 and 13 April 1862. Acting on his own agenda, Lindsay had sought an interview to ascertain whether or not the French were interested in joint recognition, with Britain, of the Confederacy. Napoleon III was frank with the MP, probably too frank. He declared that he wanted to recognise the South, but was disgusted with the treatment he had met at the hands of Russell and Palmerston. According to Napoleon, when he first formally asked the British government to join him in recognising the South, his communication had somehow ended up in the hands of the North. As a result,

> He was undoubtedly much displeased, intimating, as I understood him, that after the way in which he had been treated he could not <u>on American affairs</u> hold further official intercourse with our Government, or rather make any further suggestions unless he was satisfied that our government was prepared to act with him.[10]

There is no evidence establishing that Palmerston or Russell did, in fact, pass on the emperor's message to the Union. What had probably happened was that the North, recognising that the French would not act against the Union without Britain's help, had threatened Napoleon with dire consequences if he

---

8   *Illustrated London News*, 26 July 1862, 98.
9   *Saturday Review*, 26 July 1862, 91.
10 Lindsay papers, LND 7, 157–64 [the underlining is Lindsay's].

followed such a course. That this threat was made after the emperor had contacted the British government convinced Louis Napoleon that Perfidious Albion was double-dealing. Besides suggesting just how little trust existed between the French and British governments, this accusation of Napoleon's would prove to be crucial during Roebuck's motion a year later.

That was in the future. For now, Napoleon III asked Lindsay to act as an emissary – to sound out Palmerston and Russell on joint recognition of the South. The emperor also requested that Lindsay sound out the leader of the Conservative Party, Derby, and Disraeli as well. Lindsay recognised that his actions were, to say the least, unorthodox. But by this time, he was already virtually the member for the Confederate states of America (in the same way as Cobden and Bright were the 'Members for America'), due to his dealings with Mason and Slidell, and wanted to goad the cabinet into action.

The cabinet's two leading lights were unimpressed. When approached by Lindsay for an interview regarding what the emperor had said, Russell replied in a simple letter, 'I think the best way for the two Governments to communicate with each other is through their respective embassies.' Lindsay was even less lucky when it came to seeing Derby. The Tory leader simply refused him an audience outright. Lindsay did secure an interview with Disraeli, but the latter gave nothing away and told him that the conservatives believed all such questions should be left to the government.[11]

Lindsay, discouraged, returned to France to inform Louis Napoleon of his failure. Upon arrival in there, however, Lindsay discovered that Palmerston and Russell had already been active. As Lindsay noted, the British ambassador, Lord Cowley, had recently informed the French that 'the Emperor should not have sent "proposals" to England through me and not the usual channels'. Russell and Palmerston were clearly determined to nip in the bud Lindsay's amateur diplomacy.[12]

Whether or not Louis Napoleon was, as the cliché has it, not one to take 'no' for an answer, or whether he believed that Russell was the prime mover behind the diplomatic rebuff, he persuaded Lindsay to approach Palmerston instead. Lindsay obliged, writing to the prime minister on 21 April 1862, asking for an audience. He did not get one. Palmerston was polite, but firm: 'with regard to any message or communication from the Emperor of the French, I would wish you to say to him that we think it for many obvious reasons undesirable that his majesty's communications should be made to us through any other than an official channel'.[13] Palmerston and Russell regarded any business pertaining to foreign affairs as the business of cabinet only. They were not going to be pressured into adopting a course of action by the lobbying of a troublesome backbencher pretending to be a diplomat. Nor, clearly, were they going to be pressured into adopting a course of action by the

---

[11] Ibid. 165–74.
[12] Ibid. 181 [the underlining is Lindsay's].
[13] Ibid. 186–90.

same backbencher presenting motions in the House of Commons. Lindsay, however, would be connected with another attempt to gain the recognition of the South, once more involving the French. This was Roebuck's motion, which took place a year later.

Roebuck's motion was not the only effort at southern recognition in 1863; Lord Campbell, in the House of Lords, urged the recognition of the South earlier in the year, but as Campbell received not a single vote in support from his fellow Lords, Russell had no trouble issuing a refusal.[14] Roebuck's motion was more serious because of the involvement of Napoleon III, who apparently hoped to use Roebuck to sound out the British government on the possibility of either mediation or intervention, but was effectively foiled by the member for Sheffield's indiscreet revelations in the House of Commons. Despite, or more probably because of, the emperor's involvement, Roebuck's efforts, like Lindsay's, were completely in vain. Although all historians of our subject discuss Roebuck's motion to some extent, as D. P. Crook admits, 'Much ink has been spilled on the Roebuck affair, and it is still not completely solved.'[15] Lindsay's personal papers do, however, shed some new light on the subject.[16]

Lindsay observed that soon after Roebuck gave notice of his proposed motion, 'a rumour became current – by whom circulated I cannot tell – that the Emperor of the French had changed his well-known views on American affairs and that he would not be prepared to join England in the recognition of the Southern States'. This alarmed Roebuck. Despite Lindsay's obtaining a letter from the Confederate commissioner in Paris, John Slidell, disproving this rumour, Roebuck insisted he would be satisfied only if he were to hear such sentiments from Louis Napoleon himself. Accordingly, as Lindsay put it, 'at great inconvenience to myself and with much reluctance I accompanied Mr. Roebuck to Paris and I was alone induced to do so by the express request of Mr Mason'. The amateur diplomats arrived in Paris on 21 June and met the emperor at the Tuileries the following day.[17]

Lindsay had reason to be apprehensive. After his past experience as messenger-boy for the emperor, he doubted much good could come out of a second encounter. As it turned out, Lindsay was to find his misgivings justified. Further, Roebuck, in his parliamentary career, had been extremely hostile to Louis Napoleon and 'had on many occasions, both in and out of the Commons, attacked in no uncertain terms the Emperor's policy and himself'. Regarding the latter point, the emperor apparently wanted bygones to be bygones and was extremely courteous to Roebuck, although Lindsay believed

---

14 *Hansard*, clxix, 23 Mar. 1863, 1714–41.
15 See Crook, *The North, the South and the powers*, 309–16.
16 Lindsay also sent an account of the meeting in a letter to James Mason that was passed on to the authorities at Richmond. The major details of the letter closely match Lindsay's recollections, which are therefore probably accurate. See Mason to Benjamin, 20 June 1863, in *Correspondence of James M. Mason*, 419–25.
17 Lindsay papers, LND 7, 195–6.

this was so the latter 'could not with any decency again attack his Majesty in public'. Roebuck put forward his case for recognition of the Confederacy, with which Napoleon entirely agreed. Indeed, he replied, if Lindsay's account is accurate, 'I believe the recognition of the South as an independent nation would restore peace and therefore I am most anxious in concert with England to adopt measures to recognize a people who have given such proofs of their abilities to maintain their independence and govern themselves.' The emperor further stated that he had just requested his ambassador, Baron Gros, to ascertain whether England was prepared to entertain the question of recognition and to suggest any mode of proceeding. He also added with regard to his views on recognition: 'I wish them to be known.' As far as Lindsay and Roebuck were concerned, so far so good, but then the emperor alluded to his conversation with Lindsay a year earlier and repeated his charge that the last time he had tried to approach Palmerston and Russell on the subject of recognition, they had forwarded his views to Lincoln's government. This, he claimed, was why it was difficult for him to make a formal application to the British. This last bit of information was to prove fatal.[18]

Roebuck and Lindsay returned to Britain, their trip having been noted by the press. As a result, when the former finally proposed his motion, he did so to a full House. Speaking on 30 June 1863, Roebuck's arguments resembled most pro-southern speeches; he cited Union aggression both before and during the war, the Morrill tariff, the hypocrisy surrounding slavery, and the impossibility of Confederate defeat.[19] Then Roebuck dropped his bombshell and announced that Napoleon III had asked for the assistance of the House in getting British support for a formal proposal of mediation that the French government was about to make. This caused a sensation – but not in the fashion Roebuck had intended. As Lindsay put it,

> he made a much more pointed allusion to our conversation with the Emperor than the occasion required. He not merely repeated nearly everything he had said to the Emperor but gave the House to understand that he had a message from his Majesty as if the House of Commons could listen to any message from a Foreign Monarch.

Roebuck had violated both diplomatic and House of Commons protocol. Worse still, from Lindsay's point of view, Roebuck referred to the emperor's statement that his previous request for joint recognition to the British government had made its way to the Americans. In the words of *The Times*, 'of course there were loud cheers from the opposition at the exposure of this meanness and double-dealing of a Liberal Government'. Although the Tories had no interest in making recognition of the Confederacy a party issue, this

---

[18] Ibid. 197–8.
[19] *Hansard*, clxxi, 30 June 1863, 1771–814.

was simply too good an opportunity to miss. Roebuck, a nominal Liberal, had hurt his own party, which swiftly closed ranks.[20]

By repeating the emperor's accusation of British perfidity, Roebuck had committed a serious blunder – as Lindsay immediately realised, noting,

> he had no occasion to refer at all to that delicate affair – it was not necessary for him to say more than that it was the pleasure of the House to adopt his resolution he <u>knew</u> that France would heartily co-incide. He had no need even to state that he had seen the Emperor for every newspaper in the Kingdom had for some days before announced the fact and therefore the members knew very well that what he stated in regard to co-operation with France might be depended upon. But it was not altogether what he stated but the <u>manner</u> in which he gave the information which startled the House.

Roebuck's tone was both sarcastic and offensive and, by questioning the honour of the cabinet, he had guaranteed that response to his motion would be hostile. To the liberals, the issue was now one of damage limitation, especially as the conservatives' taunts began to grow in volume. By the time Roebuck concluded his speech, dismissing northern military power in the face of a combined British and French alliance, and demanded that the House recognise the South, his opponents – most of them from his own party – were ready.

The first member to reply, Lord Robert Montagu, cited Ireland and rhetorically asked how Britain would respond to foreign intervention should it suppress rebellion there. Montagu called for the maintenance of neutrality and was supported by both H. M. Clifford and Gladstone. The latter went so far as to warn Roebuck that 'Recognition, though not inseparably connected with the use of force, was commonly accompanied by it.'[21] Gladstone thus challenged Roebuck's glib assertions, reminding the House that recognition of the Confederacy would not be a cost-free action. Forster, speaking next, predictably opposed Roebuck, although he did note that, regarding slavery, 'he was not one to justify the North in their conduct upon this question'.[22] Not unexpectedly, Bright also insisted on making a speech which, although a familiar refrain of praise for American institutions as a whole, was unquestionably accorded far more respect than Roebuck's – this despite the fact that Bright's speech contained as many inaccuracies and as much misinformation and hyperbole as Roebuck's, the only difference being that it was in favour of the Union. The liberals were doubtless relieved that Bright, for once, was helping them get out of trouble instead of getting them into it.

Lindsay recognised that Roebuck had blundered badly and, noting the level of abuse directed at himself and the latter, particularly by his own party,

---

[20] Lindsay papers, LND 7, 199–201 [the underlining is Lindsay's].
[21] *Hansard*, clxxi, 30 June 1863, 1809.
[22] Ibid. 1816.

stayed silent.[23] This meant that only two members spoke in Roebuck's defence: Lord Robert Cecil and Percy Wyndham. Cecil argued that ending the war would allow cotton back into England for the benefit of the operatives. This argument was obviously suspect because of the South's King Cotton tactics. Percy Wyndham's insistence, meanwhile, that many Northerners would welcome intervention sounded equally dubious so long as the Union was committed to continuing the war.

The cabinet, by this time, had had enough. The home secretary, Sir George Grey, condemned the whole involvement of Napoleon as irregular and demanded that debate be adjourned until such time as news from the French arrived. Grey got his wish and the debate was suspended. If Napoleon had ever asked Baron Gros to sound out the British government on southern recognition, Roebuck's antics ensured that any such orders were swiftly rescinded. Baron Gros quickly denied that he had ever received any such instructions and, with that, Roebuck's entire motion was discredited. Although Lindsay later observed that Baron Gros had declared he had received no 'official' instructions, meaning that he might have received unofficial ones, no one was interested in this distinction.[24] Roebuck was thus forced to withdraw his motion a few days later, his credibility in shreds.

As *Reynolds's Weekly* remarked, the pantomime's 'principal performers', Bright and Roebuck, had both abandoned previous positions: Roebuck had always opposed Louis Napoleon, while Bright had usually supported him.[25] *Reynolds's* dismissed the whole performance as a farce and it was not far wrong. Roebuck's motion had not just ended in farce but rather, thanks to the unwelcome debate's mysteriously bizarre diplomatic justification, it had run as a farce from beginning to end. Indeed, the only clear result of the motion was that it convinced the Confederacy that Britain would not intervene in the war, which ultimately led to Mason's withdrawal.[26]

There remain two issues regarding Roebuck's motion that have not been properly considered by historians. The first is that, although Roebuck's motion actually took place during the same week as Gettysburg, the English were almost a fortnight behind events in America. In the first days of May, Robert E. Lee, although greatly outnumbered, routed Joseph Hooker at Chancellorsville and, after resting and refitting the following month, invaded Pennsylvania with an army 75,000-strong. This invasion, unlike that of Maryland in 1862 that ended bloodily at Antietam, was not only larger, it was much better prepared.[27] Indeed, Lee's invasion of Pennsylvania was arguably the height of southern success and was partially why Roebuck made his attempt to gain recognition. The Union had its back against the wall, yet,

---

[23] Lindsay papers, LND 7, 200.
[24] Ibid. 204. See also, Lindsay to Palmerston, 11 July 1863.
[25] *Reynolds's Weekly*, 5 July 1863, 5.
[26] Owsley, *King Cotton diplomacy*, 466.
[27] McPherson, *Battle cry of freedom*, 638–51.

despite this, the House of Commons refused to consider recognition. This must surely cast serious doubt on allegations of a pro-southern parliament.

The second issue is the general hostility in England towards notions of military alliance with France, a probable necessity if Britain did enter the Civil War on the side of the Confederacy. As Miles Taylor has shown, France was widely (and probably wrongly) blamed for the unsatisfactory end to the Crimean War.[28] Having had France as an ally in one war and found it wanting, Britain was in no mood to find itself relying on France again. There was serious distrust in the House of Commons regarding Louis Napoleon's government – France was simply not a nation on which the British wished to rely – or, at least, not in these circumstances.

If Conservative members of parliament were amused at the trouble Roebuck's antics had caused the government, the press was not. *The Economist* argued that as long as the Union continued trying to conquer the Confederacy, recognition was an act of war:

> Mere recognition would, therefore, when the subject is examined, be a breach of international law, without even the base merit of a corresponding advantage. It would not shorten hostilities; it would get us no cotton; it would not relieve our manufacturing districts. If we chose to intervene by war, to break the blockade, to create the 'South' . . . we should at least gain as much. But the objections to this course are so many and so obvious, that no one even proposes it.[29]

Of course, someone had proposed such a course – namely Roebuck. The journal's point, however, was that support for such a course was the preserve of a small minority – a minority, the journal concluded, who had lost sight of basic logic.

The *Illustrated London News* did not even grant Roebuck's motion any great attention but instead filed it away under its 'Parliamentary Sketches' column. This was hardly the location a journal would have placed a political debate if it assumed it was an important one. Nor was the journal overly impressed with Roebuck's theatrics: 'He does so concentrate his sarcasm and bitterness – delivers his opinions with such assertion of their being unanswerable . . . that he never fails to interest, if he does not actually convince.'[30] Indeed, the *Illustrated London News* thought more highly of Bright's equally histrionic performance.

Most violently opposed to the motion was the *Saturday Review*, which remarked, 'Mr. Roebuck, in his ungenerous and studiously indiscreet speech, virtually accepted the natural consequence of the policy of which he supported.' By 'natural consequence' the journal meant war, even though it

---

28 Taylor, *The decline of British radicalism*, 258.
29 *The Economist*, 4 July 1863, 732–3.
30 *Illustrated London News*, 4 July 1863, 10.

believed 'it is perfectly true no effective resistance could be afforded to the maritime power of England and France'. Furthermore, the *Saturday Review* argued,

> The persistent attempt to conquer the South may be regarded by many as a blunder, and by some as a crime, but it is impossible to suggest that the incidental injury which it inflicts upon England is a just cause for hostilities. . . . Mr. Roebuck, indeed, attempts to strengthen his case by pointing out the expediency of diminishing the formidable strength of the former Union. If he had wished to deprive his speech and his motion of all moral weight, both in England and America, he could not have avowed an unworthy motive with more damaging candour. The legitimate greatness of a foreign country is no excuse for projects against its prosperity. . . . It is, however, a waste of time to discuss the possible interest of England in union or in separation. It was not for the sake of Europe that the Southern States declared their independence, or that the North has expended half a million lives in the attempt to reconquer their allegiance.[31]

The journal completely opposed Roebuck's motion; although it took care to dismiss Bright's 'singular speculations' as well.

Lindsay made a (and the) last attempt at recognition of the South in the House of Commons in July 1864. Lindsay again asked Palmerston if the British government would mediate. Unlike in 1862, however, Lindsay found no backers and Palmerston's curt refusal ended the matter.[32] Not long after this, Lindsay, whose health was never particularly good, had a stroke. Although he eventually recovered – and lived until 1877 – the stroke kept him both out of the House and away from the political scene until after the Civil War ended. The South had lost one of its most vocal, if not effective, champions.

Lindsay and Roebuck must be regarded as the two members of parliament who made the greatest effort to obtain British recognition of the Confederacy in the House of Commons. Neither of them were the reactionary conservatives they should have been in accordance with the traditional interpretation. Indeed they were both liberals with impeccable radical credentials. If, then, they were supporters of democracy, what motivated them to propose British intervention on the side of the Confederacy? As we have seen, in Chapter 1, Lindsay was a committed pacifist who believed that as the South was unconquerable and because the war was not one of emancipation, there were no moral grounds for it – peaceful separation was the best result. In no small part thanks to his friendship with the southern commissioners, Lindsay carried these beliefs to the point of becoming, to all intents and purposes, an agent for the Confederacy. Determining Roebuck's motivations, however, is slightly more problematic.

---

[31] *Saturday Review*, 4 July 1863, 1.
[32] *Hansard*, clxxvi, 25 July 1864, 2018–19. See, in addition, Lindsay papers, LND 7, 441.

Like Lindsay, Roebuck was a self-made man. His political background was not only radical but Chartist. A friend of William Lovett and Francis Place, Roebuck had helped draft the People's Charter. Although Roebuck disliked the revolutionary element of Chartism, he none the less, as a barrister, defended numerous Chartists charged with sedition and similar crimes. Many of these cases he took on *pro bono*. Considering that Roebuck was not a wealthy man, his actions in this instance show a genuine commitment to the cause. Indeed, Roebuck's sobriquet was the 'poor man's lawyer' because of such work.[33] In his parliamentary career, Roebuck, like Bright, called for, among other things, the extension of the franchise and separation of church and state, and constantly lambasted the British aristocracy, holding it up to ridicule whenever possible. His strong support for free trade would have made him a natural ally of the Manchester school but for his dislike of Cobden and Bright. As he observed, 'The [Anti-Corn Law] League and its leaders have never been cordial with me. I would never run in their harness or strut at their word of command. This species of independence was deemed treason by the potentates of Lancashire.'[34] Roebuck, however, also fell out with Cobden and Bright because of their opposition to the Crimean War – a conflict Roebuck, and many other liberals and radicals, viewed as a campaign for liberty, especially as it would weaken Russia, the oppressor of Poland.[35]

Besides his activities as a Chartist, Roebuck came to prominence during the Crimean War when he called for an inquiry into the British government's activities in the conflict (although Roebuck supported the war, he predictably opposed the military incompetence associated with it). Roebuck's motion for 'a committee to inquire into the state of the army before Sebastopol' was put forward on 26 January 1855, after William Howard Russell writing for *The Times*, made public knowledge the news of the condition of the army. Despite opposition from the House, public opinion was behind Roebuck, and he soon found himself heading the committee. Although Roebuck's efforts were, according to his biographer, Sarah Wilks, only partially effective at best, his activities none the less brought down the Aberdeen administration.[36]

Despite the fact that Roebuck is best known for his activities during the Crimean War, he had also earlier distinguished (or disgraced, depending on whom one talked to) himself by his support of the French Canadians in Lower Canada in the 1830s. During that period, Roebuck was in correspondence with the province's speaker of the assembly, Louis Joseph Papineau, and, sympathetic to French Canadian demands for more accountable (i.e. democratic) government, raised them in the House of Commons. Parliament

---

33 Sarah Wilks, 'An independent in politics: John Arthur Roebuck, 1802–1879', unpubl. DPhil. diss. Oxford 1979, 47.
34 Ibid. 154.
35 Taylor, *The decline of British radicalism*, 223, 232.
36 Wilks, 'An independent in politics', 219–26.

ignored Roebuck only to see him vindicated when rebellion broke out in the colonies in 1837. Seen as something of a Canadian expert after this, he became involved with Lord Durham's plans for the colonies in the Durham Report, which paved the way for Canadian Confederation.[37] Most importantly, however, Roebuck found himself a celebrated champion of liberty.

Canada, however, brings us to Roebuck's views on the United States. Roebuck was born in India, but he spent his formative years in Upper and Lower Canada. When he spent them is just as important as where he spent them, for Roebuck arrived in Canada in 1815, just after the conclusion of the war of 1812. Although American traditional history blames Britain's violation of the United States' neutral rights by its impressment policies for the conflict, Canadian traditional history blames the war on American aggression and the United States' attempt to annex the colony while Britain was conveniently engaged in a war with Napoleon. Irrespective of the merits of these two interpretations, there is no doubt about which nation the inhabitants of Upper and Lower Canada blamed for the war. In short, Roebuck spent his formative years amongst a people who, as they saw it, were the victims of unprovoked American aggression. Considering the already high levels of anti-American sentiment felt by the descendants of the United Empire Loyalists in Upper Canada because of the Revolution, and by French Canadians, fearful for the future of their culture in the case of annexation, one can easily imagine what Roebuck learned of the United States – and its citizens – as a young man.

Roebuck's Canadian upbringing, and his later interests in Canada, made American threats of annexation very serious indeed. Past history, as far as Roebuck was concerned, had proved that the United States was an aggressor nation and, even if it had been rebuffed in the War of 1812, its greater strength by the time of the Civil War meant that it could undo the verdict of the last Anglo-American conflict. This explains Roebuck's constant description of the United States as both a bully and a threat to British peace and prosperity. When northern newspapers and individuals such as Seward made threatening noises, Roebuck took them seriously. So seriously, in fact, that far from being discouraged from entering the war on the side of the South, he treated such comments as evidence that Britain should enter the fray and remove this obvious threat to Canada's security for ever.

Unfortunately for the Confederacy, Roebuck was probably the worst member of parliament to champion it. Known as 'Tear 'em' after the watchdog in Sir Walter Scott's *Guy Mannering*, Roebuck wore this nickname with pride. Unfortunately, like many fierce canines, Roebuck sometimes bit the wrong people. Called 'a mock Robespierre who had no guillotine to command', by A. W. Kinglake, Roebuck's sarcastic, invective-ridden tone had made him many enemies in the House.[38] One of these enemies was

[37] Ibid. 77–145.
[38] Ibid. 222.

Russell, the foreign secretary – the wrong individual to offend if one wanted to introduce a motion involving foreign affairs. Politicians have longer memories than most, especially when it comes to personal insults. By the time of his motion to recognise the Confederacy, there were few in the House who had not felt the lash of Roebuck's tongue. His personal attacks over a long career had damaged his credibility, and, as Wilks observes, 'Roebuck never learned his lesson'[39] – the lesson being, that if he wanted support for his motions, a supply of friends was handier than a surplus of enemies.

Further, by the 1860s, Roebuck was something of an anachronism. His failure to submit to the increasing party discipline soon reduced him to the status of an outsider. Although some historians have declared that Roebuck was no longer a radical by this point in his career, they are wrong. Just prior to the war, in 1857, he helped establish the Parliamentary Reform Association, which contained men such as A. S. Ayrton and produced a manifesto in favour of reform signed by thirty-one members of parliament, including future pro-Northerners such as Cobden and Bright as well as W. Williams.[40] Further, although he angered numerous radicals by his support of Disraeli's 1859 bill, Roebuck was being true to his principles. He had always said he would support any reform bill no matter who introduced it – Liberal or Tory. Where Roebuck made an error, however, was in his refusal to join Gladstone's attack on the bill – something that earned him the enmity of his party.[41] None the less, despite the fact that Roebuck angered both his party and many of its radicals, Wilks provides compelling evidence that the labourers of Sheffield always regarded him as their champion.[42] The problem was that his unquestionably radical credentials could not serve as a substitute for support in the House. It thus seems likely that Roebuck's motion to recognise the South was doomed by the very fact that it was his motion – and the hostility he engendered both inside and outside the House points to this conclusion.

Suggestions have been made that the Confederate lobby in the House failed in its efforts largely because of poor organisation. This argument, however, fails to explain why few members of parliament were willing to champion recognition at public meetings and elsewhere. It was usually the same group of politicians, too, who supported intervention in America: Roebuck, Lindsay and Gregory – a cabal that lacked real power and influence in the House. The fact is, there was never a significant enough number of members of parliament sympathetic to the Confederacy for any attempt at recognition or mediation to succeed. It was lack of numbers, not organisation, which doomed southern hopes. The *Saturday Review* was not far wrong

---

[39] Ibid. 99.
[40] Ibid. 239.
[41] Ibid. 249–52.
[42] Ibid. ch. vii passim.

when it stated, 'no section of English politicians has either desired to make war on the North or give active assistance to the South'.[43]

Russell, Gladstone and the cabinet

The *Saturday Review*'s statement was not far wrong so far as the numerical majority of the Houses of Parliament was concerned, but the British cabinet did consider offering to mediate in the conflict on the basis of southern independence. Towards the end of September 1862, Russell (possibly with Gladstone's assistance) aired the proposal to the cabinet that Britain attempt to offer to mediate between the two sides.[44] Russell may have been influenced by the earlier appeal of Edward Everett, made in February 1861, to Lord Lyons, the British minister to Washington, to mediate between the contending parties.[45] After the war broke out, Everett supported the North's efforts, of course, but his earlier appeal unquestionably carried resonance. Russell managed to win over a couple of cabinet members to his plans, including the pro-northern duke of Argyll. He met, however, determined resistance from the secretary for war, George Cornewall Lewis, as well as from Thomas Milner Gibson, and failed to win over Palmerston.[46] Although Russell's proposal was never a formal one, Cornewall Lewis's opposition probably killed it. Cornewall Lewis was no fan of the Union, but he did not wish to involve Britain in a foreign war. He also, in a report, exaggerated the strength of the Union navy, citing the existence of ironclads in order to discourage any careless thought of conflict.[47] This was what would ultimately doom Russell's proposals. The foreign secretary did not want a war either, but mediation, to say nothing of intervention, would be seen as a hostile act by the North. Further, as there was little pressure either outside or inside parliament to interfere in the struggle – and a war would prove more expensive than supporting Lancashire's destitute – the proposals were shelved.

There was one other factor which doomed Russell's mediation plans and that was the public reception accorded to Gladstone's famous speech at Newcastle in 1862, where he pronounced, 'Jefferson Davis and other leaders of the South have made an army; they are making, it appears a navy; and they have made what is more than either, they have made a nation (loud

---

[43] *Saturday Review*, 2 May 1863, 554.
[44] The most recent and thorough examination of Russell's mediation plans is Jones, *Union in peril*, chs vi–x passim. But see also Crook, *The North, the South and the powers*, chs vii–viii passim.
[45] Jones, *Union in peril*, 5.
[46] Ibid. 218. Jones is uncertain about Palmerston's position. Certainly, there is nothing in Palmerston's papers or at the Public Record Office to suggest that the prime minister was ever in favour of Russell's plans.
[47] Ibid. 189–96.

cheers).'[48] Historians have not much remarked upon this, despite the fact that when Gladstone made this speech, the cabinet was actually debating mediation at the time, making it a 'leak' of sorts. Even though the public was unaware of cabinet discussions, many in England interpreted his remarks to mean that the government was about to recognise the South.[49] Although Gladstone from the first declared that his speech had assumed a broader meaning than he intended, speculation was rife.[50] Despite Gladstone's efforts to play down his comments, the press was either dismissive or hostile. The *Illustrated London News* was 'disposed not to place much stress on the opinions expressed by Mr. Gladstone', and did not believe that his comments reflected the opinion of the cabinet, stating, 'A good deal of emphasising has been expended on the assertion that the South had become a nation; but the phrase appears to us to have about it more of the epigrammatic turn of a sentence rather than of an intention to express a political opinion.'[51] So, as well as opposing Gladstone, the journal denied that the speech was anything more than his private opinion. The Union's sternest critics were the most hostile towards Gladstone: *The Times* condemned him and the *Saturday Review*, meanwhile, remarked, 'Although the Federals may be in the wrong, still, beyond idle and irresponsible talk, they have offered no offence to England. Annoyance at foolish obstinacy is not a cause of war, and, short of actual war, there is no opportunity of interference.' The journal remained completely opposed to any attempt to mediate in the war and particularly condemned Gladstone for even hinting at it, even if it was his private opinion: 'The arguments in favour of neutrality remain unshaken; and even if Mr. Gladstone's judgment proves to be correct, it might well have been cherished in silence, so that the policy of England might appear to be unanimous as well as moderate and consistent.'[52] The *Saturday Review* anticipated that the Union would react badly to the speech. It proved prescient. After the war, Gladstone's Newcastle speech was cited as evidence of 'conscious unfriendly purpose' towards the Union on the part of the British cabinet during the *Alabama* arbitration.[53] This, despite the fact that, as an inflammatory speech, it paled in comparison to the pronouncements of Clay, Seward and other members of the Lincoln administration. The *Saturday Review's* commentary,

---

[48] *Reynolds's Weekly*, 12 Oct. 1862, 4.
[49] Crook, *The North, the South and the powers*, 221–8.
[50] In a letter to Russell, Gladstone noted that he had met James Spence (at the latter's request) and believed that the southern spokesman 'did not appear to have put any such construction on my [Newcastle] words as that they signified any intention on the part of the Government': Gladstone to Russell, 17 Oct. 1862, Russell papers, PRO 30/22/11. Gladstone's diary also reveals the lack of importance he accorded to his speech: *The Gladstone Diaries*, ed. M. R. D. Foot and H. C. G. Matthew, Oxford 1968–94, vi. 154.
[51] *Illustrated London News*, 18 Oct. 1862, 397.
[52] Adams, *Great Britain and the American Civil War*, ii. 63; *Saturday Review*, 11 Oct. 1862, 428.
[53] Crook, *The North, the South and the powers*, 232.

and that of the rest of the press, was entirely consistent and reflected the public's non-interventionist stance. Gladstone's leak, whether intended or not, had the effect of gauging public opinion. The cabinet took the hint. In response to public speculation, George Cornewall Lewis rebutted Gladstone in a speech at Hereford on 14 October. The cabinet shelved Russell's plans for mediation – permanently.

Once the controversy died down, the *Saturday Review* made some interesting observations:

> The English nation is not so entirely of one mind in the American quarrel as in the Italian struggle for independence; but, on the whole, it has come to the conclusion that the South will have the best of the contest, and that it is not the business of foreigners to accelerate the impending catastrophe. The resentment which has been justly provoked by the silly malignity of the North is by no means strong enough to create a desire for rupture; and the wrong doers are executing poetical justice on themselves effectively enough to satisfy the most unfriendly aspirations.[54]

Clearly, even in 1862, there were serious divisions in English thinking on America, before the appearance of the anti-slavery demonstrations organised by northern supporters in early 1863. Further, the *Saturday Review* reiterated that its dislike of the North was based on the latter's aggressive and even hostile diplomacy. The most important thing to note, however, is that non-intervention by Britain was the agreed consensus. As Mason noted despairingly to Judah P. Benjamin, Confederate secretary of state, 'Both parties [Liberal and Conservative] are guided in this, by a fixed English purpose to run no risk of a broil, even far less a war, with the United States.'[55]

Press and public opinion on the South

The general unwillingness of England to become embroiled in the conflict did not, of course, necessarily mean that there was no pro-Confederate sympathy, only that the extent of the sentiment was extremely limited. Although there was a sizeable amount of anti-northern sentiment that sometimes developed into pro-southern sympathy, pro-Confederate opinion was not the preserve of any social or political class. Once we look beyond the hyperbole (not to mention paralogisms) of Bright and his allies, both the levels and the extent of southern sympathy are difficult to determine with any certainty. Further, the testimony of both sides' supporters is often contradictory.

For example, those journals which had claimed that a majority favoured the South often repudiated their own claims. The *Saturday Review*, for

---

[54] *Saturday Review*, 22 Nov. 1862, 610.
[55] Mason to Benjamin, 9 Feb. 1863, in *Correspondence of James M. Mason*, 387.

instance, remarked in May 1863, 'the New York papers scarcely condescend to notice Mr. Bright's meetings and deputations, while they denounce with affected indignation the cold neutrality or *supposed* Southern bias of the influential classes'.[56] The *Saturday Review*, however, had never been shy, at least during 1862, of accepting northern apologists' claims that most Englishmen viewed the conflict as a war for empire on one side, a war for independence on the other. Most importantly, with regard to its own case, the journal frequently denied any appreciation of the South: 'Assuredly we have no sympathies with the Southern institutions, and we are none of us at all inclined to swerve from an honourable neutrality at the instigation of men who have openly advocated the legalization of importing negroes from Africa.'[57] Slavery, as we have seen, was the bar to open support for the Confederacy. Even in 1862, the *Saturday Review* dismissed claims of southern friendship: 'It is even said that the South shares the animosity of its bitterest enemies against the former object of their common envy and dislike.'[58] On another occasion, the journal even went so far as to state, 'The truth would seem to be . . . that the people of the Southern States are deficient in the knowledge and the habits of civilization.'[59] That was a claim more worthy of Bright.

While the *Saturday Review* contradicted itself on the levels of pro-southern sentiment, other journals always argued that public opinion was split. The *Illustrated London News* remarked in mid-1863: 'Upon the war itself there may be two opinions, and there can be no doubt that there are as many British partisans of the South as of the North, though the majority of us cordially approve the policy of our Government.'[60] The *Illustrated London News* held, for the most part, a neutral course. It stated its policy in 1862 and rarely wavered from it:

> We have no sympathy with those who are seeking to crush a nation that desires to be isolated; we have no sympathy with a nation that upholds the atrocious system of slavery. But we admire the valour on both sides, and we lament the cruel and useless sacrifice of life. That is the English standpoint, and we are neither to be menaced, cajoled nor taunted into abandoning it.[61]

'Cruel and useless sacrifice of life' is the key phrase. Most commentators believed that the South could not be subdued and thus regarded the attempts to conquer the Confederacy as hopeless. Southern slavery severely curbed the level of English sympathies, but the South was expected to preserve its independence none the less.

---

[56] Ibid. 9 May 1863, 586 [my italics].
[57] Ibid. 25 Jan. 1862, 85.
[58] Ibid. 31 May 1862, 606.
[59] Ibid. 4 Oct. 1862, 407.
[60] *Illustrated London News*, 1 Aug. 1863, 106.
[61] Ibid. 13 Dec. 1862, 626.

That most individuals in England believed that the South could not be conquered is not only unquestionably true, but has also been long established. Although historians such as Keiser insist that belief in the inevitability of Confederate independence effectively made England pro-southern, this is a dangerous simplification, and most nineteenth-century commentators would have rejected this argument outright.[62] It should also be remembered that defeatism struck the North occasionally, too, particularly in July–August 1862 and two years later in July–August 1864.[63] The English, having access to Union papers, were aware of this. Certainly, it is worth quoting Henry Adams at this point, who noted in December 1861, 'As a mere question of independence I believe the thing to be settled. We cannot bring the South back.'[64] If this was the opinion of a patriotic Northerner, it should be no surprise that many English commentators believed the same.

Thus, despite what Keiser writes, the belief that the Confederacy would maintain its independence did not necessarily imply any great respect for its society, or any hatred of the North and its institutions. Even that sizeable percentage of individuals who believed the South had the right to its independence did not always have any particular affection for the South. Take the *Athenaeum* for one, which always denied any fondness for southern society. *The Economist*, although it expected the Confederacy to maintain its independence, hoped the Union would secure the border states, arguing, 'Slavery is so great an evil and so sad a wrong – as an institution it is fatal to industry, to social progress, to sound views, to real elevation of principle or purpose, that we should grieve to see it enabled to assert or consolidate its empire in any quarter where it is now doubtful or disputed.'[65] Unqualified support for the Confederacy was very rare indeed.

There were, of course, Englishmen sympathetic to the Confederacy. The trouble for the South appears to be that they were few in number and largely inactive. The *Wesleyan Methodist Magazine* accused the 'mercantile classes' of supporting the South, and condemned the fact that when asked what the war is about, 'A certain portion of the public press replies, with surprising pertinacity, "The Northerners, influenced by ambition, are waging an unjustifiable war for territory; the Southerners are fighting for their homes and independence."' The *Wesleyan Methodist Magazine*, which was always anti-South because of slavery, dismissed this as 'specious'.[66] The journal, however, was not prepared to declare which way the sympathies of the majority were directed. The journalist Cyrus Redding was also unprepared to state that a majority of Englishmen favoured the South, although he wrote,

[62] Keiser, 'The English press and the American Civil War', 39.
[63] See McPherson, *Battle cry of freedom*, chs xvi, xxv, esp. pp. 760–73.
[64] Henry Adams to Charles Francis Adams Jr., 13 Dec. 1861, in Worthington Chauncey Ford (ed.), *A cycle of Adams letters: 1861–1865*, London 1921, i. 83.
[65] *The Economist*, 30 Aug. 1862, 954.
[66] *Wesleyan Methodist Magazine* (Nov. 1862), 1026–7.

'That there is in this country a party anxious for the success of the South there is no doubt.'[67] We know there was a pro-Confederate lobby, but it lacked numbers and influence.

The southern independence societies

Some historians have pointed to the Southern Independence Association chaired by Lord Wharncliffe as evidence of strong Confederate sympathies in England.[68] Unfortunately for this argument, the impact of the Southern Independence Society was virtually nil, especially in comparison to the efforts of the anti-slavery lobbies and northern apologists. The association, which operated entirely out of Manchester with its impact limited to Lancashire, was formed in 1863, largely in response to the meetings and propaganda efforts of the anti-slavery bodies in the same year.[69] It was also formed because of growing hostility towards the Confederate states on the part of the government. As Lindsay explained to James Mason, he and other pro-Southerners decided 'to launch the association to watch over the interests of the South in this country – and it is high time, for I think that our Government grows colder and colder by the day'.[70] As we shall see, hostility towards the Confederacy was growing in England by the end of 1863, as Anglo-southern relations declined. Despite this, the Southern Independence Association did what it could to propagandise the cause of the Confederacy. As Lord Wharncliffe put it, speaking as chairman in the Clarence Hotel in Manchester in October 1863,

> He unhesitatingly said that he did not believe that anything like one third of the population of England were in favour of the North. . . . There had been more agitation on the part of the North; they had been more active in propagating their opinions; and they had been assisted by one distinguished orator in Mr. Forster, the member for Bradford. The course of action on the part of the friends of the South must be to endeavour to show this was not the feeling of the country.[71]

The society held a number of meetings in Lancashire but, lest anyone claims that it was to these that Bright referred when he stated that 'every effort that

---

[67] *New Monthly Magazine* (Aug. 1863), 441.
[68] Adams, *Great Britain and the American Civil War*, ii, ch. xv passim; Foner, *British labor and the American Civil War*, 70–1.
[69] James Mason dated southern societies as being established only by the middle of 1863. See, for example, Mason to Benjamin, 21 June 1863, in *Correspondence of James M. Mason*, 418–19. It is also worth noting that E. D. Adams states that the pro-Confederates in Britain only began agitation through public meetings in 1863 – and in response to pro-northern lobbying: *Great Britain and the American Civil War*, ii. 186–7.
[70] Lindsay to Mason, 6 Nov. 1863. Lindsay papers, LND 7, 353.
[71] *Reynolds's Weekly*, 11 Oct. 1863, 8.

money and malice could make to stimulate amongst the suffering people of Lancashire an opinion in favour of the slave states', he levelled that accusation in 1862. It must also be repeated that the Southern Independence Society's efforts at holding meetings and disseminating propaganda were paltry compared to those of the Union and Emancipation Society, and had no funding comparable to that which Washington provided for its opponents.

As it happened, the Southern Independence Association was something of a last-ditch effort on the part of the Confederacy's English supporters. Never a particularly large organisation to begin with, its membership numbers declined rapidly as the year wore on. Towards the end of 1863, Beresford-Hope despairingly wrote to Lindsay with the news that 'there are only fifteen members'.[72] Lindsay's collection of Association materials is very small and nothing can be dated after 1863, suggesting that the organisation was both short-lived and unproductive.[73]

Other Confederate societies existed. Jordan and Pratt cite both the London Southern Independence Association and the London Society for Promoting the Cessation of Hostilities in America, but the second organisation was the same society under a different name.[74] Although, under the latter name, the society managed to accumulate a petition of 350,000 signatures urging the Union to make peace, as Joseph Hernon has established, half the names were Irish.[75] The Irish signatures can be easily explained by the fact that so many Irish *émigrés* to America found themselves conscripted into the northern army – something their families back in Ireland did not appreciate. Besides this, as well as an element of pacifism, numerous individuals might well have signed the petition in light of the common belief that the South could not be conquered. Insisting on regarding such individuals as staunch Confederates is a dangerous simplification. In any event, petition aside, the number of members the London Southern Independence Association had was few and the extent of their activities was negligible. Jordan and Pratt also claim that 'Southern organizations existed in thirty-one English and Scottish towns', but there is absolutely no evidence to support this nor do

---

[72] A. J. Beresford Hope to Lindsay, 19 Dec. 1863. Lindsay papers, LND 7, 353.
[73] There is no single complete collection of the Southern Independence Association's papers. The Manchester Public Library has copies of speeches reprinted from the local press. It also has a membership list which, although it contains certain MPs and aristocrats (all well-known Confederate supporters), is overwhelmingly made up of private individuals. Unfortunately, neither their professions nor socio-economic status are listed, making observations of class support impossible: Manchester Public Library, F. 1863/7c.
[74] Jordan and Pratt, *Europe and the American Civil War*, 172–3; Owsley, *King Cotton diplomacy*, 177–8. The only known pro-southern society to exist before this was the London Confederate States Aid Association, which, as Adams has pointed out, only contained around fifty members: *Great Britain and the American Civil War*, ii. 191–2.
[75] Hernon, *Celts, Catholics and copperheads*, 104.

they provide any.[76] Certainly none of these groups received any coverage by the national press and their impact was, again, marginal.

This is what is significant about pro-southern efforts: the paltry level of their achievements. The number of pro-southern meetings – either working-class or middle-class – listed by historians is unimpressive. Most took place in destitute Lancashire and were outnumbered by anti-slavery rallies.[77] If most people in England (as it has been claimed) did indeed sympathise strongly with the Confederacy, it would surely have been simplicity itself for southern independence organisations to copy the tactics of their opponents, namely, bar individuals opposed to their stance from their rallies and meetings and fill them with southern partisans.[78] The fact that the southern independence societies were largely unable to do even this raises serious questions about the depth of pro-Confederate sympathy in England.

The southern view of Britain

Historians adhering to the traditional interpretation, who have looked at southern documents, argue that Mason's letters provide support for the argument that England was overwhelmingly pro-South. Mason certainly believed that the English favoured the Confederacy, writing to Benjamin, 'I am satisfied that so general, almost universal, is popular sentiment in England with the South.'[79] Those adhering to the traditional interpretation of Anglo-American relations, however, would have to acknowledge that such a statement, if true, would include the opinions of not only the middle and upper classes, but the working class as well. Mason, after all, used the words 'universal' and 'popular'. Further, Mason never stated, in any one of his surviving letters, either to his family or to the Confederate government, that the working class opposed the South or that any public division on the subject of the Civil War was in any way based on social class.

Mason, however, unquestionably exaggerated the levels of English sympathy for the Confederacy. His testimony is often contradictory, and he

---

[76] Jordan and Pratt, *Europe and the American Civil War*, 172.

[77] Ellison's meetings, as far as I have been able to ascertain, comprise 47 pro-southern meetings and 51 pro-northern ones. Ellison argues that most of the southern ones were spontaneous, unlike the northern ones, but, even so, this does suggest a division of opinion in Lancashire. Ellison, *Support for secession*, passim.

[78] Jordan and Pratt are oblivious to the fact that this was a regular practice of Union sympathisers. Hence their incredible explanation that southern sympathisers could not hold meetings to which admission was by ticket because these 'lacked weight': *Europe and the American Civil War*, 172. Indeed, Adams noted before Jordan and Pratt that, 'No doubt many of these pro-Southern meetings were by ticket, but that many were not is clear from the reports in *The Index*': *Great Britain and the American Civil War*, ii. 189. For Union meetings' admission policies, see Ellison, *Support for secession*, 114.

[79] Mason to Benjamin, 1 June 1864, in *Correspondence of James M. Mason*, 501.

repudiated this position as the struggle wore on. He reported to Benjamin in 1862,

> I am in full and frequent communication here with many able and influential members of the House of Commons, who confer with me in perfect frankness and candour, and who are prepared to move the question in the House whenever it may be found expedient, and the attitude of the parties here, meaning the Ministerial and the Opposition, as to the Ministry it will not move, it is not deemed prudent to enable it to make the question an issue with the Opposition, and so motions that have been projected 'hang fire'. As far as the public is concerned, all agree that there has been a complete change of sentiment as the war goes on; both my own intercourse, which is becoming large, and information derived from all quarters satisfy me that the educated and enlightened classes are in full sympathy with us, and are becoming impatient at the Government.[80]

While this sounds impressive, it is not entirely convincing. The members of parliament Mason actually names who were sympathetic to the South number only a handful and were inevitably publicly known supporters of the South such as Lindsay or Roebuck.[81] Further, if a majority of members of parliament in either party favoured the South, why was it 'not deemed prudent' to make the supposedly popular question of recognition an issue? Also, despite Mason's statements about the 'educated and enlightened classes', as we have seen, there is no evidence of any impatience for the government to recognise the South at this (or any other) period. Henry Hotze also contradicted Mason: 'We have friends in all parties', he informed Benjamin, but 'our affairs are not, and cannot be made a party question.'[82]

Mason basically confused anti-northern sentiment with pro-Confederate sentiment (he was neither the first nor the last to commit this error). For example, he reported to Benjamin in 1863,

> There is a very disturbed feeling in all circles here arising out of the aspect of affairs between the United States and this country. Men's minds are highly incensed at the arrogant and exacting tone of expression found in the public speeches and the press in the Northern States, and a strong opinion prevails that it will be difficult to avoid drifting into the war which the Lincoln Government and its advisors seem determined to provoke . . . it is perfectly understood in the House of Commons that the war, professedly waged to

---

[80] Mason to Benjamin, 23 June 1862, in *The messages and papers of Jefferson Davis*, ii. 258.
[81] See, in particular, *Correspondence of James M. Mason*, passim.
[82] Hotze to Benjamin, 14 Feb. 1863, in *The messages and papers of Jefferson Davis*, ii. 432. In the same letter, Hotze reported that Queen Victoria opposed southern recognition, a comment some historians have been quick to accept. Unfortunately, Hotze gave no source for this remark, stating only 'the personal wishes and feelings of the Queen . . . are said to be still decidedly averse to recognition'. As a result, Hotze's report must stand as unsubstantiated. None the less, according to *Reynolds's Weekly*, the North believed Victoria favoured their cause: 24 Aug. 1862, 1.

restore the Union is hopeless, and the sympathies of four-fifths of its members are with the South.[83]

All we have here is again more confirmation of the prevailing belief in England that the Union sought a quarrel with Britain. But this fear of drifting into war, as we have seen, did not necessarily lead to pro-southern sympathies. As for Mason's claim that four-fifths of members of parliament supported the Confederacy, the examination of public meetings held by politicians exposes the fallacy of these calculations. Even if we accept the possibility that 80 per cent of members of parliament did believe that the Union was permanently divided, that, as the public meetings have established, did not necessarily make them southern sympathisers.

There are other reasons, however, to believe that Mason exaggerated his estimate of the number of pro-southern Englishmen. Besides comparing his reports to those of other Confederate agents in England, several of his own letters suggest he was less knowledgeable than he admitted. For example, in a letter to Benjamin, Mason boasted of his intimacy with his neighbour, the Conservative politician W. R. S. Fitzgerald, stating that, 'we have much social intercourse'. Despite this, Mason also admitted in the same letter that he could not be certain whether W. R. S. Fitzgerald's southern sympathies were shared by the latter's party as a whole.[84]

Even the fact that Mason had social relations with so many people in England does not establish much. If his letters are to be believed, the Confederate commissioner did indeed meet numerous individuals, but although some of them were pro-Southerners, many were not. For example, while Mason met pro-Confederates such as Lord Campbell, he also ate dinner on a number of occasions with Lord Ashburton who, as we have discussed in Chapter 4, was pro-North. More importantly, Mason appears to have struck up something of an acquaintance with Richard Cobden, whom he met on several occasions. Take, as an example, the following remark: 'July 6, Mr. Richard Cobden at breakfast with me; had a long conversation on American affairs; Mr. C. decidedly Northern in his sympathies, but deploring the war; admits his sympathies with the North because of anti-slavery.'[85] Mason's reports of Cobden's courtesy are borne out by the testimony of Lindsay who reported that 'Cobden, though strongly against the South used always to mention Mr. Mason's name to me with the highest respect.'[86] By all accounts, Mason was a genial and engaging individual. As Lindsay also noted, 'Mr. Mason during his stay in this country was much respected. Even the most bitter opponents of the South had not a word to say against him.'[87] Without a

---

83 Mason to Benjamin, 17 June 1863, in *The messages and papers of Jefferson Davis*, ii. 476.
84 Mason to Benjamin, 30 July 1862, ibid. ii. 294.
85 *Correspondence of James M. Mason*, 340–2.
86 Lindsay papers, LND 7, 238.
87 Ibid. Lindsay's opinion of Mason must be taken with a grain of salt because of his pro-southern proclivities, but the fact that Mason apparently got on well with even so strong

doubt, Mason, representing a revolutionary government, enjoyed something of celebrity status in England (as did C. F. Adams, as *The education of Henry Adams* reveals), and was able to capitalise on it to a certain extent. But many people, although interested to meet a representative from such a government, did not necessarily sympathise with its aims. The Civil War was a major event. Mason, being a participant of sorts, was immediately interesting – even to pro-Northerners, to say nothing of neutrals.

Yet Mason's comments on Cobden are also important because they show a dislike of the war, even by pro-Northerners. In other words, wishing for peace did not automatically make one a pro-Southerner. Also, notice how Cobden did not refer to democracy being at stake in the struggle or, indeed, any belief that to support democracy one had to champion the Union. For Cobden, the issue at stake was slavery – but he clearly did not despise the South so much as to avoid social intercourse with one of its representatives. As we shall discuss in the next chapter, Cobden's opposition to the South being based on slavery, rather than pro-democratic sentiment, was typical of northern supporters. Yet the subject of slavery brings us to the main problem with Mason's reports.

Despite the time he spent in England socialising, Mason never really grasped how the existence of slavery militated against the possibility of widespread southern support. For example, in a letter to Benjamin, Mason observed, 'In my conversations with English gentlemen, I have found it was in vain to combat their <u>sentiment</u>. The so-called anti-slavery feeling seems to have become with them a sentiment akin to patriotism.'[88] Considering that some of these 'English gentlemen' were staunch pro-Confederates, one can imagine how neutral or pro-northern individuals felt about the institution. On another occasion, Mason writing to his family about southern impatience with Britain's refusal to recognise the Confederate states, remarked, 'It would be remarkable, indeed, had our people other than such feelings, and I share it to the utmost, yet the Government here remains unmoveable in great part, I think, to avoid any and all risk of getting into a war, but the anti-slavery feeling of England has much to do with it.'[89] Of course, the anti-slavery sentiment had much to do with it – as an examination of both the English press and public meetings reveals.

Although Mason was dimly aware of the damage slavery did to the chances of widespread pro-southern sympathy, he never really understood just how large a barrier it presented – even though several of his compatriots did. When the end of the Confederacy was apparent, Mason still failed to fully acknowledge the damage southern slavery caused, despite his admission that it had been pointed out to him throughout the conflict: 'In all my conversations

---

an opponent of the Confederacy as Richard Cobden does suggest some charisma on the Southerner's part.

[88] Mason to Benjamin, 25 Jan. 1864, in *Correspondence of James M. Mason*, 461 [the underlining is Mason's].

[89] Mason to his family, 20 Mar. 1863, ibid. 407.

here for the last three years, both in public and private circles, whilst satisfied that their sympathies were entirely with us as a people struggling for independence . . . many declared such sympathy would be even stronger and more general were it not for slavery.'[90] His underestimation of the slavery issue is shown starkly in his conversation with the earl of Donoughmore, one of the few aristocrat acquaintances the commissioner was able to name. Describing his friendship, 'I have known this gentleman more intimately, perhaps than any other of his rank in England, and have always found him a fast and constant friend of our cause', Mason reported that the earl 'remarked that but for slavery we should have been recognized long ago'. Mason professed to be surprised at this, and insisted that although 'fully aware that slavery was deplored among us, I had never heard it suggested as a barrier to recognition'. That Mason could have so casually ignored or dismissed the massive display of anti-slavery sentiment which pervaded this period casts serious doubt upon the reliability of much of his testimony regarding English public opinion – especially as the other Confederate observers in England constantly worried about the issue of slavery. Certainly, Donoughmore persisted, 'that in his opinion that it had always been in the way, and often Lee's successes in the Rappahannock and march into Pennsylvania, when he threatened Harrisburg, and his army at the very gates of Washington, he thought that but for slavery we should then have been acknowledged'.[91] Slavery was the major millstone around the neck of the South. As long as the institution existed, widespread sympathy for the South was impossible. Notice, too, how for Donoughmore, like Cobden, the issue that divided the English on the Civil War was slavery. Donoughmore, a Tory, never regarded the issue of democracy or political reform in England as in any way related to the question of public opinion on the conflict.

Besides the inherent contradictions in Mason's own letters, his superiors remained unconvinced by his reports of a pro-southern England. Benjamin, who, courtesy of blockade-runners, had access to British newspapers, was certainly sceptical. Writing to Slidell in Paris, Benjamin noted, 'without entering into any detailed examination of the curious statements and contra-statements of English gentlemen in and out of the ministry, the important fact has been saliently developed that France is ready and eager for our recognition, and that England is opposed to it'.[92] In fact, Benjamin, like the rest of the Confederate government in Richmond, always believed that Britain favoured the Union, regardless of Mason's reports. As he wrote to Slidell, 'The English Government has scarcely disguised its hostility from the commencement of the struggle. It has professed a newly invented neutrality which it has frankly defined as meaning a course more favourable to the

---

[90] Mason to Benjamin, 31 Mar. 1865, in *The messages and papers of Jefferson Davis*, ii. 710. Benjamin never received this letter; Richmond fell three days after it was written.
[91] Ibid.
[92] Benjamin to Slidell, 17 Aug. 1863, ibid. 544.

THE CONFEDERACY'S PARTISANS

stronger belligerents.'[93] Benjamin was not the only member of the Confederate government holding this opinion. President Jefferson Davis believed the same and, addressing the fourth session of the first Confederate Congress in December 1863, expressed his sentiments clearly:

> Great Britain has accordingly entertained with that Government [the Union] the closest and most intimate relations while refusing, on its demands, ordinary amicable intercourse with us, and has, under arrangements made with the other nations of Europe, not only denied our just claim of admission into the family of nations, but interposed a passive though effective bar to the knowledge of our rights by other powers.[94]

Although it is hard to see just how Britain prevented other countries from recognising the South, clearly, Davis and his ministry recognised what the Adams family never really grasped: British neutrality was a key factor in the preservation of the Union. It was because the South believed that Britain actually opposed the Confederacy, not merely because it refused recognition, that in 1863, Davis's government decided to cease and desist from any attempts at achieving diplomatic relations.

Not long after Roebuck's disastrous motion, Benjamin ordered Mason to vacate his post in August. He departed on 21 September 1863, recalled because, as the *Saturday Review* put it, 'he wanted what a neutral country could not possibly give him'.[95] After this, Anglo-Confederate relations rapidly declined.[96] By October, all British consular agents in the Confederacy were expelled, largely because they prevented the now desperate South from conscripting British subjects.[97] Indeed, according to Owsley, by 1863, Britain was considered the second worst enemy of the Confederacy.[98] Southern journals became distinctly hostile towards England, becoming increasingly so as the war turned against the Confederacy. Before long, those formerly sympathetic to the South began to return fire. The *Athenaeum* furiously remarked in November 1863,

> What shall we say of Southern effrontery? Why, from the first creation of the Union till its violent death in consequence of Abraham Lincoln's election, Southern politicians were conspicuous amongst the representatives of the Republic for their animosity against Great Britain – the birthplace of abolitionist sentiments, and the consistent friend of the African race. No candidate for public honours in the South presumed to canvass his fellow-citizens until

---

[93] Benjamin to Slidell, 10 Sept. 1864, ibid.
[94] Fourth session of first Congress, 7 December 1863, ibid. i. 357.
[95] *Saturday Review*, 26 Sept. 1863, 414.
[96] Owsley provides the most thorough examination of declining Anglo-Confederate relations – from the South's diplomatic point of view: *King Cotton diplomacy*, ch. xiv passim.
[97] Crook, *The North, the South and the powers*, 331.
[98] Owsley, *King Cotton diplomacy*, 472.

he had assured them that 'hatred of England' was the first article of his political creed. Since the rupture, the cry, 'Cotton is King', has been less often heard, and the leaders of secession have taken pains to flatter and fawn the 'old country'; but now that they see England is not to be fooled by blandishments, or goaded on by self-interest into the desertion of sacred principles, they are beginning again to bluster and rant, as they used to bluster and rant in the days of General Jackson.[99]

Here, the Confederacy's past conduct was repeated in full: the adherence to slavery, the attempts to blackmail Britain into entering the war through the King Cotton policy, and the part friendly, part menacing, diplomatic overtures. Clearly, by 1863, what southern support existed had passed its apogee. The *Illustrated London News*, neutral as always, merely stated that the English have 'borne with creditable patience all the bluster of the North and, so to speak, the feminine petulance of the South'.[100] Eventually, however, irritation set in: 'The South, now realizing that nothing can be gained from forbearance, is taking up the anti-English cry, and Mr. Davis is as "bitter", if not as vulgar, as *The New York Herald*. . . . Therefore we are well pleased at the close of the year to add to our record that the South is as angry with us as was the North.'[101] *The Economist*'s prediction, made from the first, that 'we must expect to be hated by the greater part of both sides' had come true.[102]

By 1863, some northern sympathisers, delighted to see the Confederacy's attacks on Britain and an increasing exasperation in response to them, began to announce a change in English sympathies. The *Westminster Review* declared:

The dispute, like every other, has complicated itself with every minor grief which the disputants had ever entertained against each other. All the secondary questions of commercial and political preponderance are now fairly dispersing before the cardinal point of the institution of Slavery. . . . English opinion is now, in spite of a strong partisanship of the South by one of its most influential organs, at last settling down to a clear insight into the real issues at stake.[103]

Russell certainly believed by late 1863 that most Britons opposed the South. He engaged in a very public argument with Charles Sumner, who, at a meeting in New York, accused the British government and public of being pro-South. Russell replied with a speech of his own at Blairgowrie, Scotland, where, after defending the government's record, he stated:

---

[99] *Athenaeum*, 7 Nov. 1863, 602.
[100] *Illustrated London News*, 28 Nov. 1863, 532.
[101] Ibid. 26 Dec. 1863, 650–1.
[102] *The Economist*, 1 June 1861, 590.
[103] *Westminster Review* (Apr. 1863), 575.

my belief is that the people of the United States, whether they are now called Federals or Confederates, will finally do us justice; that they will observe – as indeed they cannot help observing – that this is a free country, where there is so much difference of opinion, there are parties, very considerable in number who sympathise with the Confederates, and there are other large masses, I believe superior in numbers, who sympathise with the Federals.[104]

Although Russell was clearly feeling hostility from both the North and the South at this point, the English press, at least, agreed with him. The *Spectator*, after dismissing Sumner as 'a know-nothing', stated, 'Lord Russell truly says that the numerical majority of English people sympathise heartily with the North.'[105] For once, the *Saturday Review* was in agreement. Answering one of Seward's periodic accusations of a pro-southern Britain, the journal retorted, 'Mr. Seward cannot seriously believe that the insurgents have derived any benefit from the good-will with which their heroic resistance has been contemplated by a part of the community which, according to Lord Russell's conjecture, is not even a majority.'[106] Not everyone was in agreement with Russell's estimation. The *Annual Register* of 1863 still believed that difficult as it was to estimate the levels of public sentiment on the question of America, 'opinion in England at this time leaned rather in favour of the Southern than Northern states'.[107] It should be noted, however, that the *Annual Register* was referring to the year 1863 as a whole, and Anglo-Confederate relations had just begun to decline. Certainly, the following year, the *Annual Register* refused to comment on which way public sentiment leaned. In any event, southern hostility towards Britain was well known by late 1863 and it effectively eroded any sympathy the southern cause had engendered.

Neither permanent friends, nor . . .

By the end of 1863, then, as far as the English were concerned, both sides in the Civil War were unfriendly towards Britain. At that point, neither side was deemed to deserve much sympathy, let alone support. The conflict may have continued to attract interest, but other international events distracted English attention from America. In 1863 and 1864 major European events were under way in both Poland and Schleswig-Holstein. Europe was always nineteenth-century Britain's first priority and American news was now relegated to the back pages of journals.[108] Members of parliament referred to

---

[104] *Illustrated London News*, 23 Oct. 1863, 347.
[105] *Spectator*, 3 Oct. 1863, 2565.
[106] *Saturday Review*, 3 Oct. 1863, 443.
[107] *Annual Register*, 1863, 5. See ch. 2 above for the entire quotation.
[108] Mason certainly believed that the Schleswig-Holstein crisis distracted English attention away from American affairs. See his letter to Benjamin, 8 July 1864, in *Correspondence of James M. Mason*, 506.

America less and less frequently in their meetings, and the agitators' efforts on each side received less coverage. Certainly, each side's written propaganda was beginning to exhaust some individuals. By October 1864, before Lincoln was re-elected, the *Athenaeum* irritably stated:

> We could almost be grateful for an Act of Parliament that should prohibit the publication of more books on the American War until the termination of hostilities. . . . The book-makers and the spouters have done their best to make the American question the most intolerable and stupendous nuisance that has been imposed on English society since Mesmer.[109]

The journal was not alone. The *Saturday Review* became exhausted by Bright and Roebuck's combined hysteria in the House of Commons after the two had yet another debate on the merits of each side. Roebuck, opined the journal, 'talks of the United States the way a wild Yankee talks of England', while Bright and his friends were 'as bigoted and one-sided as the leading journals in America'.[110] But it was not only the press who were getting tired of the debate. Both Roebuck and Bright came in for abuse. Roebuck was particularly savaged by A. W. Kinglake who criticised the former's description of the government at Washington as 'base, cowardly and corrupt' and stated that his opinions 'do not represent the opinions of this House, nor do they represent the opinions of any party, or any fraction of any party in this House; they represent only that which no doubt the honourable and learned gentleman has a great respect for, namely, the opinions of himself'.[111] Clearly, Kinglake did not believe the House of Commons shared Roebuck's views. By June of 1864, the *Saturday Review* openly criticised the 'extravagant partisanship which induces large classes of Englishmen to identify themselves with the American Federals or Confederates'.[112]

There was, of course, some interest on the question of Lincoln's re-election, as a (initially possible) Democratic victory might change the course of the war. The press, however, despised McClellan's toleration of slavery and, once it became obvious that Lincoln was going to win, interest ebbed for all but the pro-Union lobby which, naturally enough, celebrated.[113] From that point to Appomattox, American issues were, at best, of secondary importance to English affairs.

In conclusion, historians adhering to the traditional interpretation of Anglo-American relations have failed to adequately account for the reasons for English suspicion of the Union, dismissing such criticism as irrational

---

[109] *Athenaeum*, 22 Oct. 1864, 525.
[110] *Saturday Review*, 19 Mar. 1864, 338–9.
[111] *Hansard*, clxiii, 1916–30, 1928.
[112] *Saturday Review*, 11 June 1864, 708.
[113] For commentary on Lincoln's re-election see *The Times*, 22 Nov. 1864, 6; *The Economist*, 26 Nov. 1864, 1454; *Illustrated London News*, 26 Nov. 1864, 525–6; *Reynolds's Weekly*, 27 Nov. 1864, 1; *Saturday Review*, 26 Nov. 1864, 646; *Spectator*, 26 Nov. 1864, 1343–4.

prejudice against America caused by a reactionary fear of democracy and liberalism, and then assuming this was the view of the aristocracy, conservatives, and, depending upon the historian, elements of the middle classes. They have further compounded the problem by equating anti-northern sympathies with pro-southern sentiment, a fatal assumption indeed. An examination of the criticism of the Union establishes that the role of anti-democratic sentiment was minor, nor is there much evidence of aristocratic, conservative or middle-class pro-Confederate sentiment, even if there was a deep distrust of the North. Indeed, few of those hostile to the Union in England were actually pro-southern. In the end, it is impossible to escape the conclusion that, despite the hostility the North engendered, few commentators in England ever really approved of the South, either its society or its political ambitions. Even what sympathy there was, generated largely by respect for a vastly outmatched underdog, anti-British Union measures, disputes over neutral rights and, indeed, a latent pacifism, was largely reduced by Lincoln's emancipation measures and Confederate anglophobia which eventually surpassed that of the North. It is surely significant that the closest Britain ever came to entering the war, the *Trent* affair, was the result of a northern blunder. Even when southern sympathy reached its height, it never attained a degree that would have encouraged active British involvement in America. Active involvement was what the Confederacy desperately needed; English sentiment in the end was, ironically, pro-Union.

There remain, however, the opinions and arguments of the pro-Union lobby that were, in part, responsible for the foundation of the traditional interpretation of Anglo-American relations during this period. After an examination of the opinions of their opponents, alleged and real alike, the northern apologists themselves now need to be subjected to some scrutiny.

6

Who Supported the Union?

'Slavery alone was thought of, alone talked of.'

On the question of Anglo-American relations during the Civil War, no aspect is as controversial as that of radical and working-class opinion on the conflict. What is immediately significant is just how resilient the chief argument of the traditional interpretation, that radicals and their working-class allies were pro-North because they viewed the Union as the bulwark of democracy and equated democracy's survival with that of the North, has proven to be. It has survived not only the overwhelming amount of evidence produced militating against it, but has also proven resilient in the face of the recent debates surrounding the history and nature of both the English working class and radicalism.[1] For example, although Eugenio Biagini's and Royden Harrison's accounts of both the labour movement and radicalism greatly differ, and are separated by some twenty-seven years, both scholars effectively endorse the traditional interpretation that the vast majority of the forces of reform were pro-Union.[2] The traditional model, however, remains greatly flawed. Besides being anchored in a misunderstanding of English perceptions of the conflict as a whole, it is based on sources that, if not necessarily unreliable, certainly deserve a great deal more scrutiny.

Although our notions of what the terms 'working class' and 'radicalism' mean are undergoing a necessary transformation, this work is not concerned with entering the debate. Unless designated explicitly, the term 'radical' is used largely to describe those individuals who favoured an extension of the franchise, from mild reformers to resolute republicans. Likewise, unless designated more explicitly, the term 'working class' is used even more broadly, being applied to those who referred to themselves as 'workmen', 'labourers' or, in some cases, 'common people'. These criteria are very broad, but are necessarily so as far as this study is concerned. Here we are chiefly concerned with that body termed the 'pro-Northerners', a group that contained not only individuals who might properly be classified as working-class or radical, but others as well.

---

[1] See, for example, Eugenio Biagini, *Liberty, retrenchment and reform: popular liberalism in the age of Gladstone, 1860–1880*, Cambridge 1992, 69–84.
[2] Ibid. 69–84, and Harrison, *Before the socialists*, ch. ii passim. Harrison is far more critical of the traditional interpretation than Biagini, especially in the 1994 introduction to his second edition.

WHO SUPPORTED THE UNION?

What must be borne in mind when examining the opinions of the northern supporters and apologists is that they were, in fact, anti-slavery and anti-Confederacy rather than favourably inclined towards the Union (with its social and political make-up) as a whole. In other words, just as those commentators who have been carelessly labelled pro-South usually disliked both sides, those individuals who have been classified as pro-Union were, in fact, anti-Confederacy – with the outstanding exceptions noted below. Contrary to what has been so often asserted, the pro-northern lobby was not entirely composed of radicals, who were, in any case, divided on the subject of America. Also divided on the question of America were working-class commentators – the arguments for a solidly pro-Union proletariat being based on tenuous grounds.

The traditional interpretation is best summed up by one of its most recent defenders, Biagini: 'to liberals and radical democrats the slaveholding and aristocratic South represented the American version of the *ancien régime*, while the North fought to preserve a nation "conceived in Liberty, and dedicated to the proposition that all men are created equal" '.[3]

Having established, in the previous chapters, that neither the British aristocracy nor conservatives were, in fact, pro-Confederate and that they did not see the events in America as being relevant to political reform in Britain, we now need to examine working-class and radical views. As regards working-class and radical perceptions of the war, the traditional interpretation is based on three main sources, all of which have serious flaws. The first source is the opinions of Bright (and, to a lesser extent, Cobden) and some of his allies, which largely excludes the views of other radicals and northern apologists. The second source is the position of the *Bee-Hive*, which not only ignores the newspaper's internal struggles at the editorial level but excludes the rest of the labour and radical press as well as the opinions of the other northern-supporting journals. The third and last source is the pro-Union meetings that took place in 1863 that, upon close examination, in fact call into question the existence of high levels of pro-northern sentiment amongst radicals and the working class. This chapter examines these issues and concentrates largely on the period from 1863 to the end of the war, including Lincoln's assassination.

---

[3] Biagini, *Liberty, retrenchment and reform*, 69. Biagini's quote originates, of course, from the Gettysburg Address, which had virtually no circulation in England. Another recent defence of British labour's support for the Union may be found in John Breuilly, Gottfried Niedhart and Antony Taylor (eds), *The era of the reform league: English labour and radical politics, 1857–1872, documents selected by Gustav Mayer*, Mannheim 1995, 57–61, 76–93.

Radical and liberal views of antebellum America

There are reasons to believe that many liberals, both working-class and middle-class, had little faith in America as a suitable model by the time of the Civil War. Besides the rise in the belief in economic justice, Margot Finn has pointed out that the British labour movement was more interested in events in Europe, particularly Italy and Poland, than it was in America.[4] Even so, English radicalism's views on America had always been problematic. The republican Jeremy Bentham (1748–1832), for example, who had a profound influence on both James Mill and J. S. Mill, although willing to learn from the United States, dismissed the Declaration of Independence as 'jargon' and declared he was an 'anti-American'.[5] The radical William Hazlitt (1778–1830) also declared himself anti-American.[6] Liberals in Britain were generally suspicious of written constitutions, such as the American one, which, they believed, restricted the opportunity for change – not to mention reform.[7] This, in part at least, explains the pro-Northerner Forster's dismissal of the American constitution as an 'idol'. Certainly, critics of the American constitution could point to the fact that part of the problem of slavery (or, rather, 'persons held in service') was its constitutional protection. As a final example, there was Matthew Arnold, a supporter of democracy, but not of the American sort. He, unusually for an Englishman, saw the institution in a similar light to Europeans, in cultural terms. In many respects, Arnold was merely repeating the concerns of the American novelist James Fenimore Cooper in *Gleanings in Europe* and other works. Cooper expressed his belief that democracy, or at least the American version, led to a society characterised by mediocrity, particularly in the arts, but frequently in politics, too.[8] Arnold, however, had other beliefs such as that equality is the basis for a healthy society. In some ways he was a prototypical socialist.[9] This tied him closer to the views of those who wanted economic justice, rather than those of the Manchester school.

This is the point about English radicals' views of America, that it was always a complex relationship. Further, the argument in England by the time of the Civil War was not so much to do with the necessity of reform, but just to what extent such reform should be carried. The questions of political reform were complex and the example of America did not necessarily provide the answers the English sought.

English radicals' concerns about the suitability of the United States as a

---

4 Finn, *After Chartism*, 204n. Finn's discussion on radical working-class politics from 1848 to 1874 contains surprisingly little on the American Civil War.
5 Roper, *Democracy and its critics*, 131.
6 Crook, *American democracy in English politics*, 79–80.
7 Roper, *Democracy and its critics*, 120–2.
8 James Fenimore Cooper, *Gleanings in Europe by an American*, Philadelphia 1837.
9 Roper, *Democracy and its critics*, 156–66.

model were reinforced by the antebellum travel literature. Literature, which, after 1848, Berger tells us, showed 'a greater tendency to be fair, and to award both praise and criticism where it was due', acted as an antidote to Bright's constant (and blind) praise of the institutions and society of the United States.[10] The greatest travel writer of them all, although he was far more than that, de Tocqueville, cited the use of wealth as a touchstone of distinction in the United States.[11] As a result, the idea of a classless society certainly came in for criticism from English writers:

> Americans, they insisted, though aggressively egalitarian in their public relations with each other, were quite the contrary in their personal relations in private life. The theory of equality and of a classless society became a farce when applied to the latter, according to British visitors. Instead they avowed, a strong aristocratic feeling existed.

As Berger notes, 'This resulted in an aristocracy of wealth' which caused some writers to insist: 'In such circumstances . . . liberty and equality were mere Shibboleths.'[12] It is interesting to note that both the *Athenaeum* and the *Spectator* agreed on this point, despite their opposition on virtually every other issue. The former remarked, 'Having no peerage to distinguish the grades of society, the Americans are obliged to have recourse to another test, so that money becomes the touchstone of rank, and the possession of wealth is equivalent to a patent of nobility.'[13] The latter, meanwhile, listed wealthy Northerners holding political power, arguing that these individuals were 'just as powerful as the English aristocracy', and noted: 'America has an aristocracy just as much as England, with one remarkable difference: the English aristocrat is trained to strive for leadership in a nation, not in a district.'[14] Thus, the notion of an aristocracy of wealth clearly had circulation in England during the war, and not merely among the Union's opponents either.

British writers were also shocked at the levels of violence in American society, not merely in the South and the West, but in the North and East, too. This may have been owed to the sensational American press of the day, as Berger asserts, but it scarcely spoke well for the United States as a model for reform.[15] Nor was the American political system regarded as quite the model of enlightenment Bright presented it to be – even by writers sympathetic to the United States. Many pro-American visitors viewed its government as corrupt.[16] Harriet Martineau professed to be shocked at the levels of duplicity

---

[10] Berger, *The British traveller in America*, 20–1. This is also the judgement of Allan Nevins: *America through British eyes*, New York 1948, 205–12.
[11] De Tocqueville, *Democracy in America*, ii. 228–9.
[12] Berger, *The British traveller in America*, 58, 60.
[13] *Athenaeum*, 24 Dec. 1864, 860.
[14] *Spectator*, 27 July 1861, 806.
[15] Berger, *The British traveller in America*, 68–71.
[16] Ibid. 101.

she claimed were practised during elections.[17] The largely pro-American Alexander MacKay reported that Americans declared their government to be one of the most corrupt on earth.[18] Finally, as Berger notes, 'Not even the most liberal traveller would go so far as to recommend that England adopt the American system of political democracy.'[19] This is not to suggest that America held no lessons for radicals in England, only that many were aware of the society's problems. This, at least in part, explains why so many lacked Bright's wholehearted enthusiasm for the Union.

Mill, Cairnes, Forster, and labour leaders

An examination of the chief northern supporters' arguments reveals, once again, how our understanding of Anglo-American relations has been hampered by an over-reliance on Bright. Earlier historians such as E. D. Adams and Jordan and Pratt equate radical and working-class perceptions of the war with those of Bright. Even modern historians such as Biagini rely too heavily on Bright. Thus, despite the fact that more recent historians have openly questioned whether Bright's views on America were shared by the groups he claimed to represent, his perception of the conflict is still too often assumed to have been endorsed by the radical and working-class movements as a whole.[20] It is certainly worth comparing several of the most significant (and radical) Union supporters' views with those of Bright, including, among others, J. S. Mill, Cairnes and Forster.

As Biagini acknowledges, Mill was one of the leading radical thinkers. Mill's interpretation of the American Civil War, however, contrasted sharply with Bright's. In the February 1862 issue of *Fraser's Magazine*, Mill's article on the nature of the war was published. Appearing shortly after the sound and fury of the *Trent* affair had died down, Mill set forth his reason for opposing the Confederacy: 'The world knows what the question between the North and the South has been for many years, and still is. Slavery alone was thought of, alone talked of.' Although Mill recognised that the war was not yet one of emancipation, he correctly predicted that the issue would come to the fore: 'parties in a protracted civil war almost invariably end by taking more extreme, not to say higher grounds of principle, than they began with'. This opinion was, of course, common to those most sympathetic to the North, that

---

17 Harriet Martineau, *Society in America*, London 1837, i, ch. iii passim.
18 Alexander MacKay, *The western world or, travels in the United States in 1846–1847 exhibiting in them their latest development, social, political, and industrial, including a chapter on California*, London 1849, ii, ch. i passim.
19 Berger, *The British traveller in America*, 107.
20 Crook argues that few radicals shared Bright's blind faith in the American institutions: *American democracy in English politics*, 84–6. Biagini, meanwhile, presents Bright's views as being those of radicals as a whole. For example, he uncritically accepts Bright's fulminations against the opinions of 'privilege' regarding the war: *Liberty, retrenchment and reform*, 70.

the Union would be forced to fight a war of emancipation rather than freely choosing to do so.

Mill did not endorse the notion that democracy's future depended upon a Union victory. In relation to questions of reform or democracy being raised by the spectacle in America, the only thing Mill had to say remotely connected with these issues surrounded the democratic impetus behind secession, of which he was dismissive:

> Secession may be laudable, so may any other kind of insurrection; but it may also be an enormous crime. It is one or the other, depending upon the provocation. And if there ever was an object which, by its bare announcement, stamped rebels against a particular community as enemies of mankind, it is the one professed by the South.

Mill never referred to the Confederacy as an aristocracy or *ancien régime* of any kind; indeed, like many in England, he regarded the South as essentially barbaric, citing the prevalence of lynching and the burning of blacks (and abolitionists) alive. The only discussion of democracy in the entire article was about whether or not secession could claim to have had a mandate from the people of the southern states: 'it is questionable if there was in the beginning a majority for secession anywhere but in South Carolina'. Mill blamed secessionist politicians' 'terrorism' for their success at the ballot box, but noted, 'yet even so, in several of the States, secession was carried only by narrow majorities. In some [States] the authorities have not dared to publish the numbers; in some [States] it is asserted that no vote has ever been taken.'[21] Thus, it was not an aristocracy behind secession, but corrupt and dishonest elected officials. Without overstatement, the above paragraph could be read as a warning that popular democracy required safeguards. This view was entirely in harmony with Mill's thoughts on the subject. Mill believed that political democracy would come to Britain, but he worried about the form it would take. Accordingly, his version of democracy was an elitist one and he drew up various plans to bring it into effect.[22] Despite his views, or more probably because of them, Mill did not regard the United States as a model suitable for Britain. Indeed, as Crook has pointed out, Mill had serious reservations about both American society and its political system.[23] Finally, what must be remembered about Mill's arguments in *Fraser's* is that they were anti-South rather than pro-Union. He expressed irritation at what he termed the *Trent* outrage, and regarded re-union as 'a moot point' – a position he retained until the end of the war.[24] A position, it scarcely

---

[21] *Fraser's Magazine* (Feb. 1862), 261–5.
[22] Roper, *Democracy and its critics*, 145–52.
[23] Crook, *American democracy in English politics*, 184–5.
[24] Mill to Cairnes, 15 June 1862, Mill-Taylor Collection, London School of Economics, vol. LV.

needs to be added, which was incompatible with that held by Lincoln's government.

Cairnes, one of Mill's disciples, shared his mentor's views that the cause of the war was slavery. In his work, *The slave power*, which we have already examined, Cairnes argued that the expansionist Confederacy would inevitably come into collision with Britain over the slave trade; thus, it was in Britain's interests to have friendly relations with the Union as a counterbalance. Far from being enamoured with either the North or its institutions, Cairnes was frankly dismissive. For example, he made a point of denying any admiration for the American political system.[25] Cairnes was not in favour of re-union either, but instead hoped only that the South would be confined to its present borders, causing slavery to die out. In a defence of the Union, published in *The Economist*, before he had finished writing *The slave power*, Cairnes explicitly stated: 'I do not expect, nor desire to see the Union restored.'[26] This position was maintained in *The slave power*, where Cairnes argued that the societies of the North and the South were too divergent for effective political co-operation.[27] As we have seen, this was an argument made by anti-northern commentators in England; it also loaned credence to the notion that the South, being an inherently different society, should remain independent of the Union. Cairnes's outlook, like Mill's, was not compatible with the views of the Lincoln administration.

Cairnes did not accept American re-union as possible, let alone desirable, until February 1865 – two months before Appomattox.[28] Considering that *The slave power* was the seminal text for English northern apologists, including Harriet Martineau, Mill, Leslie Stephen, Dr John Chapman and Forster, Cairnes's dismissal of the American system of government becomes even more noteworthy. Certainly, none of the journals that gave the work a positive review, such as the *Spectator*, the *Westminster Review*, *Fraser's Magazine*, the *National Review*, *Macmillan's Magazine* or the *English Woman's Journal*, expressed the slightest disquiet about Cairnes's views on American institutions; indeed, some used the opportunity to criticise the Union.[29] For both Cairnes and, it appears, most of his readers and supporters, the only reason for sympathising with the Union was the fact that its opponent upheld slavery; not because the South was an aristocracy or that the future of democracy depended upon a northern victory.

W. E. Forster's views on the Union were also ambivalent. Certainly, any comparison between Forster's speeches on the American Civil War and

---

25 Cairnes, *The slave power*, ch. ix passim.
26 *The Economist*, 1 Mar. 1862, 232.
27 Cairnes, *The slave power*, xiv, 30–1, 267–79, 308–37.
28 The earliest example of Cairnes's conversion is in a letter to Mill: Cairnes to Mill, 5 Feb. 1865, Mill-Taylor Collection, vol. LV1 A.
29 For the reviews see *Spectator*, 21 June 1862, 690–2; *Westminster Review* (Oct. 1862), 489–510; *Fraser's Magazine* (Oct. 1863), 419–37; *National Review* (July 1862), 167–98; *Macmillan's Magazine* (Feb. 1863), 269–76; *English Woman's Journal* (Feb. 1863), 370–81.

Bright's betray a clear difference of opinion. Whenever Forster spoke at public meetings or in parliament, the only issue he dwelt upon was slavery – he did not praise either the Union or American institutions. Indeed, sometimes he did just the reverse. In September of 1863, speaking at Leeds, Forster dismissed the American constitution as an 'idol'.[30] The *Spectator* also noted a clear distinction between Forster's position and Bright's: 'The member for Bradford does not, of course, endorse the unreasonable complaints in which the American press indulge, for he does not belong to the school which prefers America to England, and is disposed, like most Englishmen, to meet menace with a very clear defiance.'[31] Even on the issue of the North's emancipation intentions, Forster expressed suspicion. As we have seen, he predicted that the Union would be forced to fight a war against slavery in 1861, and refused to defend the Union's conduct as regards slavery in the House of Commons during Roebuck's motion. Forster supported the North despite its often-dubious stance on emancipation because the South was the society based on slavery. Forster's parents had been leading abolitionists and the Confederate states was the last powerful slave-owning nation.[32] For Forster, the best chance for the destruction of slavery was a Union victory, hence his support. None the less, Forster largely endorsed Cairnes's opposition to re-union. Besides failing to champion it, while speaking in the House of Commons during Roebuck's motion, Forster expressed his desire that the war would end with the capture of Vicksburg. This would, of course, mean the independence of the South – a position unacceptable to the North.[33]

Revisionist historians have, for a long time now, identified leading radicals (both middle- and working-class) who were anti-Union. It was two radical politicians, Roebuck and Lindsay, who made the most concerted efforts to obtain the recognition of the Confederate states. Further, as we have already seen, politicians who were in favour of reform made many of the most vociferous pro-southern speeches. Ellison, besides identifying numerous Lancashire radicals who opposed the North, has revealed that the region's radical press was almost entirely anti-Union.[34] Considering the significance of the local press in this period, if the radical journals in Lancashire did not represent a significant portion of the support for reform in the region, the question must be asked, who did?[35] Cobden and Bright again appear to represent a minority view. While it is possible that Lancashire was a special case because of the cotton famine, to dismiss it as an anomaly on such speculative

---

[30] *Spectator*, 26 Sept. 1863, 2538.
[31] Ibid. 2537. Notice how, by extension, the journal tried to distance its support for the North from Bright's.
[32] Lorimer, *Colour, class and the Victorians*, 127.
[33] *Saturday Review*, 4 July 1863, 1.
[34] Ellison, *Support for secession*, 8–14.
[35] For a discussion on the significance of the local press during this period see Brown, *Victorian news and newspapers*, 47.

grounds would be dangerous.[36] Moreover, Lancashire was not the only area where there existed pro-reformers who expressed antipathy towards the Union or sympathy for the Confederacy. Besides those radicals and politicians in favour of reform mentioned in previous chapters, Harrison lists numerous London radicals such as George Potter, T. J. Dunning, W. Newton, J. F. Bray, Thomas Vize, John Bedford Leno, and, of course, Reynolds.[37]

Harrison's explanation that it was the older generation of labour leaders, especially former Chartists (whose influence was waning), who disliked the Union because of their opposition to Bright, is not entirely convincing.[38] Certainly there is no evidence of Reynolds's influence waning; his paper remained the leading republican journal throughout our period and long after. John B. Leno's *Workman's Advocate*, meanwhile, likewise remained an influential and important labour journal during our period.[39] In the case of Potter, whose southern sympathies were well known because of his activities in the *Bee-Hive*, he was responsible for the huge working-class demonstration in favour of the Polish rebellion in St James's Hall in 1863.[40] The overwhelmingly positive reception Potter, and his speech received, left no doubt about his status.[41] Certainly no one challenged him for his southern sympathies and, considering it was an open meeting, some criticism surely would have been made if the working class was as overwhelmingly pro-Union as some historians would have us believe.[42] The only criticism Potter appears to have received from any radical working-class quarters for his southern proclivities came from the pro-northern *Bee-Hive*. Indeed, after the war, Potter was still in the forefront of radical working-class politics. He organised a meeting of

---

36 Biagini's criticism of Ellison is largely based on the grounds that there are also examples of pro-northern radical sentiment in Lancashire (which Ellison never denied existed), and he writes that 'Britain cannot be reduced to Lancashire'. This misses the point. What is significant about Ellison's study is that she has found that so many Lancashire radicals, possibly a majority, were sympathetic to the South. Further, while Britain indeed cannot be reduced to Lancashire, the opinions there cannot simply be dismissed: Biagini, *Liberty, retrenchment and reform*, 75–6.
37 Harrison, *Before the socialists*, ch. ii passim.
38 Ibid. 55–64. Harrison acknowledges that there are several outstanding exceptions.
39 Finn, *After Chartism*, 232.
40 *Reynolds's Weekly*, 3 May 1863, 1. It must be noted that there is some confusion regarding Potter's position on the war. Harrison believes Potter may have switched sympathies in 1863. Foner, however, notes that Potter was still considered by the *Bee-Hive* to be pro-southern up to the time of Lincoln's assassination. Considering the decline of Anglo-Confederate relations at the end of 1863, it is quite possible that Potter abandoned his pro-southern proclivities but still declined to support the North: Harrison, *Before the socialists*, 70; Foner, *British labor and the American Civil War*, 87.
41 *Reynolds's Weekly*, 3 May 1863, 1.
42 For example, the criticism Foner cites of Potter come from the pages of the *Bee-Hive* after it switched sympathies in 1862. The problems of the *Bee-Hive* are discussed below: Foner, *British labor and the American Civil War*, 28–31.

between 20,000 and 25,000 workers in London in November of 1866 to agitate for the franchise.[43]

Biagini is also sceptical of a generational split in the ranks of the labour leaders and cites several former Chartist leaders who expressed sympathy for the North, and argues that this establishes that the American Civil War united, rather than split, the labour leadership.[44] This, however, misses the point. No one – including Ellison – has ever claimed that there was no middle-class and working-class radical support for the Union. The evidence is overwhelming that there was. What revisionists have argued is that there were a sizeable number of middle-class and working-class radicals who were either indifferent or hostile to the North, and some who were actively pro-southern. Although these individuals might not have comprised a majority, they may have formed a large minority – an important point to note when it is remembered that it is highly doubtful that the majority of radicals were in fact pro-Union.

It is interesting to note that the Confederate propagandist Henry Hotze did not believe that the majority of the working class was pro-North. Writing to Benjamin, in February 1863, Hotze noted, 'A better knowledge of us, a higher appreciation of our national character, and a more reasonable view of our institutions are visibly gaining ground every day. Even among the masses these juster ideas gain ground. And Mrs. Beecher Stowe and negro fanaticism are satirised and ridiculed on the public stage.'[45] Thus, if Hotze is to be believed, and there is no reason to suppose he was lying, contemporary popular culture was anti-North in sentiment.

More revealing, however, is the opinion of Hotze's opponents. Although Bright never admitted it, other pro-northern radicals openly acknowledged that the Confederacy drew support from their allies. Ellison tells us that 'Goldwin Smith admitted in 1866 that all classes, including the lowest, had misguidedly sided with the South.'[46] Goldwin Smith, another vocal pro-Northerner, probably exaggerated the extent of pro-southern sentiment (it is clear the majority of Englishmen never sided with the South), but other, more reliable, sources paint a similar picture. Forster, for example, speaking at a public meeting in Leeds in September 1863, remarked,

> There are men – I confess it fills one with wonder and surprise – men who have done good service to the Liberal cause in past times – who have fought hard for that cause – who yet profess that it is a matter of fanaticism to carry on

---

[43] Finn, *After Chartism*, 249.
[44] Biagini, *Liberty, retrenchment and reform*, 70–5. In all but a few cases, Biagini simply assumes that these individuals endorsed Bright's interpretation of the war, rather than showing that they did.
[45] Hotze to Benjamin, 14 Feb. 1863, in *The messages and papers of Jefferson Davis*, ii. 435. Considering that this is when the activities of the northern apologists were at their height, Hotze's observations become even more noteworthy.
[46] Ellison, *Support for secession*, 83.

this great question of whether slavery shall or shall not rule over the continent of America.[47]

Forster was clearly referring to men he had worked with such as Lindsay and Roebuck as well as William Scholefield, but he was not alone. J. S. Mill writing in the *Westminster Review* explicitly stated in 1862 that liberals, radicals and reformers, expressed anti-Union sentiment too.[48] This still appeared to be the case two years later when Cobden expressed concern at the possibility of a split in the reformers' ranks over America. Speaking at Rochdale in November 1864, promoting the nascent Reform Union, Cobden made a point of offering an olive branch: 'I wish to be tolerant towards everyone who differs from me about this dreadful civil war in America. I have most intimate friends who differ totally from me on this question. It never drove me from their doors, nor prevented me from associating with them.'[49] Cobden had personal reasons for making this statement: he and Lindsay were friends, despite their diametrically opposed views on the merits of the conflict.[50] Cobden's urge for a truce on the subject of America is probably the best explanation for the fact that the reform movement did not split over the conflict, despite the fact that large numbers of reformers could be found amongst each side's partisans: to be divided by the issues of the American Civil War could jeopardise opportunity for reform.

This was certainly the case as far as Reynolds and his journal were concerned. *Reynolds's Weekly*, despite its reservations about Bright, gradually abandoned its hostility towards him as he reversed his opposition towards trade unions. By early 1862, the journal accepted Bright as one of the leaders of reform, despite the fact that it disagreed with him on the subject of America. Indeed, even at the height of its pro-southern agitation, *Reynolds's* criticism of Bright was based only on the question of America and it did not seek to undermine him on the issue of reform:

> How long will this stalwart, and we believe sincere, champion of reform, persist in occupying untenable positions, and thus continue to furnish the enemies of freedom with the means of achieving further triumphs? How long will it be before he learns the elementary lesson that, to defend the inconsistencies, the absurdities, the infatuations, and the inequities of democracies, is *not* to defend democracy? Wonderful, is it not, that a man of Mr. Bright's unquestionable ability should not seemingly be able to discriminate between the idiotic blunders and tyrannical pretensions of Mr. Lincoln and his underlings,

---

47 *Reynolds's Weekly*, 27 Sept. 1863, 1.
48 *Westminster Review* (Oct. 1862), 503.
49 *Reynolds's Weekly*, 27 Nov. 1864, 5. Cobden also admitted that many individuals leaned southwards in their sympathies for liberal reasons. Interestingly, Bright was absent on this occasion because of the recent death of his son.
50 Ellison, *Support for secession*, 8–9.

and the eternal truths for which Washington, and Jefferson, and Franklin and their immortal compatriots fought and conquered?[51]

The writer continued, 'The original sin committed by Bright was in being false to the true principle of democracy, which amounts to this – that a people have a right to govern themselves.'[52] Even though *Reynolds's* became less hostile towards the Union after the Emancipation Proclamation and the arrival of the American ship the *George Griswold* loaded with supplies for the Lancashire cotton spinners (this convinced Reynolds that the North had abandoned its previously aggressive course), the journal never changed its belief that the South had a right to independence or questioned its republican credentials. None the less, this did not prevent it from championing Bright.

This raises the question of whether or not all of Bright's erstwhile supporters endorsed his peculiar views on America. This is an important question. As Margot Finn has established, by 1859 (two years before the Civil War began) opposition to the *laissez-faire* ideas of the Manchester school and liberals such as Goldwin Smith was beginning to grow in the ranks of organised labour. Demands for economic justice – not something practised by the United States – and curbs on the powers of the market were beginning to grow in volume.[53] This is not to say that the radical working class was in opposition to Bright, but rather that it did not share all his views, including those on America. Radicals, by and large, wanted reform. If Bright's influence and leadership could possibly bring this about, it made sense to support him – whether or not one agreed with his strident pro-Unionism. Further, liberals and radicals in England had good reason for wanting to 'agree to disagree', as the phrase has it, in order to promote reform because of their experiences during the Crimean War. There, they had allowed themselves to divide over the merits of the war and, as a result, unquestionably slowed the pace of reform.[54] Radicals and liberals clearly learned from the mistakes made during the Crimean. The job at hand was to bring about political reform in Britain and no American diversion was going to be allowed to prevent that. Thus, despite what Biagini asserts, the forces of reform united *despite* the American Civil War, not because of it.[55]

This was true of not only Bright and Reynolds but of George Potter and P. A. Taylor, the first anti-North, the second distinctly pro-Union. The two amicably shared a public stage together in order to welcome Giuseppe Garibaldi to England in 1864.[56] An even better example is the phenomenal rise of that very public southern supporter, Gladstone. Biagini tells us that by 1862

---

51 *Reynolds's Weekly*, 23 Feb. 1862, 1 [their italics].
52 Ibid.
53 Finn, *After Chartism*, 196–8.
54 Taylor, *The decline of British radicalism*, 265.
55 Biagini, *Liberty, retrenchment and reform*, 72.
56 Finn, *After Chartism*, 220.

(the very year of the 'Jefferson Davis has made a nation' speech), 'Gladstone and working-class radicals were entering into an alliance that perhaps began as "a parallel movement of fairly distinct forces", but soon became a full symbiosis.'[57] Although the Grand Old Man did not renounce his open Confederate sympathies until well after the war, his widespread popularity with the working classes and impact on reform have been well documented. Indeed, Gladstone was as much credited as Bright (if not more so) with the passage of the 1867 Reform Act. Bright certainly co-operated with Gladstone, despite the fact that he never forgave him for taking the opposite view of the conflict.[58] We also know that some northern sympathisers, such as W. E. Adams, became followers of Gladstone.[59] Of course, radicals sympathetic to the South, such as Reynolds, could (and did) easily fall in behind Gladstone.[60]

The labour press

A first glance at the opinions of the *Bee-Hive* certainly supports the argument that working-class radicals were pro-North. Several historians cite its opinions on the war in defence of their arguments for a pro-Union working class.[61] The *Bee-Hive*, however, was not quite the free forum for debate that it has been presented to be. Harrison and Kevin Logan have revealed the internal struggles that took place within the paper during the conflict.[62]

Originally edited by George Troup, a radical whose antipathy towards America arose during the 1840s because of its tariff policies, the *Bee-Hive* began the war supporting the South; however, in 1862, the board of directors, some of whom had connections with the Union and Emancipation Society, replaced Troup with Robert Hartwell, a northern sympathiser who turned the paper's sympathies towards the Union.[63] Besides Hartwell, the northern apologists E. S. Beesly and Edmund Beales also wrote leading articles and

---

57 Ibid. 380. Biagini is quoting from E. J. Feuchtwanger, *Gladstone*, London 1975, 116.
58 Herman Ausubel, *John Bright: Victorian reformer*, New York 1966, 127.
59 Biagini, *Liberty, retrenchment and reform*, 72.
60 See, for example, *Reynolds's Weekly*, 22 May 1864, 1, 3.
61 Biagini, *Liberty, retrenchment and reform*, 69–82; Foner, *British labor and the American Civil War*, ch. vii passim; Harrison, *Before the socialists*, ch. ii passim. Once again, Harrison remains more sceptical.
62 Harrison, 'British labour and the Confederacy', *International Review of Social History* ii (1957), 78–105; Kevin J. Logan, 'The *Bee-Hive* newspaper and British working class attitudes toward the American Civil War', *Civil War History* xxii (1976), 337–48. Additional information may be found in Stephen Coltham, 'George Potter, the Junta and the *Bee-Hive*', *International Review of Social History* ix (1964), 391–432.
63 Harrison, 'British labour and the Confederacy', 97, and Logan, 'The *Bee-Hive* newspaper', 342–3. Logan errs in assuming that the anti-slavery society was a working-class body. See below.

quickly repudiated all that Troup had written.[64] From this point on, the *Bee-Hive* became an essentially uncritical pro-Union paper.

Beesly, being a friend and political ally of Bright by 1862, adopted the latter's views on the conflict, including the belief that the future of democracy depended upon a Union victory. Indeed, Beesly's public addresses and his articles appear to have been lifted verbatim from Bright's Rochdale pronouncements. For example, upon news of a southern victory in mid-1863, Beesly wrote: 'The insolent chuckle of the upper classes ought of itself to be sufficient to stir the blood of every workman who means to stand by his order. Every defeat suffered by the North is a blow to the hopes and prospects of the masses here.'[65] This, of course, was merely the old calumny repeated by Bright, that the aristocracy was pro-South and that the advancement of democracy depended upon a Union victory.

Beesly did not, however, have it all his own way. In the name of open discussion, Troup was given a chance to respond to the former's unsubstantiated remarks and did so, along with the assistance of Dunning and others.[66] Open debate, however, was not to Beesly's taste and he threatened to resign unless the correspondence ceased. As Harrison notes, however, 'the Federal supporters were not strong enough to drive Troup and Co. from the pages of the paper'. Hartwell eventually closed the correspondence in 1864 – after Confederate hostility towards Britain became pronounced – but by that time Beesly had resigned in disgust.[67]

The *Bee-Hive* then essentially fell under the control of working-class radicals who were sympathetic to the North. Did its views represent the majority of the radical English working class as it claimed, not only under Hartwell, but under Troup as well? The answer appears to be no. The problem with the *Bee-Hive* is that it was not mass-circulated, despite its being classified as more 'official' or 'intellectual' than the other workers' weeklies by some historians.[68] Further, the working-class radical press as a whole did not share its views on the American Civil War.

Apart from the *Bee-Hive*, the working-class radical press expressed antipathy towards the Union. As Harrison has pointed out, 'it is a problem to find a single influential working-class paper which consistently favoured Lincoln and opposed British intervention. The predominant tendency was decidedly the other way – and this is scarcely less evident in the later than in the earlier

---

[64] Harrison, 'British labour and the Confederacy', 97; Foner, *British labor and the American Civil War*, 68–9.
[65] *Bee-Hive*, 23 May 1863, 1.
[66] Harrison, 'British labour and the Confederacy', 102–3; Foner, *British labor and the American Civil War*, 69.
[67] Harrison, 'British labour and the Confederacy', 103–4; Foner, *British labor and the American Civil War*, 69. Foner's and Harrison's accounts of the struggle within the *Bee-Hive* and, indeed, the trade unions differ somewhat. Harrison's, however, is unquestionably the more balanced view.
[68] Biagini, *Liberty, retrenchment and reform*, 25.

period of the conflict.'[69] Keiser, who also finds very few pro-northern journals amongst the working-class press, supports Harrison's examination.[70] Harrison argues that part of the reason may have been because 'the editors of working-class papers had little or no independent source of news in America and that they were completely dependent on the middle-class press'.[71] This, however, assumes that the middle-class press in its entirety either falsified events or was inherently anti-Union, neither of which is true. There is also at least one example of the working class rejecting a pro-Union radical journal. The circulation of the *Daily News*, which had a large working-class readership, plummeted during the conflict, suggesting, once again, a lack of pro-northern sentiment amongst some sections of the radical working class.[72]

Although Harrison has a point when he states that 'It is a notoriously suspect procedure to make inferences from the opinions of newspapers as to those of their readers', the consistent lack of support for the Union amongst the working-class press cannot be dismissed.[73] Historians of the press consistently tell us that the views of journals must have some bearing on their readership.[74] In most cases, profits for newspapers depended mainly on sales, rather than advertising, and therefore on their appeal to a readership.[75] As Biagini rightly points out, journals could try to make, rather than reflect, public opinion.[76] A periodical, however, could hardly actively promote a doctrine or cause to which its readers were militantly opposed – such as, we are told, the Confederacy's.

The contradictory nature of at least a portion of working-class radicalism's perceptions of America is revealed by an examination of *Reynolds's*. We may immediately dismiss Foner's assertion that the British ruling class worked to inflame the working class against the Union to the extent that even '*Reynolds's Weekly Newspaper*, the "sole great and widely circulating workers' organ still existing", had been purchased for the one purpose of contributing to the campaign of inciting the British working class.'[77] The origin of this remarkable information appears to be Karl Marx, who expressed a vaguely similar opinion in 1861.[78] This allegation, however, was and is, false. Besides

---

69 Harrison, *Before the socialists*, 53. For his discussion of the labour press see pp. 47–55.
70 Keiser, 'The English press and the American Civil War', 285–92. Despite my reservations about Keiser's simplifying opinion ambivalent towards the Union into pro-southern sentiment, his findings do, at a minimum, suggest working-class press antipathy towards the North. The fact that his findings support Harrison's is also significant.
71 Harrison, *Before the socialists*, 53.
72 Brown, *Victorian news and newspapers*, 51; Jordan and Pratt, *Europe and the American Civil War*, 85.
73 Harrison, *Before the socialists*, 53.
74 Koss, *The rise and fall of the political press*, i. 146–8.
75 Biagini, *Liberty, retrenchment and reform*, 21–2.
76 Ibid. 23.
77 Foner, *British labor and the American Civil War*, 12.
78 Marx did not actually state that *Reynolds's* was 'purchased' by the 'ruling class', only that

the fact that the 'ruling class' neither favoured the Confederacy nor tried to inflame the working class against the Union (as we have seen, the chief fear was that the distressed Lancashire operatives would force a war upon the nation), *Reynolds's* remained a fiercely radical journal which did not shy away from republicanism. Biagini notes the 'enthusiastic empathy' between *Reynolds's* and its readers and the fact that it was 'avidly' read in the industrial districts of the Midlands and north of England by the most radical and democratic of manual workers.[79] Stephen Koss, meanwhile, notes conservative alarm expressed at the 'pernicious doctrines' that '*Reynolds's* spread on Saturday nights through the length and breadth of the country'.[80] We should also remember that *Reynolds's* had a huge circulation which rose from roughly 60,000 in 1860, to 150,000 by 1865.[81] This, it should be noted, was well in excess of the *Bee-Hive*.[82]

Initially, *Reynolds's* adopted the belief that opponents of democracy were delighted to see America torn apart. The journal noted that 'British royalty and aristocracy, with their votaries and parasites, have enjoyed a more than ordinarily merry Christmas, and they expect a most delightful new year'. The reason for these festivities, according to the journal, was obvious: 'The news from America of the threatened breaking up of the great democratic confederation, has, in our liberty-hating circles, been held as a slight compensation from Providence for the magnificent achievements of the democratic and heroic Garibaldi.'[83] Leaving aside the fact that support in England for the Austrians, rather than for the Italians, was minuscule, among all social and political groups, this was also the period when public opinion in England was, at almost all levels, anti-secession. This establishes, once again, that when studying the opinions of social groups like the aristocracy, and political groups like conservatives, sole reliance on the charges of their critics and opponents almost infallibly leads to error. Not that this mattered to *Reynolds's*, which insisted,

> The cardinal mistake into which our Jenkinses and Tom Noddies have fallen, with respect to the present crisis in the United States, is, that, they confound the *confederation* of the *democracy* with *democracy* itself: much the same sort of error as if one were to confound Lord Tom Noddy's breeches with his Lordship himself; as if a disastrous rent in the fundamental region of the 'unmentionable' garment were to be considered as a fatal accident to the illustrious and invaluable wearer.[84]

---

it 'sold itself to Messrs. Yancey and Mann' (the first Confederate envoys). If this is Foner's source, his use of it is odd: Karl Marx, *New York Daily Tribune*, 1 Feb. 1862, 6.
[79] Biagini, *Liberty, retrenchment and reform*, 24.
[80] Koss, *The rise and fall of the political press*, i. 184.
[81] Keiser, 'The English press and the American Civil War', 245–6.
[82] Biagini notes that the *Bee-Hive* was not mass-circulated and only a few thousand copies were printed: *Liberty, retrenchment and reform*, 25.
[83] *Reynolds's Weekly*, 6 Jan. 1861, 8.
[84] Ibid. 26 Jan. 1861, 8 [their italics].

Sarcasm aside, this argument is crucial. While *Reynolds's* approved of a society with no official aristocracy, and a much wider electoral franchise, there was no belief that democracy's future depended upon what occurred in America. *Reynolds's* continued in this vein, arguing that peaceful secession spoke well for the United States. The journal, like the rest of the London press, began to turn against the Union after the controversy surrounding the Proclamation of Neutrality and the passing of the Morrill tariff, and became increasingly hostile as Anglo-Union relations declined.[85] Finally, in September 1861, *Reynolds's* went beyond the mainstream journals and demanded that the northern blockade be broken.

In an article headlined 'England Must Break the Blockade or Her Millions Will Starve', *Reynolds's* blamed the 'criminal obstructions of our rulers and the stupid apathy of our capitalists' for having failed to develop the cotton capacities of India and other regions in order to relieve Britain's 'degrading dependence on the Slave States of America', and demanded that the northern blockade be breached, even at the cost of war with the Union.[86] This position was to be retained until March of 1862.[87]

What is important to note at this point is *Reynolds's* condemnation of the so-called ruling classes' failure to break the blockade – by going to war if necessary – in order to help the Lancashire operatives. For example, in November 1861, remarking on the non-interventionist position adopted by most English politicians, *Reynolds's* columnist Gracchus sneered,

> the Duke of Argyll and other smug and oily-tongued orators, say there is no help for it. They, the comfortable well-to-do class, feel assured that, 'the good sense and manly spirit of the English workman will enable him to bear up against every hardship, privation, and suffering that the stoppage of work may originate, rather than join in the cry which has been raised to break the Northern blockade!' The plump, well-fed bishop preaches temperance and abstention to his admiring listeners, but, generally speaking, the lawn-sleeved fraternity themselves live upon the fat of the land. It is easier to preach than practise.[88]

Reynolds's views are yet another challenge to the notion of an English establishment being excessively pro-southern in its views or, at the very least keen to become involved in the conflict. The question is where did the call for the breaking of the Union blockade originate if not from the 'lawn-sleeved frater-

---

[85] For example, see *Reynolds's Weekly*, 3 Mar. 1861, 8; 5 May 1861, 1; 9 June 1861, 1; 11 Aug. 1861, 1.
[86] Ibid. 29 Sept. 1861, 1.
[87] Ibid. 16 Mar. 1862, 1. After this edition, calls for interference were sporadic, although anti-northern hysteria lingered. It is also worth noting that *Reynolds's* was among the minority of periodicals that praised Gladstone's Newcastle speech and, believing that the speech foreshadowed recognition of the Confederacy, proudly announced that this had been the journal's position since October 1861: ibid. 12 Oct. 1862, 4.
[88] Ibid. 10 Nov. 1861, 7. The charges were repeated: see 16 Mar. 1862, 1.

nity', that is, the aristocracy and political conservatives? The cry, apparently, was taken up by radicals such as Reynolds and, as Ellison has established, radicals in Lancashire.[89] It is certainly interesting to note that, during its anti-northern period, *Reynolds's* received letters of thanks for its continued championing of working-class issues from public meetings of unemployed Lancashire cotton-spinners.[90]

As Anglo-Union relations declined, *Reynolds's* admiration for the Confederacy and distaste for the North exceeded even that of *The Times* and the *Saturday Review*. *Reynolds's* remarked, 'Indeed, we are not by any means certain but that, barring the one damnable point of negro slavery, the Southern men are better and heartier Republicans than their Northern brethren.' The reason this was so, according to the journal, was because the people of the North 'seem to have carried the most objectionable characteristics of the English middle class to their most extreme and exaggerated logical development'.[91] For *Reynolds's Weekly*, this was about as serious an insult as it could level. Even the notion of the United States being 'the fairest experiment ever tried in human affairs', as American nationalists put it, came under attack: 'The very form of their government, the principles of civil and religious liberty which are embodied in their institutions, were elaborated in England in the course of some hundreds of years. All their noble thoughts and ideas are the product of British brains.'[92] Faced with the aggression of Seward, Clay and much of the Union's press, *Reynolds's* quickly denied that the North represented the future of democracy and, instead, as we have seen, promoted reform (and republicanism) independently. *Reynolds's* consistently argued for the first two years of the war that the Union's activities proved nothing about the merits of democracy – a view endorsed, as we have seen, by numerous conservatives. 'Democracy', concluded the journal, 'is no more responsible for the present troubles in America, than Christianity is responsible for the excesses of a drunken parson.'[93]

Reynolds's, as the war progressed, and certainly by early 1863, largely followed the views of the rest of the press. Its hostility towards the Union declined as emancipation finally became a war aim and as Anglo-Confederate relations deteriorated. Where *Reynolds's* differed from the rest of the national press was in its accusation upon the arrival of the *George Griswold* that this was proof the North did not hate the English people, 'though the servile organs of the British court and aristocracy are never tired

---

[89] Ellison, *Support for secession*, passim. Harrison cites other labour journals that favoured breaking the blockade; *Reynolds's* was not an isolated case. Harrison, *Before the socialists*, 50–1.
[90] See, for example, *Reynolds's Weekly*, 25 May 1862, 3.
[91] Ibid. 11 Aug. 1861, 1.
[92] Ibid. 1 Dec. 1861, 1. This was, of course, written during the *Trent* affair, which added impetus to the journal's dislike of the North.
[93] Ibid. 17 Nov. 1861, 4.

of telling us that such is the case'.[94] This was an interesting accusation, coming from the journal that had been the chief organ that agitated for active interference against the Union. Clearly, whatever stance *Reynolds's* took, it was going to use its position to condemn the aristocracy – just like Bright and Beesly. Further, the journal never championed re-union, but retained its support for Confederate independence, even though it claimed not to be anti-North.[95] This stance could be dismissed as hypocritical, except that it was, as we have seen, the position taken by leading Union apologists such as Cairnes and Forster.

It seems then, at least as far as *Reynolds's* was concerned – although there is no reason to believe that this was not a view held by many other working-class radicals, especially when we consider Ellison's findings and the rest of the labour press – that America was a useful stick with which to beat the drum for reform. It was also an ephemeral stick. As soon as the United States broke down and the Union became belligerent towards Britain, it was cast aside as an example. Certainly, as far as the press is concerned, radical working-class opinion was never overwhelmingly pro-northern on the scale portrayed by the traditional interpretation.

The pro-Union press

It is also worth examining those journals that, more or less, remained consistently sympathetic to the North throughout the conflict.[96] In some cases, these were indeed radical, but in others, not at all. Even when radical, slavery appears to have been the only reason they (rather inconsistently) threw their support behind the Union. Certainly, the opinions of the *Westminster Review* and *Spectator*, among others, are worth examining.

Despite the *Westminster Review*'s radical views, it also failed to equate the cause of Union with that of democracy. Indeed, it initially adopted the views of those commentators who argued that, regardless of the Confederacy's adhesion to slavery, it had the right of self-determination. In late 1861, it commissioned an article by one Thomas Ellison, who remarked upon news of the North's attempts to conquer the South:

---

[94] Ibid. 15 Feb. 1863, 4. It should still be noted, however, that as late as July 1863 the journal remarked that 'the professional politicians and present rulers of the North ... appear to have behaved abominably': ibid. 26 July 1863, 1.

[95] Ibid. 27 Dec. 1863, 1; 6 Mar. 1864, 1; 18 Sept. 1864, 3.

[96] It is difficult to find a single English journal (this of course excludes northern-owned propaganda pamphlets such as the *London American*) which defended the Union with complete consistency simply because events such as the *Trent* affair caused problems for northern supporters. The only journal I have found which was consistently pro-Union is the *Morning Star*. This, however, was Cobden and Bright's organ, which effectively made it a propaganda pamphlet like the *London American*.

How, above all, could this *despotic* work be performed by a *republican* government? What would become of the doctrine of *the people's inherent right to govern themselves*, which is the foundation of all democracies? It is of no use for us to be told that the North *does not intend to subjugate* the South – it is trying to do it.[97]

Like *Reynolds's*, the *Westminster Review* did not regard the Confederacy as an aristocratic government, but as a republic like the Union. Although the journal detested slavery and was by no means pro-South, the issue of self-determination trapped it. It was not until 1862 that the *Westminster Review* found an escape in the form of Cairnes's *The slave power*. Publishing an ecstatic review in the October 1862 issue, the journal endorsed all of Cairnes's arguments and, from that point on, completely opposed the Confederacy, equating its success with the establishment of a slave empire. The issues of democracy and republicanism were unmentioned by the *Westminster Review* throughout the duration of the war.[98] Like most northern supporters, it was the issue of slavery and only slavery which motivated this radical journal's opposition to the South.

Slavery was, without doubt, the only reason the *Spectator* sympathised with the Union. Aside from the criticism levelled at the North already mentioned, the journal made its opinion of the Union known by the end of 1861: 'We have as little respect as any of our contemporaries for the American democracy of the last twenty years and its irritating and blustering foreign policy.'[99] The *Spectator*, like Mill and numerous other pro-Northerners, believed that the Union would be forced to fight a war of emancipation and that this was the only reason for sympathising with the Union. None the less, the journal noted, 'our sympathy is with the *cause* of the North, not with its people or administration'.[100] Indeed, after the *Trent* affair, the *Spectator* turned quite anti-northern, announcing that if the Confederacy were to begin some form of emancipation it would be recognised in a week. 'Europe cares nothing about the preservation of the Union *as such*',[101] the journal added. The *Spectator* was never a dependable champion of re-union. Besides accepting, if not supporting mediation on more than one occasion, throughout 1863 it insisted that the North did not intend to conquer the South, but merely isolate it. Not until October 1864 did the *Spectator* begin to support re-union.[102] Nor was the journal impressed by the American system of

---

97 *Westminster Review* (October 1861), 501 [Ellison's italics].
98 The journal only discussed these arguments in the latter half of 1865, after the war was over. For a discussion of this, see below.
99 *Spectator*, 14 Sept. 1861, 1001.
100 Ibid. 16 Nov. 1861, 1253 [their italics].
101 Ibid. 25 Jan. 1862, 91 [their italics].
102 Support for mediation: ibid. 14 June 1862, 650–1; 11 Oct. 1862, 1125. Predictions of southern independence: ibid. 14 Feb. 1863, 1633–4; 15 Aug. 1863, 2365; 29 Oct. 1864, 1232.

government, frequently referring to 'the marvellous badness of the American constitutional system'.[103] When the *Spectator* finally abandoned its constant ridicule of Lincoln and his 'bad grammar', it used the opportunity to contrast the political systems of Britain and the Union, to the disadvantage of the latter:

> While Lord Palmerston's success is the legitimate offspring of our parliamentary system, Mr Lincoln's modest and somewhat vulgar but respectable statesmanship is strictly a godsend, – and, such as it is, has been achieved in spite of every obstacle which an elaborate political machinery could manage to place in his way.[104]

Thus, even what the journal deemed to be positive about the North was in no way owing to its political system.

It was unsurprising that the *Spectator* expressed no particular respect for America or its institutions. The *Spectator* was generally cool to the idea of an expansion of the franchise and was largely hostile to the labour movement. For example, although the journal approved of the pro-northern sentiment expressed at the St James's Hall meeting, it made its opposition to Bright and the elements of the trade unions present at the gathering perfectly clear: 'We do not share his [Bright's] wish, and that of the Trades' Unionists, to see a democracy take the place of our present constitution, because we believe that a far truer freedom and higher kind of liberty may be secured under it than can ever be secured under any mere democracy.'[105] The career of the *Spectator*, traditionally regarded as one of the most staunchly pro-northern journals in England, establishes not only that most so-called periodicals were actually more anti-South than pro-Union, but that not all such journals were even in the liberal or radical camp. This is a fact that needs to be continually remembered.

The equation between reform and the success of the Union was conspicuous by its absence in the pages of other journals that supported the North, such as *Macmillan's* and the *Wesleyan Methodist Magazine*. Some journals sympathetic to the Union such as the *Eclectic Review* were actually staunch opponents of reform.[106] The pro-northern Edward Dicey, writing in the *National Review*, meanwhile, like the *Spectator*, was highly critical of the American political system and society, claiming, 'In politics, as in everything else, the North is the home of *aurea mediocritas*.'[107] With the chief exceptions of the *Bee-Hive* and the *Daily News*, not only were there few pro-reform or radical journals which supported the North, but precious few of the periodicals sympathetic to the Union were especially enamoured with the American

---

[103] Ibid. 19 Sept. 1863, 2513.
[104] Ibid.
[105] Ibid. 28 Mar. 1863, 1800.
[106] *Eclectic Review* (May 1865), 346.
[107] *National Review* (Oct. 1862), 426.

political system. In the end, it was the simple issue of slavery rather than any particular party political stance that determined most journals' position during the conflict.

The public meetings chimera

Even the anti-slavery meetings are by no means the convincing display of pro-northern English radical working-class opinion that they have been represented to be. The source of the allegedly vast number of working-class pro-Union rallies is E. D. Adams, whose findings need to be reprinted in full.[108]

Year	Number	Anti-slavery and religious	Working men
1861	7	7	–
1862	16	11	5
1863	82	26	56
1864	21	10	11
1865	5	4	1

The trouble is, these numbers do not actually mean a great deal. There is the problem of Adams's sources. He depends on the American William Lloyd Garrison's *Liberator*, the abolitionist periodical, and C. F. Adams's reports to Seward, neither of which are reliable.[109] Leaving aside Ellison's forty-seven pro-southern meetings in Lancashire alone (many of which were attended by Lancashire operatives), which must be compared to the number of anti-slavery rallies, Adams's sources are American and, as Crook has pointed out, there is a problem with these. To the North the idea that the disenfranchised and genuine progressives could desert the chosen people, the beacon of freedom that was the United States, was unbearable. The only explanation was that the people of Europe were still in chains, their opinions suppressed by the governing classes. Hence, from the start of the war, the northern press searched for the slightest evidence of sympathy from groups outside the centres of power, manufacturing such proof as was necessary.[110] There certainly can be no other explanation for the *New York Times*'s insistence, in November 1862, that the 'dumb masses' were the Union's only allies in England.[111] At that point in the war, virtually the entire labour press, even

---

[108] Harrison relies almost completely on Adams's numbers, as does Biagini. Foner, meanwhile, merely cites a small handful of already well-known pro-Union meetings: Harrison, *Before the socialists*, 65; Biagini, *Liberty, retrenchment and reform*, 77; Foner, *British labor and the American Civil War*, ch. iv.
[109] Adams, *Great Britain and the American Civil War*, ii. 223.
[110] Crook, *The North, the South and the powers*, 272–3.
[111] Quoted in Foner, *British Labor and the American Civil War*, 47–8. This, however, should be contrasted with the *New York Herald*'s fulminations against the British working class for its lack of sympathy. See *Reynolds's Weekly*, 20 Apr. 1862, 4.

the *Bee-Hive*, was anti-North and some, such as *Reynolds's*, had gone beyond the mainstream press in demanding that Britain go to war against the Union. If we use Adams's calculations, the only factor offsetting this widespread hostility was five pro-northern meetings, which were, in turn, offset by pro-southern gatherings. One cannot escape the conclusion that northern commentators saw only what they wanted to see.

Not that C. F. Adams's reports are as impressive as they appear at first glance. Adams was routinely sent copies of resolutions by meetings held in favour of the North, which he forwarded to Lincoln through Seward. Not all the meetings, however, from which these resolutions originate are indicative of very much. For instance, in January 1864, Adams was sent an address of support for Lincoln, ostensibly from a meeting held by Ashton-under-Lyne's workingmen.[112] Part of the address contained the exhortation that:

> Believing the interest of remunerated labour to be a paramount one in your war, as working men we regard your cause as ours, and rejoice with you that victory is crowning your efforts to suppress a most wicked and infamous rebellion, and restores to your country that unity without which it can have no true prosperity or lasting peace.[113]

Adams's reply is also worth noting:

> Sir – I am directed to apprise you of the reception by the President of the United States of the interesting address of the citizens of Ashton-under-Lyne, which was transmitted to him some time since through this legation. It is with lively satisfaction that he accepts their assurances that, under all the disadvantages of a distant position, they have not been unable to understand the policy of the Government, and to comprehend how a fixed and unswerving determination to rescue the state from the assaults of domestic faction is compatible with the policy of lawfully extinguishing the chronic evil of African slavery – I have the honour to be, Sir, your obedient servant, Charles Francis Adams.[114]

Read through the medium of the Adams papers, this meeting apparently utterly vindicates the traditional interpretation, and gives the impression of distressed operatives rallying behind the Union. In actual fact, it proves nothing of the sort. The meeting, far from being a gathering of the working class, was, in fact, a private soirée, held in a small tearoom by middle-class members of the Union and Emancipation Society, at 47 Charles Street.[115] This, of course, raises the obvious question, if the Ashton-under-Lyne operatives shared the views of their self-appointed spokesmen, why was no open and public meeting held? Indeed, when we compare this private gathering to the large working-class meeting held at Ashton-under-Lyne in favour of the

---

112 *Reynolds's Weekly*, 4 Mar. 1864, 3.
113 Ibid. 10 Jan. 1864, 4.
114 Ibid. 4 Mar. 1864, 3.
115 Ibid. 10 Jan. 1864, 4.

South in January 1863, the question becomes even more pressing.[116] The fact is this 'Address' represented only the view of a small lobby group and, despite its fraudulent claim to be otherwise, cannot be treated as the opinion of the workmen of Ashton-under-Lyne, let alone Lancashire. None the less, Adams (probably through no fault of his) clearly treated it as such by forwarding it to his president. After receipt of addresses such as this, there is little wonder that Lincoln was convinced of the Lancashire operatives' 'sublime Christian heroism that has not been surpassed in any age or in any country'.[117]

Even when so-called pro-Union meetings appear genuine, the resolutions passed did not necessarily take a position inherently different from that of the nation as a whole. For example, a meeting of the working population of Marylebone took place in the New Hall on Edgware Road in January 1862. Occurring shortly after the *Trent* affair, the meeting was held to determine how Mason and Slidell should be received in England. After a fierce (and inconclusive) debate on the merits of the conflict, a resolution was passed against giving Mason and Slidell a warm reception, which was subsequently passed on to Adams.[118] This resolution is remarkable only if one is unaware of the general dislike felt for Mason and Slidell among commentators in England at the time of the *Trent* incident. Almost the entire national press argued against celebrating their arrival and this was true even of journals hostile towards the Union. For, despite the fact that *Reynolds's* was currently demanding that Britain break the Union blockade even at the cost of war, its columnist 'Gracchus' averred, 'I do not imagine that the English people will welcome the representatives of the Slave States on their arrival in England with any particular warmth or enthusiasm, although we have risked war in order to rescue them.'[119] The anti-northern and scarcely proletarian *Saturday Review* meanwhile sneered, 'by a curious change of circumstances, Mr Mason has been saved from a dungeon by the action of the very Government which it had been the business of his life to threaten and denounce'.[120] Indeed, it was a large but silent crowd that greeted Mason and Slidell upon their arrival at Southampton; there were no pro-Confederate or anti-Union celebrations whatsoever.[121] The resolution passed at the New Hall meeting, then, scarcely represented an opinion unique to the working class.

We should also be careful before accepting pro-northern meetings as being actually representative of any area's sentiments as a whole. For example, Foner cites a working-class meeting held in Edinburgh on 19 February 1863 in support of Lincoln's Emancipation Proclamation, as proof of the Scottish

---

[116] Ellison, *Support for secession*, 74.
[117] Lincoln, *The collected works of Abraham Lincoln*, vi. 63–5.
[118] *Reynolds's Weekly*, 2 Feb. 1862, 6.
[119] Ibid. 19 Jan. 1862, 3. 'Gracchus' was, in fact, Edward Reynolds, Reynolds's brother.
[120] *Saturday Review*, 25 Jan. 1862, 87.
[121] *Reynolds's Weekly*, 2 Feb. 1862, 1.

labour movement's support for the North.[122] Besides the fact that the meeting contained a small number of individuals, it was far more anti-slavery and anti-Confederate than pro-Union. Also, this meeting must be compared to the working-class meeting Lord Brougham addressed in the same city in October of the same year, which has already been discussed in Chapter 4. Further, Scotland cannot be reduced to Edinburgh. In April 1863, for example, Palmerston attended a working-class meeting in Glasgow consisting of some 50,000 persons. Here, Palmerston promoted his government's conduct during the war to cheers, and although he stated that British mediation would be unwelcome, he nevertheless hoped, 'If a different state of things should arise, that the friendly counsels of England should be listened to with success (cheers).'[123] As Palmerston referred throughout his speech to the North and South as separate countries, he was obviously referring to peace through separation. Thus, the possible demise of the Union did not seem to overly disturb the working population of Glasgow. Having said that, it is important to note that no one isolated meeting can be cited as definitive evidence of a city's population's opinion – never mind the sentiment of a country, such as Scotland. It merely reinforces the point that isolated examples in specific locales need to be treated with more caution.

Indeed, the issue of location is extremely important when it comes to a discussion of the meetings expressing sympathy for the North (and, indeed, gatherings as a whole). Most of Lancashire's pro-northern meetings took place in Rochdale, where Cobden and Bright routinely held pro-Union rallies.[124] These numerous meetings, which only represent the opinion of that region of Lancashire, greatly increased the grand total number of pro-northern rallies held. This is yet another problem with Adams's calculations. Although the veteran abolitionist George Thompson, while on a visit to America, bragged that the Emancipation Society 'had waged war with Confederate sympathisers wherever they were to be found', he was not being entirely honest.[125] The fact is, there were regions of England that were effectively 'no-go' areas for Union supporters. Besides some of the areas in Lancashire Ellison cites, there were no sizeable pro-Union rallies held in the region's major city, Liverpool, or in Sheffield.[126] Indeed, in the case of Liver-

---

[122] Foner, *British labor and the American Civil War*, 55–6. Foner acknowledges that the Edinburgh Trades Council was divided by an eight to six vote to hold the meeting, which again suggests a serious division of opinion.
[123] *Reynolds's Weekly*, 5 Apr. 1863, 3.
[124] Ellison, *Support for secession*, 40–1. Meetings held by Bright in Rochdale often sent copies of their resolutions to Adams, adding to the minister's numbers.
[125] *Reynolds's Weekly*, 20 Mar. 1864, 1.
[126] As late as September 1864 the Liberal member for the West Riding of Yorkshire, Sir Francis Crossely, speaking to a gathering of the Sheffield cutlers, was effectively shouted down when he argued that the cause of the war was slavery: *Spectator*, 1 Sept. 1864, 1001. Meanwhile, although there were, of course, some northern sympathisers in Liverpool, the few meetings held there were always lacking in numbers: Ellison, *Support for secession*, 49.

pool, Bulloch noted that the Union consul was unable to get Liverpudlians of any class to testify against Confederate ship building, and this included the far-from-secret Laird's Rams.[127] In the end, the North had to rely on the testimony of private detectives (many of whom, if Bulloch is to be believed, were borderline criminals) when trying to halt such activities through the British courts.[128] It should also be borne in mind that there was never a shortage of English sailors willing to serve, not only on the blockade-runners, but on the Confederate privateers as well. While the recruitment pitch reproduced in Bulloch's memoirs suggests that many sailors believed that they were serving the cause of liberty by serving in the Confederate navy, doubtless many served solely for profit. This, however, is another example of economic considerations outweighing abstract political arguments for certain members of the working class, such as sailors.[129] An investigation of the sympathies of the rank and file of the British merchant marine would prove interesting. Location, not to say profession, has been an all too easily overlooked factor in the case of meetings.

The one meeting which has been repeatedly cited as the radical working-class endorsement of the Union and the idea that a northern victory represented a victory for democracy, is the one held in St James's Hall in London on 26 March 1863 by a portion of the London trades councils.[130] While this meeting is significant, there are a number of problems surrounding it. For one thing, it was organised by pro-northern agitators who invited Bright to speak.[131] For another, it was by ticket, which could (but not necessarily) suggest great demand – it also ensured that individuals such as Dunning and members of his union did not disrupt the proceedings. Further, the glowing reports of the meeting all originate from the *Bee-Hive*, from the pens of the organisers such as Beesly, ignoring the views of the rest of the labour press.[132] Further, the two chief speakers who linked the future of democracy and the future of the United States were Bright and Beesly. Although the meeting was (and has been) cited as a demonstration of the trade unions of London, this was immediately disputed.

---

[127] Thomas Dudley, the northern consul in Liverpool, admitted much the same in July of 1862, stating, 'The feeling is deep and strong against us, and the whole town seems to take sides with those who are building the vessels.' Charles C. Beaman, *The national and private 'Alabama Claims' and their 'Final and amicable settlement'*, 102, quoted in Ellison, *Support for secession*, 27.
[128] Bulloch, *The secret service of the Confederate States*, i. 339–43.
[129] Ibid. 244–9.
[130] See Harrison, *Before the socialists*, 69–77; Foner, *British labor and the American Civil War*, 56–62; Biagini, *Liberty, retrenchment and reform*, 76–7.
[131] Foner and Harrison disagree over who actually organised the meeting, Marx or Beesly. Harrison insists on the latter; Foner argues a case for the former: Harrison, *Before the socialists*, 70–1; Foner, *British labor and the American Civil War*, 57–8. Harrison's rebuttal appears in the introduction to the second edition, xxx–xxxi.
[132] Harrison's, Foner's and Biagini's reports on this meeting all originate solely from the *Bee-Hive*.

Take, for example, the letter submitted to the *Bee-Hive* by the committee of the London Society of Compositors:

> Sir – It having been represented to the committee of the London Society of Compositors that an impression prevails that our society was represented at the late meeting of Trades' Unionists, held at St. James's Hall, I am directed to inform you such was not the fact, no person having been authorised to appear on our behalf; it being the invariable rule of this society to avoid in any way mixing up, as an associative body, with political questions. Your insertion of this disclaimer will much oblige, Sir, your most obedient servant, W. M. Beckett, Secretary For the Committee of the L. S. C.

Although no individual was named, the letter referred to the fact that because a member of the Society, E. S. Mantz, had spoken at the meeting, it was apparently assumed that he had been an official representative of the union. The *Bee-Hive* admitted that, initially, they were not going to print the letter because its 'contents [were] of an injurious tendency', but decided to do so because Mantz wished to reply. This came dangerously close to manufacturing consent. Besides the fact that the letter was in no way injurious to Mantz – he was neither mentioned nor criticised – that such disclaimers would be suppressed solely because their alleged opponents declined to reply is noteworthy. Such is what would have happened to this letter had Mantz not been willing to unnecessarily vindicate himself. One cannot help wondering if other such disclaimers remained unpublished.[133]

Mantz's rebuttal, besides being largely irrelevant, reveals the typically wild accusations the pro-northern lobby levelled at its critics, perceived or real. For example, Mantz stated that the letter 'disclaims the object for which the meeting at St. James's Hall was convened', and accused the committee of being pro-slavery. Yet neither charge was true. The committee had neither disparaged the meeting nor expressed any pro-slavery views. Mantz also accused the committee of 'constituting themselves the censors of my political acts'. This was also false. The committee had not tried to censor Mantz, they had merely made it clear that his opinions did not necessarily reflect those of the London Society of Compositors; of Mantz's views themselves, the committee had said nothing.

Mantz further declared, 'the committee state that they authorised no one to speak on their behalf. Who says they did?'[134] In actual fact, someone at the meeting had made precisely this claim. The individual in question was Beesly, who had stated at the meeting that 'This is the first time, I believe, that the Trades' Unionists of London have met together to pronounce on a political question, but I am sure it will not be the last.'[135] This of course did imply that the speakers were representing their unions and societies. Indeed, Mantz

---

[133] *Bee-Hive*, 11 Apr. 1863, 5.
[134] Ibid.
[135] Ibid. 28 Mar. 1863, 6.

himself recognised that this was the case when he stated: 'The committee say that it "has been *represented* to them that they were represented at the late meeting of Trades' Unionists". Well, and if they were so represented, what does it amount to? Simply this – that the society of compositors, in common with the other trades, had raised its voice against the curse of slavery.' Thus, by Mantz's own admission, his speech had been regarded as the sentiment of the Society, which he had no mandate to represent. Further, by referring to 'the other trades', Mantz effectively endorsed Beesly's statement that the views of the speakers at the meeting represented the opinions of the unions and societies they came from, even though, if Mantz is any indication, these individuals probably had no mandate either. Far from repudiating the committee's letter, Mantz actually justified it. Furthermore, the St James's Hall meeting had not simply denounced slavery – it had endorsed Bright's entire misrepresentation of the war and English attitudes towards it, which was by no stretch of the imagination the same thing.

Mantz concluded by stating, 'When I wish to know the sentiment of the printing profession I shall boldly appeal to the whole trade, not a few self-inflated members sitting in select committee.' The fact is, however, no one in the Society repudiated the committee's letter, which suggests that it was indeed the committee, and not Mantz, who represented the views of the society.[136] It must also be noted that the London Society of Compositors was a radical organisation. As Margot Finn has pointed out, the Society was responsible for providing funds for the 1859 builders' strike.[137] If the traditional interpretation of radical support for the Union is correct, the Society should not have denied the claim that Mantz represented the union. Indeed, it should have made him an official spokesman or, at the very least, championed the meeting.

It appears then that, so far as the St James's Hall meeting was concerned, the rank and file of the unions was not consulted – one is forced to ask why – and that the radical trade unionist Dunning was not wide of the mark when he said of the meeting, 'The trades were not consulted at all, much less their authority given,' and further calculated that 'nine out of every ten workmen' had no confidence in Lincoln's abolitionist credentials.[138] The event of the St James's Hall meeting only establishes that there was a strong pro-northern element within the London trade unions who were able to orchestrate a meeting in favour of the North. That the meeting actually represented the majority view of the various unions' members is clearly dubious.

---

[136] Ibid. 11 Apr. 1863, 5 [Mantz's italics]. Foner predictably dismisses the committee as 'pro-Confederate elements', without providing a shred of evidence, and does not even quote from the committee's letter, but bases his argument entirely on Mantz's irrelevant rebuttal. Further, Mantz's initials were E. S. not T. J. See Foner, *British labor and the American Civil War*, 64–5.
[137] Finn, *After Chartism*, 195.
[138] *Bookbinders' Trades Circular*, 2 Mar. 1864, quoted in Harrison, *Before the socialists*, 45.

Other meetings, meanwhile, have been misinterpreted. For example, there is the 29 January 1863, Exeter Hall meeting, which was not even a radical working-class demonstration, as Biagini appears to assert, but a middle-class gathering organised by the Union and Emancipation Society.[139] Indeed, the *Saturday Review* expressly described the meeting as such, reporting it under the title, 'Opinion of the Middle Classes'.[140] Besides the fact that Exeter Hall was the traditional gathering place for anti-slavery rallies, an examination of the advertisement placed for the meeting is necessary:

> Whatever differences of opinion there may be in this country regarding the war now waging on the other side of the Atlantic, no sincere friend of the down-trodden 4,000,000, of sable bondsmen in the South can fail to rejoice at the issuing of President Lincoln's Emancipation Proclamation. We do not trouble ourselves as to the motives by which the Federal Government has been influenced in the adoption and publication of this document. We only look to results. And as there appears no probability of negro emancipation – none, at least, for some time to come – through any other instrumentality, we shall gladly give our cordial support to the Lincoln administration so far as it relates to the abolition of slavery, though differing much from its policy in other respects.[141]

Leaving aside the fact that this meeting was an organised party rally this advertisement was scarcely an overwhelming endorsement of either Lincoln or the Union and its institutions as a whole. At the meeting itself, the speakers and organisers, Thomas Hughes, P. A. Taylor, Ludlow, Beales, Revd Baptist Noel, Forster, Cairnes and Goldwin Smith (all well-known northern apologists), restricted their commentary to anti-slavery remarks and, indeed, largely repeated Cairnes's *Slave power* arguments.[142] Not only did the meeting offer little praise for the Union, but no one suggested that it was a war for democracy, nor were any republican remarks made. Indeed, the one radical remark, coming from a Revd R. Hibbs who equated the state of the poor in England to that of southern slaves, was interrupted and voted down. The platform of this meeting was an anti-slavery one, not one for reform and certainly not for republicanism.

None the less, this meeting was far more typical of the anti-slavery meetings, working-class and middle-class, held across the country than the St James's Hall meeting, or, indeed, any at which Bright spoke. One need only look at the meetings Forster, Milner Gibson and, indeed, most of the members of the Union and Emancipation Society held. This leads to the question of the meetings' organisation. E. D. Adams's numbers show that, by a wide margin, 1863 was the year most pro-Union gatherings were held,

---

[139] Biagini, *Liberty, retrenchment and reform*, 76–7.
[140] *Saturday Review*, 31 Jan. 1863, 137.
[141] *Reynolds's Weekly*, 25 Jan. 1863, 8.
[142] Ibid. 1 Feb. 1863, 5.

listing 56 working-class meetings and 26 anti-slavery meetings (making the automatic assumption that there was a practical difference). The year 1863, however, was when Abraham Lincoln's Emancipation Proclamation took effect and when the anti-slavery forces in Britain made a concerted effort to swing public opinion (at all levels of society) around in favour of the North.[143] For example, Thomas Bayley Potter, a prominent Lancashire businessman, founded the Emancipation Society (later the Union and Emancipation Society) in early 1863 and invested some £6,000 pounds in the organisation. Containing known pro-Northerners such as J. S. Mill, Hughes, Cairnes, Goldwin Smith, Beesly, Leslie Stephen and Edward Dicey, and basing its tactics on those previously used by the Anti-Corn Law League, the Society issued and circulated some 400,000 books, pamphlets and tracts. Nor did the Society rely solely on publications, it also held a vast number of meetings.[144] Apart from London (most famously, the Exeter Hall meeting), they were active in Lancashire, holding meetings with restricted entry.[145] Both before and after the first six months of 1863, according to Adams's own statistics, mass meetings on the subject of the American Civil War were few and far between.[146] The phenomenon of the rallies of 1863 had more to do with the propaganda battle regarding the Emancipation Proclamation rather than spontaneous outpourings of pro-northern sentiment as a whole. If the meetings were spontaneous mass displays of support for the Union and its institutions, as it has been asserted, it is highly unlikely that the gatherings would have been confined to the first six months of 1863 – they would have continued throughout 1863, 1864 and 1865 while the war was still raging. The fact that they did not should immediately make us suspicious.

Certainly, a quote from the *London Herald*, in mid-1863, is worth noting. The journal accused the pro-Union lobby of having overstated its case, and remarked that

---

[143] This has been acknowledged by E. D. Adams: 'Northern friends in England were early active in organising public meetings and after the second emancipation proclamation of January 1, 1863, these became both numerous and notable.' Adams is, however, uncritical of the pro-northern lobby's claims: *Great Britain and the American Civil War*, ii. 186.

[144] The exact number remains unknown. Adams and Villiers and Chesson claim that as many as 500 meetings were held, but that was probably an exaggeration, especially as it cannot be independently verified. For example, the national press was conscientious in reporting public meetings of any reasonable size held for any reason. The number 500 could only be arrived at if the Society was counting tiny meetings numbering only a few bodies, such as that held at 47 Charles Street, Ashton-under-Lyne, mentioned above. We should also remember that these were probably the same anti-slavery individuals holding multiple meetings. See Villiers and Chesson, *Anglo-American relations*, 101–9. Adams cites the number 500 in a footnote, citing Goldwin Smith as his source: *Great Britain and the American Civil War*, ii. 223.

[145] Ellison has noted how many of these organised meetings were very small and 'carefully picked' and thus hardly representative of overwhelming operative support for the Union: *Support for secession*, passim, esp. pp. 67–71.

[146] This is not only based on Adams's figures, but on my reading of the national press as a whole.

the anti-Confederates have overdone their parts, and a reaction has set in, the originators of which are striving to place matters in their true light. The operatives, finding they have been misled, naturally feel irritated at the deception which has been practised upon them, and we now find that in Lancashire there is springing into existence a strong party whose sympathies are entirely with the Confederates.[147]

The journal was pro-southern and, because it accepted submissions from Confederate agents such as Hotze, its opinions were biased and must be treated with caution (though no more so than Bright's or most other northern apologists'). None the less, it is interesting that the *London Herald* not only detected an organised lobby group behind the meetings in Lancashire and elsewhere, but that it also detected that a counter-reaction had set in. Certainly, from this date on, there were very few pro-northern meetings of any real size held in Lancashire (with the signal exception of Rochdale).

It is also worth bearing in mind the view of the *Spectator* regarding large meetings. Reporting on one of Roebuck's pro-southern meetings at Sheffield, the journal remarked,

We attach no great importance to the numbers of the meeting, since it seems a curious fact that Englishmen seldom go in any considerable force to the meetings of the opposite party. Had Mr. Bright called the meeting instead of Mr. Roebuck, no doubt he could have carried with him nine thousand, nine hundred and ninety nine men out of the ten thousand instead of a mere large majority. On the whole, Englishmen, when they have made up their minds, do not go to hear the other side; they do not even like to read the newspapers on the other side. When settled in mind they do not care to be unsettled, and praise those arguments only which make them feel their balance steadier.[148]

Considering that this was when the pro-northern lobby was making a concerted effort to hold meetings identical to the one mentioned above, the journal's dismissal is even more noteworthy. If the *Spectator* is to be believed, it seems that members of the working class who were anti-North or pro-South, or more likely neutral, simply boycotted meetings held by their opponents. Certainly, this would explain why so many of the pro-northern meetings in Lancashire lacked numbers.

None the less, the pro-Union forces in England were usually assisted by, and often part of, a very experienced lobby, namely, the anti-slavery movement, which still existed, despite the general decline in public support for naval action against foreign slave trading.[149] Seymour Drescher's description

---

[147] Quoted in *Reynolds's Weekly*, 31 May 1863, 4.
[148] *Spectator*, 30 May 1863, 2055.
[149] Seymour Drescher, 'Two variants of anti-slavery: religious organization and social mobilization in Britain and France 1780–1870', in Bolt and Drescher, *Anti-slavery, religion and reform*, 54.

of the anti-slavery movement's tactics is noteworthy: 'At critical moments it used mass propaganda, petitions, public meetings, lawsuits and boycotts, presenting anti-slavery action as a moral and political imperative.' These are exactly the same tactics we see repeated at the time of the Emancipation Proclamation. The British anti-slavery societies also, according to Drescher, accepted working-class members – individuals who could thus be counted upon to appear at, and indeed hold, meetings.[150] Hence, there certainly were opponents of slavery within the working class, but they did not make for a pro-northern majority. It also is no coincidence that the largest single pro-northern gathering was that held in Exeter Hall, discussed above, which had previously been a favourite meeting place for the anti-slavery societies. Thus, there was an already solidly established anti- Confederate movement in England long before secession ever occurred. Although some societies such as the Union and Emancipation Society were only formed during the war, they were obviously able, in many cases, to attract committed abolitionists such as Forster and George Thompson.[151]

In looking at the pro-northern rallies, generally, it should be remembered that all the advantages were on the side of the pro-Union lobby. Organisers of a pro-southern rally had to call for what amounted to active intervention when, as we have seen, most in England wished to avoid becoming entangled in the fray. The pro-Northerners, of course, only had to push for neutrality. Further, as we have also seen, very few of those opposed to the North were actually pro-Confederate. Even Dunning and Troup denied that they favoured the South.[152] Such individuals were hardly likely to agitate for recognition of the Confederacy. It should also be remembered, as has been discussed elsewhere, that the national press repeatedly warned the Lancashire operatives about King Cotton and urged them *not* to agitate against the Union blockade. Hence, the fact that there were some pro-northern meetings (only a fraction of which have been conclusively established as genuinely working-class), such as that held at Stalybridge in October 1862, where the audience passed a resolution 'That, in the opinion of this meeting, the distress prevailing in the manufacturing districts is mainly owing to the rebellion of Southern States against the American constitution', should come as no surprise.[153]

With a national press consistently preaching that the South was withholding its cotton in order to force Britain to enter the fray and thus blaming the distress in Lancashire on Confederate intransigence, the real surprise is

---

[150] Ibid. 43–4.
[151] Thompson was associated with the abolitionist movement long before the American Civil War: Harrison, 'A genealogy of reform in modern Britain', 124. See, in addition, Fladeland, *Abolitionists and working-class problems*, 109.
[152] Harrison, *Before the socialists*, 49.
[153] *Bee-Hive*, 4 Oct. 1862, 1.

that the region was not, in fact, overwhelmingly pro-Union. That there was some pro-southern agitation by operatives was not only due to the distress suffered, but to the persistent demands of *Reynolds's* and other radical working-class journals that Britain should break the northern blockade. What effectively killed pro-southern agitation in Lancashire was that the distress caused by the cotton famine peaked during 1862 (the period of the height of anti-northern sentiment) and declined precipitously thereafter.[154] Motivation for agitating for intervention was thus sharply reduced. Finally, it has long been acknowledged that Washington not only provided money to assist Union lobbyists in organising meetings, but that some meetings were entirely set up by northern agents.[155] Beesly's challenge to his pro-southern opponents, that they hold meetings of their own, which he made only in 1864, was not only disingenuous, it was frankly dishonest.[156]

This is not, however, to suggest that all the anti-slavery or pro-Union rallies were bogus; some were undoubtedly open and the resolutions passed represented the general opinion of the region or the body they claimed to represent. The question is which meetings (pro-North or pro-South) can be fairly treated as such. When dealing with public gatherings convened for specific purposes, a number of facts must be determined (where possible) if they are to be treated as proof of anything. First, under what circumstances the meeting was held needs to be known – in other words, whether or not it was open, as well as who organised it and why. Second, the size and composition of the audience. Third, the location of the meeting needs to be determined. Fourth, a close examination of the resolutions themselves, whether or not they actually passed and by what majority if they did is also required. Fifth and finally, an examination of the meeting's opponents' opinions, instead of just the organisers', would also be useful. As they stand, E. D. Adams's numbers, one of the foundation stones of the traditional interpretation, establish very little, least of all that the working class of England was overwhelmingly pro-Union.

The Confederacy's collapse and Lincoln's assassination

It was only after the complete collapse of the South in April 1865 that radical support for the Union appeared to be virtually unanimous. This is easily explained by the fact that there was little political capital to be made in defending the now defeated and discredited South; especially when it is

---

[154] By January of 1863, the number of persons on relief had fallen from 500,000 to 203,000: Jenkins, *Britain and the war for the Union*, ii. 233. See, in addition, Eugene A. Brady, 'A reconsideration of the Lancashire "cotton famine" ', *Agricultural History* xxxvii (1963), 156–62.
[155] Martin P. Clausen, 'Peace factors in Anglo-American relations', *Mississippi Historical Review* xxvi (1940), 511–22.
[156] *Bee-Hive*, 12 Mar. 1864, 1.

recalled that Anglo-Confederate relations had suffered a precipitous decline by the end of 1863. The anti-northern radicals simply contributed to the agitation for reform and generally forgot their former hostility to the Union or, in some cases, their outright support for secession. The pro-northern lobby was also greatly assisted by the assassination of Lincoln, who was quickly transformed into an unassailable martyr.

Much has been read into the outpourings of sympathy Lincoln's death received; however, the mourning itself needs to be seen within the context of its time.[157] Take, as a comparison, the eulogies of the *Spectator* and the *Daily News* for the Confederate general Thomas 'Stonewall' Jackson, killed during the South's victory at Chancellorsville in May 1863. The former compared Jackson to Oliver Cromwell, and, raving about the general's religiosity, remarked, 'There can be no question – not only of the man's heartfelt piety, but of that intensity and depth of character in connection with it which is now so rare in the world.'[158] The latter, meanwhile, noted, that 'It is not only in America that the loss of Jackson will be felt', but also that

> This American war, it has often been remarked, has been singularly barren of great men, and its spectacular interest has suffered accordingly. Jackson, the only man of whom the most vigorous imagination has attempted to make a hero, is therefore one whom the observer can ill afford to lose.... The Jackson mythology has grown and is growing.[159]

These tributes were far more generous than those given by journals such as the *Saturday Review*. That two such anti-southern journals should so fulsomely praise one of the Confederacy's greatest commanders during the height of the war should be borne in mind when reading tributes to Lincoln.

Lincoln certainly had some supporters amongst Union apologists, but his stature had been improving in England, even among those unsympathetic to the North. Besides the credit accorded to him for the successful resolution of the *Trent* affair, in comparison to individuals such as Seward and Clay he certainly appeared a more responsible politician to many observers.[160] There was also an appreciation, if often muted, for his emancipation efforts. None the less, as Keiser observes, a lot of the eulogies for Lincoln were formal nineteenth-century ones, and, in some quarters, criticism appeared not long afterwards.[161] Less surprising is that the working-class press was divided over the

---

157 Thomas J. Keiser was the first historian to establish that the obituaries for Lincoln, far from being overly laudatory, were in fact, standard for their time and place. A small number of historians have subsequently noted this, but have failed to give Keiser the credit he is due.
158 *Spectator*, 30 May 1863, 2056.
159 Quoted in *Reynolds's Weekly*, 31 May 1863, 2. Note the lack of enthusiasm for the Union.
160 See, for example, *The Times*, 29 Apr. 1865, 8; *The Economist*, 26 Nov. 1864, 1454; *Illustrated London News*, 24 Dec. 1864, 627; *Saturday Review*, 24 Dec. 1864, 761.
161 Keiser, 'The English press and the American Civil War', 412. While I agree with Keiser that a large number of the eulogies were simply formalities, he has clearly exaggerated the

assassination, especially in light of their opinions on the merits of the conflict in the first place.[162] Of course, for some in England, Lincoln's assassination meant little. Sir John Ramsden broke his silence on America only to scrawl in his diary, 'We have heard that President Lincoln has been assassinated in the theatre at Washington (being at the theatre on Good Friday sounds a little queer).'[163] It is interesting that there was an almost complete absence of any but token sympathy among English commentators, even among northern apologists, for Seward, who was injured having also been the target of an assassin. Clearly, his previous activities had not been forgotten, much less forgiven.

The pro-northern lobby, of course, did its best to elevate Lincoln to sainthood. A meeting was held on 4 May 1865, in St Martin's Hall, London, at which T. B. Potter, now the member of parliament for Rochdale because of the death of Cobden, spoke, as well as the same familiar crop of northern apologists. As expected, the *Bee-Hive* provided glowing reports and numerous untenable statements were made – particularly by Potter – such as that the working classes, unlike everyone else, had been pro-Union and that they had prevented Britain from helping the South.[164] Lest we be too credulous accepting pro-Northerners' claims of English working-class admiration for Lincoln, it is worth noting what the anti-Confederate *Spectator* reported upon news of the assassination: 'The mass of workmen here are indifferent, and it is only from them that any brutalities have been heard.'[165] Lincoln may have become a symbol for English radicals, but such sentiment became widespread only after his death. Thus, contrary to what some historians assert, Lincoln's personal popularity was largely created by his assassination, as opposed to merely increased.[166] This later overwhelming adulation should not be confused with the opinions at the time of Lincoln's death.

The formation of the traditional interpretation was, however, already under way. The St Martin's Hall meeting in London, although by far the largest such gathering, was just the beginning, as northern sympathisers claimed (and contradicted themselves) that only the working classes in England had been solidly pro-Union while everyone else had been hostile.

---

amount of criticism directed at Lincoln. Keiser's evidence for 'the sneering', as he puts it, comes from the Confederate agitator, James Spence, and some of Lancashire's provincial press, which, in light of the region's sufferings, should not be too surprising. Keiser also states that the *Westminster Review* was hostile to Lincoln – which it most certainly was not. See *Westminster Review* (July 1865), 43–76. See also Ellison's findings of indifference, even on the part of radicals, towards the assassination: *Support for secession*, ch. viii passim.
162 Keiser, 'The English press and the American Civil War', 429.
163 Sir John Ramsden, diary, entry for 16 Apr. 1865, Ramsden papers, RA 48.
164 *Bee-Hive*, 6 May 1865, 5–6.
165 *Spectator*, 29 Apr. 1865, 453.
166 Biagini, *Liberty, retrenchment and, reform*, 78–81. Biagini's sources of radical admiration for Lincoln are largely derived from known pro-northern sources such as the *Bee-Hive* and from reports written *after*, and, in some cases, long after, Lincoln's assassination.

Henry Fawcett, speaking to a pro-northern crowd in Bradford, declared that while the working classes had been pro-Union, the House of Commons had been almost wholly pro-Confederate.[167] Union apologist members of parliament, such as Forster, claimed that Lancashire workers' supposed unwillingness to agitate for the Confederacy proved their pro-northern credentials and that they deserved the vote. This conveniently forgot not only the efforts made to alleviate the distress, but also that, from the war's outset, the national press and politicians – the lawn-sleeved fraternity – had denounced King Cotton and urged the people of Lancashire to be patient.

Bright remained the most bombastic, however, and indeed travelled to join the victory celebrations in the country for which he had served as chief propagandist throughout the conflict. Once there, he continued to damage already deteriorated Anglo-American relations by repeating his calumny that most of Britain had been pro-Confederate and had done everything possible to destroy the Union. The *Saturday Review*, reporting on his (it hoped permanent) departure, could scarcely refrain from remarking, 'Luckily for the commander of the steam-frigate, the voyage to America is not too long.'[168] Other commentators simply welcomed the break. Despite the service he had given it during the war, to the extent of traducing his own country, Bright's relationship with America, like most passionate love affairs, was eventually to sour. His opposition to Home Rule for Ireland ultimately placed him in opposition to American public opinion. That was in the future, however, and for the present he enjoyed what he doubtless regarded as the justification of all his activities.

Despite the extravagance of some of the northern apologists' claims, some individuals began to believe them, establishing that if something is repeated often enough it may well become accepted as true. The *Westminster Review*, for instance, announced in 1865, three months after Lee's surrender at Appomattox, that the American Civil War was, after all, a test of republicanism, and that the upper classes feared the triumph of democracy more than that of slavery.[169] Forgetting not only its own previous defence of secession, it continued its bout of amnesia by declaring that most in England were pro-South, despite its own claims in 1863. It was scarcely an unpredictable tactic to claim that the outcome of the war proved the stability of republicanism once the verdict was known. On the other hand, there is no reason to doubt that the *Westminster Review* would have found in favour of democracy regardless of the war's result. This, after all, was the position *Reynolds's* took. Once again,

---

[167] *Reynolds's Weekly*, 30 Apr. 1865, 1. It is worth noting that this was Forster's constituency – in other words, probably an area in which pro-northern sentiment already existed. There is, however, some evidence that Bradford was sympathetic to the North beyond the influence of Forster: D. Wright, 'Bradford and the American Civil War', *Journal of British Studies* viii (1969), 69–85.
[168] *Saturday Review*, 19 Aug. 1865, 233.
[169] *Westminster Review*, 17 July 1865, 43–4.

radicals were interested primarily in reform and were going to continue promoting it regardless of what happened across the Atlantic.

It must be noted that some commentators recognised that a myth was being formed and immediately denounced it. The *Saturday Review*, which had previously exposed Bright's less tenable claims, remarked, 'Since the termination of the American war, and in consequence of the murder of Mr. Lincoln, the partisans of the Federal cause have enjoyed a clamorous and almost unopposed triumph.' It then noted that Roebuck, who had 'been conspicuous *in the small number of members who advocated the recognition of the Confederate States*', received 'all but unanimous applause from the working men of Sheffield'.[170] Thus, the journal noted, not only had the pro-Confederate lobby (as opposed to those who had little sympathy with the Union) always been very small, it also contained a measure of working-class support. If the *Saturday Review*, however, seriously believed this would justify the claim of unanimous pro-Union support among the working class, it was to be disappointed.

The *Saturday Review* continued to serve reminders to the triumphant pro-northern lobby. The journal noted that 'The victorious Republicans are constantly assured that the majority of the people were always on their side, and they are entreated to forget and forgive the criminal delusion which prevailed widely among the most enlightened classes.' This was, the *Saturday Review* remarked, 'absurd'.[171] Deciding that a little reminder was due, the journal noted, 'It might be said with perfect truth that the English supporters of the North were as fully convinced as their opponents, during two or three campaigns, that the combatants were practically fighting only to determine a frontier.'[172] This charge, being true, was unanswerable and, as a result, a lobby in full triumph ignored it.

It was not, however, an altogether easy triumph. For a period after Appomattox, it appeared as if the now re-United States would use the so-called Alabama claims as a pretext for war against Britain. Some of the declarations made by the pro-northern lobby smacked of appeasement. Britain, now faced with a huge northern army and the resurrection of demands from some quarters in America for an invasion of Canada, regarded the aggression seriously. Contrary to E. D. Adams's claims, there was no 'panic' about the issue.[173] There was a debate in the House of Commons regarding the security of the colony, which took place on 13 March 1865, over a month before the news of Richmond's fall. Several members of parliament expressed concern about American intentions, which were played down not only by northern apologists such as Forster, but by neutrals such as C. Fortesque and Disraeli. None the less, a sizeable number insisted that a formal declaration be made that an

---

170 *Saturday Review*, 17 June 1865, 717–18 [my italics].
171 Ibid. 1 July 1865, 3.
172 Ibid. 4.
173 Adams, *Great Britain and the American Civil War*, ii. 255.

attack on Canada would be an act of war – a position Disraeli endorsed. Ever consistent, Bright used the debate to both misrepresent British neutrality and sentiment as pro-Confederate and declared that Canada was indefensible. He concluded by insisting that the only reason for the debate was 'the pricking of conscience' on the part of his fellow members of the House.[174] In fact, the only accurate charge Bright could have levelled was that the House of Commons had failed to wholeheartedly support the far stronger side in the conflict – unlike him.

It is unfortunate that the historians who largely accept the latter's shrill accusations have not noted Palmerston's response to Bright. Palmerston's explanation for the deteriorated Anglo-American relations was, in substance, far closer to the truth than Bright's utterances. If Britain had been (and was) so pro-South, Palmerston asked rhetorically, why did both sides hate it?

> No doubt during the contest there has been expressed, both in the North and the South, feelings of irritation against this country. The irritation was caused by the natural feeling of the two parties against a third who does not espouse their cause, and who therefore think he is doing them an injury. The North wished us to declare on their side and the South on theirs, and we wished to maintain a perfect neutrality.[175]

Palmerston also rejected Bright's craven suggestion that Canada be abandoned and promised that an attack on the colony by the United States would be treated as an act of war. It is difficult to tell if Palmerston intended this as a warning to the United States or even if he was bluffing. Certainly, although Canada had been defensible during the conflict, it most probably was not now. None the less, despite their supposed fear of 'Grant's juggernaut', the British press (including those periodicals friendly to the North) fell in behind the prime minister, and announced that Canada would be defended if attacked.[176]

Had the United States been as bellicose as it was in 1861, a third Anglo-American war would have been a distinct possibility. It was, however, 1865, and the United States had just fought a major war which had cost millions of dollars and the lives of over 600,000 men. In addition, the future of a sullen and resentful South had to be determined. The period of Reconstruction was about to begin and the United States had other priorities. A war against what was reckoned to be the world's leading power, for territory which, if conquered, would only provide more resentful citizens, was not

---

[174] Hansard, clxxvii, 13 Mar. 1865, 1620.
[175] Ibid. 1634.
[176] See, for example, The Economist, 25 Feb. 1865, 218; 11 Mar. 1865, 279–80; 18 Mar. 1865, 307–8; Illustrated London News, 18 Mar. 1865, 250; 25 Mar. 1865, 270; Saturday Review, 7 Jan. 1865, 9; 11 Feb. 1865, 155–6; 11 March 1865, 276; 18 Mar. 1865, 298–9; Macmillan's Magazine (Nov. 1864), (Apr. 1865), 419; Spectator, 25 Feb. 1865, 199–202; 18 Mar. 1865, 287.

seriously contemplated. Although the United States was determined to drive the French from Mexico – brazenly acting as a defender of the country from which it had carved large chunks of territory – an attack upon Canada was not on the agenda. President Andrew Johnson took pains to assure the new British minister, Sir Frederick Bruce, that Britain and America were on friendly terms – even Seward was quick to announce that the United States had no military designs on Canada (although regular denunciations of Britain would reappear as a staple of his repertoire).[177]

The general condition of Anglo-American relations would fluctuate until the Alabama claims and damages cited by Britain for northern raids into Canada were finally settled. It is interesting to note that, during this period, some Union apologists actually began to regret their former stance. The *Spectator*, for example, fell out with its American correspondent who had kept them abreast of events (from a Northerner's point of view) throughout the last two years of the conflict. The correspondent's contempt for African Americans, previously carefully concealed, was made explicit once the war was over. As the *Spectator* grumbled, 'We publish, though with regret, a letter from our able "Yankee" correspondent expressing in full measure the hatred felt by many persons in the North towards the negro. As a sketch of opinion, it is valuable, but we can endorse neither his facts nor the arguments.'[178] The correspondent's letter was a long harangue against inter-racial marriage and blacks having access to political power, and it castigated the English for believing that support for abolition meant any particular respect for African Americans. No one in the North, sneered the writer, ever thought that they were fighting for the benefit of the blacks.[179] The *Spectator*, to its credit, denounced its own correspondent, arguing, 'He says the presence of negroes in congress is impossible; we say that it is found easily in Jamaica', and stated that people should be free to marry whom they liked.[180] Further, the journal added,

> unless the ultimate purpose of abolishing slavery is to let the negro become everything that he can qualify himself to become, – even the social and political equal of the white, if he can really raise himself to the moral and political level of the white, – unless that is so, we do not hesitate to say that the anti-slavery motive *was* a mere pretence.[181]

Fortunately, not everyone in the United States shared the *Spectator*'s correspondent's views. The long struggle known as Reconstruction began and, although many blacks found themselves promoted from slaves to second-class citizens, some improvements were made (although many were lost once

---

177 *Illustrated London News*, 22 Apr. 1865, 367; 6 May 1865, 422.
178 *Spectator*, 26 Aug. 1865, 935.
179 Ibid. 947–9.
180 Ibid. 26 Aug. 1865, 935.
181 Ibid. 2 Sept. 1865, 968 [their italics].

Reconstruction ended). Unfortunately, views like those expressed by the *Spectator* were already on the decline in England. The Jamaican rebellion in October 1865 and the rise of social Darwinism meant that although one battle was won, another was lost.

These issues, however, are beyond the scope of this work, as are the Alabama arbitration and Britain's counter-claims. While the majority in England were astonished (and readily admitted so) that the apparently unconquerable Confederacy had been vanquished, few lamented its abolition. By mid-1865, for the vast majority of English commentators, who had never accorded the Confederacy much admiration, especially after 1863, the verdict delivered at Appomattox was easily accepted.

Conclusion

Towards the end of 1865, Leslie Stephen published his pamphlet *The Times and the American Civil War* which simply misrepresented the paper's views on the war by either selective quotes or outright fabrication. Stephen claimed, for example, that *The Times* blamed the war on democracy which, as we have seen, was wholly false; he also sneered at English anger towards the Morrill tariff, which took a lot of nerve, considering, as we have also seen, that he had objected to it himself in *Macmillan's Magazine* in 1862.[1] This, of course, merely highlights the difference between what pro-Northerners said during the war and what they said after it. In 1867, *Essays on reform* appeared, containing treatises by James Bryce and Goldwin Smith – the ones that attracted the ire of Robert Lowe – which, although predominantly concerned with political reform, also repeated many of the Civil War myths (particularly that the Conservative Party supported the Confederacy) that the pro-Union lobby was currently perpetuating.[2] Bryce was to repeat many of these myths in his *magnum opus*, *The American commonwealth* (1888).[3] It is perhaps worth noting as an aside, that Bryce declared, contrary to Henry Adams, that Oxford University was pro-northern in sentiment.[4] If Bryce was correct, Oxford's reputation as the home of lost causes should probably be revised. Goldwin Smith, meanwhile, published his memoirs in 1911 in which he repeated virtually all the myths that would become the traditional interpretation in its entirety (although Goldwin Smith, to his credit, admitted that he had initially sanctioned southern secession).[5] By that time, however, the individuals who might have corrected this interpretation, such as Roebuck, Lindsay and Scholefield, not to mention Cobden, were all conveniently dead.

The writers above are important to note, because they must be counted along with John Bright as the individuals who made the greatest effort to equate the forces of progression with the Union and the forces of reaction with the Confederacy. During the course of the conflict, they formed an alliance with the Manchester school and, to varying degrees, accepted Bright's arguments on the war. It does seem a fact that whenever one reads of someone equating pro-democratic sentiment with the Union and anti-democratic sentiment with the Confederacy, one always uncovers a connection to

---

1 Leslie Stephen, *The Times and the American Civil War*, London 1865.
2 *Essays on reform*. Bryce's essay is number X, and Goldwin Smith's is number IX.
3 James Bryce, *The American commonwealth*, London 1888.
4 Harvie, *The lights of liberalism*, 110.
5 Goldwin Smith, *Reminiscences*, London 1911, 319–21.

CONCLUSION

Bright. It also must be noted, in addition, that Leslie Stephen, James Bryce, and Goldwin Smith, were all friends of the Adams family, who, being Americans, naturally believed that whatever their country did was for the good of democracy as a whole. The above group also visited the Union during the war, particularly Massachusetts – the most militantly abolitionist state – where they certainly heard more than one eloquent defence of the North.[6]

Their and Bright's misrepresentation of events was further supported by the very public dispute that took place between Thomas Carlyle and Walt Whitman in 1871. Carlyle had earlier dismissed America as the land of 'Eighteen Millions of the greatest *bores* ever seen in this world before'.[7] One might have thought that the 'bores' became more interesting once the Civil War began, but Carlyle largely ignored the conflict – and its participants. In 1867, however, he published 'Shooting Niagara and after?', in direct response to the political pressure in Britain which resulted in the 1867 Reform Act. America did not feature as an example of either the benefits or flaws of democracy in any great detail, but Carlyle described the Civil War thus:

> A continent of the earth has been submerged, for certain years, by deluges as from the Pit of Hell; half a million (some say a whole million, but surely they exaggerate) of excellent White Men, full of gifts and faculty, have torn and slashed one another into horrid death, in a temporary humour, which will leave centuries of remembrance fierce enough: and three million absurd Blacks, men and brothers (of a sort), are completely 'emancipated'; launched into a career of improvement, – likely to be 'improved off the face of the earth' in a generation or two![8]

In other words, to the racist Carlyle, the Civil War was an even more pointless exercise if it was a war of emancipation, because it meant that the lives of whites had been sacrificed for blacks. To Carlyle, the conflict was an exercise in futility. Although Carlyle did not expressly say so, it seems he regarded the Civil War as a blot on the American system of government. The poet Walt Whitman was stung by this, as were many other Americans who had previously respected Carlyle, and responded in 1871 with *Democratic vistas*, refuting 'Shooting Niagara' on every point, especially as regards the morality of the war.[9]

The importance of this debate to our discussion is that Whitman, like most Americans, treated Carlyle's rant, especially regarding American democracy, as the voice of English conservatism. Indeed, it doubtless confirmed many suspicions, particularly those voiced by the Adams family, that English conservatism was hostile to them and their efforts in the war. But

---

[6] Harvie, *The lights of liberalism*, 105–15.
[7] Thomas Carlyle, *Latter-day pamphlets*, London 1850.
[8] Idem, 'Shooting Niagara and after?', in *Thomas Carlyle: critical and miscellaneous essays*, v, London n.d.
[9] Walt Whitman, *Democratic vistas*, New York 1871.

as Jon Roper has cogently pointed out, politically Carlyle ultimately spoke only for himself. He was as much at odds with the British political establishment as he was with the American. Carlyle has been labelled a proto-fascist, but the description is problematic, not least because many of his views placed him in the socialist camp. He was certainly no democrat, however, but an authoritarian with an unhealthy belief in the virtues of force. Because of his opposition to liberty, Carlyle was attacked on both sides of the British political spectrum, including by conservatives. In short, he was an intellectual maverick, and his views were unique.[10]

This, however, was not seen in America. All opponents of the Union were immediately lumped together with Carlyle, a logical result of the North's mythologising about both its own democratic mission in the world and the Civil War – the war fought to ensure that 'government of the people, by the people, for the people' would not 'perish from the earth', as Lincoln put it so pithily at Gettysburg. If, to all of the above, one adds the pronouncements made by Bright on his trip through the United States and some of his supporters after 1865, it should come as no surprise that the American diplomat and historian John Lothrop Motley felt confident enough to declare that the Union's victory in the Civil War paved the way for political reform in Britain.[11] In many respects, the final plank of the traditional interpretation had been laid. The Americans, who misunderstood English opinion of them during the war, were not about to understand it now.

The traditional interpretation was buttressed by Bryce's *The American commonwealth* and Goldwin Smith's *Reminiscences*, which we have already mentioned, as well as Henry Adams's *The education of Henry Adams* (1907) which basically confirmed the American view of events.[12] Adams was followed in 1919 by Brougham Villiers and W. H. Chesson's work, *Anglo-American relations 1861–1865*. Writing during the period of the 'great rapprochement', Villiers and Chesson based their work almost entirely on the papers of Chesson's father, F. W. Chesson, who worked for the Union and Emancipation Society, and the writings of the Adams family. Although Villiers and Chesson did acknowledge occasional unreasonableness on the part of the Union, their work was broadly a plea for the Anglo-American unity, created by the First World War, to continue and grow. By 1922, the great Whig historian, George Macaulay Trevelyan, accepted the ideas of Bryce, Smith and Adams, selected some from Villiers and Brougham, and, after placing conservatives and the aristocracy on the Confederacy's side and radicals and the working class on the Union's side, declared that the result of the Civil War was one of the causes of the 1867 Reform Act.[13]

---

10 Roper, *Democracy and its critics*, 171–81.
11 Quoted in Harold Hyman (ed.), *Heard around the world: the impact abroad of the Civil War*, New York 1969, introduction at p. vi.
12 Henry Brooks Adams, *The education of Henry Adams*, Washington 1907.
13 G. M. Trevelyan, *British history in the nineteenth century, 1782–1901*, London 1922, 339.

CONCLUSION

Trevelyan was the son of Sir George Otto Trevelyan, a close friend of Leslie Stephen, Goldwin Smith, Bryce and, of course, John Bright.[14] Indeed, G. M. Trevelyan's work concentrated almost exclusively on the views of Bright and the radical's closest allies. Although Trevelyan's was not a full-scale study of Anglo-American relations during the Civil War, one appeared three years later – namely, E. D. Adams's *Great Britain and the American Civil War*. With the publication of Adams's work in 1925, which was written with the assistance of C. F. Adams Jr., the traditional interpretation was established once and for all. In short, it was a tradition based almost wholly on the views of the Adams family and Bright and some of the latter's acolytes – eventually to be joined by Marxist historians. Later, when historians examined evidence that did not originate with the opinions of these fervent pro-Northerners, a different picture of Anglo-American relations during the Civil War arose – as might have been expected.

Having established in the course of this work that the traditional interpretation is untenable, the question remains, what direction can studies of Great Britain and the American Civil War take? Two areas that have been touched upon in this work but still require much more investigation are regionalism and trade. Certainly, when dealing with British opinion, regionalism appears to be a consistent factor. As this work has established, some areas in England were far more pro-Union (or, conversely, pro-Confederate) than others. The reception Roebuck's pro-southern speeches were accorded in Sheffield, for example, leaves little doubt about that city's sentiments. The subject of regionalism is closely related to that of Anglo-American trade, an area of study where much more needs to be done. The most obvious, and best-documented, study of this issue remains Ellison's examination of Lancashire. Unfortunately, regarding Lancashire, too much attention has been paid to King Cotton. For example, Ellison cites Oldham as an area with high levels of pro-southern sentiment. By 1860, however, the majority of male workers in Oldham worked in large-scale engineering firms, rather than in the cotton industry.[15] These industries suffered from the Morrill tariff rather than the cotton blockade. Hence, Oldham's opinion on the war was probably unaffected by King Cotton, unlike other regions of Lancashire.

The Morrill tariff, in turn, is still only part of the picture. It is certainly true that specific economic activities such as the Confederate Erlanger loan have been studied.[16] Indeed, some historians such as Harrison have pointed to the loan as evidence of pro-southern sympathy amongst the aristocracy for investing £3 million in the Confederacy.[17] What is being forgotten here is

---

[14] Harvie, *The lights of liberalism*, 105–15.
[15] Gareth Stedman Jones, *Languages of class: studies in English working-class history, 1832–1982*, Cambridge 1983, 28.
[16] Judith F. Gentry, 'A Confederate success in Europe: the Erlanger loan', *Journal of Southern History* xxxvi (1970), 157–88.
[17] Harrison, *Before the socialists*, 66.

that investors in the Erlanger loan were essentially either buying set amounts of cotton or buying bonds fixed on future cotton prices. The cotton famine, however, made the Erlanger loan an extremely profitable investment at best, a financially good risk at worst.[18] Although those who believed the Confederacy was an immoral cause were quick to heap opprobrium on the investors, those who judged the South to be no worse than the North simply saw the Erlanger loan as an opportunity to make money. Profit was the motive for investment in the Erlanger loan, not love for the Confederacy.

In any event, the £3 million invested in the Erlanger loan is a paltry sum compared to the levels of British investment made in the United States, and, in particular, the North. Indeed, the role of economics is the least understood aspect of what influenced English opinion on the American Civil War. British investment in the United States was in excess of £60 million by 1860.[19] Virtually all of this was invested in the industrialising North, not the South. Considering that the Union would almost certainly have seized all British assets in the event of a war (indeed, the idea was bruited during the *Trent* affair), these investors must surely have toed a peaceful line out of fear of such patriotic theft. It is probable too, of course, that these same investors hoped for peace in America – no one, after all, likes to see chaos where their money is involved. We have no idea, as yet, who these investors were, and this needs to be discovered, because it is inconceivable that these individuals made no effort to prevent a breakdown in Anglo-Union relations. It is also quite probable that some of these same investors held positions of power and prestige and this would certainly affect our thinking on the subject of Anglo-American relations. There is, however, one thing of which we can be reasonably sure: whoever these investors were, they were unlikely to be members of the industrial proletariat.

Other areas of enquiry that fall under the subject of trade which have been only partially studied are those who sold munitions to both sides in the war and the blockade-runners (including the latter's investors). The latter were known to make profits of 700 per cent at comparatively little risk.[20] Regarding the former, Owsley calculates that Britain sold over $100,000,000 of war supplies alone (thus, this excludes materials such as clothes, shoes, tents, leather goods, etc.) to both sides in the American Civil War.[21] Like those individuals who invested in the Erlanger loan, these too were profiteers rather than partisans. Nonetheless, neither of these groups would have been particularly keen on war with the Union nor, it must be added, any attempts at mediation. Both war with the North and peace between the belligerents would either sharply reduce their profits or put them out of business. Once

---

18 Lester, *Confederate finance and purchasing*, ch. ii passim.
19 Allen, *Great Britain and the United States*, 91. This investment increased between 1860 and 1876, particularly in the railways.
20 Lester, *Confederate finance and purchasing*, ch. ii passim.
21 Owsley, *King Cotton diplomacy*, 553–4.

CONCLUSION

again, a lot more needs to be known about who these individuals were and their impact upon public sentiment. English support for non-intervention may turn out to be a very broad church indeed.

Having noted this, none of the above should be treated as an attempt to minimise the significance of King Cotton who fatally wounded his subjects in two ways. In the first instance, as Lester has established, had cotton been sold to Britain from the war's outset, the South might have purchased enough munitions to turn the tide in some earlier, crucial battles – including Antietam.[22] By withholding their cotton, the Confederate states blockaded themselves before Lincoln's embargo even began, much less became effective and, by the time they realised their error, it was too late. Southern historians have known this for some time. What they have not been aware of is the second, equally serious, effect of the King Cotton policy – its negative impact upon English opinion.

King Cotton alienated the very nation the South needed on its side. It was primarily French help that turned the tide against Britain during the American Revolution. So long as the Union was prepared to fight a total war against the Confederacy, the latter was probably doomed. Alienating Britain was a move the South could not afford. Small nations need allies at birth. In light of the experiences of 1776, it appears incredible that the Confederacy forgot this fact. Before the war, Southerners were fond of affirming that a strand of cotton could hang the world. King Cotton did not hang the world – he hanged his subjects.

It was not, of course, only King Cotton that alienated the English. Despite historians' constant minimisation of its significance, slavery was unquestionably the great millstone about the neck of the South. Initially, slavery was also to prove to be the great handicap of the North as well. Lincoln, of course, did not pursue an emancipation policy from the war's outset because he could not afford to alienate conservative Northerners or the border states – especially during the first eighteen months of the conflict when the verdict hung in the balance. Lincoln also believed that there were many loyal Unionists in the South whom he could still win over – provided he left slavery alone. In following this course, 'though, Lincoln had to settle for a lesser evil – that, abroad at any rate, the Union cause would be identified with simple conquest, not liberation. As this study has shown, very few English observers understood Lincoln's difficulty, and the constant, indeed, specific, insistence that the Union would not follow an emancipationist course was, in modern terminology, a public relations disaster. In fairness to the North, the English were unquestionably far too sceptical regarding Lincoln's emancipation efforts, but, even here, there are a few points that should be remembered.

One, that the preservation of the Union was always Lincoln's first priority

---

[22] Lester, *Confederate financing and purchasing*, ch. i passim.

– emancipation came a poor second. As one of Lincoln's admirers has frankly pointed out, had the Confederacy been defeated in 1862, slavery would have survived.[23] Indeed, it is probably not an exaggeration to say that Lincoln embraced emancipation *because* it was the only way to preserve the Union. Lincoln, the 'Great Emancipator', was never an instinctive abolitionist; he freed the slaves largely because circumstances forced him to. When one combines this with America's past history regarding slavery, English suspicion of the Union regarding emancipation becomes understandable, even if it proved – with the advantage of hindsight – to be wrong.

Two, that if the English took a self-righteous position regarding American slavery, it was not a stance for which they had no justification. It should be remembered, for example, that the much-maligned Palmerston and Russell have been cited by at least one major historian as the chief reasons for the decline of slave trading during the nineteenth century.[24] Palmerston and Russell fought slavery not only in their own country, as Lincoln did, but in the world as a whole. In the end, Lincoln freed the slaves out of necessity; Palmerston and Russell did so out of humanity, and this is something about 'those two dreadful old men' (as Queen Victoria put it) that ought not to be forgotten.

Finally, the English correctly recognised that the chief issue of the war was not in fact slavery, but whether or not the United States would become two nations. Irrespective of how much (or how little) slavery underlay the cause of southern secession, the fact remains that the North fought primarily to preserve the Union. Whether this cause is called national self-preservation or defence of national integrity, it nonetheless entails forcibly imposing upon a people a political structure of which they no longer wish to be part. It is only a slight exaggeration to call this activity defence of empire, and this, like slavery, was another subject about which the English needed no lessons from the North.

Although none of the three sides behaved in a creditable fashion, a point needs to be made about Palmerston. Namely, that there was no war between Britain and the northern states is, in no small measure, owed to him and his policy of neutrality. Although, until recently, historians have believed that the Union's victory at Antietam ended Russell's ideas for mediation, Howard Jones has established that Antietam actually added impetus to the foreign secretary's intervention plans.[25] If cabinet and Conservative opposition ended plans for mediation, so too did Palmerston's unwillingness to embark upon a war with the Union. We have seen, in this study, how intervention was unpopular in England. Palmerston, it seems, read the public mood well;

---

23 McPherson, *Drawn with the sword*, 158.
24 Roger Anstey, 'The pattern of British abolitionism in the eighteenth and nineteenth centuries', in Bolt and Drescher, *Anti-slavery, religion and reform*, 33.
25 Jones, *Union in peril*, chs viii–x passim.

his quote from *Hudibras*, 'They who in quarrels interpose, oft must wipe a bloody nose', was not simply made for effect.[26]

The one individual who deserves no credit whatsoever for the fact that there was no breakdown between Britain and the Union is Bright. His constant refrain of an England on the side of the Confederacy bedevilled not only Anglo-American relations then, it has also misled historians since. This is inexcusable, especially when some nineteenth-century commentators recognised the damage Bright caused. While Bright's contribution to reform in Britain must be acknowledged, so too must his wilful misrepresentation of English attitudes towards the American Civil War. That there were no dire consequences of this in no way mitigates Bright's activities. It is almost incomprehensible that certain historians have actually credited Bright with the fact that Britain and the Union did not go to war. The fact is he has usurped Palmerston's right to the credit for this for far too long.

On the subject of war, it has been too easily argued that Britain did not intervene out of fear of Union might. This is an argument that cannot be substantiated, especially when it is remembered that Palmerston (and the nation) was prepared to go to war over the *Trent* affair. There has been, for example, too much written of the vulnerability of Canada and the effect of this on discouraging British involvement in the conflict. Simply put, the British did not assist the South because they were afraid of losing Canada to the North. This argument appears to be based largely on an ignorance of two things: Canadian geography, and the relative military strengths of Britain, the Union and the Confederacy; or, indeed, a combination of the above.

Aside from discounting any Anglo-French alliance or the fact that the Union relied on British munitions until the end of 1864, or that the Royal Navy, with its ocean-going ironclads, was always more than a match for the northern navy, even if the latter adopted privateering, Canada was never quite the soft target some historians have presented it to be.[27] From the Union point of view, the strategic problems were enormous – it would all be very well for the North to invade Canada, but unless they conquered the entire eastern seaboard, the Union was faced with the prospect of British

---

[26] Jordan and Pratt, *Europe and the American Civil War*, 174.
[27] Although the myth that Britain had no ironclad ships, unlike the Union with its *Monitor*, has been discredited since Owsley, it is still being repeated. Susan Balée, for example, tells us that the *Merrimac–Monitor* duel worried the English because, 'England, you see, had no iron-clad ships of her own': 'English critics, American crisis, and the sensation novel', *Nineteenth Century Contexts*, vii/2 (1993), 125–32, p. 125. As Crook points out, Britain had a marked world lead in armoured warships and, unlike both *Merrimac* and *Monitor*, the British vessels were made for the high seas, whereas the Americans' ships tended to capsize: *The North, the South and the powers*, 186–9. Indeed, Roebuck, during his motion for recognition, stated that HMS *Warrior* could single-handedly sweep the Union navy from the seas. Even while acknowledging Roebuck's hyperbole, the fact remains that Britain's naval power was far greater than that of the Union.

troops landing in Halifax and moving southwards into the Union or westwards to attack any occupying forces. Worse still – from the North's point of view – unlike both the American Revolution and the War of 1812, Britain was not engaged in a life-or-death struggle with any European rivals. Indeed, the situation was reversed. The British could turn their undivided attention to a North already engaged in an all-out war.

The only realistic hope the Union had was a lightening strike along the eastern coast, conquering and occupying the entire region before Britain could reinforce the colony by landing troops. This, of course, assumes virtual non-resistance from some three million Canadians, both the French Canadians and the descendants of the United Empire Loyalists – the very groups who successfully defended the colony against the American invasions in the War of 1812. It also assumes an unrealistic negligence on the part of Russell and Palmerston to initiate hostilities without first reinforcing the colony.

In any event, considering the problems the Union had in raising sufficient troops to defend itself against Confederate attacks, not to mention to invade and conquer the South, how and where the North was supposed to raise the troops for this 50,000–100,000-strong army (depending upon the historian), minus the foreign recruits a British blockade would deny, to invade Canada, is a question to which no satisfactory answer has yet been provided. Unless, of course, the Union simply let the Confederacy go and turned to Britain. Yet even this argument assumes a great deal. It would be no easy task to simply break off hostilities with the South when the Confederacy claimed several border states (most importantly, Maryland) and might very well hold out for an alliance with Britain in order to obtain these. Simply put, until around late 1864, the northern seizure of Canada is at least as speculative as any other venture involving British intervention in the war – and should properly be treated as such.[28]

Some historians have pointed to European problems, such as Poland and Schleswig-Holstein, claiming they diverted British attention. These, however, did not come into play until 1863 and 1864. European affairs are important to note, but not because they diverted attention away from America. For example both Poland's and Italy's causes won widespread sympathy in England, sympathy far in excess of that accorded to the South. Yet there was little call for intervention in these struggles either. If public opinion was disinclined to become involved in European struggles it supported, it seems impossible that there would have been widespread support for intervention in America. Despite Russell's mediation plans, public opinion was never interested in becoming entangled in the American Civil War. Here, again, we arrive back at Palmerston who noted that Britain had neither permanent friends nor permanent enemies – only permanent interests. The Confederacy was not one of these.

[28] A good examination of relative military strengths at this time is Kenneth Bourne, *Britain and the balance of power in North America, 1815–1908*, London 1967, chs vii–viii.

CONCLUSION

Public opinion can be further researched through the medium of personal influences. It has been noted how mail between England and the Union doubled in volume during this period.[29] Numerous English observers, such as Elizabeth Gaskell, only took a pro-northern stance because of American friends. In an interpersonal age, this area needs more research. A closely related area is that of organisations such as the peace societies and the temperance societies that were often transatlantic in membership.[30] It is inconceivable that individuals attached to these were not susceptible to the Union point of view. These, too, may have had a profound influence on Anglo-American relations.

On the subject of societies, we still need to know a great deal more about the anti-slavery societies and each side's propaganda efforts. Their activities and, indeed, even which groups constituted their memberships are known only in the most general way. An examination of the Union and Emancipation Society's papers, for example, would shed a great deal of light on the vexed question of public meetings. Even an idea of each side's numbers would prove to be useful to our understanding of this period.

Regarding each side's supporters, 'though, the point that needs to be repeated is that historians have been far too accepting of northern supporters' ambitions and claims while similarly denigrating southern supporters' activities and opinions. Just as neither the North nor the South had a monopoly on either virtue or venality, the same must be said of each side's English partisans. Confederate sympathisers' support for the self-determination arguments of the South have been too easily dismissed, while their opponents have been attributed only the most noble of motives. Ellison has pointed to Cobden and Bright's investments in the Union; some of the other northern apologists should certainly be examined on these grounds – the duke of Argyll, to name just one. More scepticism should be applied to northern commentators, too. Henry Adams's self-righteous denunciations of England are certainly entertaining, but so too is the fact that, although in his twenties during the war, he did not serve on the battlefields of America but instead acted as his father's secretary and thundered at the Confederacy from the safety of London. This is, of course, denigration but it is mentioned to underline the point that balance is needed.

On the question of self-determination, for example, it is certainly worthwhile to mention Ireland and the anti-Irish sentiment expressed by numerous northern apologists. It is interesting that the pro-Confederates, Gladstone and Acton, were pro-Home Rule, while the pro-Northerners, Bright and Forster, were opposed to it. This raises another question: did the North's defeat of the South teach England the wrong lessons regarding Ireland? Did Irish nationalism later become compared to or associated with (figuratively

---

[29] H. C. Allen, 'Civil War, reconstruction and Great Britain', in Hyman, *Heard around the world*, 3–96, 9.
[30] Idem, *Great Britain and the United States*, 121–2.

speaking) the discredited Confederacy, especially as Irish nationalists favoured the South?

There remains the question of reform and the American Civil War's impact upon it. Judging by English opinions on the war, its impact upon political reform in Britain was probably negligible. As this work has established, those historians who detect a distinct link have inevitably overrated the numbers of reformers who were pro-North while similarly underrating the numbers of reformers who were anti-Union or, indeed, pro-Confederate.[31] As we have seen, numerous members of parliament who disliked the North, and, in some cases, supported the South, were staunch supporters of reform during the war. The event in 1865, which cleared the way for reform in Britain, was the death of Palmerston, not Lee's surrender at Appomattox.

There has been much made of the idea that the northern victory advanced the cause of democracy in Europe, but even this cannot be substantiated. Where the North's victory might have advanced the pace of reform was in France, for French liberals seem to have supported the Union. Nonetheless, despite the frequent comparisons made to English radicals, we should remember that French liberalism always had more respect for the United States, originating from the American Revolution. Elsewhere in Europe, the question is still an open one. Garibaldi's Italians seem to be the only liberal movement that supported the Union. Otherwise, the most consistently pro-northern regimes in Europe were the despotisms of Prussia, Austria and Russia. Their support for the North was probably owed to the fact that in the case of the last two, they themselves were facing secessionist (nationalist) movements of their own, while in the case of the last, it was trying to build an empire through German unification. The fact that the democratic Union was willing to put down revolt and a nationalist movement proved a useful justification for their own activities. It may turn out that democracy in continental Europe was actually retarded by the surrender at Appomattox.

It has often been alleged that the English never really understood the complexities of the American Civil War. Even this seems a dangerous simplification. While it is certainly true to say that the English never grasped the North's devotion to the Union, it is also true that they recognised the South's determination to form a separate nation before the North did. That the English public's judgement on the war was sometimes incorrect is irrefutable, but then, at one point or another, so was everyone else's, too. What does need to be noted, is that the English saw the war through their own perspective – a perspective very different from that of the North or the South – and one which has never been fully appreciated or acknowledged.

When it came to Anglo-American relations during the conflict, each of the three parties themselves – Britain, the Union and the Confederacy –

---

[31] The most detailed argument for the impact of the northern victory on the Reform Act of 1867 is idem, 'Civil War, reconstruction and Great Britain'. See, in addition, Pelling, *America and the British left*, chs i–iii passim.

considerably damaged their own cause. Britain should have been more rigorous in its neutrality. Although generations of Americans have believed (and some historians still believe) that the British deliberately unleashed the *Alabama* on American shipping, the fact remains that its escape was due to blundering, not malice. This was, nonetheless, a major mistake by the British, especially in light of the fact that such shipbuilding activities were inimical to their own interests as the world's leading naval power. Russell's plans for mediation were also ill conceived. Absolute non-intervention was the only course Britain could have followed in the war. Both activities must count as major mistakes.

In the case of the North, it should have saved its belligerence for the Confederacy. Threats of annexing Canada and the activities during the *Trent* affair were the primary cause of English hostility towards the Union and were at least partially responsible for the Palmerston government's errors. If the North was concerned about British intervention, it should have issued a formal declaration that either recognition of the South or offers of mediation would be treated as hostile acts. This would probably have been enough to discourage Palmerston's government – it might also have silenced claims from individuals such as Roebuck that recognition would not be an act of war.

The South, finally, was arrogant and presumptuous. It should not have expected the issue of slavery to be simply ignored by the very nation that had worked hardest to eliminate it. Nor should the Confederacy have tried to use King Cotton to blackmail Britain into intervention. Britain had no outstanding reason for becoming involved in the American quarrel – the South, facing an uphill battle to gain British intervention, effectively foiled itself.

These were all major blunders on the part of the three parties. In retrospect, it appears incredible that they were committed. On the other hand, it is easy to be wise after the fact.

It is unfortunate that, despite the revisionists' research, the myth that the English were pro-southern is still with us. For example, a recent historian has written of 'the predominantly pro-Confederate stance of the British press at this period' which 'led to pressure on the British government to abandon its policy of neutrality and take the Confederate side, break the Northern blockade of Southern ports and even enter the war'.[32] Far from pressurising their government to aid the Confederacy, neither the English nor their press were pro-southern – they simply did not regard the Union's cause as any more valid than that of the Confederacy. Nor is this simply semantics – it meant the difference between intervention and neutrality.

It was believed by Matthew Arnold that the middle classes of England, upon hearing of the South's defeat, persuaded themselves that they had

[32] Clare Midgley, *Women against slavery: the British campaigns, 1780–1870*, London 1992, 179.

always desired that result.[33] In actual fact, this seems to be applicable only to the northern apologists. The most accurate summation of England's attitudes towards the conflict was Lord Shaftesbury's pronouncement: that the English sympathised with neither side because there was no sincerity on either side.[34] In a war that left well over half a million dead, the real truth of the American Civil War is that there was too much sincerity on both sides. Nonetheless, as regards English views of the war, Shaftesbury's pronouncement holds true. When dealing with English observations of the conflict, we must abandon the unsustainable traditional interpretation and that of its heavenly kingdom containing the small group of English northern partisans in their sublime, but lonely, campaign for freedom, equality, democracy and emancipation against the reactionary hordes. As far as the vast majority of English commentators were concerned, their nation was the freest, wealthiest and most powerful on the globe. They were already in the heavenly kingdom – it was the Americans, Union and Confederate alike, who were outside in pandemonium, and the English had no desire to admit them, far less join them.

---

[33] Joseph M. Hernon, 'British sympathies and the American Civil War; a reconsideration', *Journal of Southern History* xxxiii (1967) 356–67.
[34] Jenkins, *Britain and the war for the Union*, i. 120.

APPENDIX 1

MPs' Proclivities During the Civil War

Southern sympathies
W. Angerstein
A. S. Ayrton*
G. W. P. Bentinck
E. P. Bouverie
J. Bramley Moore*
Lord Bulwer-Lytton
Sir J. Ferguson
J. T. Hibbert*
J. A. Roebuck*
Sir C. Wood*#
F. Peel
W. E. Gladstone*#
W. N. Massey
W. Scholefield*
Lord Russell*#
W. Gregory
W. S. Lindsay*
W. R. Seymour Fitzgerald
Lord Vane Tempest
J. Whiteside
J. T. Hopwood
Lord R. Cecil
P. Wyndham
G. W. M. Peacocke
Col. Orville
T. C. Haliburton
H. Jervis
Sir J. Ramsden
Lord H. F. Thynne
<u>W. E. Duncombe</u>
<u>W. Vansittart</u>
<u>Sir E. C. Kerrison</u>

Neutral
Lord Fermoy
J. Harvey Lewis
A. W. Kinglake
W. Roupell
C. Gilpin*
Lord Henley*
A. M. Dunlop
R. P. Collier
W. Morrison
C. Buxton*
J. Locke
R. A. Slaney
E. Horsman*
Lord Palmerston#
B. Disraeli
Lord Derby
H. B. W. Brand
J. G. Blencowe
C. P. Villiers#
T. M. Weguelin
H. Berkeley*
D. O'Donoghue
C. N. Newdegate
J. Walter
S. Gurney
Lord Paget
E. K. Hugessen
T. Bazley*
W. H. Sykes
J. M. Cobbett
Sir G. Grey#
W. Wood
H. M. Clifford
J. Ewart
Sir G. Cornewall Lewis#

Northern sympathies
J. Bright*
R. Cobden*
W. E. Forster*
W. Coningham*
J. White
J. Stansfeld*
duke of Argyll#
E. A. Leatham*
J. E. Denison
F. Doulton
W. Williams*
H. B. Sheridan
P. A. Taylor*
Sir S. M. Peto*
T. Baring
A. H. Layard
R. M. Milnes
Sir R. Palmer
F. Crossley
T. Milner Gibson#

Totals: 32 southern supporters, 20 northern sympathisers and 35 neutrals, for a total of 87
* denotes MP favoured reform
\# denotes MP held a cabinet position
<u>Underlined</u> denotes position derived from Jordan and Pratt (see below)

APPENDIX 1

The categorisation of the MPs has been determined by their speeches in their constituencies and in parliament. Unless listed below, the MPs' speeches in question have been cited in this work. Those names that are underlined are derived from Jordan and Pratt who produce no evidence for their claims, nor have I found any. The names are nonetheless reproduced here.

This list increases the support for the Confederacy because of the criteria used in categorising the MPs' positions. For example, some MPs have been classified as southern supporters solely on the grounds that they believed a divided Union was to Britain's benefit. Thus, Bulwer-Lytton is included among the pro-Confederate MPs even though there is no evidence to suggest that he had any respect for the South. On the other hand, to be labelled a Union sympathiser required that the MP in question had to actively speak in favour of the North. Thus, MPs clearly tolerant towards the Union, such as Newdegate, or vocally opposed to southern slavery, such as Gurney, have been placed in the neutral category, because neither actually agitated on behalf of the North. Jordan and Pratt claim that Villiers was pro-Union, but my own interpretation of Villiers's speeches places him in the neutral category.

Lists of this sort are always inherently imprecise. Historians basing their categorisation on different criteria will certainly challenge certain individuals' positions. My placement of Palmerston and Derby, for example, will not go unquestioned, but as no historian has yet produced evidence of Confederate sympathies on the part of either man, this allows me to place them in the neutral category, based on what they said in the House of Commons and elsewhere. Nonetheless, while one or two of my decisions may be open to challenge (and this would be in favour of either side), the vast majority of MPs have been placed in the correct category and thus the general conclusions hold.

The fact that only 87 members out of well over 600 in the House of Commons chose to speak on the American Civil War suggests that the impact of the conflict on British politics was of comparative unimportance. Furthermore, this view is reinforced when it is recalled that the affairs of both Poland and Schlesweig-Holstein largely replaced those of America as a source of interest from 1863 to 1864.

Although the southern sympathisers outnumber their northern opponents by a ratio of approximately 3:2, this is less impressive when it is remembered that my categorisation is biased in favour of the Confederacy. The significant number is the neutrals, and if one combines them with the pro-Northerners, the pro-Southerners are outnumbered by a ratio of almost 2:1. Further, the cabinet ministers who spoke on the American Civil War largely remained neutral. Those in favour of either the Union or the Confederacy were almost equally divided – two for the North, three for the South. These statistics show a clear lack of political support for the South, thus providing an explanation for why the Confederacy failed to obtain recognition.

Sources

J. Walter: *Reynolds's Weekly*, 29 Nov. 1863.
T. Bazley: ibid. 25 May 1862.
D. O'Donoughue: ibid. 25 Feb. 1864.
R. A. Slaney: ibid. 11 May 1862.
J. Ewart: ibid. 1 Feb. 1863.
Col. Sykes: ibid. 13 Sept. 1863.
Lord C. Paget and E. K. Hugessen: ibid. 2 Feb. 1862.
W. Roupell: ibid. 9 Feb. 1862.
J. Bramley Moore and C. Buxton: ibid. 16 Nov. 1862.
R. Monckton Milnes was a friend of the Adams family.

APPENDIX 2

Aristocratic Proclivities During the Civil War

Southern sympathies	Neutral	Northern sympathies
earl of Donoughmore	Lord Brougham	duke of Argyll
Lord Vane Tempest	earl of Hardwicke	Lord Ashburton (Baring)
Lord Strathenden (Campbell)	Lord Henley	Lord Houghton
Lord H. Thynne	Lord Fermoy	Lord Bryce
Lord Robert Cecil	Lord Paget	earl of Carlisle
Lord Eustace Cecil	duke of Somerset	Lord Denison
Lord Acton	Lord Hurlington	<u>Lord Cavendish</u>
Lord Wharncliffe	earl of Granville	<u>earl de Grey</u>
Lord Lothian	earl of Malmesbury	<u>Lord Dufferin</u>
Lord Robert Montagu	earl of Carnarvon	
Lord Teynham	earl of Clarendon	
marquis of Bath	Lord Churchill	
marquis of Clarincarde	earl of Shaftesbury	
	Lord Coleridge	
	Lord Enfield	
	<u>Sir Stafford Northcote</u>	
	<u>Lord Stanley</u>	

The source of the underlined names is Jordan and Pratt. Once again, as in the case of the members of parliament, although I have found no evidence to support Jordan and Pratt's claims, I have added their names to my list.

Jordan and Pratt list the radical Lord Teynham as a pro-Northerner. Lord Teynham's name, however, appears on the roster of the Manchester Southern Independence Society, placing him firmly on the side of the Confederacy.

This list, like that of MPs, is composed of Lords who spoke on America at public meetings and in the House and are placed according to where their sympathies appeared to lie. Once more, I have weighted the criteria for selection in favour of the Confederacy (see Appendix 1). Yet again, there are only slightly more individuals sympathetic to the South while the neutrals make up the largest single number. Once again, it appears that only a very small minority of the Lords, like the Commons, concerned themselves sufficiently to speak on the American Civil War.

Sources

Earls of Malmesbury and Carnarvon: *Reynolds's Weekly*, 23 Feb. 1862.
Lord Churchill: ibid. 26 Apr. 1863.
The earl of Carlisle was a vocal supporter of J. E. Cairnes.

Lord Lothian wrote a pro-Confederate book.
Lord Coleridge was neutral according to Whitridge: 'British liberals and the American Civil War', 692.
The marquis of Bath was a member of a pro-southern society.
Lord Houghton was a member of the Union and Emancipation Society.
Lord Bryce was neutral according to E. D. Adams: *Great Britain and the American Civil War*, ii. 188.
Lord Enfield was named a neutral by the pro-Confederate MP William Schaw Lindsay. Lindsay papers, LND 7, 639.
Lord Denison was pro-North according to Villiers and Chesson: *Anglo-American relations*, 205.

Bibliography

Unpublished primary sources

Dublin, National Library of Ireland
John Elliot Cairnes papers, MSS 8940–68

Greenwich, National Maritime Museum
William Schaw Lindsay papers, LND 7

Kew, Public Record Office
John Russell, 1st Earl Russell, papers, PRO 30/22

Leeds, West Yorkshire Archives
Sir John Ramsden papers RA 17, 48, 66/8

London, British Library
John Bright papers, MSS 43,152–551
Richard Cobden papers, MSS 43,676, 44,099–938
Henry John Temple, 3rd Viscount Palmerston, MSS Add. 48405, 48575–6; MS Microfilm 881

London, London School of Economics
John Stuart Mill papers, Mill-Taylor Collection, Vols LV, LV1 A

Southampton, University of Southampton
Palmerston papers, GC/RU/685

Published primary sources

Anderson, Edward C., *Confederate foreign agent: the European diary of Major Edward C. Anderson*, ed. W. Stanley Hoole, Alabama 1976
Chase, Salmon P., *Inside Lincoln's cabinet: the Civil War diaries of Salmon P. Chase*, ed. David Herbert Donald, New York 1954
Ford, Worthington Chauncey (ed.), *A cycle of Adams letters: 1861–1865*, London 1921
Gladstone, William E., *The Gladstone diaries*, ed. M. R. D. Foot and H. C. G. Matthew, Oxford 1968–94
Lincoln, Abraham, *The collected works of Abraham Lincoln*, ed. Roy P. Basler, New Brunswick 1953–5
Marx, Karl and Friedrich Engels, *The Civil War in the United States*, ed. Richard Enmale, London n.d.

Mason, Virginia (ed.), *The public life and diplomatic correspondence of James M. Mason with some personal history by his daughter*, Roanoke 1903

Moran, Benjamin, *The journal of Benjamin Moran*, ed. Sarah Agnes Wallace and Frances Elma Gillespie, Chicago 1948

Richardson, James D. (ed.), *The messages and papers of Jefferson Davis and the Confederacy, including the diplomatic correspondence, 1861–1865*, New York 1966

Official documents and publications
Hansard. Parliamentary debates, 3rd ser., London 1830–91

Newspapers and periodicals
All the Year Round
Annual Register
Athenaeum
Bee-Hive
British Quarterly Review
Eclectic Review
The Economist
English Woman's Journal (*Alexandra Magazine*, after 1863)
Fraser's Magazine
Illustrated London News
Macmillan's Magazine
National Review
New Monthly Magazine
New York Herald
New York Tribune
Once a Week
Quarterly Review
Reynolds's Weekly Newspaper
Saturday Review
Spectator
The Times (London)
Wesleyan Methodist Magazine
Western Morning News
Westminster Review

Contemporary books and articles
Adams, Henry Brooks, *The education of Henry Adams*, Washington 1907

Beresford Hope, A. J., *The social and political bearings of the American disruption*, London 1863

Bryce, James, *The American commonwealth*, London 1888

Bulloch, James D., *The secret service of the Confederate States in Europe: or, how the Confederate cruisers were equipped*, New York 1959

Cairnes, John Elliot, *The slave power, its character, career and probable designs*, 2nd edn, London 1863

Campbell, John Francis, *A short American tramp in the fall of 1864, by the editor of 'Life in Normandy'*, Edinburgh 1865

Carlyle, Thomas, *Latter-day pamphlets*, London 1850
———, *Thomas Carlyle: critical and miscellaneous essays*, London n.d.
Cooper, James Fenimore, *Gleanings in Europe by an American*, Philadelphia 1837
Corsan, William Carson, *Two months in the Confederate States: including a visit to New Orleans under the domination of General Butler by an English merchant*, London 1863
Day, Samuel Phillips, *Down South: or, an Englishman's experience at the seat of the American war*, London 1862
De Tocqueville, Alexis, *Democracy in America*, New York 1945
Dicey, Edward James Stephen, *Six months in the federal states*, London 1863
Essays on reform, London 1867
Fremantle, Arthur James Lyon, *Three months in the southern states, April–June, 1863*, Edinburgh 1863
Grant, Ulysses S., *The personal memoirs of U. S. Grant*, London 1885
Hopley, Catherine Cooper, *Life in the South. From the commencement of the war. By a blockaded British subject. Being a social history of those who took part in the battles from a personal acquaintance with them in their homes. From the spring of 1860 to August 1862*, London 1863
Kemble, Frances Anne, *Journal of residence in America*, London 1835
———, *Journal of a residence on a Georgia plantation in 1838–1839*, London 1863
MacKay, Alexander, *The western world or, travels in the United States in 1846–1847 exhibiting in them their latest development, social, political, and industrial, including a chapter on California*, London 1849
Martineau, Harriet, *Society in America*, London 1837
Montagu, Robert, *A mirror on America*, London 1861
Russell, William Howard, *My diary, north and south*, London 1863
Smith, Goldwin, *Reminiscences*, London 1911
Spence, James, *The American union; its effects on national character and policy with an inquiry into secession as a constitutional right and the cause of the disruption*, London 1861
Stephen, Leslie, The Times *and the American Civil War*, London 1865
Trollope, Anthony, *North America*, London 1862
Wheaton, Henry, *Cases argued and decided in the Supreme Court of the United States*, Albany 1883
Whitman, Walt, *Democratic vistas*, New York 1871

Secondary sources

Adams, Charles, *When in the course of human events: arguing the case for southern secession*, Lanham, Md. 2000
Adams, E. D., *Great Britain and the American Civil War*, London 1925
Allen, H. C., *Great Britain and the United States: a history of Anglo-American relations, 1783–1952*, London 1954
———, 'Civil War, reconstruction and Great Britain', Hyman, *Heard around the world*, 3–96
Anstey, Roger, 'The pattern of British abolitionism in the eighteenth and nineteenth centuries', in Bolt and Drescher, *Anti-slavery, religion and reform*, 19–42
Ausubel, Herman, *John Bright: Victorian reformer*, New York 1966

Balée, Susan, 'English critics, American crisis, and the sensation novel', *Nineteenth Century Contexts* xvii/2 (1993), 125–32

Bellows, Donald A., 'A study of British conservative reaction to the American Civil War', *Journal of Southern History* li (1985), 506–36

Bennett, Lerone, Jr., *Forced into glory: Abraham Lincoln's white dream*, Chicago 2000

Berger, Max, *The British traveller in America, 1836–1860*, New York 1943

Best, Geoffrey, *Mid-Victorian Britain*, London 1971

Biagini, Eugenio, *Liberty, retrenchment and reform: popular liberalism in the age of Gladstone, 1860–1880*, Cambridge 1992

Blackett, R. J. M., 'Pressure from without: African Americans, British public opinion and Civil War diplomacy', in May, *The Union, the Confederacy and the Atlantic rim*, 69–100.

Blake, Laurel, and others (eds), *Investigating Victorian journalism*, London 1990

Blumenthal, Henry, 'Confederate diplomacy: popular notions and international realities', *Journal of Southern History* xxxii (1966), 159–67

Bolt, Christine, *Victorian attitudes to race*, London 1971

—— and Seymour Drescher (eds), *Anti-slavery, religion and reform: essays in memory of Roger Anstey*, Folkestone 1980

Bourne, Kenneth, 'British preparations for war with the North, 1861–1862', *English Historical Review* lxxvi (1961), 600–32

——, *Britain and the balance of power in North America, 1815–1908*, London 1967

Brady, Eugene A., 'A reconsideration of the Lancashire "cotton famine"', *Agricultural History* xxxvii (1963), 156–62

Breuilly, John, Gottfried Niedhart and Antony Taylor (eds), *The era of the reform league: English labour and radical politics, 1857–1872, documents selected by Gustav Mayer*, Mannheim 1995

Briggs, Asa, *Victorian people: a reassessment of persons and themes, 1851–67*, Chicago 1955

Brogan, Hugh (ed.), *The American Civil War: extracts from* The Times, *1860–1865*, London 1975

Brook, Michael, 'Confederate sympathies in north-east Lancashire, 1862–1864', *Lancashire and Cheshire Antiquarian Society* lxv–lxxvi (1977), 211–17

Brown, Lucy, *Victorian news and newspapers*, Oxford 1985

Burnet, Alastair, *The Economist America, 1843–1993: 150 years of reporting the American connection*, London 1993

Butterfield, H., *The Whig interpretation of history*, London 1931

Clausen, Martin P., 'Peace factors in Anglo-American relations', *Mississippi Historical Review* xxvi (1940), 511–22

Clinton, Catherine, *Fanny Kemble's civil wars: the story of America's most unlikely abolitionist*, New York 2000

Collini, S., R. Whatmore and B. Young (eds), *History, religion and culture: essays in British intellectual history, 1750–1950*, Cambridge 2000

Coltham, Stephen, 'George Potter, the Junta and the Bee-Hive', *International Review of Social History* ix (1964), 391–432

Conacher, J. B., *Britain and the Crimea, 1855–56: problems of war and peace*, New York 1987

BIBLIOGRAPHY

Corsan, William Carson, *Two months in the Confederate States: an Englishman's travels through the South*, ed. Benjamin H. Trask, Baton Rouge 1996

Coulter, E. Merton, *Travels in the Confederate States: a bibliography*, Oklahoma 1948; Baton Rouge 1994

Crawford, Martin, *The Anglo-American crisis of the nineteenth century: The Times and America, 1850–1862*, Athens, Ga. 1987

Crook, D. P., *American democracy in English politics, 1815–1850*, Oxford 1965–

—— 'Portents of war: English opinion on secession', *Journal of American Studies* xxxiii (1967), 163–79

——, *The North, the South and the powers: 1861–1865*, New York 1974

Donald, David Herbert, 'Died of democracy', in Donald, *Why the North won the Civil War*, 81–92

——, *Lincoln*, London 1995

—— (ed.), *Why the North won the Civil War*, Baton Rouge 1960

Drescher, Seymour, 'Two variants of anti-slavery: religious organization and social mobilization in Britain and France 1780–1870', in Bolt and Drescher, *Anti-slavery, religion and reform*, 43–63

Ellison, Mary, *Support for secession: Lancashire and the American Civil War*, Chicago 1972

Evans, Eric J., *The forging of the modern state: early industrial Britain, 1783–1870*, London 1983

Felix, David, *Marx as a politician*, Carbondale 1983

Fermer, Douglas, *James Gordon Bennett and the New York Herald: a study of editorial opinion in the Civil War era*, Woodbridge 1986

Ferris, Norman, *Desperate diplomacy: William H. Seward's foreign policy, 1861*, Knoxville 1976

The Trent affair: a diplomatic crisis, Knoxville 1977

Feuchtwanger, E. J., *Gladstone*, London 1975

Finn, Margot C., *After Chartism: class and nation in English radical politics, 1848–1874*, Cambridge 1993

Fladeland, Betty, *Abolitionists and working-class problems in the age of industrialization*, Baton Rouge 1984

Foner, Philip S., *British labor and the American Civil War*, New York 1981

Foote, Shelby, *The Civil War: a narrative*, New York 1958–74

Freehling, William W., *Prelude to Civil War: the nullification controversy in South Carolina, 1816–1830*, New York 1965

Fremantle, Arthur J. L., *Three months in the southern states, April–June 1863*, ed. Gary Gallagher, Lincoln, Neb. 1991

Fulton, Richard D., 'The London Times and the Anglo-American boarding dispute of 1858', *Nineteenth Century Contexts* xvii/2 (1993), 133–44

Furnas, J. C., *Fanny Kemble: leading lady of the nineteenth century*, New York 1982

Gentry, Judith F., 'A Confederate success in Europe: the Erlanger loan', *Journal of Southern History* xxxvi (1970), 157–88

Grob, Gerald N. and George Athan Billias (eds), *Interpretations of American history: patterns and perspectives*, 3rd edn, New York 1978

Hall, Catherine, *White, male and middle-class: explorations in feminism and history*, Cambridge 1992

Harrison, Brian, 'A genealogy of reform in modern Britain', in Bolt and Drescher, *Anti-slavery, religion and reform*, 121–38

Harrison, Royden, 'British labour and the Confederacy', *International Review of Social History* ii (1957), 78–105

———, 'British labor and American slavery', *Science and Society* xxv (1961), 291–319

———, *Before the socialists: studies in labour and politics, 1861–1881*, London 1965

———, *Before the socialists: studies in labour and politics, 1861–1881*, 2nd edn, Ipswich 1994

Harvie, Christopher, *The lights of liberalism: university liberals and the challenge of democracy, 1860–86*, London 1976

Hernon, Joseph M., 'British sympathies and the American Civil War: a reconsideration', *Journal of Southern History* xxxiii (1967), 356–67

———, *Celts, Catholics and copperheads: Ireland views the American Civil War*, Columbus 1968

Hyman, Harold (ed.), *Heard around the world: the impact abroad of the Civil War*, New York 1969

James, Lawrence, *The Iron Duke: a military biography of Wellington*, London 1992

Jenkins, Brian, *Britain and the war for the Union*, i, ii, Montreal 1974, 1980

Jones, Howard, *Union in peril: the crisis over British intervention in the Civil War*, Chapel Hill 1992

Jones, Wilbur Devereux, 'British conservatives and the American Civil War', *American Historical Review* lviii (1953), 527–43

Jordan, Donaldson and Edwin J. Pratt, *Europe and the American Civil War*, London 1931

Kaufman, Will, ' "Our rancorous cousins": British literary journals on the approach of the Civil War', *Symbiosis: A Journal of Anglo-American Literary Relations* iv/i (2000), 35–50

Koss, Stephen, *The Rise and fall of the political press in Britain, volume one: the nineteenth century*, London 1981

Lester, Richard, *Confederate finance and purchasing in Great Britain*, Charlottesville 1975

Lillibridge, G., *Beacon of freedom: the impact of American democracy upon Great Britain: 1830–1870*, Philadelphia 1955

Logan, Kevin J., 'The *Bee-Hive* newspaper and British working class attitudes toward the American Civil War', *Civil War History* xxii (1976), 337–48

Lorimer, Douglas A., 'The role of anti-slavery sentiment in English reactions to the American Civil War', *Historical Journal* xix (1976), 405–20

———, *Colour, class and the Victorians*, Leicester 1978

———, 'Race, science and culture: historical continuities and discontinuities, 1850–1914', in West, *The Victorians and race*, 12–33

McPherson, James M., *Battle cry of freedom: the civil war era*, New York 1989

———, 'The whole family of man: Lincoln and the last best hope abroad', in May, *The Union, the Confederacy and the Atlantic rim*, 131–58

———, *Drawn with the sword: reflections on the American Civil War*, Oxford 1996

Mahin, Dean B., *One war at a time: the international dimensions of the American Civil War*, Washington 1999

Mandler, Peter, 'Race and nation in mid-Victorian thought', in Collini, Whatmore and Young, *History, religion and culture*, 224–44

Maurer, Oscar, '*Punch* on slavery and civil war in America', *Victorian Studies* i (1957), 5–28

May, Robert E. (ed.), *The Union, the Confederacy and the Atlantic rim*, West Lafayette 1995
Merli, Frank J., *Great Britain and the Confederate navy: 1861–1865*, Bloomington 1970
Midgley, Clare, *Women against slavery: the British campaigns, 1780–1870*, London 1992
Nevins, Allan, *America through British eyes*, New York 1948
Owsley, Frank Lawrence, *King Cotton diplomacy: foreign relations of the Confederate States of America*, 2nd edn, rev. Harriet Owsley, Chicago 1959
Parish, Peter J., *The American Civil War*, New York 1975
Pelling, Henry, *America and the British left; from Bright to Bevan*, London 1956
Pelzer, John D., 'Liverpool and the American Civil War', *History Today* xl (1990), 46–52
Rapson, Richard, *Britons view America: travel commentary, 1860–1935*, Seattle 1971
Ridley, Jasper, *Lord Palmerston*, London 1970
Roper, Jon, *Democracy and its critics: Anglo-American democratic thought in the nineteenth century*, London 1989
——— and Duncan Campbell (eds), *The American Civil War: literary sources and documents*, Mountfield 2000
Semmell, Bernard, *Liberalism and naval strategy; ideology, interest and sea power during the Pax Britannica*, Boston 1986
Shane, C., 'English novelists and the American Civil War', *American Quarterly* xiv (1962), 399–421
Smith, Paul, *Disraeli: a brief life*, Cambridge 1996
Stedman Jones, Gareth, *Languages of class: studies in English working-class history, 1832–1982*, Cambridge 1983
Taylor, Miles, 'The Sheffield steel inquiry of 1869', *Transactions of the Hunter Archaeological Society* xv (1989), 38–47
———, *The decline of British radicalism, 1847–1860*, Oxford 1995
Thomson, David, *England in the nineteenth century, 1815–1914*, London 1950
Trevelyan, G. M., *British history in the nineteenth century, 1782–1901*, London 1922
Turley, David M., ' "Free air" and fugitive slaves', in Bolt and Drescher, *Anti-slavery, religion and reform*, 163–82
Van Auken, Sheldon, *The glittering illusion: English sympathy for the Confederacy*, London 1988
Villiers, Brougham and W. H. Chesson, *Anglo-American relations, 1861–1865*, London 1919
Warren, Gordon H., *The fountain of discontent: the Trent affair and freedom of the seas*, Boston 1981
Weinberg, Adelaide, *John Elliot Cairnes and the American Civil War: a study in Anglo-American relations*, London n.d.
West, Shearer (ed.), *The Victorians and race*, Aldershot 1996
Whitridge, Arnold, 'British liberals and the American Civil War', *History Today* xii (1962), 688–95
Wills, Gary, *Lincoln at Gettysburg: the words that remade America*, New York 1992
Winks, Robin W., *Canada and the United States: the Civil War years*, Baltimore 1960

Wright, D., 'Bradford and the American Civil War', *Journal of British Studies* viii (1969), 69–85

Unpublished theses

Botsford, Robert, 'Scotland and the American Civil War', PhD diss. Edinburgh 1955
Keiser, Thomas J., 'The English press and the American Civil War', PhD diss. Reading 1971
Smith, Robert Trumbull, 'The Confederate *Index* and the American Civil War', PhD diss. Washington 1961
Smith, Van Mitchell, 'British business relations with the Confederacy, 1861–1865', PhD diss. Texas 1949
Wilks, Sarah, 'An independent in politics: John Arthur Roebuck, 1802–1879', DPhil diss. Oxford 1979

Index

abolitionism, *see* emancipation
Acton, Lord 4, 243
Adams, Charles Francis 6, 10, 60, 66, 111, 115, 128, 131, 142, 160, 187, 189, 215–17, 235
Adams, Charles Francis, Jr 6, 10, 60, 102, 189, 235, 237
Adams, Henry 1, 5, 6, 8, 10, 60, 67, 181, 187, 189, 234–6, 243
Africa 1, 20, 22, 47
African Americans, *see* blacks
Alabama Arbitration 178, 230, 232, 233
All the year round 45
American Civil War
    historiography of Anglo-American relations during 2–12
    English writers on 117–24
    aristocratic views of 134–9
    conservative views of 140–50
    pro-southerners' views of 163–93
    pro-northerners' views of 194–226
    MPs' views of 151–62
American Revolution 28, 35, 56, 59, 77, 104, 175, 239, 242, 244
Anderson, Edward 46, 127
Anderson, John 26, 27
Andrew, John 69, 70
Angerstein, William 152, 153
Annual Register 19, 36, 44, 59, 94, 191
Antietam, battle of (1862) 103, 171, 239, 240
Appomattox 94, 126, 158, 192, 200, 229, 230, 233, 244
Argyll, duke of 4, 11, 55, 177, 210, 243
aristocracy, British 2, 5, 11, 14, 76, 86, 96, 101, 134–9, 151, 162, 174, 193, 195, 197, 207, 209–12, 229, 236
Arnold, Matthew 196, 245
Ashburton, Lord 139, 186
Ashton-under-Lyne 8, 158, 216, 217
Athenaeum 23, 58, 122, 123, 128, 131, 149, 181, 189, 192, 197
Austria, 20, 105, 209, 244
Ayrton, Acton Smee 159, 176

Beales, Edmund 206, 222
Beecher, Henry Ward 98, 99

Bee-Hive 5, 195, 202, 206, 207, 214, 216, 219, 220, 228
Beesly, E. S. 206, 207, 212, 219–21, 223, 226
Benjamin, Judah P. 114, 117, 131, 179, 184–9, 203
Bennett, James 36–40
Bentham, Jeremy 196
Beresford-Hope, Alexander 120, 183
Berkeley, F. H. 143
Bigelow, George 69
Blacks 9, 23, 24, 27, 75, 118, 119, 122–33, 140, 189, 199, 232, 235
Blair, Montgomery 70
Blenclowe, J. 81
blockade, Union 6, 17, 25, 29, 32, 50–4, 56, 62, 64, 83, 86, 118, 137, 157, 210, 217, 225, 226
boarding dispute (1858) 20–2, 31, 138
border states 132, 181, 239, 242
Boston 57, 69, 93
Bouverie, Edward 154
Bowen, Charles 89
Bradford 55, 83, 182, 229
Brand, H. 81
Brazil 21, 129
Bright, John 2, 4–6, 8–10, 50, 51, 56, 87, 98, 99, 107, 120, 135, 139, 141, 144–7, 153, 154, 158, 161, 162, 167, 170–4, 176, 179, 180, 182, 192, 195, 198, 201–5, 207, 212, 214, 218, 219, 222, 224, 229, 230, 231, 234–7, 241, 243
    during *Trent* affair 71, 76, 77–80, 83, 91–3
    at Birmingham 155, 156
    at St James' Hall 219–21
British Quarterly Review 34, 42, 48, 52, 54, 73, 94n.138, 124, 130, 132, 149
Brougham, Baron 137, 138, 218
Bryce, James 99, 100, 142, 234, 235, 237
Buchanan, James 30, 41
Bull Run, first battle of (1861) 31, 54, 59, 60, 70, 74, 121
Bulloch, James 46, 139, 219
Bulwer-Lytton, E. 115, 116
Butler, Benjamin 24, 106, 109
Butler, Pierce 121–4

261

Cairnes, J. E. 116, 123, 124, 149, 198, 200, 201, 212, 213, 222, 223
Calhoun, John C. 43, 102
Campbell, Lord 98, 135n.4, 168, 186
Campbell, John Francis 117
Canada 9, 13, 26, 28, 30, 32, 33, 35, 37, 42, 66, 68, 69, 79, 93, 94, 113–16, 174, 175, 230, 231, 232, 241, 242, 245
Carlyle, Thomas 125, 126, 235, 236
Cass, Lewis 20, 21, 138
Cecil, Lord Robert 100, 146–8, 171
Charleston 44, 62, 75, 101, 105
Chartism 82, 174, 202
Chase, Salmon P. 70
civil liberties (Union's suppression of) 11, 104–10, 147
Clay, Cassius 18, 28, 31–5, 54, 78, 110, 178, 211, 227
Clay, Henry 44, 48
Cobbett, J. M. 83, 84
Cobden, Richard 2, 4–6, 8–10, 35, 38 n.115, 53, 56, 76, 80, 98, 114, 139, 141, 144, 147, 153, 161, 162, 167, 174, 176, 186–8, 195, 201, 204, 218, 228, 243
Collier, Robert 154
Confederacy, the
English perceptions of 47–54, 74–6, 90–1, 97–102, 117–24, 124–33, 179–82
pro-northerners' views of 198–215
pro-southerners' views of 163–79, 182–4
views of Britain 184–91
collapse of 226–33
Confederate States of America, *see* the Confederacy
Congress (US) 21, 48, 70, 93, 132, 140
Coningham, W. 82, 152
Conservatives 2–5, 7, 9, 11, 21, 41, 55, 59, 81, 96, 100, 134, 140–62, 164, 169–72, 176, 186, 193, 195, 209, 211, 234, 235, 236, 240
views of American Civil War 140–50, 165
Conway, Moncure 109
Cooper, James Fenimore 196
Corsan, William 117, 118
cotton 5, 6, 43, 49, 50–4, 56, 78, 85, 136, 155, 156, 171, 172, 238, 239; *see also* King Cotton
cotton famine 5, 6, 29, 50–4, 86, 136, 137, 154, 172, 201, 227
Cracroft, Bernard 132

Crimean War 12, 21, 57, 63, 64, 71, 74, 78, 80, 83, 103, 107, 121, 172, 174, 205
Cuba 12, 13, 21, 22, 30, 62
Cushing, Caleb 33, 69

Daily News 14, 46, 208, 214, 227
Davis, Jefferson 1, 15, 109, 133n.181, 177, 189, 190, 206
Day, Samuel Phillips 120
Dayton, William L. 112
Delane, John 38
democracy (American) 2–6, 9–11, 78, 100, 109, 140, 142, 146, 148–52, 193, 195, 196–200, 209, 211, 213, 214, 219, 222, 229, 234, 235
Democratic Party 13, 20, 76, 108
Denson, J. E. 162
Derby, Lord 21, 167
De Tocqueville, Alexis 11, 23, 43, 71, 101, 108, 147, 197
Dicey, Edward 37, 99, 116, 120, 128, 129, 214, 223
Dickens, Charles 45, 107
Disraeli, Benjamin 100, 141, 143, 167, 176, 230, 231
Donoughmore, Lord 188
Douglass, Frederick 126
Doulton, F. 160
Drummond-Davis, Francis 42
Dunlop, Alexander 153
Dunning, T. J. 202, 207, 219, 221, 225

Eclectic Review 75, 214
Economist 19, 23, 24, 26, 30, 33, 38–7, 51–3, 58, 60, 68, 69, 71–4, 86, 87, 90, 105, 108, 116, 124, 130, 131, 172, 181, 190, 192n.113, 200, 231n.176
Edinburgh 137, 138, 217, 218
Ellison, Thomas 24, 212
emancipation 2, 15, 17–19, 22, 24, 25, 27, 28, 45, 49, 82, 96, 118, 120, 124, 128, 129, 133, 138, 144, 149, 152, 159, 164, 193, 199, 201, 211, 213, 221, 222, 227, 235, 239, 240
Emancipation Proclamation (1862) 2, 6, 11, 15, 24, 25, 122, 125, 127, 138, 151, 159, 160, 205, 217, 222, 223, 225
reception in England 130–33
Emancipation Society, *see* Union and Emancipation Society
Empire, British 6, 12, 49, 102, 129
Enfield, Lord 162
English Woman's Journal 26, 45n.150, 94n.138, 200

INDEX

Erlanger Loan 237, 238
Europe 1, 49, 53, 56, 58, 83, 196, 213, 215, 244
Everett, Edward 69, 177
Exeter Hall 99, 130, 222, 223, 225

Fawcett, Henry 99, 229
Fermoy, Lord 84, 139, 158, 159
Fitzgerald, W. R. S. 164, 186
Forster, William 32, 46, 55, 83, 99, 105, 106, 161–5, 170, 182, 196, 198, 200, 203, 212, 222, 225, 229, 243
Fort Sumter 17, 18, 30, 37, 54
France 20, 29, 33, 34, 65, 83, 105, 112, 113, 130, 166–73, 188, 232, 239, 241, 244
Fraser's Magazine 44, 47, 48, 52, 58, 72–5, 89, 94n.138, 109, 124, 145, 148–50, 200
   Mill's article in, 198–200
Fremantle, J. L. 102, 118, 119, 129
Frémont, John 20, 24, 25, 55
Fuller, Hiram 148, 149

Garibaldi, Giuseppe 157, 205, 209, 244,
Garrison, William Lloyd 215
George Griswold 159, 211
Gettysburg, battle of (1863) 97n.2, 102, 103, 118, 171
Gilpin, Charles 151, 152
Gladstone, William E. 6, 8, 10, 11, 58, 86, 87, 99, 100, 110, 116, 138, 170, 176–9, 205, 206, 243
   'Jeff Davis has made a nation' speech 177–9, 206, 210n.87
Glasgow 98, 218
'Gracchus' (Edward Reynolds) 210, 217
Grant Ulysses S. 12, 102, 231
Granville, Earl of 138
Greeley, Horace 102, 129
Greg, William Rathbone 48, 72
Gregory, Sir William 18, 54, 56, 58, 163, 164, 176
Grey, Sir George 171
Gros, Baron 169, 171
Gurney, Samuel 162

Hardwicke, Earl of 136
Hartwell, Robert 206, 207
Hazlitt, William 196
Henley, Lord 151, 152
Hibbert, J. T. 160
Hopley, Catherine, *see* Jones Sarah
Hopwood, John T. 164

Horsman, Edward 81, 157
Hotze, Henry 14n.36, 130, 185n.82, 203, 224
House of Commons, *see* Parliament
House of Lords, *see* Parliament
Hughes, Thomas 39, 40, 47, 222, 223
Hunt, James 126
Hurlington, Lord 139

Illustrated London News 25–7, 33, 36, 39, 44, 49, 52, 58, 60, 68, 71, 73, 79, 90, 104, 109, 110, 113, 114, 116, 132, 165, 166, 172, 178, 180, 190, 192n.113, 231n.176
Index 14
India 50, 59, 98, 126, 152
Indian Mutiny 12, 67, 97, 98, 126
Ireland 6, 15, 59, 99, 100, 106, 136, 150, 160, 170, 229, 243
Irish 99, 100, 160, 183, 243, 244
Italy 97, 98, 100, 196, 209, 242, 244

Jackson, Andrew 43, 44, 148, 190
Jackson, Thomas 'Stonewall' 131, 227
Jamaica 232, 233
Jamaican Insurrection 126, 127, 233
Jervis, Henry 56, 58
Johnson, Andrew 232
Jones, Sarah (Catherine Cooper Hopley) 119

Kemble, Francis (Fanny) 121, 122
King Cotton 3, 15, 18, 49–55, 58, 86, 137, 157, 171, 190, 225, 229, 237, 239, 245
Kinglake, A. W. 82, 83, 157, 175, 192

labour press 5, 206–12, 215, 227
Lancashire 2, 5–8, 50, 53, 54, 78, 83–5, 136, 137, 153, 155–7, 159, 160, 177, 182–4, 201, 202, 209–11, 215, 217, 218, 224–6, 229, 237; *see also*, cotton famine
Layard, A. H. 56, 126, 141, 156
Leatham, E. A. 154
Lee, Robert E. 118, 119, 131, 171, 188, 244
Leno, J. B. 202
Lewis, George Cornewall 177, 179
Lewis, J. H. 84, 158, 159
Liberals 1, 4, 5, 9–11, 41, 80, 82, 96, 106, 108, 129, 141, 142, 151–62, 165, 170, 173, 176, 196, 198, 204, 205, 214
Lincoln, Abraham 2, 7, 9, 11, 13, 15, 17, 19, 24, 25, 28, 29, 35, 37–9, 45, 55, 70,

263

71, 73, 77, 80, 84, 87, 90, 93, 94, 96, 99, 102, 104, 105, 107–9, 111, 125, 127–32, 135, 138, 140, 146, 147, 151, 155, 156, 159, 164, 185, 189, 192, 193, 200, 204, 207, 214, 216, 217, 221, 222, 223
  assassination of 3, 195, 226–8, 230, 239
Lindsay, William Schaw 56–8, 161–71, 174, 176, 182, 183, 185, 186, 201, 204, 234
  meetings with Louis Napoleon 166–9
  motions to recognise South 156n.86, 163–6, 173
Liverpool 1, 5, 67, 218, 219
Locke, John 56, 154
London 15, 67, 203, 223, 228, 243
London American 14, 212n.96
London Herald 14, 120, 223, 224
London Standard 14, 150
Lowe, Robert 82, 141, 234
Lower Canada, *see* Canada
Ludlow, J. M. 42, 46, 126, 212n.96, 222
Lyons, Lord 29, 115, 177

MacKay, Alexander 198
Macmillan's Magazine 39, 40, 42, 45, 47, 58, 84n.120, 89, 94n.138, 120, 128, 200, 214, 231n.176, 234
Manchester Courier 8
Manchester 7, 8, 53, 98, 182
Manchester Free-Trade Hall 7, 8
Manifest Destiny 12, 13, 30
Mantz, E. S. 200, 221
Martineau, Harriet 46, 122, 130n.162, 197, 200
Marx, Karl 6, 8, 10, 50, 71, 86, 87, 208
Mason, James 61–3, 66, 69, 70, 75, 77, 79, 82, 84–9, 91–3, 110, 117, 131, 137, 161, 162, 168, 171, 179, 182, 184–9, 217
Massey, William 152, 160
Mediation (Cabinet consideration of) 177–9
Meetings (public) 5, 8, 9, 14, 85, 122, 124, 133, 136, 139, 151, 183, 184, 195, 215–26
Members of Parliament 11, 14, 80–7, 112, 134, 143, 151–66, 169–72, 176, 186, 187, 191, 229, 244
Mexico 12, 29, 30, 115, 116, 232
middle class (English) 2, 3, 7, 11, 53, 184, 196, 203, 211, 216, 222, 245
Mill, John Stuart 11, 46, 89, 99, 108, 147, 149, 196, 204, 213, 223

Article in *Fraser's* 198–200
Milner Gibson, Thomas 86, 141, 158, 177, 222
Missouri 24, 26
Montagu, Lord Robert 120, 170
Moran, Benjamin 142, 144, 164–6
Morning Star 14, 212n.96
Morrill tariff 7, 15, 18, 41–8, 53, 54, 57, 58, 113, 117, 118, 139, 153, 169, 210, 234, 237
Morrison, W. 154

Napoleon, Louis (Napoleon III) 61, 83, 166–73
Napoleonic wars 42, 63, 103, 104
National Review 48, 53, 58, 72, 73, 132, 200, 214
neutral rights 11, 65, 79, 86, 88, 89, 92
Newcastle 55, 58, 110, 177
Newcastle, Duke of 28, 29, 113
Newdegate, Charles Newdigate 80, 81
Newman, Francis William 44, 47, 52
New Monthly Magazine 46, 48, 58, 72, 105, 114, 119
New Orleans 75, 102, 106
New York 21, 35, 37, 44, 57, 68, 69, 72, 105, 113, 114, 118, 129
New York Herald 21, 36–40, 45, 48, 54, 69–72, 78, 93, 111, 112, 115, 190
New York Times 21, 38, 112, 113, 156, 215
New York Tribune 36, 86, 113
North, the, *see* the Union
Northern press 18, 31, 35–41, 70, 78, 83, 87, 114, 129, 135, 137, 175, 180, 211, 215
Northerners 10, 13, 17, 23, 25, 27, 30, 38, 40, 57, 71–3, 81, 100, 103, 107, 121, 129, 139, 166
Northern states, *see* the Union
Nullification Crisis 43–4, 57

Olmsted, Frederick Law 23, 25, 75
Once a Week 107

Palmerston, Lord 13, 22, 27, 32, 65, 67, 71, 76, 78, 85–8, 91, 92, 94, 130, 134, 141, 153, 155, 164–7, 173, 177, 214, 218, 231, 240, 242, 244, 245
Papineau, Louis Joseph 174
Parliament 11, 18, 34, 36, 54, 91, 111, 113, 122, 135, 136, 142, 144, 156, 162, 163–77, 185, 192, 201, 229, 230, 231
Peel, Jonathan 159
Pierce, Franklin 30, 146

INDEX

Polish Rebellion (1863) 96, 98–100, 109, 191, 196, 202, 242
Polk, James 115, 146
Potter, George 98, 202, 205
Potter, Thomas Bayley 223, 228
Prince Albert 87, 88
Proclamation of Neutrality (Queen's) 17, 18, 31, 32–7, 48, 54, 57, 64, 68, 112, 113, 148, 210
pro-northerners 5–11, 18, 19, 27, 32, 39, 46, 47, 50, 54–6, 76, 96, 97, 122, 125, 134, 143, 150, 156, 180, 182, 187, 193, 194, 195, 200, 203, 205, 206, 216, 218, 219, 220, 222, 224–30, 234, 237, 243, 244, 246
propaganda literature, *see* travel literature
pro-southerners 6–11, 15, 54, 67, 97, 118, 123, 154, 156, 163–93, 169, 179, 182–4, 186, 187, 195, 203, 206, 210, 215, 216, 218, 224–7, 237, 243, 244
Prussia 20, 244

Quarterly Review 59, 142, 145, 146
Queen Victoria 33, 46, 61, 81, 113, 185n.82, 240

race 11, 124–33
racism 11, 20, 22, 124–33
radicals 2, 6, 7, 9–11, 80, 109, 173, 176, 194, 195, 198, 201, 203–11, 214, 222, 227, 228, 230, 244
Ramsden, Sir John 84n.103, 85, 142–5, 147, 159, 228
Redding, Cyrus 105n.31, 119, 181, 182
reform (political) 4, 76, 134, 141, 143, 145, 152, 157, 159, 160, 176, 195, 196, 199, 201, 204, 205, 214, 222, 227, 230, 234, 236, 241, 244
Reform Act (1867) 3, 142, 206, 235, 236
Republican Party 13, 37, 41, 76, 108, 113
republicanism 2, 4, 76, 194, 209, 222
Reynolds, George W. M. 109, 202, 204, 206
Reynolds's Weekly Newspaper 14, 52, 68, 98, 99, 105, 150, 155, 159, 171, 192n.113, 202, 204, 208–13, 216, 217, 226, 229
Richmond 120, 127, 130, 188, 230
Rochdale 77, 79, 155, 156, 158, 204, 207, 218, 224, 228
Roebuck, John Arthur 111, 118, 153, 163, 167, 185, 192, 201, 204, 224, 230, 234, 237, 245

Motion to recognise South 156n.86, 168–76, 189, 201 214n.27
Russell, Lord John 22, 55, 57, 64, 71, 76, 112, 128, 137, 141, 166–8, 176, 177, 178n.50, 190, 240, 242, 245
Russell, William H. 29, 70, 120, 121, 174
Russia 20, 29, 35, 59, 65, 98, 99, 110, 174, 244

St. James's Hall, London 135, 156, 214, 219–21, 222
Sandars, Thomas 44, 48, 52
San Jacinto (USS) 60, 62, 66
Saturday Review 14, 19, 22–7, 30, 33–5, 39–44, 48–50, 59, 60, 67, 68, 74, 75, 78, 79, 90, 91, 105–7, 109–11, 114–16, 123, 128–33, 135, 145, 166, 172, 173, 176–9, 189, 191, 192, 217, 222, 227, 229, 230, 231n.176
Schleswig-Holstein Crisis (1864) 96, 109, 144, 191, 242
Scholefield, William 155, 156, 204, 234
Scotland 15, 218
Secession 11, 17, 18, 37, 41, 47, 48, 55–7, 99, 100, 121, 123, 128, 129, 149, 150, 152, 155, 156, 160, 199, 209, 210, 227, 229, 240
Seward, William H. 10, 13, 18, 27–31, 33–5, 38, 42, 43, 48, 54, 58, 64, 66, 68–74, 78, 87, 90–4, 110, 111, 113, 115, 157, 175, 178, 191, 211, 215, 216, 227, 228, 232
Shaftesbury, Lord 110, 246
Sheffield 117, 118, 153, 176, 218, 224, 237
Sheridan, H. B. 82, 161
slavery 2–7, 11–14, 18, 19, 23–7, 46–52, 54–7, 75, 77–9, 81, 82, 84, 90, 96–8, 101, 105, 106, 118–30, 138, 139, 149, 151–3, 155–61, 164, 169, 170, 180, 182, 186–8, 190, 192, 195–201, 204, 211–16, 221, 222, 229, 232, 239, 240, 245
slave trade 13, 20–2, 31, 47, 65, 75, 81, 90, 116, 161, 168, 180, 200, 224
Slidell, John 61–3, 66, 69, 70, 75, 77, 79, 82, 84–93, 161, 168, 188, 217
Smith, Goldwin 99, 100, 142, 203, 205, 222, 223, 234, 235, 237
Somerset, Duke of 136
South, the, *see* the Confederacy
South Carolina 17, 43, 44, 62, 199
Southern planters 44, 49

265

Southerners 13, 23, 30, 40, 49, 74, 76, 101, 103, 121, 166
Southern states, see the Confederacy
Spectator 23, 25, 27, 30, 33, 38, 42, 45, 53, 54, 59, 60, 68, 69, 78, 79, 89, 94, 105, 107, 111, 114, 120, 128, 129, 132, 191, 192n.113, 197, 200, 201, 212–14, 224, 227, 228, 231n.176, 232
Spence, James 67, 123, 124, 127, 178n.50
Stansfeld, Sir James 157
Stephen, James Fitzjames 149, 150
Stephen, Leslie 45, 46, 100, 200, 223, 234, 235, 237
Stephens, Alexander 55, 130
Stowe, Harriet Beecher 27, 55, 99n.10, 125, 203
Sumner, Charles 53, 80, 190, 191

tariffs 41–4, 48, 57, 101, 206
Taylor, P. A. 162, 164, 165, 205, 222
Thompson, George 218, 225
Times of London 12, 14, 15, 18, 21, 22n.21, 24, 26, 32, 35–7, 38n.115, 42, 58, 60, 74, 77, 79, 89, 113, 121, 127, 129, 131, 149, 169, 174, 178, 192n.113, 234
trade 11, 41–5, 48, 50, 56, 57, 76, 152, 174, 238
traditional interpretation 2–12, 17, 52, 80, 82, 86, 92, 112, 114, 137, 138, 141, 142, 159, 192–5, 212, 216, 221, 237, 246
travel literature 101, 117–24, 197, 198
Trent (RMS) 60, 62, 64, 66, 88, 94
Trent affair 13–15, 28, 40, 47, 58, 61, 63, 65, 68, 86, 91–4, 96, 110, 112, 113, 115, 129, 130, 147, 158, 159, 164, 193, 198, 199, 212n.96, 213, 217, 227, 238, 241, 245
Trollope, Anthony 120–1, 148
Troup, George 206, 207, 225

Uncle Tom's Cabin (1851–1852) 27, 55, 125
Union, the
   English suspicions regarding emancipation 18–28, 124–33
   Hostile diplomacy of 28–35, 58, 110–17
   MPs' views on 54–8, 151–62
   British writers' views of 117–24
   Conservatives views of 140–50
   Pro-northerners' views on 196–206, 212–15
   Pro-southerners' views on 163–77
   Meetings in favour of 215–26
   Victory of 226–33
Union and Emancipation Society 98, 111, 183, 206, 216, 218, 222, 225, 236, 243
United States of America 1, 3, 4, 7, 10–13, 15, 20–3, 26, 30, 33, 34, 43, 48, 65, 76, 81, 88, 100, 101, 116, 138, 144, 175, 196, 211, 229, 230, 232, 236, 238
Upper Canada, see Canada

Vane Tempest, Adolphus 164, 165
Vaughn, Robert 132
Villiers, C. P. 160, 161

War of 1812 (1812–1815) 34, 64n.10, 104, 175, 242
Washington 29, 60, 66–9, 73, 91, 102, 105, 115, 183, 192, 226, 228
Weed, Thurlow 113
Welles, Gideon 69, 70, 112
Wesleyan Methodist Magazine 40, 60, 75, 85, 91, 181, 214
West Indies 21, 94, 112, 125, 128, 136
Westminster Review 24, 58, 124, 190, 200, 204, 212, 213, 228n.161, 229
Wharncliffe, Lord 182
Whiteside, James 164, 166
Whitman, Walt 235
Wilkes, Captain Charles 60–5, 67, 69–74, 76, 77, 87, 88, 93, 94, 112, 136
Williams, William 82, 160, 176
Wood, Western 153, 154
Wood, Sir Charles 157
working class (British) 2–10, 52, 96, 98, 137, 156, 184, 194–8, 203, 205–9, 216–19, 222, 224–30, 238
Wyndham, Percy 171

Yancey, William 49, 61, 76